THE EARLY HISTORY

OF

ELORA, ONTARIO

AND VICINITY

by

John Robert Connon

Reissued with an Introduction by

Gerald Noonan

SECOND REVISED PRINTING © 1975

ISBN 0-88920-012-2

WILFRID LAURIER UNIVERSITY PRESS
WATERLOO, ONTARIO, CANADA

CONTENTS

(Listings taken from subheadings in Connon's text are in quotation marks; other listings are the editor's).

LIST OF ILLUSTRATIONS	v
BIOGRAPHY OF JOHN ROBERT CONNON	vii
INTRODUCTION	ix
"PART 1 – FIRST THINGS"	5
"TOWNSHIP OF PILKINGTON–THE FIRST SETTLERS: WHO THEY WERE AND WHERE THEY CAME FROM"	19
"ELORA–ITS EARLY HISTORY"	46
LETTERS BY WILLIAM GILKISON	53
"HOW ELORA RECEIVED ITS NAME"	58
"THE BON-ACCORD SETTLEMENT"	64
INDIAN VISITORS	97
THE SEARCH FOR A LOST SETTLER	105
"ELORA–ITS EARLY HISTORY CONTINUED"	110
THE FOUNDING OF SALEM	123
FIRST NEWSPAPERS	136
THE VOLUNTEER RIFLE COMPANY	137
"HISTORY OF CHALMERS CHURCH"	159
A SYNOPSIS OF ELORA'S HISTORY	169
NOTES FROM CAPTAIN GILKISON'S DIARY	175
"LIST OF VOTERS WHO WERE PRESENT AND VOTED AT THE FIRST CONTESTED ELECTION IN THE TOWNSHIP OF NICHOL IN 1842."	191
"NAMES FROM ASSESSMENT ROLL OF NICHOL FOR 1850"	192
"NAMES FROM ASSESSMENT ROLL OF NICHOL FOR 1851"	195
"A LIST OF THE LEADING MEN AND HEADS OF FAMILIES LIVING IN ELORA IN 1853, WHEN THOMAS CONNON CAME. WRITTEN AS HE GAVE THEM FROM MEMORY.	197

"LIST OF NAMES FROM ASSESSMENT ROLL OF ELORA
FOR 1855"   198

"MEMBERS OF THE ELORA MECHANIC'S INSTITUTE,
ORGANIZED THURSDAY EVENING, 26TH NOVEMBER,
1857"   199

"ELORA", POEM BY ALEXANDER MCLACHLIN (SIC).
(McLachlan, 1818-1896, was a pioneer poet, from Scotland,
whose work is still being republished. He farmed near Stratford,
operated a tailor shop in Erin, and retired to Orangeville where
he died).   200

"INDEX"   201

"CORRECTIONS" AND ORIGINAL PAGE 31½   208

LIST OF ILLUSTRATIONS

	Facing Page
THE ELORA FALLS	3
ELORA FALLS, 1899	5
THE HOME OF CAPTAIN SMITH, 1903	6
DOUBLE DOVETAILED CORNERS IN CAPTAIN SMITH'S HOUSE	7
IRVINE BRIDGE	on pg. 18
JESSE PENFOLD	20
HUGH ROBERTS	21
THE CASCADE	32
ROCKY BANKS OF GRAND RIVER	33
THE CAVE WHERE THE WAMPUM BEADS WERE FOUND AND THE HOLE IN THE ROCK	44
THE OLD INDIAN BRIDGE, 1860	45
JOHN MATTHEWS	48
MRS. JOHN MATTHEWS	49
CAPTAIN WILLIAM GILKISON	58
THE GRAND RIVER AT ELORA, 1892	59
JOHN KEITH	86
MRS. JOHN KEITH	87
GEORGE BARRON	92
THE OLD MILL AT WINTERBOURNE, 1892	93
LT.–COL. JASPER T. GILKISON	112
AUCTION NOTICE FOR THE GILKISON ESTATE	113
ANDREW GEDDES	120
CHARLES ALLAN	121
SEM WISSLER	124
SALEM IN NOVEMBER, 1856	125

WISSLER'S MILL AT SALEM	125
RESIDENCE OF SEM WISSLER	125
SALEM IN 1870	125
DAVID FOOTE	128
ALEXANDER SPALDING	129
ANDREW GORDON	132
CHARLES CLARKE	133
REV. JOHN SMITHURST	146
REV. JOHN SMITHURST'S GRAVE	147
JOHN MCLEAN	152
REV. JAMES MIDDLEMISS, D.D.	153
DAVID BOYLE, LL.D.	164
ICICLES ON THE BANKS OF THE GRAND RIVER, 1885	165
THOMAS CONNON	188
MRS. THOMAS CONNON	189
THE WHOLE-CIRCLE PANORAMIC CAMERA	Back Cover

LIST OF MAPS

MAP OF UPPER GRAND RIVER BASIN	xiii
MAP OF AREA TOWNSHIPS, 1877	xiv

BIOGRAPHY OF JOHN ROBERT CONNON

Born: May 26th, 1862.   Died: January 18th, 1931.

John Robert Connon was the elder son of Thomas Connon and his wife, Jean Keith, and was born May 26th, 1862. His father was a native of the parish of Udny, Aberdeenshire, Scotland, who, after receiving a good education, served an apprenticeship as a wholesale grocer in the city of Aberdeen. He emigrated to Canada in 1852, and came to Elora, Ontario, in March, 1853. He engaged in the general store business, became interested in photography, and in 1859 engaged in it for profit, selling his general store business in 1867. Mrs. Connon was the eldest daughter of John Keith, one of the first settlers at Bon Accord, upper Nichol. It is worthy of note that she was the first white child born on the west side of the Grand River in what is now the Village of Elora, perhaps in Wellington County, on March 19th, 1835. Mr. and Mrs. Connon were married on November 4th, 1854.

With such a background, it is not to be wondered at that the subject of this sketch should be particularly interested in the early settlement of this country and in his father's art, in which he, too, was a pioneer.

John R. Connon received his education in the Public and High Schools at Elora, and with the exception of a short sojourn in New York city, practically his whole life was spent in his native village. He early began to take an active interest in his father's business, became an expert photographer, particularly at outside work. His photographs of scenes along the Grand and Irvine Rivers are of outstanding merit, and those who possess one or more of them have something which they should prize very highly.

Of all his school-teachers, the late John Connon was most influenced by David Boyle, Principal of the Elora Public School, afterwards David Boyle, LL.D., first Provincial Archaeologist of Ontario, first Superintendent of the Provincial Museum, and first Secretary of the Ontario Historical Society. With Mr. Boyle he maintained a life-long friendship. As a result, he took a more than ordinary interest in geology, and was also interested in astronomy, having one of the best telescopes in this part of Ontario. It was also through Mr. Boyle's influence that he finally commenced the preparation of the history of the early settlement of Elora, including also an account of the first settlers in the Townships of Woolwich, Pilkington and Nichol. This work first took definite form in January of 1906, and was completed and published in the latter part of 1930, just a few weeks previous to the author's decease. The subject matter was first published in weekly instalments in the "Elora Express", then put into book form. An interruption occurred in this arrangement at the time of his mother's death. She it was who spurred his literary efforts, and after her death he seemed for a time to lose heart in the enterprise. When later the work was taken up again it was largely through the influence of Mr. Hugh C. Templin, the Fergus historian, and the same arrangement as with the "Elora Express" was carried out with the Fergus "News-Record." The book was illustrated with pictures provided by Mr. Connon's camera. An edition of 400 copies was printed, and in face of the unprecedented depression, commercially and industrially, the History had a good sale, and today only a comparatively small number of copies are available. It is a pleasing thought to the writer of this biography to remember that Mr. Connon lived long enough to receive many congratulatory letters and messages, and to know that his History of Elora was not only appreciated by those whose opinions he valued, but was a financial success as well.

While the History will probably be Mr. Connon's most enduring monument, it is worthy of recording that he and his father made outstanding contributions to the advance and improvement of photography. Mr. Connon, Sr., in 1881, designed what was afterwards called a roll-holder, in which the gelatine emulsion on which the photograph was made was placed upon something like a roll of ribbon, instead of, as formerly, on a glass plate. In August of 1887, Mr. John R. Connon received his American Patent for the first camera ever made which would photograph the entire circle at one exposure, familiarly known as a Panoramic Camera. Unfortunately, neither he nor his father reaped much financial reward as a result of their inventions, as the story told in the closing pages of the "History" reveals.

Mr. John R. Connon was also a pioneer in the electrical field, and the writer remembers a motor designed by him, assisted by Mr. Wm. Walker, a Fergus machinist, which was in use in the Fergus "News-Record" office, where we were an apprentice, over 40 years ago. He was also a musician of no mean order, and played the piano, organ and violin with more than ordinary ability.

The author of the "History of Elora" was buried in the family plot in the Elora Cemetery, the last resting place of many of the pioneers whose story he has so graphically told, and whose names he has perpetuated. As a man, he was loyal to his friends, sympathetic and helpful to the aged, and ever ready to give aid and counsel to those who consulted him, and they were legion. He was always especially interested in the newcomer to this country, and many an immigrant, especially the foreign-born, has occasion to remember him with the deepest gratitude. He was generous to a fault to his friends and to those whose condition aroused his sympathy. To fellow-authors, historians, newspaper men, or to those seeking information about Elora or the Elora community, he was always available, and out of the abundance of his knowledge was usually able to meet their needs. His memory will long be cherished by those who were privileged with his friendship, and we believe succeeding generations will acknowledge the debt of gratitude which the whole community owes to him, appreciate him more and pay a tribute to his life and life-work that his contemporaries sometimes failed to accord.

—Richard E. Mills.
[Editor, *The Elora Express*
1901-1924.]

Reprinted, with permission, from *Waterloo Historical Society Annual Volume*, No. 23 (1935), pp. 177-179.

INTRODUCTION

This book provides little-known details about the settlement and development of the Elora area from the time the first log shelter was built by Roswell Matthews within sight of the Grand River's falls in 1817. From then until 1833, John Connon writes, "Elora seemed to be at the end of the civilized world. On the west side of the river there was not a settler between Elora and Lake Huron" (p. 62).

Connon's book, *The Early History of Elora, Ontario, and Vicinity* (as it is named in full on the original title-page) is a compilation of material that first appeared in *The Elora Express* between 1906 and 1909, plus additional material written, it appears, in 1926. The book was published in a 10 x 6½ inch, hard-cover edition in December, 1930, a few weeks before the author's death. Any of the 400 copies of that first printing have long since become rarities. This reissue of the 1930 work in a sense fulfills Connon's prophecy that "long years after this it will prove useful to those who really want to know the history of our country" (p. 171).

His purpose is "to trace the progress of the very first settlers as they pushed their way, one by one, to the vicinity of Elora" (p. 7). "In a country closely covered with bush as Ontario was, the course followed by the pioneers must be up the streams. It has been so in all countries that are difficult of access. In Canada it was up the St. Lawrence, up Lake Ontario, and, in the part we are about to follow, it was up the Grand River and up the smaller streams" (p. 6).

Connon begins at the point where the Grand River meets the Conestogo, near present-day Conestogo village, and works up river, along the river road to Elora, Fergus, and Bon-Accord, giving an account of the first owners of each farm, their families and descendants, and some of their triumphs and hardships. "For the human vine to grow that distance ... fifteen miles, it took thirty years—from 1806 to 1836" (p. 99).

After 1843, when Elora acquired a new grist-mill, store, and bridge, the pace of development increased. "For fifteen years Elora went ahead fast. It was the market for all the country toward Lake Huron" (p. 170). Railroad building and the Crimean War sent prices soaring. Sem Wissler founded a model village at Salem and it prospered for twenty years. "The little village of Alma sold by auction in January, 1856 for $18,500.00. That was when it was all bush. Now [1926?] with the buildings in it, no one would want it at that price". Later, at Elora, "the first Ingrain Carpet Factory in Canada" was so successful it was appropriated to Toronto.

Development, inevitably, brought the railway. In 1870 it reached Elora and veered east to Fergus. "In 1873 the railway was continued north-west to Southampton and at once every small place to the north became as good a market for farm produce as Elora had been" (p. 170).

The waterway that led the first settlers into the area, and the Falls that attracted the first developers were superceded by the railway and Hydro power. "The reason for Elora's existence was the Falls on the Grand River. There was no other reason. The cause of its decline is that the land about the sources of the river has been completely denuded of the trees that grew there. ... The water-powers are of little use now. They can not be depended upon for power".

But, with or without dependable waterpower, the Falls and the Islet

Rock that attracted pioneer Roswell Matthews, Captain William Gilkison, the founder of Elora, and Hon. Adam Fergusson, the founder of Fergus, as well as many others, continue to attract visitors. As Connon notes: "Summer tourists come in ever-increasing numbers to see the rocky gorge on the Grand and Irvine Rivers" (p. 170).

To read Connon's work is to become aware of the dictum he so evidently lived by: "No fact is isolated. No event is solitary.... No life exists but as a part of all other lives." His *History* is not a coherent narrative that subordinates peripheral material; the details he presents branch out into unsuspected families, places and events. More than once, he receives information from the only person who knows, just a short time before that person dies. Years later, the information completes or uncovers the account of a separate matter. "Experience in collecting local history," Connon writes, "shows that very often the most important information is found where one would least expect to find it" (p. 145).

What is true for him is often true, in a sense, for the reader, who may well discover unexpected information. Here, for instance, is the story of Florence Nightingale's secret love (Rev. John Smithurst, pp. 145-149); of David Boyle, the Middlebrook schoolmaster who became the first provincial archaeologist (pp. 161ff.); of Charles Clarke, eight times reeve of Elora, member of the Provincial Legislature 1871-1892, Clerk of the Ontario House of Assembly 1892-1907, and author of *Sixty Years in Upper Canada* (pp. 135ff.); of John McLean, discoverer of Labrador's Grand Falls, a 25-year employee, and trenchant critic of the Hudson's Bay Company who became the victim of a bank swindle in Guelph, and retired to Elora. The data concerning John McLean that Connon collected and preserved was put to good use shortly after Connon's death. W. S. Wallace, editor of a 1932 edition of *John McLean's Notes of a Twenty Five Year's Service in the Hudson's Bay Territory* (Toronto: The Champlain Society) pays tribute to "the late Mr. John Connon ... whose father had known John McLean in Elora, and who devoted a great deal of effort to recovering the facts about John McLean's life. Not only in this [McLean's family connections] but in other respects, I am deeply indebted to Mr. Connon's researches" (p. xi).

Here, too, is the story of John Connon's invention of the world's first full-circle panoramic camera, of his father's invention of a roll-holder for film (pp. 188-190), of the invention of the Opthalmoscope by Rev. James Middlemiss, pastor of Elora Chalmers Church, 1855-1893 (p. 157).

Among briefer items, one of the most striking for anyone who has ever walked across Elora's Irvine Bridge is apt to be the mention of Andrew Gordon's run across the projecting timbers, outside the railing of the bridge (p. 133). Other noteworthy items might be: Captain Gilkison's concern lest "the bridge builders ... destroy the effect of the little island" and the Falls (p. 115); and John Connon's rescue of a slotted door from Elora's first post office (p. 116).

The most sustained narrative in the book is the account of the Bon-Accord settlement (pp. 64-85) by George Elmslie, a participant. He describes a voyage from Aberdeen in 1834, and trips in Upper Canada to inspect Nottawasaga Bay, Niagara, Zorra, Elora, and Fergus before the choice of the Bon-Accord land was made. The details of settlement, the raising-bees, wolves, first crops, new arrivals, and first death, create in the reader an impression of shared experience.

Somewhat similar in impact is the account of the first Volunteer Rifle Company of Elora (pp. 137ff.), organized in 1861 to meet any threat from the Civil War "in the neighboring Republic." It was maintained for five years and made two trips to the "Front" to meet a Fenian invasion. The regulars drilled earnestly—74 times in one 12-month period—while, at the peak of the threat, other volunteers in Salem "drilled in the oatmeal grainery at Wissler's mill." On the Alma road "in a pasture field at Ewing's Corners . . . some thirty or forty men on horseback were drilled by a retired cavalry officer. Every young farmer had a gun and knew how to use it . . ." (p. 142). As Connon suggests, a sense of the urgency and patriotism of the time is recreated by these details without which it is too easy, from the security of hindsight, to dismiss the whole process as frivolous.

One final illustration of the ramifications of Connon's work stems from his genealogical studies. The Alexander Grant who became Commodore of the Great Lakes naval department in 1777, and acting Lieutenant Governor of Upper Canada in 1805, was married to a Therese Barthe, daughter of a prominent Detroit family (pp. 172ff.). One of their daughters married Captain Gilkison, Elora's founder. Another daughter married Thomas Dickson, a brother of William Dickson, the founder of Galt. (John Galt, the city's namesake, was the cousin of Captain Gilkison; both were born at the town of Irvine in Ayrshire, Scotland [the source perhaps of the name of the Irvine River?] Connon says it was Gilkison who told Galt about Upper Canada, not, as is sometimes intimated, the other way about.)[1] A third daughter of Commodore Grant married William Richardson of Brantford, a brother of Major John Richardson, the author of *Wacousta,* an important early novel in Canadian literature. A granddaughter of Commodore Grant "married Colonel Robert Nichol after whom the township of Nichol received its name." And it was a friend of Nichol's who "on August 28th, 1832, suggested to Capt. Wm. Gilkison that he should buy half of the Township of Nichol"—which gave him the site for Elora.

Gerald A. Noonan,
Department of English,
Wilfrid Laurier University,
Waterloo, 1974.

---

[1] Another prominent native of Irvine was Adam Ferrie who with his sons, Adam Jr. and Robert, founded Doon village, now in the southernmost area of present-day Kitchener. Adam Sr. was born in Irvine, Ayrshire, Scotland in 1777.

Ayrshire also has associations with Doon's neighbouring village of Ayr; the large number of settlers from Ayrshire is believed responsible for the choice of the name, Ayr, in 1840.

Note on the text

The first 144 pages of Connon's 1930 edition, and of this reissue, were published in *The Elora Express,* from January, 1906 to February, 1909. The remaining pages were compiled between 1926 and 1930 with the encouragement and "the kindness," Connon says, of *The Fergus News-Record.* With the exception of one photograph by Thomas Connon, p. 44, the photographs are believed to be the work of the author, John Connon. The original order of the illustrations, however, has been altered for convenience in printing. Similarly, the original half-page, numbered 31-1/2, has been moved with the author's corrections to page 208.

Additional material in this photocopy edition consists of the cover, the Introduction, the Contents page, the Biography of the author (reprinted with the permission of the Waterloo Historical Society), the List of Illustrations, the map of Wellington County Township and Woolwich Township, and the map of the Grand and Irvine Rivers. The maps were drawn by Agnes Hall of Wilfrid Laurier University.

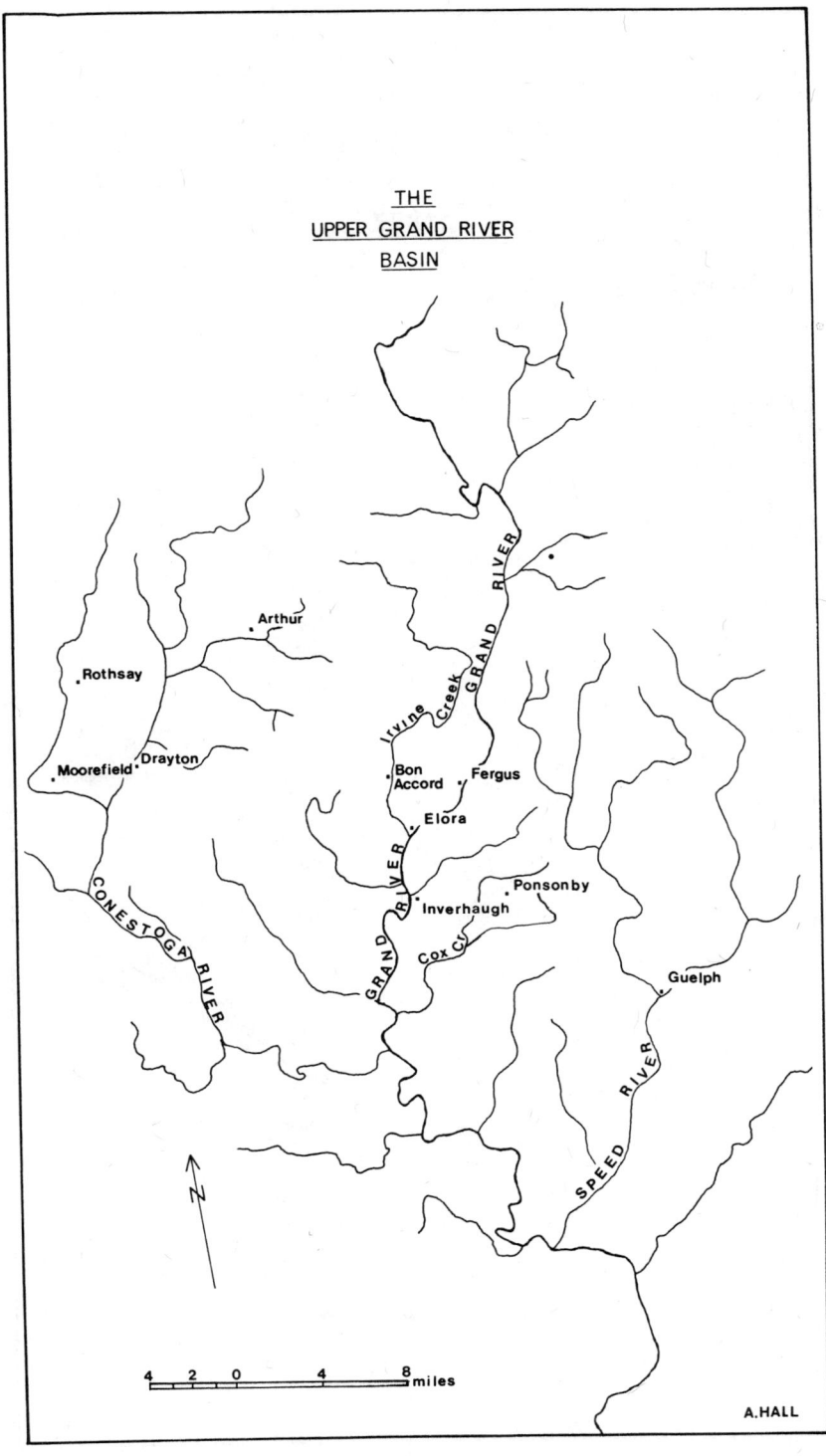

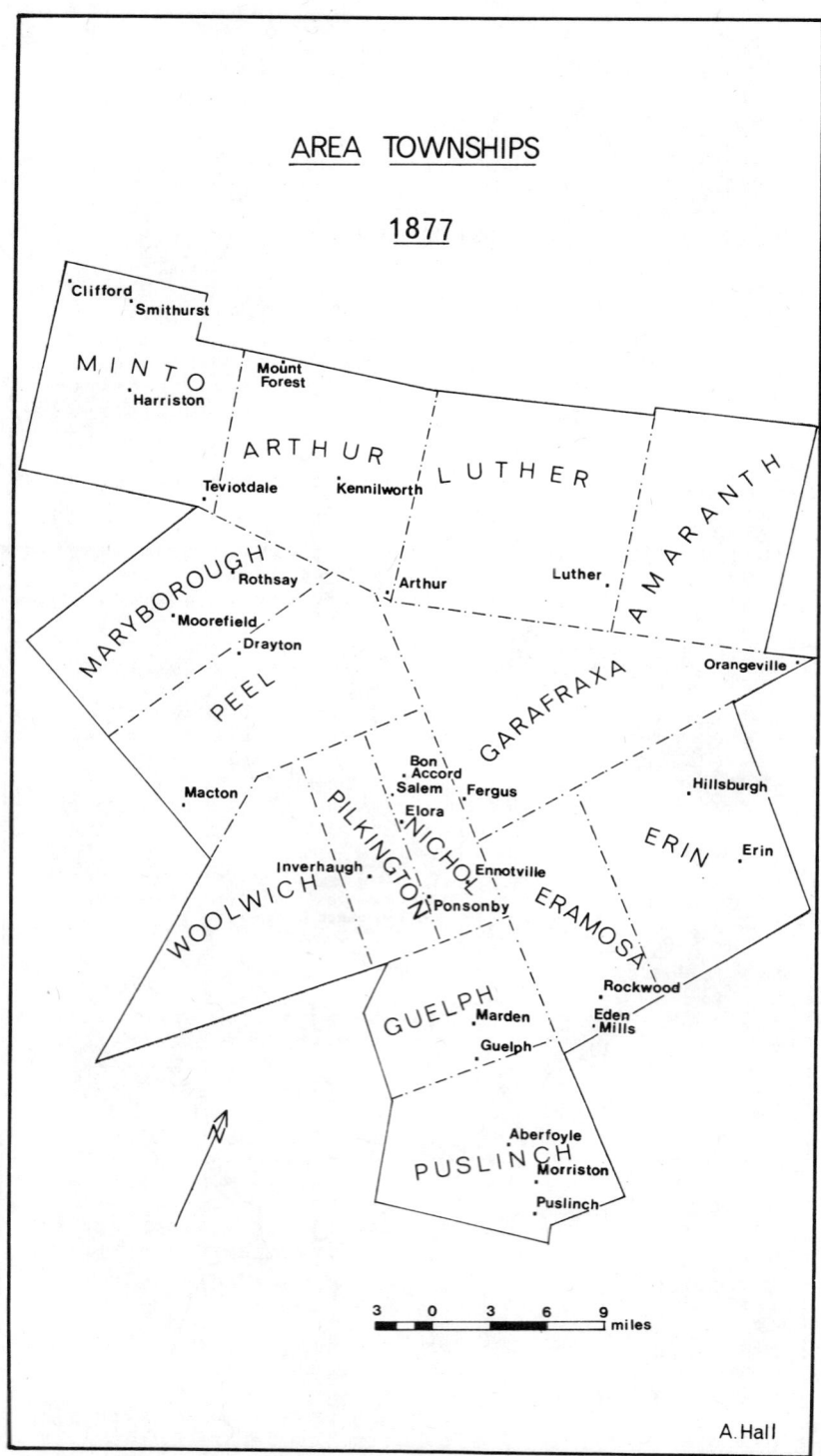

"ELORA"

BY

JOHN R. CONNON

WITH ILLUSTRATIONS AND INDEX

PRINTED BY
THE ELORA EXPRESS AND
THE FERGUS NEWS-RECORD
COMPLETED 1930.

(From an Oil Painting by Thomas Connon)

THE ELORA FALLS
As it appeared when Roswell Matthews came

INTRODUCTORY REMARKS

TO THE READER :

A few years ago my old friend and teacher, Mr. David Boyle, Secretary of the Ontario Historical Society and Curator of the Ontario Provincial Museum in Toronto, was visiting in Elora. He took the first opportunity of lecturing me, in his own peculiar way, for having made no effort to preserve the early history of this locality.

After hearing what he had to say, I brought out a collection of old books, newspapers, memorandum books and slips of paper on which I had written many stories of the early days, which were told to me by old friends who now occupy their long, last resting place upon the hill.

Mr. Boyle kindly said that he was agreeably surprised, and advised me to arrange this material in such a way that it might be of some benefit to others. This I have endeavored to do, and in the following pages will relate something of what I have learned of the early settlement of Elora, including also an account of the first settlers in the townships of Woolwich, Pilkington and Nichol.

Elora, January 3rd, 1906. JOHN R. CONNON.

ELORA FALLS
Photographed in 1899

PART I.—FIRST THINGS.

There is an element of romance about first things. They have a charm of novelty and freshness. As items of biographical interest they cannot be superseded, for however important any similar later experience may be, it can never be the first of that kind. That place is permanently occupied. There can be no second first. For this cause, if for no other, a history of the first settlers in Elora and vicinity may not be without interest.

The first European to visit the Grand River in Western Ontario was Father Daillon, a Franciscan Friar. In 1626 he was a missionary to the Huron Indians among their many villages situated between Lake Simcoe and Georgian Bay.

Father Daillon, in company with two other Frenchmen, and against the advice of his friends, the Huron Indians, set out on his perilous journey. After his first reception, which was more friendly than he had been led to expect, Father Daillon sent back his two companions and went on alone. He travelled the length and breadth of what is now the central portion of western Ontario. A rumor of his death having reached the Huron Mission, one of his former guides was sent to find out whether this was true, and, returning, brought Father Daillon back, alive.

As described in the glowing language of the Frenchman this was the most beautiful country he had ever set eyes on. The Indians living around Lake Simcoe and about the south-eastern corner of Georgian Bay were the Hurons. Here, within an area of sixty or seventy miles, was the home of this nation, who were in a state of social advancement when compared with the roving bands of Eastern Canada. The Hurons lived in villages and tilled the soil.

A little to the west of the Hurons, and along the south shore of Georgian Bay were the Tionnontates, or Tobacco nation.

From the source of the Grand River to Lake Erie and eastward towards the Niagara River, he found a tribe who called themselves the Attiwandarons. The surrounding tribes called them the Neutral Nation, from the fact that during the continued strife which had existed between the Hurons on the north and the Iroquois, or Six Nation Indians, to the south, they had remained strictly neutral.

Father Daillon described the Neutral Indians as of superior physique, intelligent, patriotic and inclined to live at peace if left alone, but under their great war chief, Tsohahissen, could put many thousand braves on the war path, and had recently carried fear to the hearts of their enemies even as far West as Lake Michigan.

In 1640 and 1641 a second attempt was made to Christianize the Neutrals. This time two Jesuits, Chaumonot and Brebeuf, are said to have visited the Canyon of the Grand River, near Elora, in winter. Their missionary efforts were not a success, but with an eye to the practical, as well as the beautiful, they noted the abundance of game and the large number of fur bearing animals that were to be found along the banks of the Grand River.

On the second of November, 1640, Brebeuf and Chaumonot set out to visit the Neutrals. After a dreary march of five days through the forest they reached the first Neutral town, Kandoucho, which may have been where Elora now stands. They visited eighteen towns, stopped four months, and commenced their return. On their way home they met with a genuine act of kindness. A heavy snow storm arresting their progress, a woman of the Neutral Nation took them to her lodge, entertained them for two weeks with her best fare, persuaded her father and relatives to befriend them, and aided them to make a vocabulary of the dialect. Bidding their generous hostess farewell, they journeyed northward from the village where they had been befriended, the site of which is supposed to be on Lot 12, Con. 7, of the Township of Beverly, and reached the Mission among the Hurons in safety.

The Hurons had long been allies of the French, and in the same way the Iroquois sided with the Dutch, who besides their settlements at Manhattan, now New York City, had trading posts at different points, among others, at Albany. To stop, if possible, the increasing power of the French, and assist Indians friendly to them, the Dutch at Albany gave fire-arms to the Iroquois. Armed with these match-locks, or as the Indians called them, "Irons with indwelling devils," the Iroquois set out to try the effect they would have on their old foes, the Hurons. On the fourth of July, 1648, the Iroquois attacked the Huron town of Teanaustaye. Father Daniel faced them and was killed, having first advised the feeble inhabitants to flee. The village and mission Church were burned. The Iroquois started for home with seven hundred prisoners, but killed many of them on the way.

Next spring, on the sixteenth of March, 1649, one thousand Iroquois attacked the Huron town of St. Ignace. They entered the town at early dawn and attacked the Hurons while they slept. Of the four hundred inhabitants at home at that time only three escaped. On the same day they attacked another Huron town, St. Louis, where they took Brebeuf and Lallemont prisoners, whom they tortured and burned to death.

Some of the Hurons who escaped fled for refuge to the home of the Neutrals. But the Iroquois no longer respected the neutrality and the turn of Neutrals came next. The campaign of 1650 was not decisive. Although the Iroquois had stormed a large village, they had afterwards been defeated with the loss of two hundred warriors. In the spring of 1651 they returned with reinforcements and landed at what is now Hamilton. This was really the key to the Neutral land from the side of Lake Ontario, for it commanded the portage that led through the Dundas valley to the Indian town of Ootinawataoua on the Grand River. At the landing place a great battle was fought, in which the Neutrals suffered overwhelming defeat. At news of this disaster inland towns were abandoned to their fate and the survivors fled to the shores of the Upper Lakes.

From 1651 until the arrival of the first white settlers, this beautiful country was visited only by a few wandering hunters of the Objibway nation from the shores of Lake Huron.

In a country closely covered with bush as Ontario was, the course followed by the pioneers must be up the streams. It has been so in all countries that are difficult of access. In Canada it was up the St. Lawrence, up Lake Ontario and, in the part we are about to follow it was up the Grand River and up the smaller streams.

The restless spirit of those pioneers of the wilderness, although a benefit to the community and the race, was at the expense of their own domestic comfort. No sooner had they made a clearing on the farm and a little appearance of comfort, than they began to feel uncomfortable. Seldom did they remain on a farm till the stumps decayed, but on the first appearance of having

THE HOME OF CAPTAIN SMITH
Photographed in 1903

DOUBLE DOVETAILED CORNERS
In Capt. Smith's House

a clear field to plough over, they began to look for a purchaser. Most of them were Americans or Canadians. Those from the "Old Country" loved comfort, and especially home, so well that nothing but necessity would make them leave the place.

The first settlers came to the Township of Ancaster about the year 1795. Shortly afterwards individuals came from the States of Pennsylvania and New Jersey. Many of the present inhabitants, and the early pioneers of the Grand River are descendants of these. The village of Ancaster started about 1798 ; Dundas a little later ; Hamilton in 1813 ; Galt in 1816, and the first settler came to Elora in 1817.

It is our purpose to trace the progress of the very first settlers as they pushed their way, one by one, to the vicinity of Elora.

Captain Thomas Smith was born in the state of Vermont in the year 1767. He was among those who came to Canada a few years before the close of the eighteenth century. Capt. Smith married Mary Weaver, whose parents had come, along with many others, from the State of New Jersey, and lived in a small place called Jerseyville, near Ancaster. They first lived in the township of Beverly ; moved to the township of Waterloo, and as early as 1807, were in the township of Woolwich. The site of Capt. Smith's house was on the east side of the Grand River and opposite the mouth of the Conestogo, which here flows into the Grand from the west. Mr. George Stroh has lived on this farm for many years, and Capt. Smith's old house stood within a hundred feet of Mr Stroh's residence. The old house was well built of hewn logs, 26x28 feet, and was two stories high. The ceilings were 6 feet 7 inches high. The kitchen was 12x24, with a large fire place and just inside of the front door, in the corner between it and the fire-place, was a winding stair which led to the four rooms above. It was here, on January the third, 1808, that their daughter Priscilla was born. She was their fourth child, but the eldest daughter, and the first white child born in the township of Woolwich.

Capt. Smith was a Lieutenant in the Canadian Forces during the war of 1812. At the battle of Lundy's Lane a musket ball struck his knee and the same shot killed the horse upon which he rode. In an old newspaper published at St. David's in the year 1816, there is a list of those who were entitled to receive pensions because of injuries received during the war of 1812-14. In this list is the name of Lieut Thomas Smith, late of the 2nd York. He was wounded at Lundy's Lane on the 25th July, 1814, and was entitled to receive a pension from and after the 23rd November, 1813. The pension amounted to twenty two pounds, two shillings, eight pence, one farthing yearly.

Many of the settlers up the river were much indebted to Capt. Smith and his family for many kind services. His home was always open to them whenever they were led that way, and for years this was the only outlet. It was here that Roswell Matthews stopped on his way up the Grand River in the fall of 1817. Here he left his wife and younger children for three months, during the winter, while he and the older sons went on up the river to cut the first tree and build the first house in Elora.

It was at Capt. Smith's, in 1821, that the Wilbee's, a family of English settlers going to the Pilkington Estate, found shelter. Some of them were sick witn typhus fever and were here nursed back to health. During the voyage out, on a vessel called the "Asia," a baby girl had been born and she was called "Mary Asia." At Capt. Smith's the young mother died of the hardships of the voyage, leaving her baby girl to be nursed and cared for, for two years, by Capt. Smith's family. One of the sons was especially kind to the mitherless bairn. The others in the family teased him by saying she would be his wife some day, never thinking that it might be true, but again was truth stranger than fiction for Mary Asia Wilbee became Mrs. Cushman Smith.

With that large hearted kindness so characteristic of Captain and Mrs. Smith, they, in 1832, adopted Catherine Kennedy, who, like Mary Asia Wilbee, had been left motherless when a child. Catherine Kennedy grew up with the younger ones in the family until she married the late William Stork and is at present living in Winterbourne.

Like many other pioneers, Capt. Smith had neglected to secure a proper title to his property and was ejected by the Hon. James Crooks' estate. He then took up another farm half a mile north of Winterbourne; made another move and tried hotel keeping on the roadside south of Winterbourne and, giving that up, he returned to the Holmwood farm. For many years he carried the mail from Preston. Capt. Smith was described as "stout, well built, about 5 ft. 10 in., limped from the wound in his knee, and was a great one to tell stories." Mrs. Smith died on November 5th, 1845, at the age of 67 years. In later years the Captain lived with his younger son. During a religious meeting which was being held in the house he fell from his chair, stricken with paralysis, and died a few days later, on the 15th of April, 1850, at the age of 82 years and 5 months. Both are interred in the Methodist Cemetery at Winterbourne. The sons were: Alpheus, who married Ann Weaver. Alexander, who married Louisa Moss. They lived at West Montrose and died in Michigan. Cushman, who married Mary Asia Wilbee. Thomas married Sarah Heartwell. Stephen married Betsy Smith. William and Peter died young. Samuel married Jane Hanna. Their first home was a little north of Winterbourne, now known as the Holmwood farm. Here the old Captain died. Later they moved to the vicinity of Mt. Forest. The daughters were: Priscilla, married to Williams Sexton. Azubah, married to Willard Clemons; they lived at St. George. Mary, married to Emanuel Gaukel. Roxy, married to Milton Woodward, and Elisheba, unmarried.

Mary Smith, who died at Winterbourne in March, 1901, at the age of seventy-one years and six months, was a daughter of Alpheus Smith, and to her we are especially indebted for much of the family history here given.

When coming up the road, on the east side of the Grand river, past the village of Bloomingdale, we soon reach the townline between the townships of Waterloo and Woolwich. Here the road forks like the letter "Y." The left fork is the road past the old home of Captain Smith to the bridge which crosses the Grand river and thence on to the village of Conestogo. The right fork turns to the north, passing through the village of Winterbourne and on through the townships of Woolwich and Pilkington to Elora and Fergus. This is commonly called the "river road" because it follows the general course of the river.

At this corner, where the road divides, several of the earliest settlers made their homes.

The first to take up land near Capt. Smith's was Elisha Hewitt, who was born in Cayuga, in northern New York State, in January 1800. His mother was a native of Maryland. He came to Canada in 1819, giving a jacknife to get across the Niagara River at Black Rock. He first worked for John Brubacher, near Berlin, and after that, for four years, at any job he might find. When he came to the township of Waterloo his capital consisted of half a dollar and an extra pair of socks. He sold his socks and then he had enough to buy an axe. From this small beginning he acquired several hundred acres of land. Not only this, but he was married three times and raised a family of fifteen children.

In the fall of the year 1823 Elisha Hewitt took up his farm in the township of Woolwich and in the same year married Rachel Cress, who, with her father, mother, two brothers and a sister, had come along with Mr. Erb in 1806. The Cress family settled at what is now St. Jacob's, in Woolwich, while Mr. Erb was in Waterloo township. One thing that is remembered of Elisha Hewitt is that he made large quantities of maple sugar.

Rachel Cress, Hewitt's first wife, died Dec. 2nd, 1846, at the age of 49 years and eight months. In the first family were: Ephriam married Jane Wright, moved to Wisconsin. Eliza married to Josh. Scheidel, lives in Berlin. Elisha married Catherine Benner, lived on the next farm north of C. D. Bowman's near West Montrose, and is now living in Berlin. Elizabeth married to Alex. Singer, moved to Michigan. Mary married to James Woolner, lives in Peel township. Peter married Margaret Donaldson; their home was in Winterbourne. Rachel, who is Mrs. Pollock, now living near the old home. It is a remarkable fact that of the first family of seven all are yet living but Elizabeth and she was killed by a runaway accident.

Hewitt's second wife was Elspet Meldrum, who died Jan. 28th, 1860, at the age of 48 years and 3 months. In this family were: Margaret married to John Hillcock, Peterborough. Charlotte married to Daniel Kennedy, Toronto. Annie married in Tonawanda, N. Y. Jessie married to Joseph Benner, moved to Culross township where she died. Helen married Rev. Mr. Groff, lived near Breslau. Alexander died when a young man.

The third wife was Ann Hamilton, and their two children were Elsie and Wilhelmina, who with their mother, who married again, went to live at Ripley, near Kincardine.

Elisha Hewitt died October 8th, 1863, at the age of 63 years and 9 months.

. .   . .

On the east side of the road near Hewitt's was another American whose parents had lived in Vermont. Zephaniah Sexton with his wife and family, lived on that farm which was long owned by the late Samuel S. Bowman and is now owned by his son, Leander Bowman. Zephaniah Sexton was married three times. His third wife was Elvira Clemons, from the township of Dumfries, who came to Winterbourne to teach school. In the first family were four sons: William, Manly, Jonathan and George. By the third marriage, two daughters, Polly and Dolly. This family moved to Bright, Michigan.

. .   . .

Williams Sexton came to Woolwich a little later than his uncle Zephaniah. His parents had lived at a place called Plum Hollow, back of Brockville. By trade he was a shoemaker. He was lame and walked with a crutch and cane. At an early date he taught school in Woolwich.

Williams Sexton married Priscilla, the eldest daughter of Captain Smith. There was a family of three: Amanda, Mrs. Robert Lawrason; Laura A., Mrs. George Stork; and Jonathan. Of these Mrs. Stork is at present living in Winterbourne with her daughter, Priscilla, who is Mrs. James Hamilton, and their son, Sexton Hamilton, is named after his great-grandparent.

Williams Sexton moved, first to Harrisburg, Ontario, where he lived for many years, and then to Ada, near Grand Rapids, Michigan. He died there on August 17th, 1872, in his sixty sixth year. Mrs. Sexton, who was Priscilla Smith, died in Michigan, September 23rd, 1890, in her eighty-third year.

Lumon Woodward, an American, was born in 1792. He came to the township of Woolwich in the spring of 1824 and took up the adjoining farm north of Hewitt's. This is the farm upon part of which is the Presbyterian cemetery. Lumon Woodward was married three times. Those in his family were : John Milton, married Rozy Smith. Alba, died in April, 1848, at the age of twenty-seven. Ebenezer, married Charlotte Peterson and lived at Hawkesville. William, married Helen Webster and they also lived at Hawkesville ; at their home Lumon Woodward and his third wife died. George married a Miss Brown and now lives in the town of Waterloo. Emmeline married George Taylor, and lived in the township of Maryborough. Laura married Louis Brace. Mabel married a Mr. Green, lived in Elmira ; and Alice. Lumon Woodward died on February 19th, 1860, in his sixty-eighth year.

Benjamin Bowman Bemis was born at Cornish, New Hampshire, on March 14th, 1792. Many stories are told of his early life which had been a remarkably eventful one. As a young man living in a New England seaport town he took part in some stirring events during the War of 1812-14. Towards the close of the war he visited a brother, Asaph. S. Bemis, who was living in Buffalo, and was there in 1814, when Buffalo, then a village, was burned. Shortly after that he was in Woolwich. After trying other places, the farm on which he settled was on the east side of the road, opposite Woodward's, and north of and adjoining Zephaniah Sexton's. Later he built a hotel in Winterbourne and in this way was well known to all the first immigrants. From one and all comes the same story that his house was always open to them. Few had any money in the days of the Pilkington settlement but that made no difference to Mr. Bemis ; he was hospitable and kind to every one.

Benjamin Bowman Bemis married a widow whose maiden name was Mary Pollard. There were two in this family,—Aurelia, born in 1821, was married to David Chalmers ; and Benjamin Bowman Bemis, jr.. born in 1823, was married in February 1850 to Christina McKay, and died December 13th, 1900 at the age of seventy-seven.

In 1834 Mr. Bemis, sr., married the widow of William Singer, from the Township of Nichol, and the children by this second marriage were : Mary Ann, married Matthew Durrant ; Angeline, married Alex. McCloy ; Catharine, now living in Winterbourne ; and Thomas, who died quite young.

Benjamin Bowman Bemis died on March 13th, 1870, at the age of 78, and his second wife, whose maiden name was Katharine Coon, died October 16th, 1869, in her sixty fourth year.

James Davidson came to Winterbourne in 1834, from Aberdeen where he had been engaged in the cotton manufacturing. He was born at Walthamstow, Essex, England, on the 31st of March 1776. His wife was Elspet Blackhall, born at Aberdeen in 1777.

The family lived in a log house on the same lot as that upon which now stands the Rev. A. M. Hamilton's residence. This was known as Lower Woolwich post office while the Davidson's had it, and old Captain Smith carried the mail twice a week from Preston. The log house was pulled down about the year 1860 by our old friend Sandy Imlay, who is now living in Winterbourne.

In the Davidson family there were : John, James, William, Alexander, Ann, Elizabeth, Isabella, Mary, and Elsie. All except Ann and Alexander had lived at Winterbourne.

Ann was the eldest and she was married in 1824 to Alexander Allan, a lawyer in the city of Aberdeen. They came to Canada in 1843 and lived near Preston. Mr. Allan was the first Superintendent of Schools in the Wellington District, and held that position until 1853, when the County of Waterloo was set apart, and was the first Village Clerk of Preston. He died in 1855, and his wife died at Salem in 1878. One of their sons, Absalom Shade Allan, was M. P. P. for West Wellington from 1886 to 1894, and is now Sheriff of the County of Wellington. The late William Allan, of Salem was another son.

Isabella married Absalom Shade. the man who in company with the Hon. William Dickson founded the town of Galt in 1816. She afterwards married Dean Boomer and resided in London, Ontario.

Mary married John Geddes, son of the late Andrew Geddes, Crown Land Agent at Elora.

Elsie married William McKenzie and they went back to Scotland and lived at his estate " Fortrie," near Aberdeen.

.. .. ..

William was a merchant in Liverpool, and Alexander was a merchant in Malta. John was a banker in Galt, and was afterwards Postmaster. His wife was a sister of the late Dr. Tassie of Galt.

James Davidson, sr., about 1845, removed to Galt and died at Spring Hill on the fifteenth of August, 1852, the result of being injured by a runaway team of horses. His wife died on the sixth of August 1853, aged seventy-six years.

.. .. ..

Thomas H. Lanphier lived a mile east of Winterbourne, where he owned three hundred acres of land. He married Jane Gordon and they had two daughters, Lucia, who is Mrs. Andrew Brown, living in her father's home, and Eliza, Mrs. Albert Gordon, living on the old Gordon homestead.

Thomas H. Lanphier died on October 31st, 1872, at the age of sixty-one years, while Jane Gordon, his wife, died on May 2nd, 1881, in her seventy-sixth year.

.. .. ..

As we go farther north on the river road' we reach a stream which comes from the lower part of the township of Nichol, through Lower Pilkington, and, after crossing this road, where it drives Mr. James Hamilton's mill, it flows into the Grand River. On the south side of the creek, on the west side of the road, about where Dr. Nairn's residence now stands, there lived an early resident by the name of Michael Cox, a blacksmith. In the natural order of things this stream became known by the name which it still retains, Cox's Creek.

.. .. ..

Andrew Geddes came to Canada in September, 1834, and, with his family settled in Winterbourne, where they remained for about three years. They lived across the road from the Davidson family where Mr. Geddes owned the land west of the road to the river. Mr. Geddes was in Elora for a short time about 1839 and 1840, but went to live in Hamilton. In 1844 he was appointed Crown Land Agent at Elora, a position which he held for twenty-one years, to the great satisfaction of all with whom he had dealings, until his death on March 7th, 1865. He will be referred to more particularly later.

William Mann came from Norfolk, England, in the year 1840, and settled in Winterbourne. At this time the land east of the river road at Winterbourne was owned by the Geddes family. Mr. Mann bought this land and held it for some years, selling it to Captain Lanphier.

William Mann married Jane Holmwood from Sussex, England, who died in 1876, at the age of sixty-seven years, while Mr. Mann died in 1860, at the age of forty-five. Their son, Charles H. Mann, is now living on the 'James Dow' farm, west of the Grand river.

Captain Henry Lanphier, who was a brother of Thomas H. Lanphier, was in Canada but a comparatively short time, but in that short time he had much to do with this place. It was he who had the first dam built across Cox's Creek, the first mill, and that fine residence which is now the Presbyterian Manse. Then, in April, 1855, the land having been surveyed into village lots for Allan & Mathieson, it was Captain Lanphier who gave it the name of Winterbourne, after the ancestral home of the Lanphiers in England. He shortly afterwards went back to his home in England.

. .   .   . .

So far those mentioned have, with the exception of Capt. Smith, been situated along the road which follows the general course of the river northward. There was only one other spot, so far as can be learned, where a settlement had been made up to the year 1825. Simon Cress and his wife, Rachel, with their two sons and two daughters, came to Waterloo along with Mr. Erb, in 1806. They settled on land upon part of which the village of St. Jacob's stands now. In doing this they followed the rule by going up the Conestogo river. Simon Cress died in October, 1863, and his wife twenty years before him. Those in their family were: Ephraim, the oldest; Polly, who married John Beatty; Jacob, died at Port Elgin, and Rachel, the wife of Elisha Hewitt. In the family of Ephraim Cress were: Simon; Levi, now living retired in St. Jacob's; John, also in St. Jacob's; Elizabeth, Mrs. Bricker; Polly, Mrs. John Whiteman; Rachel, Mrs. Bernard Meyer.

A son of Jacob Cress, who died at Port Elgin, is Peter Cress, living in St. Jacob's, and a daughter is Mrs. David Puttock, living at Blair, near Preston. Henry, son of Levi, is now on the old Cress farm at St. Jacob's.

. .   . .

High up on the hill, on the east side of the road and north of Cox's Creek at Winterbourne, there is a log house on the same site as a former one. It was here, at the home of Alpheus Smith, that the prayer meeting was being held, on a Sunday evening, during which Alpheus Smith's father, the old captain fell to the floor unconscious and remained in that state until the following Sunday when he died. Alpheus Smith married Ann Weaver, from Ancaster, and it was their daughter Mary, or Polly, a life long resident of Winterbourne, who told me the story of Captain Smith, which she alone could tell, and that but three weeks before her death.

. .   . .

John Holmwood came to the township of Flamborough from Brighton, Sussex, England. In his family there was John, who lived in Flamborough; George married Margaret Brander and lived near Winterbourne; Henry kept a hotel in Dundas; Walter married Mary Ann Thompson; Robert Penfold Holmwood, who married Elizabeth Millard; Leah married Robert Britton and after his death taught school in Winterbourne, about 1850; while Jane married Wm. Mann, who then owned the land that most of Winterbourne is on; and Emma was the wife of Thomas Crooks, of Crook's Hollow, in West Flamborough.

ELORA

When the Crooks estate put Capt. Smith off the farm, which had for so long been his home, it was Thomas Crooks who came to live on it. The Crooks Tract, as it was called, included all the land for some distance on either side of the river road from Capt. Smith's old home, which is now the Stroh farm, up to and including part of the Millard farm. The German Company's Tract is said to have taken in from what is now the north part of the Millard farm to the town line between the townships of Woolwich and Pilkington.

After Thomas Crooks had come to live in Capt. Smith's old home, his brother in law, Walter Holmwood, came to what was then Cox's Creek and started the first store, the site of which was half way up the hill, on the north side of the creek and on the west side of the road. Having opened this store, his brother, Robert P. Holmwood, came to clerk for him and remained in Winterbourne until his death. His son, Robert Penfold Holmwood, is now living in his father's home, and this is the house that Capt. Smith built after he had to leave his first one. As a specimen of a well-built log house it is well worth examining, while the historical incidents associated with it make it still more interesting. To many this house will be better known by explaining that it is the one which is close to Holmwood's cider mill.

. .   . .   . .

John Gordon was one of a party that came to Elora in October, 1834. He there married Fanny (Frances) Martin, and built a house, but shortly afterward settled on the farm which is now owned by their son, Albert Gordon, on the east side of the road, a little north of Winterbourne. John Gordon's father, mother and three sisters came out from Scotland a few years later than he did and lived with him. The father and son were master cabinet makers in the City of Aberdeen.

For some time after the Davidson family left, the Gordon home was known as the Lower Woolwich post-office, and the old, original letter box is said to be still in use in the present Winterbourne office.

One of John Gordon's sisters, Jane, was the wife of Thomas H. Lanphier.

Of the children of John Gordon and Fanny Martin : John married Leah Britton and lives in Eramosa ; William married Miss Quarry, of Dundas, and is now in Stratford ; Eliza married Dr John Douglas, now in Chicago, and Albert married Eliza Lanphier and now lives on the old home.

. .   . .

From Cox's Creek to the nearest house in the township of Pilkington there lay five miles of a dense bush, with several black ash swamps. This was called the long woods and a sort of a road was opened through it at the expense of General Pilkington. As late as the year 1833, the only clearing in this five miles of bush was one made by Wm. Letson on what is now known as the 'Howlett' farm.

Daniel Letson was the name of this William Letson's father, and his house stood between his son's and the river, which is here, because of one of the numerous bends on the river, quite a distance from the road. Daniel Letson was born in Pennsylvania, lived for a time in Utica, N. Y, and came to Canada in 1827. His wife and family came with him but some of them soon returned to New York State and married there. In the Letson family there were: William, born in 1801, married Catharine Longhouse ; Rhodes married Helen LeBarr ; Daniel was married and lived at Oswego, N. Y. Jeremiah married Eleanor Lasby ; George married his brother's widow, Eleanor Lasby ; Henry married Caroline Pinder ; Nancy was married to Daniel Alvous and lived near Lockport, N. Y ; Roxy was married to a Mr. Frost, near Lockport. N. Y. ; Julia was married to Mr. James Smith and lived near West Montrose,

Thomas Smith, a son of Capt. Smith, made a clearing on a farm west of the river road and opposite to the one that has long been known as the 'Millard' farm. He sold his clearing to his brother-in-law, Emanuel Gaukel, and, with his family, went to live in the township of Beverly.

Emanuel Gaukel was his right name but he was oftener called Mongowgkil. He was a son of Frederick Gaukel, who came from Wurtemburg, Germany, to Berlin, and for some years he had a hotel, where now the Walper House stands. Emanuel Gaukel married Mary Smith and came to live on the farm upon which his wife's brother, Thomas Smith, had made a clearing. Mongowgkil was a large man, an auctioneer and a constable. At one time he had a saw mill near West Montrose. When the Wellington, Grey and Bruce Railway was opened through to Southampton he went there. He had a saw mill and kept the post office at an Indian village called Chippewa Hill, about two miles from Southampton. Here Emanuel Gaukel died about October, 1893, and Mary, his wife, on March 18th, 1887. Of their family: Frederick married Alma Meisener and lived between Lynden and Jerseyville; Washington married Jessie Glennie, he was drowned at Port Elgin on October 25th, 1874 at the age of twenty two; Elizabeth was married to Hiram McKay and now lives near Port Elgin; Zuby (Azubah) married Ira Kilborn, a Methodist Minister, and went to Iowa; Polly (Mary) was married to William Douglas and is now in Chicago.

John Millard and his wife, Elizabeth Wilton, came from Somersetshire, England, where Mr. Millard had been a paper maker. They were first in Orleans County, New York State, in 1831, then, in 1843, came to the farm on the east side of the road, opposite Emanuel Gaukel's, where their son, Mortimer Millard, resides. Those in the family were: John, died at the age of 19; George married Susannah Wismer and they lived on the north part of the Millard farm; Mortimer married Catharine Shields and lives on the old homestead; Matilda married Henry Wilcox, of Toledo, Ohio, and Elizabeth married Robert Holmwood

John Millard died on May 31st, 1877, at the age of eighty three, and his wife died Dec. 28th, 1876, at the age of eighty two and a half.

As we go farther up the river road we pass the 'Big Ridge,' where the roadway has been cut through a gravel hill and then we come to a cross road, where, on the south east corner, Jacob Zuber has lived so long that it is now called Zuber's Corners. The road to the west, winding down the hill, passes the West Montrose school house and on through one of the prettiest woodland roads in this locality, crosses the river to the village of West Montrose. The bridge which here crosses the Grand River was long called Benner's Bridge, after Jacob Benner, who for a number of years had a store, a saw mill and a woollen mill at that place.

Mr. and Mrs. Tribe, with their family, came from Sussex, England, in the year 1832. Mr. Tribe died during the first winter that the family was in Canada and was buried near Cornell's, on the site of which is now the 'Cress House' in Preston. In this family there were: Benjamin, who married Mary Ann Lepard and lived in Pilkington; Johnathan married Martha Cornell, while Harry and Richard were not married. The daughters were Sarah, who was Mrs. Rapson; Charlotte was Mrs. Evans, and Mary was Mrs. Thomas Irvine, of Paisley, and it was at her home that her mother, Mrs. Tribe, died. Jane Tribe was married in Sussex, England, to Jesse Penfold, who had been a soldier and in service at the City of Quebec about 1814. They, with Mrs. Penfold's parents, came to Canada in 1832.

The home of the 'Tribe' family was first in the township of Dumfries, then the mother and some of the family came to the township of Pilkington and lived in a log house which stood between the road and the river, not quite half way between what is best known as the 'James Ross' farm and Inverhaugh post office.

The members of this, the older Penfold family, children of Jesse Penfold and Jane Tribe, were: Matilda, born in Sussex, England, on the same day as Queen Victoria, May 24th, 1819, and came to Canada in 1832. She was married to Thomas Adsett and they lived on a farm on the east side of the river road, which was the next farm south of Mr. Wollis'. They afterwards removed to Guelph, where Mr. Adsett died on April 21st, 1870, at the age of seventy. Mrs. Adsett was again married to the late James Hall, of Winterbourne, and died April 24th, 1896, at the age of seventy-six years and ten months. Jesse Penfold married Hannah Wismer; Caroline married Henry Wilbee, a son of Henry Wilbee, of Elora, and now lives in Brussels; Esther, born on board ship in 1832, married Owen Roberts and lived for many years where the Cascade Creek crosses the road near Thomas Cleghorn's farm in Pilkington, but, with a large family, moved to Kansas; Harriet married John Scully and their family all live in Berlin.

Jesse Penfold, son of Jesse Penfold and Jane Tribe, was born in Sussex, England, on December 30th, 1823, and with his parents and his mother's parents, came to the township of Dumfries in 1832. He was there married, in 1842, to Hannah Wismer, who was born May 30th, 1825, and died in April, 1903.

In the year 1844, Jesse Penfold took up the farm on which he has lived for sixty-two years, and he was the first settler on the west side of the river, between West Montrose and Elora, which is a distance of eight miles. His farm is known as Lot 64 in the German Company's Tract, west of the Grand River, in the township of Woolwich. Among those in this family there are: Susannah, married Thomas Batters, lives in Saskatchewan; Thomas married Margaret Annette Harvey and lives in Port Arthur; Elizabeth married Jacob B. Hewitt and is now in South Dakota; John married Emma Holzworth and lives on a farm a short distance north from his father's; Phoebe was married to Robert Peel Winfield, and is now living in Elora; Hannah was married to John Mitchell and lives on the 'George Lawrence' farm near the West Montrose school, and Jesse Penfold, jr., married Jessie (Janet) Darby, from Parry Sound, and lives on the old homestead with his father.

Continuing along the river road to the northward, on the east side of the river, we come to the new Guelph & Goderich Railway, which has been under construction during the past year The first to take up a farm in this neighborhood was one by the name of Isaac Kepke. He was followed by Michael Spiez and then, on the same farm, west of the river road and that through which the railway is built, was Jonathan Tribe.

Jonathan Tribe married Martha Cornell and those in their family were: Nathaniel married Phoebe Lawrence; Thomas married Annias Sugg; Martha was unmarried; Miriam married Oscar Woodward; William married and lived in Michigan; Joseph and Alice went west to Alberta.

Jonathan Tribe died on March 12th, 1872, at the age of forty nine years and nine months. Mrs. Tribe went west, and died near Calgary, Alberta.

The one who followed Jonathan Tribe on part of this farm was Richard Moreill, who was born in Robin Hood's Forest, Mansfield, Nottinghamshire, England, on April 10th, 1809. He lived at Markham, Toronto and Brampton before coming to this farm in Woolwich.

Richard Moreill was married in England to Annias Gravies and in their family were: Helen married Samuel Sugg, they live in Clifford; Hannah married William Sugg and lives in Winterbourne; Mary married William Goodwin and lives near Inverhaugh; Richard married Ann Stafford, living in Harriston; Robert married Sarah Howse and they also live in Harriston; Thomas married Helen Letson, living near West Montrose; and George married Mary Brohman and lives at Elmira.

.. ..

On the west side of the road, between Zuber's corners and the railway, is the farm that was the home of the Lawrence family.

George Lawrence was born at Byfield, Northamptonshire, England, on August 8th, 1817. When he was eleven years of age he came to the township of Pilkington with King Reeves, who had gone back to England for a trip, and lived at his home because Mrs. Reeves was his aunt.

When he had taken up a farm for himself, George Lawrence married Harriet Singer and they had a family of twelve, of whom two died young: Phoebe married Nathaniel Tribe; Catharine married Frederick Lasby; Benjamin married Delilah Copeland; William married Jane Stewart; Mary married Sylvester Lasby; Merab married Charles Stockford; Angeline married Thomas Shaw; George married Laura Kerr, and he is for the second time Mayor of Palmerston; and Charles married Elizabeth Seaton.

George Lawrence died at Palmerston, at the home of his son, on May 22nd, 1892, and Mrs. Lawrence in August, 1899, at the age of seventy five.

.. ..

Edmund Wollis was born at Barnoldby-Beck, near Grimsby, Lincolnshire, England, on January 27th, 1823. In the year 1844 he came to Canada and for about two years worked in the townships of Darlington and Pickering. One morning in the spring time of 1846 he landed in Elora and then walked to Winterbourne to see the land in Waterloo County, of which he had heard. The river road through the long woods was only chopped out to about half its proper width, the logs forming the corduroy road were floating about in the many swamps, while, from the James Ross farm at the 'big bend' to the 'big ridge,' a distance of more than three miles, was without a clearing on either side of the road. Mr. Wollis soon took up his farm on the east side of the river road, at the 'little ridge.' To the south of him was Thomas Adsett's farm, while across the road from Adsett, on the west, was Richard Moreill and opposite to Mr. Wollis was, a little later, Stephen Webster. Each of these made clearings on the corners of their farms adjoining, so that, as Mr. Wollis says, "they soon let daylight in."

Mr. Wollis was married in August, 1855, to Jane Mackie, whose parents had come to Winterbourne, from Aberdeenshire, in October, 1837. Of their family: Margaret married John Elsley and lives near Mt. Forest; Mary died in September, 1900; George married Esther Gillies, near Mt. Forest; Annie married Samuel Burnett, lives near Listowel; Edmund married Alice Kirkness and lives near Mt. Forest; Elizabeth married William Glennie, lives in Eramosa, and Sarah, living with her parents, who, a few years ago, retired and now live in their comfortable home on the Elora and Salem road.

Cushman Smith, born at the Conestogo on November 11th, 1806, was named after an uncle of the same name at Lewiston, N. Y. Cushman Smith is the son of of Captain Smith who married the girl that he had helped to care for when she was a baby. This was Mary Asia Wilbee, who was born on the Atlantic ocean on June 11th, 1821, when the Wilbee family were on their way to settle on the Pilkington estate. She remained at Captain Smith's until she was two years old, when, her father having married again, she went to the home he then had for her in the township of Pilkington. When she had grown to womanhood Mary Asia was for a time at the home of Alpheus Smith at Cox's Creek, and it was at his brother's home that Cushman Smith again met the girl who, it would seem, was destined to become his wife.

Cushman Smith was one of those pioneers who made a clearing on a farm' built a house, began to have some comfort in his surroundings, then sold out to commence all over again the toilsome work on another bush farm. Half a dozen farms were mentioned that Cushman Smith lived on. The last one in this neighbourhood was that farm on the east side of the river road and just within the township of Pilkington. The remains of an orchard is all that marks the spot now.

Nowadays those who are looking for new farms to settle on go to New Ontario, or to the Great Canadian West, but when the Wellington, Grey and Bruce Railway had been built through to Lake Huron it was there, where the timber could be shipped by boat or railway that for men accustomed to bush life the prospects were brighter. Therefore, in the year 1874, although at the age of sixty-eight, Cushman Smith removed to a farm in the vicinity of Port Elgin, upon which some of his family still reside.

Long after he had left Pilkington, when old men who knew him were asked about him they would say, "no one hereabouts ever made better axe-handles than Cush. Smith ; he could beat them all."

Cushman Smith died at the home of his son Henry, near Port Elgin, on September 28th, 1891, at the age of nearly eighty five years, while his wife died on March 23rd, 1899. In their family were: Edward, who taught school at West Montrose and died there on June 30th, 1878 ; Thomas also died at West Montrose, January 6th, 1872; Stephen died at Berlin on November 10th, 1905 ; Elizabeth went to Petoskey, Michigan ; Henry and his sister, Amanda, are living on the farm near Port Elgin ; Angus is at Leland, Idaho ; Sarah lives on a farm near Southampton ; Ira lives at Wolverine, Michigan ; and Charlana died at Port Elgin, February 13th, 1891.

When commencing the history of the first settlers in Lower Pilkington, Elora and Upper Nichol, it was not intended that the early settlers in Woolwich should be included, but a study of the early settlement shows that a history of Pilkington would be incomplete without them. As has been shown, the first settlers in Woolwich had been Americans. As will be seen some of the first in Pilkington and Nichol were Americans. The first family in Elora was American. These American pioneers were at home in the bush. They had been brought up in it and their early training taught them many ways of living in comparative comfort under their great hardships which were unknown to to those from the 'Old Country.' Several old choppers, who came from England to Pilkington when boys, told how thankful they were to have been shown by their American neighbours how to use an axe instead of having to learn, as many did, by their own hard experience.

The first settlers sent out by General Pilkington were from the central counties of England. They knew nothing about bush life and had it all to

18   ELORA

learn. There was no 'Canada Company' to help them. Few of them had any money and the nearest settler was ten miles from a mill, while, for years, there were no roads.

Up to the year 1852 the township of Woolwich included what is now the township of Pilkington and was usually referred to as Upper and Lower Woolwich. The total population of the township of Woolwich in the year 1825 is said to have been eighty four. In the absence of any written records giving the names of settlers and their families the lists which are here given, for Woolwich and for Pilkington, have all been prepared from careful enquiries from many different persons, and, in most cases from relatives who would be most likely to know. There are many chances for mistakes to occur and, if they do, the reader is asked to remember that all that is claimed is that it is an effort to preserve a history that would, otherwise, be lost.

Township of Pilkington

THE FIRST SETTLERS: WHO THEY WERE AND WHERE THEY CAME FROM.

The first to settle, and make a clearing, in what is now the township of Pilkington was one by the name of William Wolcott, an American. He came about the year 1817 and was the first to occupy that farm, Lot 1, on the 2nd Concession east of the Grand River, which has since been the home of so many.

At this point the Grand river is free from its rocky channel, the valley widens, and the last rock disappears in the high but rounded hills. On top of the hill, high above the river, and overlooking the tall trees growing on the flats below, a fine spring of water rises, and, murmuring as it tumbles down the steep brae, wearing for itself a channel in a bed of marl, it joins the brimming river.

Beside this spring, on top of the hill, Wolcott built his log house. He made a clearing and other improvements which he sold to Squire Smith and, in company with the 'Two French Refugees,' went to New York to keep a school there.

Wolcott's farm will be known to many when it is stated that after Squire Smith and his son, Theophilus, died, this farm was sold to Thring, in 1844; to Bonallie in 1851; to George Ross in 1870, and now it is owned by Joseph Thomson, of Elora, and rented by Alexander Farquhar.

.. ..

Just when the 'Two French Refugees' came to Pilkington is not known, but it was probably not long after Napoleon's disastrous retreat from the Battle of Waterloo. They may have been here before Wolcott but they made no clearing and could not be called settlers. They are supposed to have done something in France that compelled them to travel for their health, and as they were in search of "a lodge in some vast wilderness, some boundless continuity of shade," they came up the Grand river. Seeking seclusion they followed up Mill Creek for half a mile and on the slope of a hill facing the south they built their log cabin. Not far from it was a spring of water, while the stream into which this spring flowed was an angler's Paradise.

The site of the Frenchmen's cabin is on Lot 4 on the 3rd Con., and a little west from the house that has long been owned by Alexander Holman.

.. ..

When the American Colonies rebelled against Britain the Six Nation Indians of New York State remained loyal to the British and at the close of the war for American Independence came over to Canada. The Indians now living near Brantford are descendants of these. It was felt by the then Government of Upper Canada that the loyalty of the Indians should be suitably acknowledged. Therefore, on the 25th of October, 1784, Sir Frederick Haldimand granted to the Six Nation Indians a tract of land six miles in width on either side of the Grand river. Some years later, finding that this was more land than they could use, the Indians, on November 2nd, 1796, executed a formal power of attorney to Captain Joseph Brant, one of their principal Chiefs, by which they authorized him to surrender certain portions of this land to the Government that it might be sold, and the proceeds invested, for the benefit of the Indians. The tract of land which Captain Brant was authorized to surrender was described in the power of attorney referred to and was stated to contain 310,391 acres. Under this authority several blocks of land were sold, among them being one to William Wallace, a carpenter at Newark, or Old Niagara. This was known as Block No. 3, and was said to contain 86,078 acres.

By deed dated May 10th, 1799, and registered on June 10th, 1799, William Wallace conveyed to Robert Pilkington part of Block No. 3, being all of the present township of Pilkington east of the Grand river, and by deed of May 10th 1799, and registered on June 11th, 1799, all that part of the township west of the river.

Robert Pilkington was a Captain in the Corps of Royal Engineers in service in Canada, and for several years before and after 1799 was resident at Toronto and Niagara. On his return to England, Captain Pilkington was promoted to be Major-General and was Colonel Commandant in the Corps of Royal Engineers. As such he was overseer, or inspector of fortresses and barracks. A military barracks was being erected at Weedon-Beck in Northamptonshire, England. Weedon-Beck is a parish of 1710 acres and was the Central Depot in England for Military Arms and Stores. It is right in the heart of 'Old England.'

As the land which he owned in Canada was of little use to him in its wild state 'General' Pilkington persuaded some with whom he had become acqainted at Weedon to emigrate and settle upon his land. One of the inducements offered was that each man would receive one hundred acres of land free. This they never received.

General Pilkington had been a busy man and he was much respected by those who knew him. He had owned this land for twenty years before he could get any one to settle upon it. Then there was not a road of any kind but merely a track through the bush, the same that had been followed by the Iroquois when they came up the Grand river to exterminate their enemies. General Pilkington spent considerable sums in opening roads. The Waterloo, or 'river road,' was opened at his expense and long crossways made. The Guelph and Elora road was also chopped out from the township line to Elora to the width of half a chain. The site for a future town was chosen on broken front, Lot 1, on the 2nd Concession, the foundation for a Church was dug, the stone quarried, a lime kiln built, a saw mill, grist mill, etc. All this cost money, and yet brought no return.

It is not certain that General Pilkington ever saw the land that was his, but the probability is that he did. It seems that he intended to make his home here 'when he retired.' Such is the tradition, and this is given as the reason why the land on the west side of the river was not surveyed until after his death, as he was reserving this as a home for himself. The house was to be on Lot 4, Concession A, west of the river, where the late Hugh Roberts lived for many years, and which is now owned by his son, Griffith Roberts. Without having any other evidence that General Pilkington had seen his land we would be inclined to believe that only one with the training and experience of a Military Engineer like himself would have made such an admirable choice for the site of a future town. Nor is it likely that he would leave such an important personal matter as the location of his home to be decided for him by others. Of his family little is known. It is said that a son visited at the home of Squire Reynolds after his father's death and a daughter was the wife of Robert Tylee, of the firm of Maitland, Tylee & Co., at one time merchants in Montreal. Major General Pilkington died at London, England, on the 6th of July, 1834. He had made his Will on the 15th of May previously leaving as his executors, his wife, Hannah Pilkington; John Simcoe Macaulay, a Capt.

JESSE PENFOLD

HUGH ROBERTS

in the Royal Engineers; Edward Tylee, Solicitor, London, and George Tylee, Gentleman, of Devizes, in Wiltshire, with power to deliver Deeds, etc. By a deed poll under the hands of John Simcoe Macaulay, George Tylee and Hannah Pilkington bearing date on or about the 26th day of August, 1834, they renounced and disclaimed all the real and personal estate leaving Edward Tylee as the only acting executor. Nothing was done until 1842 when James M. Strachan and John Beverley Robinson, of Toronto, came up to make arrangements with the settlers on the estate for up to this time few, if any, of the settlers had a title to the property they were living on. These gentlemen stopped at the home of Squire Reynolds for ten days, on his farm adjoining Elora. The price of the land was then fixed at four dollars an acre ; one fifth in cash and the remainder in five annual instalments.

But what of those who were promised one hundred acres free ? The executors for the Pilkington estate either could not, or would not carry out that agreement. The Provincial Government, long afterward, through the efforts of Squire Reynolds and Alexander D. Ferrier gave a grant of twelve hundred acres in the township of Flos. This was sold and the proceeds used for the payment of the farm, of 151 acres, which Squire Reynolds and A. D. Ferrier, as trustees, on September 9th, 1864, did grant unto Mary Ann Lepard, the widow of Benjamin Tribe. (This is now known as the 'Mutrie' farm). The reason for this was that Mary Ann Lepard was the granddaughter, and heir, of Squire Lepard, who, as Clerk of the Works at Weedon and an agent, as well as friend, of General Pilkington, was instrumental in bringing out many of the first settlers to this township.

Of the twelve men sent out by General Pilkington from 1819 to 1823 there are, so far as known, no descendants living in the township to-day. One by one the older ones died and the younger members of the family moved away from the scene of so much hardship and disappointment. The improvements made on their farms were sold as opportunity offered. Some of their descendants are living in Elora, while others are scattered over the continent. The remains of some are lying in unmarked graves in the corner of a field on the 'Mutrie' farm.

The following is a list of the twelve men who were induced to come to Canada and settle on General Pilkington's estate, and were promised one hundred acres each, which, owing to the death of General Pilkington, they never received.

1819.—Thomas Lepard and his wife were among the first who came from England to settle on the Pilkington estate. Lepard was Clerk of the Works at Weedon, or Weden, as it is also spelt. They are said to have been in comfortable circumstances in England, 'hired' a ship to convey the party to Canada ; even brought out their family carriage, which they could not, for want of roads, bring any farther than Galt, and there left it.

The house that Lepard built was near that now occupied by Mr. Mutrie. It is described as an odd looking structure, like three houses set down together. In the centre was a large room that was used for the transaction of business connected with the estate. It was also expected that in this room courts would be held, for, being a magistrate, the owner was generally called 'Old' Squire Lepard.

Mr. Lepard had a son who died in India leaving a widow and daughter, who was Mary Ann Lepard. These, with Katie Nevitt, as she was called, accompanied Mr. and Mrs. Lepard to Canada.

Shortly after coming to Pilkington Mrs. Lepard, jr., whose maiden name was Callaway, went to live in Dundas. She married James Taylor, who had a hotel in Galt. He died of the cholera in Hamilton. Mrs. Lepard, sr., died in

October, 1831, and was buried on that part of the farm which, it was expected, would have been the Churchyard. Squire Lepard soon went to Dundas, where he died. Mary Ann Lepard, having gone along with her mother to live in Galt, she there met, and on April 10th, 1837, was married to Benjamin Tribe, who then came to live on Squire Lepard's farm. Benjamin Tribe died in 1848 at the age of thirty-four. Mrs. Tribe continued to live on this farm until 1879, when she went along with her son, Robert Tribe, to Muskoka and died there on May 11th, 1894, at the age of seventy-seven.

In the family of Benjamin Tribe and Mary Ann Lepard there were: Robert, who was twice married, first to Mary Ann Lister, of Eramosa, then, at her death, to Margaret Gordon, daughter of the late Andrew Gordon, of Elora. They are now living at Devlin, in the Rainy River District. Thomas married Mary Kennedy and lived in Guelph ; Catharine married Robert Winfield, and one daughter, Sarah Jane, died at an early age.

Kate Nevitt, who was a niece of Mrs Lepard, sr., married John Hamilton, a lawyer, in Guelph, and died in the General Hospital there.

1819.—Robert Greenhalgh and his wife are said to have been the first of the English settlers to arrive in Pilkington in 1819. The farm they selected was on Lot 4 on the 1st Concesssion, on the Guelph and Elora road and just north of what has, for sixty years, been known as the 'Haig' farm. Up a little ravine, opposite the gate on the Haig farm, the foundation and a few fruit trees show where the house had been.

Greenall, as his neighbors pronounced his name, was a trumpeter in the artillery in England. He had one piece of property that proved very useful to himself and all his neighbors. This was a hand mill, like a large coffee mill, that was used for grinding grain, for the nearest grist mill at this time was at Preston, which was from twenty to twenty-four miles away. As it was the neighbours carried their grain on their backs to Greenhalgh's through the bush, often for two or three miles, and then, by hard work, they could grind a bushel of wheat in a day. The only alternative was to take turn about in going to Preston for a supply of flour.

Robert Greenhalgh was married to Martha Wood, a daughter of Christopher Wood, before leaving England. Their son, Rowley Greenhalgh, was, we believe, the first boy born in the township of Pilkington. But little is known of this family. They left their farm to live in Fergus where, it is said, Robert Greenhalgh died. In the family there were Rowley, Mary, Leonora, Elizabeth and Effie. Of these, Elizabeth married Samuel Coulter in Hamilton, and Leonora was Mrs. Long, and also lived in Hamilton.

1819.—Thomas Robinson and his wife settled on Lot 6, on the 4th Concession. Their house was on the east, and higher side of the river road, on the 'James Ross' farm.

By the time that the first Scotch settlers were coming to Upper Nichol, for the few years after 1834, this was the second clearing that was met with after leaving Winterbourne, Wm. Letson's being the first. One of a party that arrived in Elora on June 10th, 1835, said that at Mrs. Robinson's they found pans full of milk floating on spring water and "they were loath to leave it." Tired, mosquito bitten and tormented with the sweltering heat of their long walk through one of the roughest of swampy bush roads, the frugal fare and kindly welcome that was extended to them by Mr. and Mrs. Robinson was never forgotten and often mentioned by those who had experienced it.

Thomas Robinson died about the year 1840 and was buried on the farm, where, until recently, a fence marked the spot. Mrs. Robinson sold the farm to James Ross, the father of James Ross who is now living in Elora, and the two sons of the latter, John and Miller, are of the third generation of the Ross family to occupy this farm.

Mrs Robinson, with her son, George Robinson, who was at one time a wagonmaker in Elora, went to the township of Brant. A daughter married a Richard Jones, of Pilkington.

.. ..

1819.—George Reeve was born at Friars Maston, Warwickshire, on the 14th June, 1774 (?). His wife was Hannah Lawrence, from Byfield, Northamptonshire. Their first house was on Squire Lepard's farm, on the west side of the road, but this was burned down and the second one built on the east side of the road opposite. The site of this was between the top of the hill and the bend of the road on Lot 1 on the 2nd Concession. This is the farm on which Mr. Traill lives. The house was a log one, two stories high, with large fire places, and was a stopping place for all the first travellers coming to Elora. Although the proper spelling of the name was Reeve, this house was always referred to as Old King Reeve's place, and in this way the spelling of the name was changed so that the only one of the name, George Reeves, of Fergus, spells his name with an 's' at the end of it.

There was not an early raising, or bee, where hard work had to be done, at which Old King Reeves was not a leading spirit. He was active, supple and strong and there were few men who could outlift, outfight, outrun, or, when he took the notion, outwork the 'King of Woolwich' for, be it remembered, that up to the year 1852 this was called the township of Woolwich.

Mrs. Reeve was a good neighbour and, one might say, the only doctor for years. She became partially paralyzed, was, therefore, helpless and falling into the fireplace was severely burned, as she was alone at the time. From the effects of this and the paralysis she died on March 17th, 1851, at the age of seventy six years, and was buried in the old English Church burying ground.

After selling his farm to the late Arthur Ross, King Reeves moved into Elora He was accompanied by Lucy Colby, an adopted daughter, his best friend, who helped and cared for him. George Reeve died on July 13th, 1866 and was also buried in the old English Churchyard.

.. ..

1819.—Davies was to be the miller, but as the attempts at building a mill were not a success he went to Niagara Falls. He had charge of a mill there and while at work on the water wheel, one of the old kind, he fell off and was killed.

Among those who so kindly assisted by furnishing information about the first family in Elora, to none, as the reader will see, have we been more indebted than to the late Mrs. John Matthews, of Maquoketa, Iowa. Her early home was at Lundy's Lane, near Niagara Falls. In a letter to her son, Mr. E. L. Matthews of Minneapolis, in December, 1900, she wrote "As you take so much interest in this matter of pioneer life I will send you the letter of acknowledgement, for my reply to the questions the gentleman at Elora asked. You will see that he gives us some account of the first settlers near Elora. There is one, especially, that I well remember hearing of long before I saw your father—Mr. Davis, the miller, who was killed in a mill near Niagara Falls. I could not have been more than fourteen years of age at that time, yet it is fresh in my memory. It occurred on the 18th of October. It snowed all day, and the next day we heard of the accident. He had a wife and two daughters. A few years later his widow was married to your father's brother. These Pilkington settlers were all English and I got acquainted with some of them who called on us when we lived in Dundas."

According to this, Mr. Davis was killed on October 18th, 1828. While in Pilkington he lived on part of lot 1, con. 2, east of the Grand River, that was afterwards known as the John Marriot farm.

. .   . .

1821—Thomas Smith and his wife came two years later than those already mentioned, and lived on the Wolcott farm. He also made a small clearing on lot 1, con 1, which he sold to Wm. Reynolds in 1830. He was a Magistrate, and, like so many of the others, was called 'Old' Squire Smith. He sold his law books to William Reynolds when he became Squire Reynolds. Thomas Smith was born at Weedon Beck in April 1750, and died on the 22nd of April 1840, ninety years of age. Mrs. Smith was born at Hoo, Sussex, on October 26th, 1763, and died in Pilkington on September 8th, 1825, at the age of 62. Both were buried on the Lepard farm.

. .   . .

1821.—Theophilus Smith, a son of Thomas Smith, came to Canada with him and lived on the same farm. He married Janet MacDonald and in their family were: William, Mary Ann, Sarah, Margaret, Thomas and Christina. Of these, William was a noted rifle shot and was at Wimbledon; Margaret married Richard Ariss, and Mary Ann married James Wilson and lived in Elora, where they and their family are well known. James Wilson was by trade a moulder, and a good violinist. Their sons were James, Theophilus, Ralph and Hugh, and there were two daughters. The eldest son, James Wilson, is Superintendent of Telegraphs in British Columbia. He commenced his successful career in the Elora Telegraph Office, under the late John Hele.

. .   . .   . .

1821.—George Wilbee, his wife, three daughters and a son, Henry Wilbee, who was married before leaving England, came from Devizes, in Wiltshire, which was also the place where Edward Tylee, the solicitor for the Pilkington estate, was born.

George Wilbee was a carpenter and while his family lived on the Wolcott farm he worked much of the time for the Hon. James Crooks, of West Flamboro. From a cold, caught while working in a cellar, followed by inflammation of the lungs, he died at Crooks' Hollow about 1828. Mrs. Wilbee died in January, 1841, at the home of Rowley Wood, in Winterbourne, where he was living at that time, at the age of seventy four, and was buried in the English Churchyard at Elora.

The three daughters were Charlotte, Elizabeth and Mary.

Charlotte married Josiah Johnston and in this family there are: Mrs. Leonora Land, now living in Elora; Thomas Johnston, also in Elora; Oliver Johnston, who died at Parry Sound, on April 12th, 1904, at the age of sixty-seven; Mrs. Sophia Hutchison, Elora; Mrs. Agnes McGee, near Morpeth, Ontario; Mrs. Robert Topham, Elora; and Mrs. Elizabeth Dalby, at Toronto Junction.

Elizabeth Wilbee married Rowley Wood. They had no family, but an adopted son, John R. Wood, another Elora boy who became an expert telegraph operator in John Hele's Drug Store on Mill street, and since he left Elora, thirty five years ago, has been a prominent railroad official in Detroit.

Mary Wilbee was the wife of Wm. Reynolds and there was a large family, who will be referred to later. Of this family the only one living in Elora is Mrs. William Gibbon, to whom we are under a great obligation for her assistance in preparing this account of the earliest settlers in Pilkington Township. In the home of her father, Squire Reynolds, she had exceptional opportunities of learning this history which her retentive memory has preserved.

.. ..

1821—Henry Wilbee was a son of George Wilbee and he was married before leaving England to Sarah Sanders. On the voyage out, on June 11, 1821, their daughter, Mary Asia, was born and the mother died at Capt. Smith's as already mentioned. Henry Wilbee afterward married Mary Wood.

The farm that Henry Wilbee expected to own was part of Lot 3, on the 3rd concession, that was later known as the 'Blyth' farm, and his father George Wilbee had chosen part of Lot 3, on the 2nd Concession, that was afterward owned by George Fasken. The house in which Henry Wilbee lived was on the west side of the river road, on the Wolcott farm, and about two miles south from Elora. His father's house was on the east side of the road opposite. A small stream flowing from a spring crosses the road at this place and near by is a cross road that leads to a fording place on the Grand River. Their houses were on the side of the hill facing the south, and they lived here for some years, but there is nothing to mark the spot now.

Both father and son were carpenters, and, like his father, Henry Wilbee, had to leave his home to find employment at his trade. It was almost five years after coming to Pilkington that the City of Guelph was started by the Canada Company and he helped to complete some of the first buildings there and he also worked at Goderich. In 1833 Henry Wilbee was employed by Mr. Gilkison to build a saw mill at the Elora Falls. To serve as a shelter while doing this work he built the first log shanty west of the Grand River any where near Elora, which means that at this time there was not another habitation between this part of the Grand River and Lake Huron. Later, in 1839, he came to live in Elora in a house on the west corner of Victoria and Woolwich streets. One of his contracts was the carpenter work of the first English Church. He left Elora in 1856 and died at Dundas in March 1858 at the age of sixty-two. In his family there were: Mary Asia married Cushman Smith; Henry married Caroline Penfold and lived at Brussels, he was killed there by a falling beam; William was killed by a falling tree near Capt. Smith's; Henrietta died when young; George married Jane Penfold. He died at Doon in October 1886. (Mrs. Hiram Card, living in Elora, is a daughter); John married Bethany Cowil and lives at Grand View, near Brantford; Thomas married Elizabeth Swain, he died at Brantford; Sarah married Charles Moss and went to Flushing, Michigan; Frederick married Mary O'Neill, lives in Hamilton; Elizabeth married Thomas Turner; Edwin M. lives in Piqua, Ohio; and Leonora died young.

1823—Christopher Wood, with his wife and family, came from Hull, Yorkshire, England. They settled on the south-east part of lot 3, on the 3rd concession. This farm is on the flats near where Mill Creek joins the river. On the opposite, or west side, Carrol's Creek flows into the river also but through such a mass of fallen logs and underbrush that it escapes observation. As Carrol's Creek is fed by springs of cold water, and the place where it enters the river is quite deep, this deep hole in the river was a favorite spot for fishermen and it was long called 'Mother Wood's.' In his family there were four daughters and a son, Rowley Wood. The daughters were: Martha, who married Robert Greenhalgh; Mary married Henry Wilbee; Effie (Euphemia) married Josh. Callaway; and Leonora married Charles Heslem.

Mr. and Mrs. Wood, with two young relatives, Fred. and James Wood, went to Dundas about the fall of 1834. Their farm remained as they left it until the year 1844 when it was taken up by Sandy Watson, from Kettins, in Forfarshire, Scotland, and in this way it is best known as the 'Sandy Watson' farm. It is now owned by David Fasken, Barrister, Toronto.

1823—Rowley Wood. a son of the former, lived on the same farm. After going with his parents to live in Dundas, Rowley lived for a short time in Winterbourne and then built a house in Elora, where he was for many years a well known resident. His was one of the worst cases of injustice on the part of the executors, or agents, of the Pilkington estate. Besides the one hundred acres to which he was entitled as one of the first twelve settlers he had been led to expect, and there is little doubt that Gen. Pilkington intended him to have a farm situated on Mill Creek. As the exact boundaries were not specified the executors made that the excuse for depriving him of it. The reason why Gen. Pilkington particularly wished to befriend Rowley Wood was that he was a relative, and named after Gen. Rowley, a friend of Pilkington's in England. It makes little difference now, although it would have been a great help to Rowley Wood and his wife, but it is only mentioned in this place to show that from first to last the early settlers in the Township of Pilkington experienced nothing but disappointment.

It is not our intention to dwell at length upon the hardships and privations of these, the first settlers in the Township of Pilkington. Transplanted from the homes where their forefathers lived in the centre of England to the midst of a dense bush in the heart of Western Ontario they were left to their own resources, and under conditions entirely different from those they had been accustomed to they were to commence their struggle for existence. Buoyed up by the hope that they would soon be landed proprietors they set to work, and, while they lived in houses on the Wolcott farm they built others beside King Reeve's place on the Lepard farm. These were used until they had decided where their homes would be.

It was on a Sunday afternoon, in the fall of the year 1819. The few Englishmen who were here at that time met at King Reeve's place to talk over their prospects in this new country. They were not thinking about going to Church for there wasn't one within forty miles. They were quite satisfied about one thing and that was that "they were at the back of the world." And they also knew that their greatest present need was in some way to provide lumber for their homes for they were not like American settlers who could build a comfortable houses with no other tools than their axes. In the still air of that autumn afternoon they heard an unusual sound coming from the north east. This they could not explain, and as they had nothing else to do they decided to take a walk and explore the unknown region farther up the Grand River. So they went down past Squire Lepard's house, near where now Mr. Mutrie lives, until they came to a small stream that crossed their path and fell over the high, rocky river bank, near the 'Stone sidewalk.' Here they found a well-worn trail that had been used for centuries by the Indians when portaging past the deep, rocky channel on the Grand River. Following this Indian path for half an hour they became still more curious to know what caused the dull, deep sound that was becoming louder. Finally they came within sight of the Falls on the Grand River. The rain, which had been falling for some days, had increased the flow of water in the river until, tossing and tumbling down the forty feet of fall, it made the noise that called them, as it has called many others since that day. The islet rock that stands alone in the centre of the Falls might first have attracted their notice had not something else that, to them, was even more striking, absorbed their attention and opened their eyes in astonishment. There, before them, on the face of the hill, on the right, was a settler's log house and a clearing from which crops had been harvested. They lost no time in visiting their newly found neighbor, who, they learned, was Roswell Matthews. He, like themselves, had been lured by fair promises to make his home in this wilderness, and with his wife and family of nine children had been living here for almost two years, far from all the comforts, and even necessaries, of civilization.

Fortunate, indeed, was this meeting. To the Matthews family it was a relief from the utter loneliness of their life. To the English settlers it meant that in their new neighbors they had found those who could help them in their many difficulties incidental to bush life, for Roswell Mathews and his wife were natives of Vermont and New Hampshire, and accustomed from childhood to a life in the woods.

Why he was here, and how he came to be the first settler in Elora, or in the Township of Nichol, will be told later on, but what interests us now is that in Roswell Matthews our English friends found a millwright.

Before coming to make his home near the Falls on the Grand river Roswell Matthews lived in West Flamborough, and while there, in the year 1816, he worked for the Hon. James Crooks at the building of a mill at Crook's Hollow, which is about two or three miles west of Dundas. In those days Mr. Crooks was an agent for General Pilkington, so, when the English settlers found they were very much in need of a saw mill it was to Mr. Crooks they applied and it was he who gave instructions to have a dam and saw mill built, while the one to whom he gave the contract was Roswell Matthews.

The site selected for the saw mill was on the east bank of the river, on the Lepard farm. Here the river bank slopes down to the water's edge, and it was here that when Indians were passing up the river they removed their conoes to portage past the succession of rapids and falls farther up the river. On the west side the river bank rises to a perpendicular height of seventy feet, and, as if to leave no feature wanting in a perfect landscape, a beautiful waterfall, called the "Cascade," falls over a rocky cliff, broken into white drops as it falls from ledge to ledge, until it disappears in the river below.

It was in this lovely spot that work was commenced early in the summer of 1820. A dam was built across the river, which is here 150 feet in width between the rocky banks. Mr. Matthews guaranteed the dam to stand for three years, but not being able to find a solid rock bottom, owing to the bed of the river being worn into deep pot holes, he was forced to place the sills of the dam on the loose stones. The dam was about ten feet high, formed of logs, for until this mill was built they had no sawed lumber and few tools but axes. Behind a projecting rock at the east end of the dam they built the saw mill which was 18 by 24 feet.

In the Spring of 1822 the annual floods came in full force, washed out the stones from the deep hole in the centre of the river, undermining the dam so loosened the whole affair that it floated down stream. Not daunted with his loss, Mr. Matthews and his son again went to work, filled up the hole in the river bed with logs, brush and stones, and once more erected the dam ; this time adding a grist mill 30 by 40 feet. The running gear was made by Gillespie & White, while the other machinery, with the exception of the main gudgeons and a few smaller shafts, was made of wood. Both mills were in operation for a time, the saw mill turning out sufficient lumber to supply the wants of the settlers, but the grist mill ground very little, for Mr. Davies, who was to be the miller, had gone away and Old King Reeves, who undertook to run the mill, didn't understand the business. Many humorous stories were told of his experience as a miller but the settlers mostly did their own milling.

Seeing that the dam would not withstand the spring floods, preparations were made to erect the mills on what was then known as Frenchmen's Creek. Quite a lot of the machinery had been removed when the water again made a breach in the dam, at the end of it this time, and kept wearing it away until the dam went down the river like its predecessor having stood for three years and three days. A few timbers of this old dam may still be seen on the east side of the river near the 'Cascade' and the foundation of one of the mills is also there but hidden under cedar trees.

Some of the machinery that was washed away was secured by Mr. Matthews who built a raft and followed it. The mills were then set up on Frenchmen's Creek. This time the dam was built by a man named Blosdale, who was indebted to Mr. Crooks and took little trouble to make a good job of the dam. Both saw and grist mills were in operation again for a few years but the cedar roots in the bed of the creek caused the dam to leak. A little down stream from the bridge which crosses the creek on the road between School House number 4 and Inverhaugh Post Office, what remains of the dam may still be seen. While the mill was in working order here it was Josh. Callaway who had charge of it but after Gen. Pilkington's death everything was allowed to go to wreck. For several years after this the mills were used by the settlers themselves until the building of the grist and saw mills at Elora by Allan & Co., in 1843. This left the old mills useless. The iron was carried away by different persons, and, at last, to secure some iron which formed part of the building the mills were set on fire, the old iron taken to Guelph and sold and so finally disposed of.

Besides those already mentioned other early residents in Pilkington were: Anson and Abram Matthews, the two eldest sons of Roswell Matthews. They came to Elora along with their father and, although they lived there for several years, were yet in time to be the first to settle in what is called Lower Pilkington. They made a clearing on Lot 9, Con. 3, which they sold in 1832, to Mr. Thacker, and then made another clearing on the next lot, now occupied by Mr. Wm. Weadick.

Anson Matthews was born August 31st, 1800. He married Helen Callaway. They afterwards lived near Benton Harbor, Michigan.

Abram Matthews was born January 21st, 1804; he married Diana Nicklin. He is said to have been employed to chop for General Pilkington the west half of the Guelph and Elora road, from the lower end of the township to Elora. In 1840, with several of his neighbours, he removed to Acton, where he died in 1886, at the age of eighty two.

[Of the many different branches of the Matthews family the only descendants that came back to live in Elora were Mrs. Broley, a daughter of Abram Matthews, and her family, of whom there are four: Mrs. Godfrey, wife of Mr. Thomas Godfrey, Postmaster in Elora; Mrs. R. D. Norris, formerly of Elora, now in Toronto; Mr. Warner E. Broley, Life Insurance Agent, Elora, and Mr. Charles L. Broley, of the Merchants' Bank, Delta, Ontario.]

Charles Lasby and Margaret Challener, his wife, were from Staffordshire, England. The date of their arrival in Pilkington is uncertain, but it was not later than 1828. The farm upon which they settled was on the south side of Cox's Creek, at Ponsonby, and is now called the 'Fife' farm. Their reason for selecting this was that the timber was thin along the banks of the stream, while on the beaver meadow there was a heavy growth of wild grass with which to feed their oxen. Their house was on the side road leading to Bethany Church, and the aged parents were buried on the 'Egerton Fife' farm. They had a family of twelve, of whom Joseph Lasby was one. He lived on that corner farm northeast of the Bethany Church. In 1837 he married Matilda Crowther, and it is from their family that all in this locality by the name of Lasby are descended. Of their family of one girl and eight boys the only ones now living are Mrs. John Seaton, of Altona, Michigan, and Mr. Walter Lasby, of Northfield, Minnesota.

Joseph Lasby died in January, 1878, while Mrs. Lasby died in June of 1854.

.. ..

Josiah Johnston was from Birmingham. He also took up a farm in Lower Pilkington at an early date but left it about 1837 to live in Elora, where he worked at his trade as a blacksmith.

Josiah Johnston died March 8th, 1887, at the age of eighty-three. Mrs. Johnston (Charlotte Wilbee) died October 9th, 1891, at the age of eighty-eight years and four months.

.. ..

John Nicklin and his wife, Mary Sutton, were from Staffordshire. There were ten in the family. They came by the Erie Canal to Buffalo, intending to go to Ohio, but found that they would have to wait a month for a boat to take them, so came to Canada instead. This was in October, 1828. John Nicklin took up four hundred acres of land, part of which is now owned by Mrs. Charles Nicklin and her sons: the old home being on the farm now owned by Mr. James Lasby.

.. ..

William Reynolds, the youngest son of the Rev. Owen Reynolds, Rector of Conway, was born at Aber, near Conway Castle, in North Wales, on November 10th, 1810. When a young man it was expected that a commission would be purchased for him in the service of the East India Company, but the death of his father changed those plans and he came to Canada. Sailing from Liverpool in May, 1830, he arrived at Quebec in the latter part of June. From this he visited Montreal, Bytown and many other places in search of a locality in which to make his home, but found none to his liking. After three months' wandering he arrived at Crooks's Hollow and met the Hon. James Crooks, to whom he had a letter of introduction. Here Mr. Crooks, who was Gen Pilkington's agent, advised Mr. Reynolds to visit Upper Woolwich, which he did and found a community that suited him and he decided to remain. Another fact which, no doubt, greatly influenced Mr. Reynolds in this decision was that here he met his future wife, Mary Wilbee, to whom he was married on August 9th, 1831.

On that farm, Lot 1, Con. 1, adjoining Elora, a thirty acre clearing had been made by Squire Smith and his son, and this Mr. Reynolds bought, at the same time buying, in December, 1830, from Mr. Crooks the 100 acres of land which, we believe, was the first land paid for in the Township.

Being a young man with a good education, Mr. Reynolds was appointed a Magistrate in 1833, although he was then only twenty three years old, and not long afterward was made a Commissioner in the Court of Requests, which was a Court in vogue before Division Courts. He was also the first member of the District Council and the first School Inspector. But law cases were rare in Pilkington and for the first few years after his appointment he was oftener called upon to conduct the marriage ceremony, for it was several years before a minister was stationed here. Just how far out of the world it was may be shown by the following address, which was on a letter received by him in 1831:

                    William Reynolds, Esq.,
                      Woolwich, to the care of
                      James Crooks, Esq.,
via Liverpool,   West Flamborough,
  New York   near Dundas,
  and   Burlington Bay,
  Queenston.   Upper Canada,
                      America.

For some years after Mr. Reynolds' arrival in Pilkington he frequently read Prayers to the neighbors gathered to hear them, and also read the service at the graves of those buried on the hill near King Reeve's place and, later, in the Churchyard on his farm.

After the failure to complete the Church on the Lepard farm, Mr. Reynolds set about the erection of an Episcopal Church, giving first one acre of land and afterwards three acres more. In his efforts to build this church he was joined by two gentlemen who were then in Elora, Mr. Andrew Geddes and Mr. David Gilkison. In the design of this building Mr. Reynolds seemed to have been thinking of the church so closely associated with his boyhood days, in which his father had preached in his far off home. That the shape was the same is shown by a beautiful pencil sketch, which was made by Mr. Reynold's sister, of the old Church near Conway Castle, in Wales.

At a meeting held in Elora on Nov. 7th, 1839, a committee of three—William Reynolds, Andrew Geddes and David Gilkison—was appointed to carry out this project. The frame work was put up by John Gafney, William Day and Joseph Huxtable; the plastering was done by Thomas Irvine and the carpenter work by Henry Wilbee. While this was being done each member of the committee used his influence with friends and their appeals were generously responded to. Altogether the sum of two hundred and eleven pounds was raised. Thirty-five pounds of this was placed at the disposal of the committee by the Rev. Arthur Palmer to whom it had been entrusted. He was an Episcopal clergyman, living in Guelph, who had, as a missionary, occasionally visited and preached to these English settlers. That the leading spirit in this work was Mr. Reynold's mother is shown by her letters to her son urging and encouraging him to persevere in this work. Besides the money which at different times she sent as her own contribution, the following extract from one of her letters is interesting as it mentions who some of the other contributors were.

                                      Conway, Nov. 13, 1840.
My Dear William:—

        I received your letter via Halifax, dated Sept. 30th, early in this month and have been waiting to answer it until I heard what the Dean of Bangor had got towards your Church. He has been very kind and has done all he could to get subscriptions, so I will give you their names:

        Lady Pembroke............twenty pounds;
        Henry Reynolds ....ten pounds;
        Mrs. Oakley .... ten pounds;
        Colonel Wynne ....five pounds;
        Mrs Taylor................five pounds;
        Mr. Lear..................one pound;

making in all fifty one pounds which the Dean sent last week by a London merchant, directed to you, with a letter, so I hope your Church will be finished and that the blessing of God may be upon it and your wife and children for your zealous support in giving four acres of your own land for a Glebe for a resident Clergyman." Farther on she says, "I shall be seventy-four on the 27th of this month."

The month of August, 1842, found the building ready for public worship, but it was not until 1844 that the congregation was visited, at long intervals, by an appointed Clergyman. In this year the Rev. James Mockridge came occasionally, for his duties covered the Wellington and Gore Districts, a length of about one hundred miles. He was followed, in 1846, by the Rev. Donald Fraser, who came to this congregation once every two weeks. In August, 1849, the Rev. J. W. Marsh was appointed to the charge of Elora and parts adjacent, and this gave the congregation one service every Sunday. It was while Mr. Marsh was here that the Parsonage was built, the land for which was given by David, Alexander and Robert Gilkison. Mr. Marsh resigned his charge in 1852, and was succeeded by the Rev. John Smithurst, who remained the pastor until 1857, when the Rev. C. E. Thomson was appointed and remained for more than twenty years. He was followed by the Rev. H. L. Yewens on Jan. 1st, 1878, while he was succeeded about Christmas, 1879, by the Rev. P. L. Spencer, who remained until Jan., 1887, when the Rev. R. S. Locke was in charge until his resignation in April, 1888. He was followed from July, 1888 until June, 1903, by the Rev. Thomas Smith, when the Rev. E. F. Hockley came, and after one year was succeeded by the present incumbent, the Rev. V. E. F. Morgan.

On the 24th of September, 1848, the Church was consecrated by Bishop Strachan, of Toronto, and named The Church of St. John the Evangelist. The old building continued to be used until the present church was built and opened in October, 1875.

Mr. Reynolds left his farm to his son, Frank, and went to Morpeth, Ontario, where he died on Sept. 11th, 1877, in his sixty seventh year. Mrs. Reynolds died at the home of her daughter in Byron, Ontario, on Sept. 4th, 1887, at the age of seventy four years and eight months. Both were buried in the Elora Cemetery.

Of a family of thirteen those now living are : Mrs. William Gibbon, Elora ; Mrs O'Connor, Byron, Ont.; Mrs. Adam Douglas, Brussels, Ont.; Owen, at Stockton, Cal.; Mrs. Henry Stewart, Morpeth, Ont; George Playford, Grass Valley, State of Washington.

.. ..

No fact is isolated. No event is solitary. No force works alone. No life exists but as a part of all other lives. We cannot separate our fortunes, or arrest the influences by which we touch each other. Society is a ship in which all are passengers, and what effects one effects all.

General Pilkington going to the Parish of Weedon to superintend the building of the Military Barracks there was the first link in a chain of circumstances that influenced many from that part of England to settle in the Township of Pilkington. These, in turn, brought many others. When Mr. Reynolds came to the Township and united his fortunes with the daughter of one of those settlers, he was not only doing what was to effect his own career but also that of others who were in no way related to him. It was owing to the fact that Mr. Reynolds was from the north of Wales that a number of Welshmen came to make their homes in the vicinity of Elora. When her son had written and told her of the brighter prospects in this new country, Mrs. Reynolds persuaded one family after another to emigrate, directing them to her son in Canada, where all found a kindly welcome at Mr. Reynold's hospitable home until they could be comfortably settled on farms of their own.

Along with them this time there was Richard Williams and his brother, Hugh Williams, who lives in Brussels. While at Liverpool on their way out they met with several Englishmen who came with them. These were Edward Badley, (whose son, Mr. Robert Badley, and grandson, Mr. John Geddes, live in Salem), Joseph Small and Samuel Small. Joseph Small was better known in Elora for several years after this as "Old Doctor Small." His brother, Samuel, was a shoemaker and lived in Fergus, while Joseph, Jr., a son of the old doctor, with others in the family, went to live in Arthur.

While the Hughes family were living near King Reeve's house, in the winter of 1832-3, a man by the name of McKinney was sent out from England to build the Church around which General Pilkington expected a town to grow. The foundation was dug on the highest part of the Lepard, or as it is now known, the Mutrie farm. McKinney had gone about his work very deliberately. Although there was lots of good building stone close at hand on the banks of the river, he must have freestone for the sills and corners. This was quarried on the 'Beattie' farm, in Lower Nichol. Mr. Hughes helped McKinney to haul these stones—two at a load ; they were long, but not heavy, and with good sleighing and an ox team more might have been taken at each trip. Many cords of common limestone were quarried and piled near the river to be used in building the walls. But this church was never built ; McKinney went back to England, and it was not long after that General Pilkington died. The stones quarried were used by those who had houses to build, and the long stones, which had been intended for the sills of doors and windows, were just what was needed to reach across the top of a large, open fire place.

Of the Hughes family two are yet living : Mr. Hugh Hughes, near Moorefield, and his sister, Mrs. Hughes, in that northern suburb of Elora called Lot 18. Both brother and sister have many interesting reminiscences of those they have known since they came here as children seventy five years ago.

Others who came from the north of Wales were :

1836—Edward Jones, his wife and two children. They went to live in Galt.

1841—Peter Thomas, one of the first residents west of the river, in Pilkington, on the farm now owned by Mr. John Doyle.

1842—Owen Reynolds, lived in Elora for some years ; died in San Francisco.

James Reynolds. who was, until his recent death on August 24th, 1905, a well known resident of Lower Nichol.

1843—Richard Hughes, [in whose family there were : Robert, who was killed during the American War ; Hugh, who died in New York State. Those now living are : Mrs. Fred. Beck, Sioux City, Iowa ; Mrs. Adam Weichel, Elmira ; Mrs. Sparks, Marshalltown, Iowa ; Miss Margaret Hughes and Miss Hannah Hughes, in Elora.]

Hugh Jones, (Ned Jones' father.) [Hugh Jones went home to visit relatives in Wales. He was returning to his family in Canada on a vessel called "The Driver," and along with him were three others who were coming to this locality, but nothing was ever heard of the ship and all on board were lost.]

John Thomas, his wife and family, [among them being Mr. John Thomas and Mrs. Thomas Winfield, who are living in Elora.]

THE CASCADE

ROCKY BANKS OF GRAND RIVER
BELOW ELORA FALLS

Hugh Roberts, [in whose family there are: Griffith Roberts, living on the old homestead; Mrs. John Watt, in Upper Nichol; Dr. Hugh Roberts, in Guelph; John Roberts, in Valley City, North Dakota; Catharine, in Buffalo; Mrs. Thomas Jones, in Elora, and Llewellyn Roberts, in Pilkington.]

Owen Roberts; (not related to the former.)

Morris Jones, the first wagonmaker in Elora, [in his family being Mrs. Alex. Walsh, who died at Whitewood, N.W.T., in 1891; and Miss Mary Jones who is Matron in the Blind School at Jamaica Plains, Boston.]

Robert Jones, (no relatives here.)

Robert Pritchard, his wife and family of seven sons. They settled in Lower Nichol. The sons were: Richard, Robert, Hugh, Owen, Henry, Thomas and James.

1848—Henry Reynolds, who died near Clifford about 1885.

1849—Hugh Pritchard, and son, Thomas Pritchard, with wife and family, and Elizabeth, who was Mrs. John Street. (When Thomas Pritchard inherited his father's farm, near Elora, on which he now lives, he dropped the name of Thomas Hughes, by which he had up to that time been known, according to the Welsh custom. Richard Hughes, already mentioned, continued to be known by his Welsh name and was a full brother to Thomas Pritchard.)

Thomas Williams, his wife and two children. He was a blacksmith who lived in Elora, but some years after his death Mrs. Williams with the family— Jane, William, Richard, Grace and Katie—went to live in Cleveland, Ohio.

David Jones and wife. [In this family there are: Mrs. Thos. Pritchard; John Jones, on the homestead; Mrs. Alex. Clark, in Toronto; Mrs. George Dyce, of Meaford; David Jones, in Elora; Mrs. S. Davies, in Upper Nichol and Thomas Jones, in Elora.]

1852—Anne Reynolds, who married John McLean Bell, the first Grammar School teacher in Elora. She now lives in Chicago.

1854—William Reynolds, now, and for many years Treasurer for the County of Wellington.

1855—John Williams.

John Thomas, who was a teamster in Elora and was accidentally killed by falling under the wheel of his wagon while it was moving.

Rev. John Williams had, for a short time, a congregation to whom he preached, in Welsh, but he did not remain long here.

Note—All those in this list by the name of Reynolds were nephews or nieces of Squire Reynolds, being children of his brother, Francis Reynolds, a Captain in the Royal Navy, latterly stationed at Achill Island, off the coast of Ireland.

Because it was at Weden in Northamptonshire that General Pilkington found the first settlers for his land in Canada, the greater number of the first residents in the south half of the Township of Pilkington, which was then the only part open for settlement, were from that locality in England. Relatives, friends and neighbours came to Canada and settled near each other in their new home. For example: two of the early settlers in Lower Pilkington were William Howse and Edmund Hall. They were comrades ever since they were boys. Their native place was Aynho, but, being English, they put the 'h' in the wrong place and called it Hayno. This was "sixty five miles from Lon'on and eighteen from Northampton." As boys they played together and came to America in the same ship. Mr. Howse was eighteen years old when he came to Pilkington in 1832, and settled on Lot 8, Con. 4. Mr. Hall, "he were six years older." Along with his parents he first went to the Township of Wilmot where, as he said, "for ten years I were aworkin' for the fat man,"— that is, someone richer than he was getting the benefit of his work. Mr. Hall then came to Pilkington and got a farm as near to his friend as he could, on Lot 9, Con. 5. In their old age they lived in Elora, yet not far apart. During fine weather they visited one another. When storms prevented them from going out they would feel lonely, for, as Mr. Hall said, "they be 'appy when they be together." But some years have now gone by since the time came that they had looked forward to, when one followed the other on that long journey where they would know no parting.

George Luckitt was born at Weden in April, 1798 ; was married in December, 1825, to Elizabeth Shaw, who was then living at Aynho but was born at Weden in 1802. Mr. Luckitt came to Pilkington alone, in 1830, and prepared a home on Lot 8, Con. 2, to which Mrs. Luckitt came in the following year. Of a family of eight, Mr. Thomas Luckitt is the only one now living.

[That we are able to give the following list of families that settled in Lower Pilkington is owing to the kind assistance of Mr. and Mrs. Thomas Luckitt, who are now living in Elora. Both Mr. and Mrs. Luckitt have grown up in that locality and were personally acquainted with most of those here mentioned. While Mr. Luckitt's parents came from Weden, those of Mrs. Luckitt were from Aynho, and both have visited those places in England and their relatives living there]

Benjamin Ariss, also from Weden, came to Pilkington at the same time as Mrs. Luckitt, in 1831. He died on Sept. 19th, 1848, at the age of forty-six. His wife, Sarah Holloway, was born March 2nd, 1801, and died on August 3rd, 1892.

The children of Benjamin Ariss and his wife, Sarah Holloway, were : John, married Ann Gibson ; James, married Emma Burgess ; Eliza, married William Martin ; Richard, married Margaret Smith ; Mary, married John Maitland and lives in Elora ; George, Benjamin and David.

John Thacker was from Staffordshire. He was a carpenter and while serving his apprenticeship, of seven years, worked most of the time at Windsor Castle. Here he came under the notice of Gen. Pilkington who got him to come to his estate in Canada to help put up a church on the Lepard farm, and other buildings. Mr. Thacker came out in 1832 and remained about a year. At this time he bought from Anson and Abram Matthews the house and clearing they had made on Lot 9, Con. 3. The house that was built by these experienced axemen was of hewn cedar, with dovetailed corners, and, although now modernized, is still in use and quite comfortable.

Having procured a home, Mr. Thacker, in 1833, went back to London to marry Catharine Lisney. Early in 1834 he made preparations to return and received instructions from Gen. Pilkington, who was then living in London, about the erection of some buildings near the mill, on Mill Creek. Mr. and Mrs. Thacker arrived at their home in May, 1834, and were scarcely settled when Gen. Pilkington died and all the plans were useless. For a time Mr. Thacker found employment with the Gartshore firm in Dundas, and while he was away Mrs. Thacker taught the neighbors' children in a school in her own house.

ELORA

In their family: The eldest was Catharine Ottawa, named Ottawa after the ship she was born on; John married Annie Michie; Mary married Joseph Astell; Henriettta married George Howse; Edward, married, lived in the County of Bruce; Willlam married Eliza Larter: although he owns the old home as well as other farms, he is now living on the 'Luckitt' homestead; Ambrose married Johanna Dyment and lives in Teeswater; Alice married Frank Leslie; Benjamin married Mary Winfield.

Mr. Thacker died May 19th, 1868, at the age of sixty, and Mrs. Thacker Oct. 27th, 1894, at the age of eighty-two years and nine months.

. .   . .

Edward Patmore with his wife and family came to Pilkington at the same time as Mr. and Mrs. Thacker, in May, 1834. In this family there were: Samuel, who married Louisa Martin: their son, Edward Patmore, is living in Elora; Harriet married her cousin, Edward Patmore; Levi married Elizabeth Bastedo: he was a carpenter and at one time a resident of Elora. One sister Sarah, was Mrs. Hatton. The father, Edward Patmore, lived on Lot 8, Con. 2, and his son, Samuel, on Lot 10, Con. 2.

. .   . .

William Elkerton, generally called 'King' Elkerton, came from Aynho about 1832. He lived on Lot 11, Con. 4. He built the first and only saw mill on Keating's Creek, a branch of Cox's Creek, in that part of Lower Pilkington called Jerusalem. This mill had to go night and day while the water was high in the spring time, for there was not enough water to move it at other seasons.

William Elkerton was twice married, first to Anna Silver and at her death to a Miss Nickison. In his family: John married Marian Headley; Martha married Robert McConnel; Mary married James Hall; Thomas married Jane Smith.

. .   . .

Benjamin, Joseph and David Elkerton were three brothers who came to Pilkington about four years after their brother, William. Joseph did not remain long in Pilkington, but went to New York State. David did not marry. He died in 1903, at the age of eighty.

. .   . .

Benjamin Elkerton was born at Aynho; died Oct. 30th, 1875, at the age of seventy seven. He married Ann Cook. In their family: Hannah married Mark Tovel, Guelph; Sarah married Henry Tebby; William married Annie Tebby; Joseph married Beatrice Delgarno; Henry married Elizabeth Boyce; Elizabeth married Thomas Lyons.

. .   . .

Nathan Lines, from Chippin Warden, in Warwickshire, came to Canada about 1829; returned to fetch out some relatives, and again sailed for Canada in March, 1831. He was for some time in Galt and then in Pilkington.

Zechariah Lines was eighteen years younger than his brother. He married Jane Gibson. In their family: William married Jane Pearson, Lake Dauphin, Manitoba; Zechariah married Jane Henderson, Clifford; Jane married George Fulton, Minto; Beatrice married David Hastings, Petoskey, Mich.; Sarah married Augustus Stull, Rothsay; Annie married John Kay, Rothsay; Kate married Fred. Height, Port Elgin; Charlotte married John Fulton, Minto; Margaret married John Bennett, Minto; Benjamin married Miss McTavish, Lake Dauphin, Man.; and James, in Seattle, Washington.

John and James Allen came from Chippin Warden in Warwickshire, in March, 1831. Their brother, William had come to Galt with Nathan Lines, in 1829, and there the brothers remained for about two years and then John came to Pilkington.

John Allen married Margaret Gibson, a sister of Mrs. Lines, who was born at Belfast, Ireland. In their family: James married Ann Drewery; Ann married John Howard, lives in Flesherton; John married Mary Winfield, Cleveland; Margaret married William Howse, in Bethany; Thomas married Elizabeth Ann Howse, and is living on the old homestead.

Thomas Howse, his wife, Mary Churchley, and their family were from Aynho. They came in 1832. Of their family: William married Sarah Tolton; George; Ephraim married Jane Bye; Mary married Donald Peckover; Elizabeth married Henry Hall; Thomas married Mary Ann Boulding.

John Bye and his wife, Rachel Reeve, were from Aynho. He and his family went to the Township of Egremont. A few years after John, George Bye came. His wife was Elizabeth Borton, and all were from Aynho. John and George Bye took up adjoining farms.

In George Bye's family there were: William married Mariah Francis; Robert married Frances Francis; Charles married Margaret Dalgarno; Jane married Ephraim Howse; and Elizabeth, who is Mrs. Gilmore, in Elora.

George Bye died in Elora, on Feb. 1st, 1886, at the age of eighty-three.

John Hall and his wife, Sarah Wiggins, came to the Township of Wilmot about 1832. There the father died some ten years later, when his widow and the family soon afterward came to Pilkington.

In this family there were: Edmund Hall married Ann Ford; Thomas Hall married Ann Buckler; Mary Hall married William Betchen; Henry Hall married Elizabeth Howse; Joseph Hall married Maria Ford; Hannah Hall married George Morley; James Hall married Mary Elkerton. One thing remarkable about this family is that both husbands and wives came from Aynho.

One of this family, Thomas Hall, was born at Aynho in 1811, and came to Canada in 1827, at the age of sixteen. He stopped for some time in Quebec City and again at Belleville. There he accidentally learned that his relatives had come to Canada and were living in the Township of Wilmot, so he made his way to them. He married in Wilmot township and remained there until the year 1846, when he came to Pilkington.

The children of Thomas Hall and Ann Buckler were: Henry, who, with his wife, who was Sarah Bye, is living in Bethany; two sisters are Mrs. Thomas Luckitt, in Elora, and Mrs. Robert Mason, in Guelph Township.

The Betchen family first settled in the Township of Wilmot. They were from Switzerland, where the father had been a watchmaker and a bandmaster. The family were all musical and were said to have played the first band music in Galt.

William Betchen was married in Wilmot to Mary Hall, and came to Pilkington to be near her relatives. In this family: Mary Ann married Henry Patmore, lately in Elora, now at Cranbrook, B. C., (she died in Elora); John Betchen, living on the old farm; David married Miss Colbeck; Hannah married Rev. William Baugh; Joseph married Lottie Boulding; Kezia married Henry Boulding; Jabez married Robina Simpson.

ELORA

John Blinco and his wife, Ann Cole, came from Mixbury, in Oxfordshire, where the boundaries of three shires meet. Their two sons, George and Harry, came to Pilkington in 1844, the parents and the rest of the family coming in 1845. Of this family: George married Elizabeth Stockford; Mary married Richard Stockford, and at his death Robert Cooke; Henry (Harry) married Emma Hawes, from Garafraxa; William married Elizabeth Beale, and they now live in Elora; Emma married John Ariss; John married Ann Ariss. Mrs. Blinco was seventy seven years of age when she died on March 28th, 1870, and Mr. Blinco died two weeks later, on April 12th, 1870, at the age of eighty.

Thomas Beale and his wife, Mary Hannah Clifford, were from Mixbury. Of their family: William married Eliza Blinco; John married Ann Newman; Elizabeth married William Blinco. Thomas Beale died Nov. 5th, 1888, at the age of eighty-five, and Mrs. Beale on Dec. 8th, 1892, at the age of ninety years and ten months.

George, Charles and Henry Lawrence were three brothers who came from Byfield in Northamptonshire. George, the eldest, came to Pilkington in 1828 and was referred to among those who settled in Woolwich. Charles Lawrence came some years later. He married Mary Cox, a daughter of Michael Cox who was mentioned as one of the first residents in Winterbourne, and from whom Cox's Creek received its name. Charles Lawrence lived in Elora for many years. He was a bricklayer and plasterer. In 1851 he built the house in which he lived which is now in rear of the Methodist Church and, with bricks of a darker color built into the wall you may read the initial letters of his name and the date—C. L. 1851.

On August 2nd 1867 the contract for building the stone pier under the bridge which crosses the Irvine River was given to Charles Lawrence and James Parsons for the very low price of $1,385, and the work was completed on November 15th. It stands to day without a flaw, a monument to those men. This pier, built of limestone, measures 10x22 feet at the base, 4 feet 4 inches by 18 feet at the top and is a few inches more than 72 feet in height. From the rock in the bed of the river to the top of the planks on the driveway is 76 feet and the length of the bridge is 114 feet.

Henry Lawrence was born at Byfield, Nov. 29th, 1813; was married August 8th, 1836, to Jane Mundon In 1846, with their family of four children, they came to Pilkington. In about two years after this Henry Lawrence died in Elora after which Mrs. Lawrence went to live in Guelph where a few years later she was married to John Emery.

When their mother went to Guelph two of the daughters, Fanny and Thirza, lived at the home of Mr. Geddes and for some years were well known in Elora.

The Lawrence brothers were all musicians. Charles was a member of the first band in Elora, while for fourteen years before coming to Canada Henry played the pipe organ in the church at Byfield.

The children of Henry Lawrence and Jane Mundon were: Mary Ann who married George Howard, at one time Mayor of Guelph. She died May 22nd, 1859; Frances (or Fanny) married Thomas Robinson and lives in Guelph; Thirza married Joshua Kribs. She died Sept. 6th, 1871; George Henry married Rebecca Simpson, of Berlin. He inherited the family characteristic and up to the time of his death on October 3rd, 1897, was well known in Guelph as a musician.

Other families who came from Aynho were those by the name of Ford, Astell, Tuckey, Ward, Buckler, Borton, Stockford and Peckover. The Ford family was the first to leave Aynho, to settle in Wilmot Township, and from there, after some years, members of that and other families came to Pilkington. John Williams came from Northampton. Sam. Darby, too, who was killed at the raising of a house in Elora. Nor shall we forget to mention John Marriot, one of the kindest hearted men that ever came to the Township.

Martin Martin, from Sussex, England, came to Canada in 1832. He stopped first in Toronto but left because there was an epidemic of cholera and went to Hamilton; from that to Guelph and then to a farm in Nichol. This was the farm afterwards owned by Capt. Forster. While here a Mr. Frazer, who was a clerk in the store owned by the Gilkison family in Elora, got Mr. Martin to leave his farm to build the first tavern in Elora, which he did, but an experience of three years was enough of this and he sold out to George Gray. Mr. Martin then went on to the 'Jonathan Swift farm,' on Mill Creek, for two years; to the Tom Robinson farm for three years and then to the farm in Bethany which is now owned by his grandson, Mr. Frank Martin. In this family there was: Fanny who married John Gordon and lived near Winterbourne; Richard did not marry; Louisa married Samuel Patmore; Maria married James Mutrie; Esther married William Larter; William married Eliza Ariss.

Thomas John Grain was born at Gibraltar where his father was a Commissary General. He came to Pilkington with the Metcalfe family when he was just a boy. (The Metcalfes did not remain here).

Thomas Grain married the widow of Joseph Nicklin whose maiden name was Cecily Swan. In their family: Miss Grain, now living in Elora; Mary married Dr. Watt, of Cariboo, B. C., she died at Meaford, Ont. Henry married Francis Leary of Jamaica and afterwards Elizabeth Wade, he died in Wingham, Ont.; William married Elizabeth Broadfoot, lives in Morden, Manitoba, and Francis died when young.

Thomas Grain was born March 5th, 1818, died Feb. 6th, 1861. Mrs. Grain died April 29th, 1859, at the age of 47.

Robert Swan was the oldest son of Robert Swan, from Alemouth, Northumberland, who died in Pilkington on April 16th, 1853. He came to Canada in 1832 and was employed by the Hon. James Crooks of Crooks' Hollow. He was afterward in business for himself at Kingston and Toronto and retired, in comfortable circumstances, to live at the village of Acton, which it is said he named.

His parents, Robert Swan and his wife Cecily Wilson, with their family, came to Canada in 1833 and because their son was there they went to Crooks' Hollow. Here the father bought from Mr. Crooks two hundred acres in the Township of Pilkington which was situated on either side of the road between school house number four and the railway.

The members of this, the older Swan family were: Robert married Maria Nicklin; George Wilson, was here for a short visit, was lost at sea when returning to England; Cecily married Joseph Nicklin and at his death Thomas Grain; Mary Elizabeth married Captain Forster; John married Catharine McTavish.

John Swan cleared lots 4 and 5 on the 2nd concession, and adjoining his father's, and this is the farm that has long been known as Swan's farm. The family of John Swan and his wife Catharine McTavish were: George married

ELORA

Clara Ross; Susan and Mary on the old homestead; Annie married John Dalby, now in Victoria, B.C.; Cecily married Dr. William Anderson of Fergus; Robert lives on Texada Island, B. C.; Madeline married Alexander Cowie, Union Bay, B. C.

John Swan died February 16th, 1889, at the age of 73, and his wife on Dec. 19th, 1896, at the age of 76.

John Winfield and Mary Barker, his wife, with their family came to Canada in the same ship as the Blinco brothers, in 1844. They settled on a farm on Mill Creek. Jonathan Swift had lived on this farm but left it in 1836, and this was the farm that Gen. Pilkington intended Rowley Wood should have.

Mr. and Mrs. Winfield were from Barnsley, in Yorkshire, where most of their family were born. John Winfield died in March, 1872, at the age of 78 after which Mrs. Winfield lived in a house on the Salem road, near Elora, until her death on May 15th, 1890, at the age of 87. Those in the family were: Elizabeth married William Ormandy; Joseph, married, died in Connecticut; John married Mary Franklin; Robert married Catharine Tribe; Edwin married Jessie Haig; James married Agnes Brydon; Thomas married Elizabeth Thomas and they live in Elora; Mary married John Allan; Fanny married Ezra Wissler.

Francis Francis with his wife and family of three lived on a small farm about where the railway crosses Mill Creek. On this hundred acres there were three homes; William Everett being to the south of Francis and Edward Badley to the north, on part of the farm now owned by Alexander Keith.

In the Francis family there were: Susannah who married Samuel Barber and lived in Guelph; Robert married Rebecca Metcalfe; Elizabeth married Leonard Dickinson. Mrs. Francis died in Pilkington after which Mr. Francis went along with Robert and Elizabeth to live in the Township of Bentinck, near Hanover.

Robt. Haig and his wife, whose maiden name was Ann Grace Crabb, came from Auchinblae, in the Parish of Fordoun, Kincardineshire, Scotland.

With their family they sailed on the ship St. Lawrence, landing at Quebec and on the 10th August, 1845, arrived at the farm upon which the three surviving members of the family—James, William and Miss Ann Haig—have lived ever since.

In this family: James, (born October 25th, 1818); Alexander, married, and lived in Grand Rapids, Michigan; William, (born March 6th, 1829); Ann; Robert, who was at one time a merchant and also postmaster in Elora.

The Haig farm is beautifully situated on the banks of Mill Creek—that stream which has had so many different names. First it was called Frenchmen's Creek, because the two Frenchmen lived beside it. Then it was known as Mill Creek, for the old Mill was on it. Yankee Miller, as he was called, was the first to occupy the 'Haig' farm, and as the stream crossed the Guelph and Elora road at this place it was, while he was there, referred to by some as Miller's Creek. At other times since it has been known as Winfield's, Swan's or Haig's Creek, and many fine trout have been caught in it.

James Cruikshank, from Insch, and his wife, Margaret Mennie, from Rayne, were married on December 31st, 1833, and in June, 1836, left their home at Culsalmond, in Aberdeenshire, to come to Canada. At first they were, for a short time, on the 'Leslie farm,' in Nichol and then for the winter of 1836-7 they lived in the house that Henry Wilbee built, west of the river, in Elora. From that they went to the 'James Reynolds farm,' in Nichol and then to their home beside Mill Creek, in Pilkington, in which their daughter, Miss Barbara Cruikshank, still lives.

It was on the 29th of June, 1853, that Mr. Cruikshank bought fishing line and hooks and went down to the Grand river to fish. On the east side of the river, between the Little Falls and the Cascade there are several large blocks of stone, one of which slopes into the river, like the side of a roof. While sitting on this sloping stone, Mr. Cruikshank is supposed to have slipped into the deep hole which is in the river at this place, and was drowned. For many years afterward all the old fishermen who knew the river well spoke of this as 'Cruikshank's Hole.' Sadder still was the death of Mrs. Cruikshank, from hydrophobia, on Feb. 19th, 1865.

In their family there were: Barbara; Andrew; Elizabeth, who married Charles Preston; and George.

Hugh McDonald was born in Glengarry, Scotland, in 1746, and died in Pilkington on Feb. 16th, 1865, at the age of ninety nine, and his wife was born in Fort Augustus, Scotland, in 1768, and died March 29th, 1855. They first lived in Lower Nichol but afterwards on the 'Wolcott' farm and on the 'James Ross' farm near the 'Big Bend.' In their family there were: Alexander; Allan; Janet; Margaret and Jemima.

Jerry Ryan was a neighbor of Hugh MacDonald and lived on the hill near Inverhaugh post-office. He married Janet McDonald, the widow of Theopholus Smith. In their family there were: Mary Ann; Joseph; Hugh; Allan; Kenneth and Christina.

James Ross and his wife, Cecilia Miller, were from the Parish of Dysart, about six miles frae the lang toon o' Kircaldy, in Fifeshire, Scotland. In 1834 they came back to 'Paisley Block,' in Guelph Township, and in 1845 bought the Thomas Robinson farm in Pilkington. In later years Mr. Ross retired to Elora, where he lived in the house which is now owned by Dr. Golden.

In their family there were: James; George, who died in September, 1879; and John, who married Annie Bonallie, and lives in Pasadena, California.

Mr. Ross died December 21st, 1869, at the age of seventy-five, and Mrs. Ross on January 6th, 1874, at the age of eighty one.

James Ross, the eldest son of the former, continued to live on the farm until recently when he, too, retired and is now living in Elora.

He married Jean Bissett and in their family there are: Cecilia, who was married to Edward Patmore; James married Annie Veitch and lives in Elora; Jane married William Rose; John married Helen McLeay and lives on the old farm; George Miller married Jean Watson and lives on the 'Old Hugh MacDonald farm,' adjoining his brother's; Margaret married Andrew Aitchison (jr) and lives in Elora.

Alexander Watson, from Kittans, on the border between Perthshire and Forfarshire in Scotland, was born on March 15th, 1803. His wife was Mary Anderson and with their family they came to Canada in 1844, stopping for some months at a place called 'Fiddler's Green,' near Ancaster. It was in the spring of 1845 that they came to live on the farm that Christopher Wood had lived on prior to 1834, and it then became generally known as the 'Sandy Watson farm.'

Of their family : George (born May, 1826, died September, 1895), married Maria Carder, who now lives in Elora ; Mary married William Veitch ; Janet ; Agnes married Francis Frank, one time Editor of the 'Elora Backwoodsman' ; Margaret ; Alexander first married Johanna Marigold, then Ann Weadick, and lives in Elora ; John married Mary Hayes, then Annie Blyth, lives near Winterbourne ; James married Prudence Hayes, lives in Manitoba ; Marjrey married James Buchan and lives in Elora ; William married Ann Mitchell and is now living on the 'Allan farm,' near Elora ; Ann married William Wilson and lives in Elora. Of this family six are living, the youngest having died at the age of forty four.

Mrs. Watson died in September, 1872, at the age of sixty-nine, and Alexander Watson in March 1881, at seventy-eight.

George McKenzie was born at Garmouth, on Speyside, Moray or Elgin, shire, Scotland. With his wife, Ann McKay, and her father, Redrick McKay and his family he came to Canada in 1829. After a few months in Toronto they came to Pilkington and along with them, from Toronto, came Francis Francis and his wife. Like other early residents they lived for the first few months in one of the houses on the Lepard farm before settling on their first farm Lot 7 on the 1st Concession. Afterwards Mr. McKenzie lived on Lot 2, Con. 1, which is quite near Elora. It was October when they arrived at the Lepard farm and an interesting incident is related that happened while they were living there. The Grand River runs past this farm and on its western bank the Cascade falls over the perpendicular banks which are seventy feet high. Trees were growing above the high rocks, their leaves passing through the innumerable shades of yellow, orange and red, thus absorbing all the heat possible from the weakened sunshine. There were several in the party who were fishing on this autumn afternoon. They had filled the large pails which they had brought with fish, for those not used at once were to be salted down for winter use. They were thinking of returning home with what they had caught when they heard the distant cry of wolves and they were coming closer. Suddenly a deer leaped from the level ground above, going too fast to stop, seeing the brink too late, it fell, a broken mass, among the rocks below.

Along with his father in law Mr. McKenzie helped to build the first bridge across the Grand River at Elora. The first school in Pilkington was held in the Frenchmen's house and from what we can learn one by the name of Jennings was the first teacher and he was followed by Mr. McKenzie who for about nine years would teach on alternate weeks at this place and Bethany.

Mrs. McKenzie died March 31st, 1892, at the age of 82, and Mr. McKenzie on February 15th, 1894, at the age of 83 years and 3 months.

In their family there were : Alexander married Jane Ann Roy, living at Grand Haven, Michigan ; Margaret married Frank Maitland, now living near Harriston ; Louisa married Hiram Cassidy ; Isabella married Alexander Kerr aud is now living in Elora ; Roderick married Mrs. Rogerson, the widow of Captain Rogerson, a confederate officer of Charleston, S. C. ; William married Mary McPhee ; George married Catharine Reid ; Elizabeth married William Hall and lives in Galt ; Catharine married Thomas Brock. She died at Wyoming Ontario ; John died in Manitoba and other five died when young.

William Kilpatrick, with his wife Elizabeth McConachie, and the first five in their family came to the Township of Nichol on June 6th, 1834. He was from Argyleshire, Scotland. In this, the older Kilpatrick family there was : John ; William married Eliza Cooper ; Frank ; Thomas married Isabella Wilson ;

Elizabeth married Robert Scott; Helen married James Broadfoot; Florence married John Mowat; Hugh married Jane Milne; Robert married Elizabeth Spiers, lived, in Salem. For his second wife Mr. Kilpatrick married Ann Cromar, who survived him some years.

Thomas Kilpatrick, one of this family, came over into Pilkington in the year 1845 and took up Lot. 3, Concession 1, which is near Elora. He was born in the County Antrim, Ireland, on August 16th, 1817. Although now near the close of his eighty-ninth year Mr. Kilpatrick still does his small share of the work on the farm upon which he has lived for sixty one years.

The family of Thomas Kilpatrick and his wife, Isabella Wilson, are— Elizabeth who married Henry Kirkland, lives in California; William married Carrie Van Horne, living at Los Angelos; Sarah married Judge Adsit of Grand Rapids, Michigan; Janet lives in Los Angelos, California; Thomas married May Clarke, lives in Mexico; Isabella married W. K. Pattison, Chicago; Margaret married Steven Martin, Chicago; Rebecca married George McInnes, Grand Rapids; James married Allison Broadfoot; Florence died when young; Ebenezer married Fanny Maria Bye and they live on the old homestead; and Nellie married Henry Chesley.

William Fasken and his wife, Margaret Mitchell, were from the City of Aberdeen, but for some time before leaving Scotland had lived in Parish of Forgue, in Aberdeenshire. Mr. Fasken was an architect, contractor and expert stone cutter and his first employment after coming to Canada was at Gananoque and at Kingston where he helped to build some stone forts. He came to the Township of Nichol in 1839. In this, the older Fasken family there was— Christina married William Atkinson, lived in Guelph Township; John married Christina Wilson, lived in Nichol, near Ponsonby; Margaret married Samuel Card, lived in Guelph Township, near Marden; William died when a young man; Alexander, married, lived in Missouri; Robert married Isabella Milne; George married Sarah Carder; Marion married Alexander McDonald, lived in Guelph Township; Isabella married Alexander McCrae; Jean married John Gordon, lives in the Township of Minto; James, married, lived first in Minnesota and then in Missouri.

Robert and George Fasken were two brothers in this family who settled on a bush farm in Pilkington in 1844. This they afterward divided and each added to his share by purchasing adjoining farms Robert bought the 'Frenchmen's' and 'Cruikshank' farms. George added the 'Francis' and the 'Hughes' farms.

Robert Fasken married Isabella Milne and in their family is—John married Elizabeth Wilson, lives in Paris, Ont.; Mary married Griffith Williams, lives in Toronto; Ann married William Aitchison, lives in Lambton, Ont; Robert married Ann Aitchison, lives in Pilkington; Margaret married John Green, lives in British Columbia; David married Alice Winstanley, lives in Toronto; Sarah; William married Mabel Bye, lives on the old homestead; Isabella; Alexander married Isabella Armstrong, lives in Toronto. Robert Fasken died November 5th, 1896, at the age of seventy six. Mrs. Fasken, with her daughters. Sarah and Isabella are now living in Hamilton.

George Fasken married Sarah Carder, eldest daughter of Joseph Carder, who came to the Township of Nichol, near Elora, in December, 1833. In their family their is—William married Elizabeth Smith; Joseph married Hannah Blinco; John; James married Fanny, daughter of Robert Winfield, and they live on the old homestead; Samuel married Minnie Bye; Margaret married Henry Martin; (Rev.) George married Ida J. Gray. He is Pastor of St. Paul's Presbyterian Church, Toronto; Alexander married Jennie Angell. He died September, 1894. George Fasken died April 18th, 1883, at the age of sixty three, and Mrs. Fasken in December, 1896, at the age of seventy-two.

    David Milne and his wife, Ann Scott, came from Auchinblae, in the Parish of Fordoun, Kincardineshire, Scotland. With their family they came to Pilkington in 1844 and lived on the farm now owned by Alexander Holman.

    In their family there was—William married Helen Milne; James married Mary Barclay; Mary married James Ross, is now living in Guelph; Ann married David Black; Margaret married Andrew Smith, was in Canada but a short time and returned to Scotland; Jean married Hugh Kilpatrick, is now living in Hespeler; Elspet married Arthur Ross; David married Jane Richardson; Isabella married Robert Fasken; Jessie married Alexander Dalgarno; George married Helen Hay; Helen married John Hay. Mrs. Milne died on May 2nd, 1865 at the age of sixty-seven years and three months and Mr. Milne on June 28th, 1887 at the age of ninety-five.

    Arthur Ross came from the Estate of Arnage, in the Parish of Ellon, Aberdeenshire, Scotland, where he was born on June 3rd, 1821. In 1838 at the age of seventeen, he came to the Township of Nichol, his brother James, having preceded him two years. The brothers took up farms where the Irvine river crosses the Owen Sound road north of Fergus. In 1842 they went into partnership with Chas. Allan and David Henderson under the name of Ross & Co. and conducted a large general business in Elora. In 1855 Arthur Ross bought 'Old King Reeve's' farm in Pilkington and on this the family resided for many years until their removal to Port Elgin, Ontario.

    Arthur Ross married Elspet Milne and in their family there was—Ann, living in Port Elgin; William married Jennie Nevin, living in Portland, Oregon; (Rev.) John married Elsie Watt. He is now Pastor of the Presbyterian Church, Port Dalhousie; was formerly in Brussels. David married Mary Veitch, now in Portland, Orgeon; Robert married Annie Binnie, living in Saskatchewan; Elizabeth married George Craig, living in Winnipeg; Jane married Charles Diehl, in Portage la Prairie; Alexander married Sarah Eby, in Port Arthur; Arthur married Marion Irvine, Miniota, Manitoba; Margaret married Robert Smith, Port Elgin; Elsie married John McGillivray, Arrow River, Manitoba; James married Caroline Schrank, and lives in Toronto. Mrs. Ross died in 1897 at the age of sixty nine and Mr. Ross in 1900 in his seventy ninth year.

    Andrew Aitchison was born at Lauder, in Berwickshire, Scotland, on February 14th, 1831. He was there married to Elizabeth Ann Bathgate and in the year 1852 came to Canada, stopping first at Niagara. There he was joined in a year or two by his father, two brothers—Ebenezer and William Smith—and one sister—Janet. After their father's death, at Niagara, these came to the Township of Dumfries, then to Guelph Township, and, in 1858, Andrew came to Pilkington.

    The members of this family, who, although not early settlers in Pilkington are now related to many in the Township are :— Andrew married Nancy Larter and now lives on the 'Squire Reynolds Farm,' adjoining Elora. William married Ann Fasken. Ebenezer married Sophia Bye. Peter married Jane Bye, lives in Elora. Ann married Robert Fasken. Simon married Margaret Robina Maitland. Margaret Janet married Thomas Bye. John Alexander

Andrew Aitchison was born at Lauder, in Berwickshire, Scotland, on February 14th, 1831. He was there married to Elizabeth Ann Bathgate and in the year 1852 came to Canada, stopping first at Niagara. There he was joined in a year or two by his father, two brothers—Ebenezer and William Smith—and one sister—Janet. After their father's death, at Niagara, these came to the Township of Dumfries, then to Guelph Township, and, in 1858, Andrew came to Pilkington.

The members of this family, who, although not early settlers in Pilkington are now related to many in the Township are : — Andrew married Nancy Larter and now lives on the 'Squire Reynolds Farm,' adjoining Elora. William married Ann Fasken. Ebenezer married Sophia Bye. Peter married Jane Bye, lives in Elora. Ann married Robert Fasken. Simon married Margaret Robina Maitland. Margaret Janet married Thomas Bye. John Alexander living on the old homestead. Andrew Aitchison died and was buried on the sixty fourth anniversary of his birthday, in 1895. Mrs. Aitchison is living with her daughter, Mrs. Robert Fasken, on their farm in Pilkington, near Elora.

The Township of Pilkington is naturally divided by the Grand River into what is usually called Upper and Lower Pilkington. For more than a mile after entering the township the banks of the river are so precipitous that there are but few places where the river may be crossed, and then only with difficulty. Confined in a channel worn out of the solid rock to a depth in different places of from sixty to eighty feet this beautiful river has a never failing attraction, and to those who love to study nature the rocks have a wonderful story to tell. In that dim and distant past the limestone rock through which the river runs was formed from the remains of myriads of microscopic animals whose life was lived near the surface of an ocean. The rock so formed at the bed of an ocean was slowly lifted until this central portion of Western Ontario rose high above the water which surrounded it. Apparently this island was, for ages, about twice the size of what is now the County of Wellington and the position of several points along its shore line have been distinctly marked. Without going into particulars in this place it may be suggested that one of these is the deep ravine on the Credit River, at the Forks of the Credit ; another is that on the Saugeen River near the village of Ayton and a third is this rocky canyon at Elora. Streams, following the lowest valleys, flowed from this rocky island and their continued action wore channels in the rock. At a point about a mile and a half south west from the present site of Elora two streams fell over the rocky shore line into the still water of this old gulf. On reflection it will be noticed that a very good reason why these rapid rivers did not wear deep channels in that part of their course which is now farther down stream was that all that part was then under water. The two streams which, side by side, flowed into deep water are now known as the Grand and Irvine Rivers. They continued to flow in their ancient courses until each had worn a separate channel backward from the shore. From the south end of Victoria Bridge, in Elora, the old course of the Grand River can be traced south westerly, to where the sides of the old river bed have steep rocks ; the centre filled with swampy soil, in which evergreens are growing. If the general direction of this channel be noted it points to that place on the river, beyond the Lepard farm, where the two old streams united. But a wonderful change took place, for that stream on the east, the Grand River, changed its course. For a long time only a part of the stream flowed over to the Irvine River forming what is called ' The Cove ' ; another, and still other branches followed the first until all the water in the Grand River turned abruptly toward the west to form the beautiful Falls of Elora and unite with the Irvine River. The junction, or meeting of the

THE CAVE WHERE WAMPUM THE HOLE
BEADS WERE FOUND IN THE ROCK

THE OLD INDIAN BRIDGE

1819 — 1865

(Photographed, September 1860, by Thomas Connon)

waters, is now just within the western boundary of the Corporation of Elora. From the present junction down what is now the Grand River there are a number of ledges of rock, in some places as wide as a street, on which trees are growing. These ledges show the depth to which the channel was worn by the Irvine River when it was working alone. After all the water from the Grand River commenced to come this way the two streams made quicker work of it and those places where the rocky banks come closer together indicate where the wearing was done more rapidly. The first of these ledges may be seen on the east bank of the Grand, opposite the mouth of the Irvine River. A second, farther down stream, is also on the eastern bank and the easier way to climb down to this is by passing through 'The Hole-in-the-rock,' a large cave with the back end open, forming a natural bridge.

A few yards to the north of the hole in the rock there is a smaller cave on the face of the cliff in which some of the Neutral Indians, when driven from their homes, in 1650, left their priceless wampum beads hidden for safe keeping. More than two hundred years had gone by, when, in 1857, several Indians from the shores of the Upper Lakes visited Elora in search of the treasure which their forefathers had hidden among the rocks "near the meeting of the waters."

It was on a Sunday afternoon, in 1880, that two boys found several of the wampum beads which had been washed from this small cave by an unusually heavy rain. The boys lost no time in telling their teacher, Mr. Boyle, then Principal of the Elora Public School, who carefully sifted the fine earth from the cave and secured the treasure which the Indians had failed to find.

A third ledge is on the western bank, near the stone barn on the Allan farm, while near the Little Falls there are ledges on both sides of the river. Here, at the narrowest part of the river, the rocky banks come within thirty-three feet. The pine tree which spanned the ravine at this point for so many years, was felled in the year 1819 by a white man, (probably Roswell Matthews) and an Indian and it was always known as 'The Indian Bridge.' A hand railing was afterwards put up by the white settlers but it only lasted two years and was never replaced. The Indians and white men constantly used this tree as a bridge and for many years this was the only means of crossing the Grand River when the water was high. The stump of the tree which formed the bridge still stands, on the eastern bank. It measures 26 inches in diameter where it was chopped, and the height of the stump shows that the tree was felled during the winter when the snow on the ground was several feet deep.

One of those who lived on the east side of the river, near the Indian Bridge, was Robert Tribe, who would cross this log bridge at any season, night or day, when to slip from it would mean almost certain death. One of his companions on hunting expeditions was Tom Roberts, who lived west of the river, near where the Cascade Creek crosses the road. His mother, Mrs. Owen Roberts, was always afraid that her boy would be killed by falling from the bridge. One night Robert Tribe came over to get Tom to go with him. Mrs. Roberts said Tom was not to go, but a nudge from Bob Tribe was the signal to meet him outside later on, when they crossed the river as usual. Next day Mrs. Owen Roberts went on to the bridge and chopped it as far as she could and then, with the assistance of her second son, Harry, they shook it down. This, in June, 1865, was the end of 'The Old Indian Bridge.'

There are still two other ledges, one forming the roof of that long cave known as 'The Stone Sidewalk,' which faces the river as it flows from 'The Punch Bowl,' at 'The Little Falls,' and the last ledge is also on the eastern bank, opposite 'The Cascade,' continuing along until the river comes to where there are no more ledges and no steep rocks—the point where the old junction and shore line was.

ELORA ❧ Its Early History

A few yards up stream from the south end of Victoria Bridge, in Elora, a small creek joins the river. Before all the trees were chopped this stream never ceased to flow, for it was fed by many springs and the water from that flat, wet land on top of the hill. Now it is dried up for the greater part of the year and it is only in spring time, or after heavy rains, that it has the volume which was but the ordinary flow of some years ago. Mid way between the brow of the hill and the river, on the east side of this stream, there stood a two-story house, built of hewn logs, with a gable roof and a window at each side of the door. On the map the location would be on the north side of Walnut street, between High and Victoria streets, but many in Elora will know it better when it is said that the house in which Mr. John Thomas lives is built on the site of it. In a historical sense this is the most interesting spot in Elora, or in the County of Wellington, for the old house which stood there was built by Roswell Matthews, and there he and his wife and family lived for nine years before the city of Guelph was founded.

In an illustrated publication called 'Picturesque Canada,' there is an account of Roswell Matthews' coming to Elora, of which the following is an extract :

"The earliest white settler, Roswell Matthews, arrived here on the first day of winter, 1817. Matthews hewed his way through the jungle and around fallen trees, arriving, after days of incessant toil, on the present site of Elora. Night was then closing in. A log fire was lighted, a rude tent of hemlock boughs was set up, and, under its shelter, beds of hemlock branches were spread. During the night a heavy snowstorm set in, bearing down the woods and strewing the ground with branches of lordly trees. The morning broke grey and dismal on the shivering and benumbed settlers. * * * * * By May a clearing had been made, and sowed and planted ; the rich, marrowy soil soon responded with good crops of wheat, corn and potatoes. A few seasons onward, and there was a surplus for market. But how to get it there ? Matthews and his sons improved on their recollection of Robinson Crusoe by hollowing out a pine log thirty feet long. Eagerly launching this dug out a mile and a half below the Falls, they embarked with sixteen bags of wheat and, paddling down to Galt, they found a purchaser in Absalom Shade, who paid them fifty cents a bushel in cash. The dug-out was sold for two dollars and a half, and they returned home afoot, blithe as any birds of the forest."

This nicely written sketch was remodeled from an article published in 'The Elora Observer' of April 12th, 1866, which was the result of an interview which Mr. J. M. Shaw, the editor of The Observer, had with Mr. Abram Matthews, who was then living in Acton and to whom, by the way, tradition gives the credit of having chopped the first tree in Elora, for he and his older brother, Anson, accompanied their father on that day which should be ever memorable in the annals of Elora—Dec. 1st, 1817.

With the exception of what was published in 'The Elora Observer' nothing was known of the very first settler in Elora, and even the importance of that was lost sight of because the paper in which it appeared was published during the excitement incident to the Fenian Raid. Fortunately, some six years ago, the writer learned that two of Roswell Matthews' sons were then living. Through their kindness, and that of Mrs. John Matthews, we are enabled to place on record, and preserve, a pathetic story of trial, courage, disappointment and misfortune. This is dramatically set forth in the following letter :—

Maquoketa, Iowa, November, 1900.

Mr. J. R. Connon, Elora.
Respected Sir,—

We received your letter yesterday and as I am the only person left that would be likely to give you information concerning the experiences of Mr. Roswell Matthews on the site where the City of Elora now stands, and the circumstances which led him to settle in that unbroken wilderness, eleven miles from any inhabitant, let me introduce myself and explain why I am obliged to take this matter in hand. I am the wife of John Matthews and was brought up within a few miles of Niagara Falls. My husband's memory has so failed that there are some things he can't recall. What I know of the history of that unfortunate enterprise has been learned from my husband and other members of the family.

Roswell Matthews left the United States a few years before the War of 1812 and located on a farm between Niagara and St. Catharines, where his family resided, and where he was employed a part of the time in building fortifications at Niagara. When the war broke out he feared it was unsafe so near the American line (as he was not a British subject) and removed to Flamboro West, and engaged in business; did some mechanical work for the Hon. James Crooks, who had mills in what was popularly called "Crooks's Hollow," and also built some Block-houses at Burlington Heights during the year before the war closed. Here he met Col. Clarke, of Niagara Falls,—then owner of the Township of Nichol—who offered him great inducements to build a mill at Elora Falls. But shortly after he had taken his family to that wilderness a mill was commenced on the river two miles below by an Englishman who owned the adjoining township. Col. Clarke abandoned his enterprise, and Mr. Matthews engaged to build the dam at the mill below, which he never succeeded in getting strong enough to resist the current.

Now comes privation and toil which exceeds our imagination, the sons working in the water gathering rocks to secure the dam until the skin would be worn off their hands, and to no purpose. The family had but little bread until wheat was grown on the homestead and then it had to be taken twenty miles to mill, with an ox team, over almost impassable roads, or ground in a large coffee mill for a family of eleven persons. They sometimes boiled the wheat when in the milk, or hulled corn to eke out the scanty fare.

Col. Clarke never fulfilled the promises he made. Father Matthews never got the deed for one hundred acres for each child.

My husband often speaks of one experience which was very sad indeed to him. A brother two years older than himself was never contented under the shadow of the big trees. When about sixteen years of age, unknown to all he left home and never returned. He took John for a walk in the woods; bade him good bye, saying, "You will never see me again;" and so it was. He went to Buffalo and visited relatives, then they lost sight of him. It is supposed he went to sea and was shipwrecked. His only companion, my husband, felt his loss very much.

Thus passed the weary years, without school for the young family, no religious services, only occasionally a Methodist Itinerant would visit them, until the year that the City of Guelph began to rise from the heaps of logs, then the wilderness was left behind. With a better prospect before them the home was left unsold. After a number of years a Mr. Gilkison, of Brantford, got possession of the place, but who it was that first occupied it we do not know.

Alas for earthly hopes. Not much more than a year had elapsed before father was taken away by an accident. He was injured and, suffering terribly. He asked John to go to Galt, eighteen miles away, for a Dr. Simpson. He went on foot, sent the doctor ahead and he stayed all night to rest. During the night he imagined he saw his father's funeral, saw where he was buried, near the Court House, the first grave in the city of Guelph. All too true. His father died that night. A young doctor in the place volunteered his services and, by maltreatment, killed him.

My husband was then eighteen years of age, the only support for the family. By hard work he kept the wolf from the door for a while. Unfortunately, as he was working in company with some worthless fellows, who got into a fight with some Catholics, and they, supposing him to be the same sort, attacked him and he was obliged to flee for his life, fearing to remain in the place. The family was broken up, their home sacrificed. The mother afterwards lived with her daughters, and died at the home of her youngest, in the ninety-fourth year of her age.

My husband returned to Flamboro; learned the carpenter's trade in Dundas; went to school when he had earned enough money to pay expenses. His wandering since might fill a small volume, if written. He is now ninety-one, his hearing is dull but his health is good, and in the enjoyment of religious experience and trust in God.

Yours respectfully,
Anna Spencer Matthews.

The writer of the foregoing letter died at her home in Maquoketa, Iowa on the 31st May, 1902.

Anna Spencer was born at Lundy's Lane, near Niagara Falls, on June 14th, 1815. On February 2nd, 1836, she became the wife of John Matthews, with whom she journeyed in brave and helpful companionship for sixty-six years. Mr. and Mrs. Matthews left Hamilton in 1854 to become the pioneers in that part of Iowa in which they resided. Mrs. Matthews had been a member of the Methodist Church for upwards of two thirds of a century. The Hon. Benjamin Spencer, late of Delmar, Iowa, who served the state as a member of the Legislature, was her brother. Another brother well known was the Rev. James Spencer, for many years editor of the Methodist publication, the Christian Guardian, of Toronto.

Mrs. Matthews was the mother of ten children, five of whom survived her. These were: Mrs. M. M. Gray, of Pasadena, California; John S. and Cyrus, of Sioux City, Iowa; W. H., of Ada, Minnesota, and Edwin L., of Minneapolis.

Her husband passed the remaining years of his life at Avalon, Santa Catalina Island, off the coast of California, in one of the finest climates in the world. Surrounded by all the luxuries that earth can bestow—in striking contrast to the privations of his early days in Elora—he led a tranquil and contented life. Peacefully he passed away on December 6th, 1905, at the good old age of ninety-six years and three months, and was laid to rest beside Mrs. Matthews, near their home at Maquoketa.

Roswell Matthews, the first resident in Elora, was born in the state of Vermont, on January 8th, 1774. His father was Welsh, and probably the first of the name to come to America. While living at Cambridge, Connecticut, Roswell Matthews married Hannah Grannis, who had been born there, of French parentage, on October 31st, 1776. Somewhere about the year 1802

JOHN MATTHEWS
At the Age of Sixty-Seven

MRS. JOHN MATTHEWS

they removed to Niagara (on-the lake), and with them were other members of the Matthews family. One of these, a brother of Roswell, was Abner Matthews, a man of character and ability, who afterwards lived at Burford, Ontario, and some of whose descendants occupy prominent positions in Canada to-day. Two sisters were Mrs. Eaton and Mrs. Rounds.

For some years Roswell Matthews lived between Niagara and St. Catharines, after which he moved to Crooks's Hollow, where he engaged in business. But for several years after the war was over business was in a very unsatisfactory condition and this venture proved unfortunate. He then, in 1816, built a mill for the Hon. James Crooks, at Crooks's Hollow. In Connecticut, Roswell Matthews had learned the trade of cabinet making, but after coming to Canada his training for the finer work had to be laid aside and he developed into a contractor and millwright. This is shown by his building fortifications at Niagara and afterwards at Burlington Heights, and by his millwright work at Crooks's Hollow. It was while here that he met Colonel Thomas Clark, who had owned the Township of Nichol for ten years without getting any one to settle in it. Col. Clark now offered Roswell Matthews one hundred acres of land for each of his children if he would go to the Falls on the Grand River and build a mill there.

Leaving their home at Crooks's Hollow, Roswell Matthews, with his wife and nine children, the oldest a girl nineteen years of age, commenced their arduous journey. Passing the new town of Galt, where another American, Absalom Shade, had built a mill, they arrived at Captain Smith's home, which was on the east side of the Grand River, opposite the junction with it of the Conestogo.

Roswell Matthews and Captain Smith could not have been unknown to each other, for, had not each taken an active part in the War of 1812 ? Capt. Smith had been living at this place for ten years. He had a log house, a numerous family, and a large heart. Backwoods hospitality knows no bounds. There was not a house that they knew of farther up the river, so Mrs. Matthews and the seven younger children must just stop with them for three months of the winter, until the father and his two eldest sons could prepare a home for them near the Falls on the Grand River. By the direct road it is eleven miles from Capt. Smith's old home to Elora, but by the meandering river it is much farther. This last stage of their journey is left to the reader's imagination, and only those who have followed the windings of the river as it is at present can form any conception of the difficulties that were experienced.

Roswell Matthews was capable and methodical in business matters, and a good provider for his family, when possible. He was well educated for those days, was a great reader, and very often read aloud to his family. He was a general favorite with the Indians and while living in West Flamborough he was adopted into their tribe. Several chiefs gathered around him, laid their hands upon his head and christened him Tee-a-ho-ga, telling him to use the name if ever threatened by trouble with their kindred.

Mrs. Matthews, who died in November, 1870, at the home of Thomas Townsend, at Woodstock, Ont., was, from all accounts, of a very lovable disposition, particularly in her old age. Even up to the time of her death, at the age of ninety four, her hair was of a fine, glossy black, with scarcely a grey hair among it.

The children of Roswell Matthews and his wife, Hannah Grannis, were : Prudence married Adam Cramer, lived near Dundas, Ontario, several of their children went to Iowa. Anson, born August 31st, 1800, took up a farm in the township of Pilkington, there married Ellen Callaway, afterwards moved to Benton Harbor, Michigan. Abram, born at Niagara on January 21st, 1804, took up land in Pilkington ; there married Diana Nicklin ; in 1843 removed to Acton, Ont., where he died in 1886. One of his family is Mrs. Broley, Sr., of Elora. Roswell, born Feb. 22nd, 1807, left home when about the age of sixteen and is supposed to have been drowned in one of the Great Lakes, but never authentically heard from. John, born near Niagara, August 22nd, 1809, married Anna Spencer, lived at Dundas and Hamilton, then removed to the State of Iowa. Mary Ann, married Mr. Edy ; two of their sons were Edy Bros., one time photographers in Brantford and London. Jane, married Benjamin Sullivan ; Hannah, married a Mr. Rose, moved to Nauvo, Illinois, and then to Utah ; Caroline, unmarried, died during the cholera epidemic. Margaret, born September 9th, 1818, married Thomas Townsend, lived at Woodstock, Ontario ; died about 1900 or 1901. Thomas, the youngest, born August 19th, 1825, married Elizabeth Blatcher, lived at Sunfield, Michigan ; died at the home of his daughter Ida, (Mrs. John Hillmer, Windsor, Ontario), September 25th, 1905.

From the date of the birth of the youngest daughter, Margaret, we are led to infer that she was the first white child born in the Township of Nichol. As to the youngest son, Thomas, the following letter explains itself :

Sunfield, Michigan, November 21st, 1900.

J. R. Connon, Elora.
Dear Sir,—

On August 19th, 1825, I was born at Elora and was the first MALE child born in the Township of Nichol.

My father went to the Elora Falls to build a mill for Colonel Thomas Clark, the owner of the Township of Nichol, and I was named after him.

Yours respectfully,

Thomas Clark Matthews.

The Township of Nichol, containing 28,512 acres, was granted by the Crown to the Hon. Thomas Clark, for military services, the patent bearing date of April 17th, 1807. On the 9th December, 1808, Thomas Clark sold to Samuel Hatt, of Ancaster, the whole of an undivided moiety, or half of what was then called "Block Four on the Grand River," and by him this was again sold to the Rev. Robert Addison, of Niagara. The widow of the latter sold her right, on Nov. 23rd, 1832, to William Gilkison.

In the graveyard of Trinity Church, Chippawa, the remains of the first owner of the Township of Nichol lie buried, and on the monument there is this inscription : "Sacred to the memory of Thomas Clark, a native of Dumfries, Scotland, who died in 1837, aged 67, and for more than twenty years was an independent member of the Legislative Council of this province, having lived in this province from its earliest settlement, and by persevering industry and strict integrity procured for him general respect, while his kind disposition and becoming deportment endeared him to numerous friends by whom his death will be long and deeply lamented. His sisters, in grateful recollection of their affectionate brother, have erected this tablet to his memory."

The inscription to the memory of Mrs. Clark is : "Sacred to the memory of Mary Margaret Clark, wife of the Hon. Thomas Clark, and daughter of Robert Kerr, Esq., late Surgeon of the militia department in this province, who died in 1837, aged 45."

In St. Mark's Church, Niagara, there is a tablet to the memory of the Rev. Robert Addison, who was incumbent of that parish from 1792 to 1829.

ELORA

The Township of Nichol was so named as a compliment to Col. Nichol, who was Sir Isaac Brock's Commissary and friend. Colonel Robert Nichol, from Scotland, was an attorney and at one time in the law office of Sir John Beverley Robinson, in Toronto. Later he lived at Lundy's Lane, near Niagara Falls. One evening he dined at the home of Mr. Thomas McCormick at old Niagara, and on his way home, on horse back, he lost his way in the dark and fell over the banks of the Niagara river, between Queenston and the Whirlpool. (May 6th, 1824.) Of course he was killed. His body was found next morning near the water's edge, and was buried at Stamford.

Captain William Gilkison was born at Irvine, in Ayrshire, Scotland, on the 9th of March, 1777. His parents were David Gilkison, (born October 8th, 1747, died 1810), and his wife, Mary Walker, (born February 13th, 1757, died 1822), to whom he was married on December 18th, 1775. Of a family of six sons and five daughters, William was the eldest and John the youngest.

William had for a schoolmate his relative, John Galt, who was afterwards to become the celebrated Scottish novelist, the manager of the Canada Company, the founder of the city of Guelph and the one after whom the town of Galt received its name. After years of an eventful life, William Gilkison became the founder of Elora.

As shown by his letters, William Gilkison received a liberal education. After leaving school he at once commenced his life as a sailor boy, for that was the usual way in Irvine—to send boys to sea as soon as they left school. In those exciting times when Britain and France were at war it was not long until the merchant vessel he was on was captured by the French and he was taken prisoner. For about a year he was in France—the time well spent in learning the language—before he found an opportunity of escaping in a small boat. About three months afterward he was again a prisoner and again escaped.

Tiring of this life he arrived in New York in 1796, with letters of introduction to John Jacob Astor, who had been for thirteen years previously developing his business as a fur trader that was to make him one of the first American millionaires. Capt. Gilkison was given command of a schooner on Lake Erie, in the service of the North-West Fur Company. For six years he sailed between the Company's warehouses, nearly opposite to Detroit, and Fort Erie, coming down with furs and taking back supplies.

On Lake Erie at this time Commodore Grant was in command of the British fleet. He was the third son of Grant, laird of Glenmoriston, in Invernesshire. In 1759, young Grant came out to Canada with General Amherst as an officer in a line regiment, but the General, finding it necessary to have a naval force on lakes Champlain and George, called for officers who had been in the navy, and, as Grant was one of them, he received command of a sloop of 21 guns. Later he was given command of the British fleet between Niagara and Mackinaw. The Commodore's residence was at Grosse Point, on Lake St. Clair, ten miles above the city of Detroit, with occasional residence at Amherstburg. He married Miss Theresa Barthe, of Detroit, a French Canadian lady.

In their family there were eleven daughters and one son. On the 13th of January, 1803, Capt. Gilkison married Isabella, the sixth daughter. Eight of the daughters married and, in consideration of their father's valuable services to the Crown, both as a Commander of the fleet and a member, for twenty years, of the Executive Council, received liberal grants of land in different parts of the province.

After his marriage Capt. Gilkison helped his father-in-law in the management of his large estate. In 1811 he built the first house in the town of Prescott. At the commencement of the war of 1812 he was appointed a Quarter Master General and, along with Mr. Wm. Porteous, had charge of the military stores at Montreal, but this did not prevent him from taking an active part in several engagements.

After the war was over, and the business connected with the settlement of Commodore Grant's estate disposed of, Capt. Gilkison turned his attention to the education of his family. With his wife and family he sailed for Scotland early in the summer of 1815, and when in mid-ocean received the news from the Captain of a passing ship that the battle of Waterloo had been fought and won.

On their arrival in Scotland Capt. Gilkison made his home in Glasgow that he might carry out his intention of carefully educating his sons. Having attended to this by placing them under good teachers, he spent much of his time in travelling. Happy was their home for ten years until, on February 10th, 1826, Mrs. Gilkison died, in the forty-fourth year of her age. Her remains were interred in a church in Glasgow, a beautiful tablet of white and black marble being placed in the wall of the church to her memory. Some four years later, when returning from a voyage, her husband wrote the following, dated: " 'At Sea, 29th Sept., 1830.'

> From the dark blue sea returning,
> From far, far lands I come,
> Oh, wherefore swells my bosom,
> All silent is my home."

The seven surviving sons of Capt. Gilkison were coming to that age when he wished to have them settled in some occupation, and as, in one of his letters, he refers to Canada as "the only free country on the face of the Globe that I know anything about," we need look for no better reason why he should have come back again to make his home here. On March 1st, 1832, he sailed from Liverpool and arrived at New York. Several of his sons had preceded him. The eldest, David, was with John Galt at the founding of the city of Guelph. Archibald, Jasper and Daniel came in 1829, and Robert came to Canada later than his father.

So well did Capt. Gilkison express his thoughts in writing that we propose to give copies of some of his letters, and extracts from others, particularly those which are interesting in connection with the history of Elora. These letters were written to his son Jasper, then between eighteen and nineteen years of age, who was at that time employed in the wholesale house of Messrs. Ferrie & Co., of Hamilton. We may say that Mr. Jasper T. Gilkison, to whom these letters were written, is at present and has been for many years, living in Brantford. He is now ninety two and a half years of age. It is to his kindness and that of his daughter, Miss Augusta Isabella Grant Gilkison, that we are privileged to publish these private letters, which show in a very convincing way that Capt. Gilkison, the founder of Elora, was one of nature's noblemen.

In the first letter we find Capt. Gilkison among his old friends at Niagara Falls, renewing old acquaintances, and quietly looking about for a place to make his home and for some suitable investment. At Niagara Falls he would meet Col. Thomas Clark, the owner of the Township of Nichol, and at the Town of Niagara lived Mrs. Addison, who owned the half interest in the township, which had been purchased by her deceased husband.

St. Forsyth's, Niagara Falls,
Sunday, 12th August, 1832.

My Dear Jasper:—
I have been here for a week enjoying the beauteous scenery of the Falls and I feel pretty well. Yesterday I dined with your aunt and all the Duff,s. The day after I left you, Daniel, dear Dan, and I separated at Youngstown—his black eyes filled with tears—and he went to Rochester by steamer on his way to the Academy at Canandaigua for a year or two. Peace and happiness be with him. Archy is very well though I have not heard from him since I left Niagara on Tuesday last. I am thinking of going to Buffalo to take the warm baths—I am troubled with rheumatism, which they will alleviate if they shall not cure.

Be so good as to write me a letter to Niagara Falls and give me an account of everything. I pray you to exercise your talent in composition; few of the powers of the mind which man possesses serve to give him more pleasure —or are more useful to him—than writing his thoughts clearly and distinctly; but, to accomplish such an object, you should write frequently and well on any subject which shall occur to your young mind and do not be overpowered with regrets if you shall not succeed in your first attempts to please—even yourself —for you will succeed if you shall determine to write gracefully. You can easily spare a little time for such a useful purpose, and if you shall do so and exhibit your book of notes to me, I will be wonderfully delighted to read such a proof of your determination to gratify me and benefit yourself, so long as life shall be given to you. I am anxious on this point—let me have it in my power to say, 'My dear Jasper has wonderfully improved since he went to Hamilton.'

Your note book may have corrections on it, indeed it must be corrected, but, if you were copying any part of it at a future period, the copy should be entirely free from bad grammar, or bad spelling,—these are seldom excusable even in the most hurried composition—notice what I have told you. I am all anxiety you should improve yourself in everything, that you should become an intelligent man, a leader in society, that you may become if you shall be industrious in all your duties.

I hope to hear from you the end of next week. I remain
thy affectionate father, W. GILKISON.

In a post script he says: "I am as much delighted with the Falls as when I first saw them 33 years ago, when I came here in 1798—how time passes away!"
I have no letters on the subject of Wood's farm at Brantford. It is my intention to go to Montreal the middle of September, that is if I am well. Born 9th March, 1777, at Irvine in Ayrshire, and I was married to your late and loved Mother in the house of your aunt Duff, at Amherstburg, on 13th January, 1803,—recollect that—and recollect, too, I am greatly changed since that later auspicious period of my life—a life that soon will terminate. Be good and just, and do not fail to be sober and industrious and your life will be easy."

In a letter written at Niagara, 24th August, 1832, he says: "I have to thank you for your letter of the 19th. On several points it gives me much pleasure and I shall refer to two of them, viz.: the handwriting is improved and I see, or think I see, an obvious prospect of a steady and fair hand, a great advantage to a young man; don't look at my handwriting, or style either, for they have altogether changed for the worse and I feel reluctant to show them even to you whom I love so well."

"Spend your leisure in acquiring knowledge—time never returns; always recollect to employ it faithfully and well in youth, in old age the reflection will cheer you,—friends will visit and learn your tales of other years—of days and events long gone bye." "Don't omit calling on my good friends when you are passing Dundas or Flamborough." "I passed an hour yesterday with our friend, Mrs. Nichol; the Duffs are well." "Adieu.—You will show your gratitude for this long letter by writing me in reply on any subject you choose—but you must do your work as well as you can do it: never be careless in doing the most trifling thing, above all be correct in the store.

ever thine, W. GILKISON.

The next, like all Capt. Gilkison's letters, needs little explanation. Some time before writing it he had bought a farm, on which now stands a part of the city of Brantford. He called this Oak Bank, after his former home in Glasgow. He had also bought the south-west half of the Township of Nichol and at the time of writing this letter the surveyor, Lewis Burwell, was completing the first map of the village at the Falls on the Grand River On this map, which is dated November 10th, 1832, the surveyor mentions the necessity of giving the village a name before any conveyances of property are made. The following letter is especially interesting because in it—for the first time— Capt. Gilkison calls the place—ELORA.

(Note that 'York' was the former name of 'Toronto').

Niagara, 3rd. Nov., 1832.

My Dear Jasper:—

Your favor of the 28th ulto. is before me and I haste to acknowledge its receipt—for your letters, and your absent Brothers' epistles, never fail to give me great pleasure.

I have been at York, and propose to return there again to-morrow, to obtain a deed for Nichol—Mr. Clark is in the Capital attending to his parliamentary duties.

* * * I hope to see you in a week or two—I am anxious to return to Brantford, my future home.

* * * My things from New York are on the way to Hamilton. Tell McPherson & Co. to send them to Brantford the moment they arrive, and if there is not enough to load the waggon desire them to make up the load with salt.

The weather is delightfully pleasant—like Italy Look frequently on the scene which bounteous nature presents to your view in contemplating the starry heavens on a fine night. Our foggy climate of Scotland has nothing like it. Look attentively at the Stars—think of them—read astronomy for an explanation—it will soothe your mind and charm you.

I am going to dine with Mrs. McCormick. When at York I dined with the Chief Justice, and was to have dined with Mrs. Allan—recollect all these names as those of persons with whom I have been and am now on terms of intimacy and kindness

Pay great attention to your style of writing—you must be more attentive to that branch of your education than you seem to think necessary. I know your time is fully employed, and am glad of it, but still there are moments of your own which can be privately and usefully employed. You will not resemble the young fellows whom I have so often, and so lately seen wasting their precious time in the destructive vice of gambling and folly. Such an exhibition to me would distract me.

I am thinking of sending a few goods, under the direction of an intelligent man, to pay for work I must have done in the Village of Elora--look for that word in the Encyclopedia or some other dictionary. At a future period Elora may become a place for you to manage Mills, &c., &c., &c.

Adieu my Dear Child,
ever yours, W. GILKISON.

The next letter was written from 'Oak Bank,' the name which he gave to his new home at Brantford. The house which he mentions as the first raised in Elora refers to the first house after the village was surveyed, and received its name, for Roswell Matthews had built his house here fifteen years before this.

Oak Bank, 15th Dec., 1832.

My Dear Jasper :—
I want the following articles from the celebrated town of Hamilton, so, order them without delay that there may be no disappointment when the goods are sent up to Elora.

Two days ago I took possession of my farm house and here I am, solitary and sad enough—but, I am wrong in using the word 'sad', for, what with town building, lot selling and farming, my mind is amply employed in thinking of all these weighty affairs, which will in due time redound to my advantage, and doubtless to yours.

Mr. Frazer returns in a day or two to Elora and I hope the first house in that young and rising City will be raised this day, this very 17th December—by the by, this day was memorable in my father's family—it was the day he married his wife,—my mother, one of the best and kindest of the human race : old thoughts will revive.

By first slays for Elora let the goods now ordered go forward—I mean the weights and measures. The Tobacco (one keg) will be sufficient for the present.

Three trunks and one small box are all that have come to me from New York. Compare the printed bill of lading and tell me what remains in Store : if that which is in store was at Hamilton you could send the articles to me here as an opportunity offered. I fear the Telescope and the Map of Upper Canada we left at New York have not come up.

Archy will be up for Christmas and I shall expect you to come with him for dinner.

I am ever thine,
W. GILKISON.

During the month of January, 1833, Capt. Gilkison wrote several letters. In them is shown the sea Captain, the military Quarter Master—planning, ordering and urging on supplies for the first store in Elora.

These are some extracts from different letters : "Monday, 6th January 1833.—Tell me the amount of your check on the agency at Hamilton. I had 200 pounds there—your check must have absorbed the balance,—enquire. Keep an accurate account of every farthing you disburse for me. Archy has gone to Nichol and cannot be back again in less than a week."

"Oak Bank, 25th January, 1833.—I see Mr. Richardson's assortment of made up coarse clothing, which I think well adapted for the shop at Elora ; wherefore, if you can buy about 12 pounds worth for me I pray you to do so ; and I shall send a check on York to pay the amount. You can send the Bill to Frazer by slays : for I still hope for roads to send the goods up.

The weather is fine like that which we may expect in April.

I thank you for sending me the articles in the tin box—they are all wanted at Oak Bank.

Wednesday.—Mr. Frazer has written to me—just received—that his movements will be governed by the advice you shall send to him as to the state of the roads with you—so be particular and do not let us lose the next snow that falls, or the things may not reach Elora this winter—a great disappointment if such shall be the case. Frazer will come himself whenever the roads shall answer: hire a person to go up, as an express, (for you cannot depend on chance) with an account of the state of the roads.

If you can buy a good whip saw, and two good mill saws of Philadelphia manufacture, have the goodness to buy them for Elora: the best you can find must be had, if the Philadelphia sort is not in your market: see they are of proper lengths and send an assortment of files with them. Frazer may choose the saws if his time will permit; look out for them in the meantime. Send up a grindstone to Elora.

Your aunt and Ann Duff came and dined with me yesterday—a compliment from ladies to an old fellow.

* * * I want a saw mill maker: if you can hear of one of the best of that description let me know immediately, or rather ask him to come and see me. Tell him I want a man who can make the best description of mill on the latest improved plan; tell him of the saws I have ordered and take his advice—for I have no one to advise with."

Monday, 28th. January, 1833.—As we have abundance of snow here, I propose to send my own two teams for loads to carry to Elora: so you need not send an express to Mr. Frazer.

Johnston Richardson will go with the slays on his way to Elora and he will call on you,—a nice lad. I have heard nothing from Archie since his return to Niagara. Dan was very well on the 17th., when he sent me his quarter's bill of 30 pounds: his writing is much improved.

Mr. Richardson goes down by coach to Hamilton; assist him in hiring waggons—or slays—to carry up the goods—he is young and knows nothing of such matters, so be particular in explaining everything to him: bargain for a certain price to Guelph in case they cannot go to Elora with the goods, and tell Richardson to take an invoice of each cargo, and see them carefully stored until they can be taken up from Guelph.

Tell Frazer what has been done in case he should come down—I intend being at Guelph on Thursday if I can go in waggon or slay

Pay the teamster and I shall send you a check for the amount if Mr. Ferrie will accomodate me for a few days "

Sunday, 13th. March, 1833.

My Dear Jasper :—

Last night I returned from Elora: everything is going on there as well as a new country will permit. I believe I shall erect my first Bridge over the Grand River exactly at the Falls of Elora: it is a remarkable and beautiful spot, and I clambored directly up the precipice of the Falls. because it was wholly covered with thick ice and the water hidden from view. In a year or two, I hope for your assistance to manage and direct the operations—the various plans I have in contemplation at that new City for I cannot figure to myself a better school of instruction for you than the store of Mr. Ferrie: so be diligent and observant of everything about you, as well as the art of store keeping. In this country it is absolutely necessary one should be acquainted with everything going on in it; and, therefore, it is right you should attentively read the essential parts of every law which may be made for the Gov't. of the people; do this when you have leisure. Those laws which relate to money, and the duties we have to perform to the public should be studied with attention.

Since I wrote the above I have your favor of the 11th. and regret my Flamborough and other friends have not been able to come up—for I am all ready and prepared for them, with every delicacy which the season and the adjoining City can afford; but I will be rejoiced to see Mrs. Crooks and her friends let them come when they will—say so when you meet any of the party that were coming to me.

I have a long and pleasant letter from Archy, full of wise and intelligent remarks that delighted me to read. You can write well, too, but you will do better by and by, if you resolve to do so.

I am Dear Jasper,
ever thy affectionate
W. Gilkison.

Tuesday evening, —.—
(The date is not given. but it was probably April 5th, 1833.)

My Dear Jasper :—

I am in debt to you several letters : but I know you will excuse me when you learn how busy I am with one thing or another. Had I not determined to go to Hamilton on Tuesday to attend Sessions I should have written you before this, on the subject of your offer to go to Elora : and I would have promptly accepted your kindness, had I not thought you are better with Mr. Ferrie than you would be in the woods. It is for your interest I would wish you to continue for another year at Hamilton—after which you shall go to Elora and grow up with a fine and beautiful Country and be an ornament and an example for the settlement to follow.

I shall be sorry to miss you—try to meet me on Tuesday night or Wednesday morning. There is a place for you here when you shall come.

Adieu—it is dark !
W. Gilkison.

"Be contented and happy where you are—continue to give exemplary satisfaction to your employer—let your excellent temper never become ruffled with any circumstances and all will go well with you."

This was the last letter written by Capt. Gilkison to his son, Jasper. Having been at Hamilton, purchasing supplies for Elora, Capt. Gilkison was returning to his home at Brantford. He stopped at the Tuscarora Parsonage, the home of the Rev. Abraham Nelles, at Onondaga, on the banks of the Grand River, near Brantford. He was about to resume his journey and had given directions to his coachman to fetch the horses and carriage, when he was stricken with paralysis, and died on April 23rd, 1833, at the age of fifty-six. His remains were buried beside the Old Mohawk Church at Brantford.

What the history of Elora might have been had Capt. Gilkison lived for a few years longer to complete the plans he had in view, it would now be idle to conjecture. A few weeks before his death he wrote out instructions for his sons to follow and, on the following day, March 4th, he made his will, leaving his property to his sons, the eldest being then thirty years of age. As it is from his family that all owners of land in the south-west half of the Township of Nichol received their title, it would be well to know something of his family.

There were eleven sons, seven of whom grew to manhood. These were: **David**, who married Margaret Geddes. He was a merchant and died in **Toronto in May, 1851**. Alexander Grant, married Miss Outram; was a merchant in Glasgow, and died there in 1849. William Galt, was a ship builder. He died, unmarried, at Cawnpoor, India, in August, 1831. Robert was also a ship builder at Glasgow, and for a few years at Niagara-on-the-lake. He died, unmarried, at Leith, Scotland, in April, 1855. Archibald married Hannah McCormick, of Niagara. He was a Lawyer and a Judge at Picton, Ontario. He died in 1876. Jasper Tough, born at Johnstown, near Brockville, on the 13th March, 1814, married Mary Elizabeth McCormick, the third daughter of Thomas M. McCormick, of Niagara on-the-lake, and grand-daughter of the late Wm. Jarvis, of Toronto, Secretary to Governor Simcoe. Daniel Mercer married Georgiana Rackham. He farmed his father's farm, which is now part of the city of Brantford, and died there in January, 1861.

To show that the good advice given by Capt. Gilkison in his letters to his son was followed, it may be said that while living in Hamilton Jasper T. Gilkison was actively engaged in many enterprises which were a great benefit to the public. He was the principal promoter of the Great Western Railway Company, and its first Secretary. He was the projector of the first telegraph line into Canada via Queenston, and of the Clifton Railway Suspension Bridge across the Niagara River, all the capital stock for which was subscribed for in his office. In 1862 he was appointed Government Commissioner and Superintendent of the Six Nation Indians, near Brantford, retiring in April, 1891. Colonel J. T. Gilkison joined the Volunteer Militia in 1832 and, until prevented by advancing years, he continued to take an active part in Military matters.

HOW ELORA RECEIVED ITS NAME

The founder of Elora, Capt. William Gilkison, was the eldest of a family all the brothers in which were ship Captains. Even one of his nephews, Capt. Brown, followed the same profession and was for years Captain of the Allan Line Steamship 'Polynesian.'

The Gilkisons were in command of ships which sailed to different parts of the world, but principally to the West Indies, to Chili, and the East Indies. The youngest brother in the family was Capt. John Gilkison, who, for a few years before 1830, was Captain of a ship called the 'Fortune,' which sailed from Port Glasgow to Bombay, in India. Not far from Bombay are the celebrated Cave Temples of Elora, or Ellora, of which, during the intervals when his vessel was in port, Capt. John Gilkison must have heard, and probably visited.

In a letter written by Capt. William Gilkison, dated from London the last day of February, 1831, he, in referring to his youngest brother, John, the Captain of the 'Fortune,' says, "Johnny leaves the 'Fortune' for a new ship now building at Port Glasgow." This was a three masted vessel, technically called a 'barque.' In selecting a name for his new ship, Captain John Gilkison called her the 'Elora,' and on this ship he continued his voyages to Bombay.

After coming to Canada and determining on the sight of a future town at the Falls on the Grand River, Capt. William Gilkison called the place 'Elora' after his brother 'Johnny's' ship, the name which had been suggested by the Caves of Elora, in India.

What strange coincidences we meet with! We little know what chain of circumstances may be caused by some incident that, in itself, would seem to have the remotest connection with the consequences. When, in 1893, the writer sent some photographic views of the Grand River at Elora to be published in a Toronto daily newspaper, he had no reason to suppose that this

CAPT. WILLIAM GILKISON

.THE GRAND RIVER AT ELORA — 1892

should cause a letter to be written in London, England, which, thirteen years later, would be forwarded to him as evidence of the way in which Elora received its name.

The newspaper containing the views of Elora was received by Mr. Jasper T. Gilkison in Brantford, who sent it to his cousin in England, Miss Elizabeth Gilkison, daughter of Capt. John Gilkison, and the following is an extract from the letter which he received from her :

26 Kensington Gardens, London,
October 21st, 1893.

"What a very beautiful place that must be on the Grand River, near Elora, of which there is a sketch in the newspaper which you sent me. I suppose it once belonged to your father and probably owes its name to his memory of the good ship Elora, which was named after the **Caves of Elora** in India, and my father was her Captain at one time."

The clearing made by Roswell Matthews, on the south side of the river, became the building site for the first houses in Elora and it was on this clearance, of some thirty acres, that the town plot was surveyed. For two blocks along the top of the hill and down to the river at the Falls the ground was cleared of trees and stumps.

The solitary log house that Roswell Mathews left remained unoccupied until about the year 1831. when one by the name of Wintermute, with his wife and family, took possession of the house. They came from the vicinity of Chippawa, and, after remaining here for some months, went on farther up the river to take up a farm in the Township of Garafraxa. The house that Wintermute built in Garafraxa was near what is now the residence of Mr. James Wilson, the proprietor of Monkland Mills.

The log building mentioned by Capt. Gilkison, that was raised on the 17th of December, 1832, and was used as a store house for the goods he was sending to Elora, stood near that brick residence which is opposite the entrance of the Armory Hall. The next structure erected in the village was a small log tavern built by Martin Martin, but this was scarcely completed when it burned down and another was built across the street from it, on the west corner of High and Walnut streets, forming an extension of Roswell Matthews' house towards the east. There was also another log house completed in the winter of 1833-34, the house that was long occupied by Mr. James Chambers, and which is at present owned by Mr. Alex. McLean. This has now the distinction of being the oldest house in the village The only other building on the south side of the river, in the Fall of 1833, was the barn built by Roswell Matthews which was to the east of his house, on the north corner of Woolwich and High streets.

The Grand River at Elora in 1833 was not much like it is to day. On top of the Islet Rock, which stands alone in the centre of the Falls, the stump of a cedar tree could be seen, about eight inches in diameter. This tree was chopped by Anson Matthews without his having any apparent reason for doing it and yet it was fortunate that he did so, for, had the tree been allowed to grow, the rock might long ere this have been split by the pressure of the growing roots, which not even the hardest rocks can resist.

From near the Islet Rock, up the river to the foot of Metcalfe street, there was an island on which large trees were growing. This island was a great protection to the Islet Rock for it divided the current in the river, although, before all the land was cleared, there were no floods like those of recent years.

The first bridge across the Grand River was from the street in front of the Armory Hall to the foot of Metcalfe street. It is said that George

McKenzie and his father-in-law, Redrick McKay, built this bridge for thirty-five dollars, and glad they were to get even this small sum, for it is doubtful if, during all the three years they had been living in Pilkington, they had received as much money before.

Another Pilkington settler, Henry Wilbee, was employed by the Gilkison estate to build a saw-mill at the Elora Falls. A rudely constructed dam was built across the river, back of what has for the past twenty-eight years been well known as 'Campbell's Store'. From this point a flume was excavated along the bank of the river to the Falls, where the saw-mill was driven by an undershot, or 'flutter' wheel. It was while working at this saw mill that Henry Wilbee built the first log house west of the Grand River at Elora.

On the evening of the 6th of of October, 1833, the Hon. Adam Fergusson arrived in Elora, having left Guelph in the morning. They had been misdirected and in the course of the forenoon found themselves on the farm of Mr. Armstrong, in Eramosa. The following is Mr. Fergusson's account of his visit, slightly abbreviated : "Mr. Armstrong put us on our way to the farm of Mr. Dunwoodie. By this good family we were welcomed in a spirit of genuine hospitality, and sat down to a comfortable dinner where excellent sheep's head broth formed an acceptable item. After a glass of good whisky toddy, and being furnished with the aid of Mr. Bryden, a Scotch settler in the neighborhood, as our guide through the forest to Elora Falls, a distance of about twelve miles, we left Mr. Dunwoodie and were soon immersed in the woods. I have seldom seen a better pedestrian than our guide, who dashed away through bush and brake at a slapping pace and performed the distance in two hours and forty minutes. The soil was rich and the wood of great size and valuable kinds. Elora is in a beautiful situation with most romantic scenery and valuable mill-power on the Grand River. A bridge is at present building and extensive mills erecting. Mr. Frazer, who has acted as agent for the Gilkison family, insisted upon our taking quarters in the "manor house," as the tavern was in a rather rough state. There had been a "Bee" held for two days— (probably raising the new bridge)--and the jollification had yet scarcely subsided. We got a most comfortable supper, however, and kind reception, for which we were sincerely thankful. Some respectable settlers from the adjoining township of Woolwich (now Pilkington) spent the evening with us and communicated much useful information.

Oct. 7th.—Our host volunteered to ride with us after breakfast up the banks of the river to view the object of our visit, distant about seven miles. The day was fine and the prodigious height of the maples, elms and other trees gave a solemn character to the stillness of the forest. The only trace of a road consisted in blazes or chips taken from the bark of the trees. Occasionally some immense overthrown trunk blocked up the only passage, and we had nothing for it then but a sporting leap, a performance which the Canadian pony took his own mode of executing, somewhat to the discomposure of his rider, as it more nearly resembled the feats of a grimalkin than any equestrian movement we had ever seen."

The result of this visit was that Mr. Fergusson purchased from the Hon. Thomas Clark the north easterly quarter of the Township of Nichol, containing about 7,367 acres. Associated with him in the enterprise was Mr. James Webster, who had accompanied Mr. Fergusson from Scotland.

The Hon. Adam Fergusson was born at Edinburgh on the 4th of March, 1783, of a family long established in the Highlands of Perthshire. He was the son of an Advocate and was himself a lawyer in Scotland but scarcely practiced as he preferred the life of a country gentleman. In 1831 he made a tour of the United States and Canada—the small part that was then known—and his published account which appeared in pamphlets and newspapers in Scotland had a considerable effect in directing emigration to this country. Although he was the founder of Fergus his own usual residence was at Woodhill, near Waterdown, where he died on the 26th of September, 1862.

A village was laid out some three miles up the river from Elora and named 'Fergus,' after its founder. Building operations were commenced in the new village on the 20th of December, 1833, this being a year and three days after the first house was 'raised' for Capt. Gilkison in Elora, but more than sixteen years after Roswell Matthews had made his home here.

One of Elora's citizens was invited to the raising of the first house in Fergus. Early in the morning he tramped through the woods along the south side of the river until he came nearly opposite to the new town. The only bridge was the trunk of a tree which had been felled across the river, back of where Melville Church now stands. This was more than he had bargained for, but he managed to crawl along it on his hands and knees. On his return, later in the day, having received considerable encouragement at the raising, such a trifling matter as a narrow log swinging high above the river did not trouble him in the least and he bravely walked it with his head up, reaching his home in safety.

    ..   ..

One of the early settlers in Nichol, adjoining Elora, was the late Joseph Carder. He was born at Bow, near London, England. When a young man he was apprenticed to an Optician in London, with whom he served seven years. Failing sight compelled him to abandon his trade and he turned his attention to shop-keeping in Chapel Place, Islington. After continuing this for seven or eight years he gave it up to come to Canada.

On Sunday the 27th of August, 1833, he left the London Docks in the ship 'William Osborne,' which was towed down the Thames by a steam tug. On the Thursday following the day of sailing a fearful storm arose and continued until Monday morning. There had not been such a storm for forty years, and during its continuance one hundred and thirty-six ships were lost off the coast of France and in the English Channel. The 'William Osborne' lost all her sails, the bulwarks were swept away, three anchors were lost one after another, and as the sailors were about to abandon the ship a heavy sea swept off the boats, pigs, poultry and everything on deck, except the sailors. The ship was left to the mercy of the storm with one anchor out, close to the Goodwin sands, near the coast of Deal, the most dangerous part of the English Channel. Signals of distress were hoisted and the Deal Pilot Boat took many of the passengers ashore, but before they had taken Mr. Carder and his family the storm moderated and all were saved from a watery grave. The ship was towed into Ramsgate harbour where she remained a fortnight for repairs, which cost the owner seven hundred pounds sterling. The vessel again put to sea, and after a stormy passage arrived in New York.

Mr. Carder and family soon afterwards started for Canada, bound for Brantford. He should have left the Erie Canal at Rochester but made a mistake and went on to Buffalo. Being late in the season the boats had stopped running. After a fortnight's delay he boarded a schooner belonging to Mr. Van Norman, who had a large blasting furnace at Long Point, and, as this was to be the last trip of the season, Mr. Carder arranged with the Captain for a passage. They set sail in the evening and were at Long Point in the morning. Thus, after three months' travel, were they landed on Canadian soil.

Their first sleigh ride had been in Buffalo. They were now to experience the roughness of Canadian roads on a thirty mile trip to Brantford. Fortunately they had some beds in the waggon for the little ones to sit on.

At Brantford Mr Carder remained for about a month looking out for a Canadian home. David Gilkison, Esq., was at that time living in Brantford and had the management of his late father's estate. Mr. Richfield, Mr. Peck, and several others came from Nichol to transact some business with Mr. Gilkison and Mr. Carder happened to get into their company. Mr. Carder found that Richfield and Peck were inclined to sell out and the old gentleman, Mr. Richfield, who was Peck's father-in-law, gave such a glowing description of the place that Mr. Carder promised to come up and see it in the following week. As Mr. Gilkison's sanction was necessary to the transfer, Mr. Carder called on him first and was given every encouragement to make the Township of Nichol his home.

On the following week he started for Elora, accompanied by his brother-in-law, Thomas Seach, who had come to Brantford three years before. They arrived at Galt on the first day and on the second got as far as Cox's Creek, now called Winterbourne. There they were told that it was ten miles to Elora, so put up at Mr. Alex. Smith's, and on the next day started for Nichol. The ground was covered deep with snow so that they had hard work to get along. There were only two clearings in the first eight miles, one was at William Letson's and the other at Thomas Robinson's—the James Ross farm. On arriving at Robinson's clearing they were told that they still had four miles farther to go. The road that was cut from the 'big ridge' finished here and to escape a swamp they turned into a clearing and soon came to a place where there were two tracks. Here they were in a fix, but they left it to fate by setting up a stick and letting it fall three times. The direction in which it fell twice they followed and came to the farm then occupied by Christopher Wood. Here they got information as to their whereabouts and soon found their way to Elora.

At this time Elora seemed to be at the end of the civilized world. On the west side of the river there was not a settler between Elora and Lake Huron. Mr. Samuel Trenholme and Mr. John Mason had taken up lots west of the river but did not go on to them until after this and were living in Elora.

On arriving at Mr. Richfield's shanty, and a "splendid large" shanty it was, with a bark roof, which had the misfortune to sag in the middle, the old Yankee gave them a hearty welcome. After a good night's rest, Mr. Carder and his host went to business and Mr. Carder bought the right of Messrs. Richfield and Peck to Lots numbers one and two on the first concession of Nichol. This is on the Guelph and Elora road, half a mile south of Elora.

To get the contract finally settled, Messrs. Richfield and Peck agreed to accompany Mr. Carder to Brantford to settle with Mr. Gilkison. The price that Mr. Gilkison was selling land for at that time was four dollars an acre. Richfield and Peck had taken up these lots from Col. Thomas Clark, before Mr. Gilkison bought the west half of the Township at, according to Mr. Carder, two dollars an acre, with ten years to pay it. Mr. Carder paid two dollars and a half an acre for his two farms. There were about ten acres cleared on both farms, eight acres in fall wheat, a log house, and some bush chopped but not cleared. Mr. Carder gave sixteen dollars an acre for the clearing and eight dollars an acre for the chopping, besides paying for the wheat and the houses.

The next day they all started for Brantford. That they might see more of the country they returned by way of Guelph. There had been a heavy fall of snow during the night and the snow was more than two feet deep. Mr. Carder had never had such a hard day's travel before. They left the shanty at daylight and travelled on till an hour after dark and had walked a little more than seven miles. They called in at Mr. Knowles' to enquire how far they were from Blythe's, but were told it was of no use to travel farther as Blythe's tavern was not ready to accommodate them. They accordingly agreed with Mr. Knowles to stop the night. Here they got comfortable lodging, the good wife bustled round and got them a supper in real backwoods style. There was the large open fire-place, with a back log as big as a flour barrel, and three or four smaller ones blazing away, making it as cozy and comfortable inside as it had been disagreeable outside. While supper was being prepared the travellers were having a chat with their host, who gave them all the news of the country side. On the shelf at the side of the room there was what looked like a round cheese. The good woman reached it from the shelf and, placing it on the table, began to cut it. To Mr. Carder's astonishment it was bread. The flour had been made from smutty wheat, and it was nearly black. This was the first baked kettle loaf he had seen but, as it was newly baked, it ate first rate.

Next morning, after an early breakfast, they started for Guelph and as they advanced they found the road better, as many Ox teams had been out and broken it. In Guelph there were two taverns. Mr. D. Allan, Mr. Sandiland, Capt. Lanphier and Mrs. Worsley had stores. Mr. Allan's mill was in working order and Mr. Wright had a bakery in a log house.

The road from Guelph to Galt was better tracked. They stopped about half way, at a tavern, where they got dinner. The landlady said she had no bread, nor flour to make any, but if they could put up with buckwheat cakes she would get dinner for them. She set to work and soon had a pile of buckwheat cakes nicely buttered and Mr. Carder never enjoyed dinner better. It was late at night when they arrived in Brantford, pleased to find all well. The business with Mr. Gilkison was satisfactorily arranged and the next move was to fetch the family to their Canadian home. Then followed the hardships of the early days. When there was anything to sell there was no market nearer than Dundas or Hamilton With bad roads and slow Ox teams there were times when for several weeks there would be a scarcity of flour and other necessaries, not because they were unable to pay, but from the difficulty of getting them. On one occasion how anxiously they looked for the return of Benjamin Ariss, the teamster, who had gone to fetch a load of provisions from Hamilton ! Wheat, when they had it, sold for thirty seven and a half cents a bushel, oats for ten cents, butter seven cents a pound and eggs five cents a dozen, in trade, for cash was out of the question. Pork and beef were from two to three dollars per cwt , and a barrel of salt cost forty bushels of oats.

A couple of years after Mr Carder settled in Nichol he was appointed Bailiff, which was no small honour in those days. He had considerable administrative ability and many poor settlers did he save by originating ways and means for the payment of their indebtedness.

He was also the first School Trustee in Elora, before its incorporation as a village, and in the building of the first school and the first Methodist Church he took a great interest. On the 25th February, 1845, the Elora Branch Bible Society was organized, when Mr. Carder was elected Secretary, a position which he held to the credit of himself and the benefit of the Society for thirty-five years, until his death on the 28th January, 1880, in the eightieth year of his age.

Joseph Carder was married in England to Sarah Jones. In their family were four daughters: Sarah married George Fasken ; Elizabeth ; Catharine married Hugh Hughes ; Maria married George Watson.

* * * *

For nine years after the death of Captain Gilkison, from 1833 to 1842, Elora made but little progress. Those who came to the village during this time will be mentioned later; in the meantime it is necessary to refer to

The Bon-accord Settlement

The following narrative was written by Mr. George Elmslie, one of the first settlers in that upper part of the Township of Nichol, called the Bon-accord. As will be seen, it is both interesting and authentic.

As originally written Mr. Elmslie did not give, except in a few cases, the full names of those he refers to. These we have supplied and have prepared lists of the first settlers in Upper Nichol, which will be given in another place. But before commencing his narrative it might be well to know something of Mr. Elmslie himself.

Mr. George Elmslie was born in the city of Aberdeen in the year of 1803. After receiving a good college education, Mr. Elmslie engaged in business in Aberdeen as a Dry Goods Merchant. As one might suppose, his early experience was not that best fitted for a pioneer. Mr. Elmslie was naturally a student and an interesting book would be very apt to make him forget all about farming, with its constant round of work that should be attended to. It was no wonder, then, that Mr. Elmslie became a school teacher, first, for two winters, in his own house; then in a school that was built on his farm, and afterward, at Elora, Ancaster, Guelph, Hamilton and Alma. One morning, while on his way to school, Mr. Elmslie was stricken with paralysis and died at Alma on the 19th of October, 1869. Mrs. Elmslie, whose maiden name was Agnes Gibbon, was born at Cullerlie, in the parish of Echt, in Aberdeenshire. She died at the home of her son, William, on July 2nd, 1889, at the age of 83, and was buried beside her husband in the Elora Cemetery.

In their family: Mrs. Robert Philip, formerly of Elora, now deceased; Mrs. James Middleton, living in Salem; William, living near Clifford; George in Hamilton; Alexander in Galt; Gordon, at Lachine, and Mrs. David Spragge of Victoria, B. C.

* * * *

In 1831–32 the agitation about the Reform Bill and long continued opposition to it, had caused a great stagnation of business. Trade was dull; there were many failures; all were in difficulty, and many in distress.

A little before this time appeared Mr. Fergusson's account of his first tour in the United States and Canada, and not long after it his second tour, while the Chambers' were publishing their admirable papers on Emigration to America, containing letters from actual settlers in Canada. The eyes of thousands were turned to Canada, as a place of refuge.

Three friends in Aberdeen, afterwards joined by others, were in the habit of meeting frequently to consider seriously the advantages or disadvantages of emigrating; and at length, after obtaining all possible information, they resolved to go out, settle side by side, and thus form a little Aberdeeen colony and give it the name Bon-accord—from the motto of the town's arms.

Mr. Elmslie, as being able to wind up his business the most easily, was appointed to go before, and search out a fit location. His instructions were that it should be in a healthy situation—the land fertile, abundant in running streams—and lastly, if Fergus answered the description given by Mr. Fergusson, and a sufficient block could be got in its neighborhood, to prefer it.

All preparations having been completed, and abundant stores of clothing, etc., laid in, on the 30th of June, 1834, Mr. Elmslie set sail from Glasgow, in the Fania, Capt. Wright, Commander. The voyage was pleasant. We reached safely the banks of Newfoundland where we were becalmed two days. One terrible danger, through the goodness of Divine Providence, we escaped. A drunken steward sculked down to the spirit hold to get a stolen draught and, in his hurry and trepidation, spilled a quantity of rum, which caught fire from the candle. Happily he was just able to give instant alarm and it was speedily put out, the danger was past ere we knew of it. Our passage up the St. Lawrence was very rough—the wind ahead and constant tacking. At length we reached Grosse Isle, the quarantine station, and were immediately boarded by the authorities. Here first we met with Mr. Watt and his party—a blythe sight—for I had known him in Aberdeenshire. On the second day we reached Quebec, the next morning set sail for Montreal, which we reached in two days more From there we proceeded up the river to Ottawa, and by the Rideau Canal to Kingston. We reached Kingston on the ninth day after leaving Bytown (Ottawa) and boarded the steamer for Toronto. On Sabbath, 14th August, a bright, beautiful day, we were walking its streets.

The cholera had preceded us, and there had been a great many deaths daily. Unfortunately for us, one of our party, through fatigue and the hardship of the Durham boats, took sick in the inn where we intended to remain. The landlord refused us rooms, pretending that they were all occupied, and we found great difficulty in obtaining lodgings. Next day we rented, by the month, the upper flat of a newly built house on Adelaide street. The most strange and appalling thing to us was the sight of the carts for the dead going their rounds several times a day.

We spent a day or two in looking round the city. The chief streets then were King St., Yonge St. and Bay St. These were of brick, well built and filled up, and in them were handsome shops and extensive warehouses. The other streets, such as Church St., Adelaide St., &c., had large gaps in them, without pavements, and the houses mostly frame.

Having letters of introduction from the Secretary of State for the Colonies to the Lieutenant Governor Sir J. Colborne, we set out for the Government House and found it to be a large, old, frame building, dingy looking, without any ornament, and situated in a garden surrounded by a high board fence. We entered by a small porch, in which stood the sentry, and were conducted by another soldier into the presence of His Excellency. Sir John Colborne seemed but little past his prime—tall, not burdened with much flesh, his countenance conveying the impression of one accustomed to command, yet frank and open withal He wore a plain blue surtout, the one sleeve empty and attached to his breast, for he had left the left arm in the Peninsula.

He answered frankly the numerous questions we put to him, and gave a glowing description of the prospects of Upper Canada. He advised us to visit and examine the recently surveyed township of Nottawasaga, receiving from his secretary a note to the chief Surveyor, Mr. Rankin.

In the afternoon I called on Archdeacon Strachan and spent two hours very agreeably with him. Our conversation turned more on Scotland than on Canada and was now and then carried on in the 'guid auld Mither tongue'.

Having seen our families comfortably lodged, a fellow passenger, Mr. William Gibbon, and I took the stage to Newmarket, and thence to Holland Landing. In the morning, we took the steamer, sailing by the western shore of Lake Simcoe, and keeping close to the wild rice fields which grow luxuriantly on its borders. The noise of our wheels and the snorting of the engine scared large flights of birds that were feeding on the rice. When nearly two-thirds across, and so close to the shore that our wheels were almost clogged by the weeds and rushes, a she bear and two cubs burst from their concealment, scarcely twenty yards from us. Instantly rifles and fowling pieces were brought out, and many shots were fired, but harmlessly for Bruin, who kept dashing along by great bounds, nearly parallel to our course, disappearing among the thick rice, and we saw no more of her. We reached Barrie about one o'clock, and, after resting a while, took the great road through Sunnidale. Here, at least, we met with something new, though, we could scarcely say, pleasant. The road was just brushed, only here and there short detached pieces cut down to the width, and but partially logged ; our feet, accustomed to the smooth pavement of the city, were constantly tripping on snags, causing us now and then, an awkward tumble ; the afternoon was close, sultry and moist, around us an interminable forest of gigantic pines ; and for miles and miles no sign of a house, or flocks, or herds, or human face divine. Lest, however, we should fall asleep, our hands and arms were kept in constant exercise, trying to defend ourselves from clouds of mosquitoes, which till then we had little more than heard of. At last, at nightfall, we reached a rude inn where we put up for the night, making our supper on salt pork and sugarless, creamless, green tea and a certain liquor which they called by courtesy "Canada Whiskey," of which "aqua fortis" was the chief constituent part.

"Aqua fortis as ye please,
He can content ye."—Burns.

Next afternoon we found the headquarters of Mr. Surveyor Rankin, to reach which we had to descend the high bank of the Nottawasaga river—a dull, brown, stagnant stream, so dead that we could not tell in which direction it flowed—to a flat near the water's edge. His summer place was roofed with cedar bark, carpeted with hemlock branches, fronted by a huge, smoky fire, now illuminating the woody banks, and now quenched by the dense smoke, which, suffocating as it was, by putting to flight our tormentors, felt tolerable and even pleasing. The utmost kindness and attention was shown us by Mr. Rankin and he gave us his best room. We sank into a feverish sleep, speedily broken by the awful hum and the tormenting stings, to be succeeded by another short slumber, and again to be rudely roused by the tormentors. And thus passed our first night's bivouac in the forest, on the banks of the Nottawasaga.

The observations of the few days since we left Toronto had satisfied our minds that Nottawasaga Bay was not an eligible sight for our projected colony. We took a good long circuit round the Bay, bathed in it, and left on the third day. A heavy rain had fallen—the weather was much cooler—and our return was much less painful than our outset. We reached Barrie about mid afternoon and, there being no steamer, and we anxious to get to Toronto, we hired a Highlander to take us across in an open flat bottomed boat. After getting over very agreeably one half of the navigation, a thick mist came upon us, about nightfall, and enveloped us so closely that we had no help but to lie to and wait the morning, or at all events, a clear atmosphere. We were quite unprepared for passing a night on the lake—no great coat, no cloak, no blanket, not even a glass of their despised Canadian whiskey. But we were not so badly off as we dreaded, for our boatman had some salt pork and he contrived to get up a fire and boil the pork, and he had some uncouth looking substance in the shape of bread, so that, night coming down on us and mist, we had really a dainty supper, finished off with green tea infused in the hot water in which the pork had been boiled, of course ornamented with pork beads. Our only pillow was Jacob's—the stones on which he made the fire that had boiled our supper. Without shelter of any kind the night drove heavily along, but about six o'clock next morning the mist evaporated as suddenly as it had come down upon us, and we reached Barrie in time to meet the stage to Toronto, where we arrived in the evening, tired and fagged out enough.

We remained at Toronto a few days, for the sake of rest, in which time we again met Mr. Watt and his relatives. We gave them an account of the late excursion, and our opinion of that part of the country, telling them it was now our intention to go West, to see the Canada Company's Lands, and especially the Huron Tract. Mr. Watt offered to go along with us and we gladly accepted his company.

On the following Monday, Mr. Watt, Mr. William Gibbon and I took the steamer to Niagara, where we arrived in the afternoon. It had then all the appearance of a falling village : the frame buildings, grey and ricketty, few new buildings, scarcely any going up, and no signs of activity or improvement. We took the stage thence to Drummondville, where we remained all night. Next morning we visited the Falls. We stood for a long time with our eyes rivetted upon them, and the longer we gazed the more vast and magnificent they grew. I certainly felt no disappointment, but was quite of the Irishman's opinion, who, on being told that many persons were disappointed when they saw the Falls, exclaimed : "By japers, I don't know how anybody could be disappointed, unless they went to see a river fallin' up." But in truth the Falls must be studied. Every part of the vast amphitheatre is on so grand a scale—their height, their depth, their volume, the boiling surge below, the hills and landscape all around—measure and weigh each particular part in the mind's eye, then with the eye and the mind, and endeavor to comprehend the grand whole—then only will you have some faint idea of the overwhelming magnitude of the panorama before you. To attempt to describe more minutely a scene which any one may now view by a pleasant day's excursion, would be an abuse of the reader's patience and of the Queen's English. We went down the stair to the foot of the fall, and I, as many others have done, attempted to go in between the projecting torrent and the rock, but a mighty rushing wind, driving a dense spray, so blinded and almost choked me that after penetrating about three yards, I was fain to get back. We then ascended and stood on Table Rock, which at that time projected so far as almost to touch the edge of the torrent, so that lying down on my breast and stretching out my arm, I could put my hand in the fall. The look down here was awful.

We left for Chippewa, and thence took passage in a covered barge of the Welland Canal, to Dunnville. The evening was rainy and all on board had to take shelter in the narrow and crowded space below. Our fellow-passengers seemed all to be Canadian farmers,—old settlers—comfortable looking persons in their grey homespun. Their talk was of the weather, the crops, the prices, the poor markets, the canal and such topics. But what shocked us much was the universal swearing. Though the conversation was carried on in a quiet, calm tone, without anything exciting, every other word was an oath, often a strange one. But we had no help but to sit still and hear it with what patience and resignation we could. At length the long, painful evening came to a close, and we were in Dunnville.

It was dismally dark, the rain pouring down, and what was called the street seemed a mud lake. We plunged through the darkness, occasionally falling foul of a stump, and got to the chief Inn, where we found every room filled up, the village being crowded with workmen and artisans, employed at the canal and dam. We were told we might perhaps be better accommodated at another house, but we chose to remain and rough it with the rest. We therefore bivouacked on the floor along with many others. We started next morning early to go up the Grand River side to Brantford.

* * * We reached Brantford late in the afternoon, tired out. We remained there over Sabbath, and on Monday took the stage to Oxford along the London road, and towards evening reached the clearing of the Messrs. W——, in Zorra.

The ground we had gone over since morning was rolling and hilly ; we saw but few streams ; and the long poles with bucket and balance attached to the draw wells showed they were very deep. The Messrs. W—— had the true spirit of backwoodsmen, and talked with pleasure, almost enthusiasm, of their roughings, discomforts, and privation, and of the feeling which their success had inspired. Next morning we started to examine their and the neighboring clearances ; but, oh, how rough and uncouth these irregular, zigzag fence fields seemed to our inexperienced eyes ! The fencing, the stumps, the irregularly cut stubble, about a foot and a half high, the profusion of weeds in the angles of the fences and about the stumps, and the shoots from the stumps, made us wonder how any crop could grow there, or having grown, be taken off or drawn in. And yet the crop had been a rich one, the thick, strong stubble bore witness to its luxuriance, and with all these drawbacks we were told it had exceeded twenty bushels an acre.

The houses, too, were strange and novel ; for, unlike the shanty hovels we saw in Nottawasaga and Sunnidale, they were something like houses ; they had at least a door and two windows in front, and the corners were roughly squared, although the perpendicular and the square were not always rigidly adhered to ; but on the inside, the round, bark-covered logs, the rough chinking (not altogether impervious to the air and light), the huge, wide chimney built of cedar and mortar, the blazing log pile on the hearth, sending the heat to the farthest corners ; the rough deal partition, with its door and wooden latch, the axe hewn stools and tables, alternating sometimes with the round blocks sawn from the trunk of a tree ; the baking kettle covered with live coals ; the rough deal shelves all around with their various utensils ; the strong wooden pegs driven into the logs—these things, though afterwards perfectly familiar to us, were then altogether new, and conveyed to us the idea, not of squalid poverty, but of rude comfort and independence. On mentioning our purpose of settling in a little colony on some favourable situation, all, as may be easily believed, were extremely anxious that we should settle somewhere near them, and pointed out several blocks which they thought might suit our purpose ; but on visiting them, the want of running streams, and especially of one considerable stream, proved an insuperable objection.

We then left, and travelling in the direction pointed out, came upon the road leading through Waterloo, where was a tavern kept by one Freivogel.

* * * *

At Elora, having taken lodging at the tavern, and got some refreshment, which we greatly needed, we enquired for Mr. Gilkison, (the late David Gilkison) and were told that he owned the large log house we had seen on entering the clearance, and kept a store there. We rested a while and then called there, when we learned that he was from home, but was expected to return next day.

From the door of the store we observed that a part of the opposite river bank was cleared, with a small shanty upon it—a saw mill,— beneath which were "the Falls." We also observed a bridge on a line with the store. We hastened down to the saw mill, which was not then working, being out of repair, and from beneath it got our first view of the Falls, which, notwithstanding our having so lately seen Niagara, appeared to us really magnificent and extremely picturesque. We then returned to our lodgings at Mr. Martin Martin's. Next morning, finding that Mr. Gilkison had not returned, we resolved to visit Fergus.

We were shown the brush road, the only road leading to it, and on enquiring for Mr. Wilson, who had left Aberdeen some months before us, were told that his clearance was right on our way, and would be the most direct route to Fergus.

We soon got there, and found him in his logging habiliments—picturesque, withal, but certainly not white as snow. We spent an hour very agreeably, and greatly admired the romantic position of his cottage, perched on a projecting ledge of rock, commanding a view of the Grand River, with its steep rocky banks and lofty trees, for a long way up and down—nor less admiring the comfort and even elegance within, embellished with old country ornaments and some wild flowers of the forest. He led us through his chopping, where we first saw the process of logging, into the path to Fergus, near which we met Mr. Webster and two of Mr. Ferguson's sons, in the light deshabille common in those days, carrying axes.

On mentioning our object, Mr. Webster said he would be at home in the evening, and would be glad to show us his maps and further our object in any way he could.

We were soon in Fergus, then consisting of a tavern, unfinished; a smithie; two or three workmen's shanties of the rudest kind; and Mr. Webster's house, a neat log cottage with the best finished corners, roofing, and windows we had yet seen.

As a matter of course, we went to the tavern, where were workmen in every part of it, fitting up, planing, plastering and chinking. We sauntered about, seeing the little that was to be seen, looking at the dam, the falls, the black pool under the rude half finished bridge, and the stumps wherever there was any clearance, which was mostly confined to the village site; and the banks of the river, which appeared to us much less majestic than at Elora—although the lofty, precipitous, water worn, rocky banks attracted much of our attention. We then went to Mr. Webster's, and saw the plan of his lands, but found that all the choicest situations, all the lots nearest Fergus, all the lots bordering on the rivers and streams, were already sold; and he had not a block left of any extent nearer than four or five miles from Fergus. On pointing out this to Mr. Webster, he then advised us to examine Mr. Gilkison's land that, as far as he knew, very few lots of his had been sold, and we would therefore have the pick of the block and many choice sites on the Irvine and other streams. We then took our leave.

When we entered the tavern in the evening, it was swarming like a hive with artizans, millwrights, and carpenters, together with several young men with capital, sons of Scotch proprietors—mostly intelligent young men from Perthshire, Dumfries, and the south of Scotland; and from all we received a cordial welcome in the genuine Scotch style and in hamely Scotch. On asking if we could be accomodated for the night, "I kenna what ye'll ca' accomodated; but ye'll just get yer share o' the flure—we'll no can do mair for ye—an' yer bite an' yer sup wi' the lave".

The night was very joyous: The novelty of the situation—the rudeness of accomodation—the drollery of the make shifts—the mixed yet entirely Scotch character of the society—the hopes upspringing in the breasts of all—imparted a loveliness, a zest, and a joyousness to the conversation such as I have rarely experienced. The hackneyed lines, "The nicht drave on wi' sangs an' clatter, An' aye the yill was growin' better," was not on that occasion a poetic fiction, but a literal fact, for, up to that evening I had small liking for " this Canada."

We returned to Elora next morning, and found Mr. Gilkison, who showed us the map of his lands, pointing out how beautifully they were watered. We therefore resolved to spend the next two days in exploring a part, at least, of them.

Proceeding along the Fergus brush-road between the eleventh and twelfth concessions, we followed it up to the Irvine river, crossing a stream which falls into the Irvine, and diverging occasionally to the right or left to examine the land; thence we came to the stream falling into the Irvine, called, on the earliest maps, "Elmslie water." Passing on to the north-west, we diverged to the left to see the Beaver Meadow which Mr. Gilkison had told us of, and soon found it—a very beautiful Beaver's clearance of some acres, covered with natural grass, very thick and tall, studded with shrubs and small trees, whose spreading tops reminded us of "home," and fringed about with an ugly hedge of brambles, canes, and brakes, though which we now and then had some difficulty in struggling. In looking about this pretty spot we almost lost our bearings, and it cost us some time to recover the "blaze." Passing onwards as far as lots four and five, we came upon the stream already mentioned, and went up and down its banks a considerable distance the land gently rolling, the trees large, the under-brush thinner than in other places. The sun now descending low, warned us that it was time to return if we would escape a bivouac in the woods.

Next morning we passed on the line between the twelfth and thirteenth concessions, and following the "blaze" we came upon the largest and thickest swamp we had yet seen. We had great difficulty in penetrating it and keeping the blaze, owing to the underwood, the water dammed up, and the fallen trees. After crossing a rivulet we came to the Irvine spreading out to a considerable width—the opposite bank steep and high. Thence we came to the stream at Mr. Michie's and thence to lots 4 & 5.

As on the day before we spent a considerable time examining the land to right and left, every now and then coming on some small stream. At length in our search we fairly lost the blaze and failing to recover it, we directed our course towards the Irvine, which we came upon, somewhere in the neighborhood of "Dolachar." Keeping therefore, the west bank, we followed it down holding close to the river; partly because we knew not its windings, and were afraid to lose sight of it, less we might again lose ourselves. We found it in some places spreading out beautifully, with flats sometimes on one side and sometimes on both. Now and then the west bank was lofty and steep even to the water's edge, and in several places the river was marred and blocked up by accumulations of fallen timber and drift-wood. We thus reached again the line between the 11th. and 12th. concessions, and following it, reached Elora when it was quite dark.

I was now satisfied. We had found a block suitable in all respects for our projected colony. The quality of the soil, as indicated by the trees and their size, was equal to any we had seen ; watered in such a manner as we had nowhere seen ; the streams living, clear, rapid, and the chief of them on a limestone bed, and therefore healthy ; the society was superior to what we could have anticipated—the newer settlers almost entirely Scotch, the older, around and in the neighbourhood of Elora, respectable, intelligent Englishmen ; the block bordering on the new and rapidly rising settlement of Fergus, with the immediate prospect of having a Church and Schools ; the only drawback—far in the woods and the roads execrable. We therefore immediately called on Mr. Gilkison, to ascertain on what terms a block of 2000 or 2500 acres could be purchased. His reply was that he could make no reduction from four dollars per acre, but he referred us to his brother in Toronto, Mr. Archibald Gilkison, who was agent for the estate of his late father. It now only remained that we should hasten to Toronto, which hitherto had been our headquarters, and we set off next morning. Nothing worthy of recording that I can remember, occurred on the journey back to Toronto. Conveyances there were none; as yet stages were not, at least northward from Hamilton; for ten years after that there was only a weekly conveyance by waggon from Guelph, so that we had to perform the whole journey to Hamilton on foot. On arriving at Toronto, we called together our party, ladies included, gave them a description of our travels, and, in particular, of the location we had in view, its appearance and the society, and an eager and almost unanimous wish was expressed to settle there. Mr. Watt alone hesitated; he had visited Whitby, and seemed to have a partiality for it, partly, I believe, because it was not so far back; partly, because he had several old acquaintances settled there; partly, it might be, because, being farther advanced, it would be more advantageous for one with some capital to settle there. The ambitious resolution, however, of his sisters and brother-in-law, Mr. John Keith, at length determined him to cast in his lot with the new colony.

We lost no time in going to Mr. Gilkison and finishing the bargain. He would make no deduction in the price, four dollars per acre, but agreed to allow half a dollar of the price per acre to be expended within the block in cutting roads and making bridges.

We remained in Toronto two or three days to make what arrangements were necessary, and Mr. William Gibbon having gone on the day before to secure waggons, on Friday the —— day of October, we took steamer to Hamilton and landed amid an outpour of rain, through which we proceeded up a street of glutinous mud to Burleigh's tavern. We dined at one common table there and I could perceive that our travelling costumes and drenched appearance caused some surprise as well as amusement to some of the diners.

Mr. Gibbon had engaged six waggons, including a light one for the ladies and children, and, it clearing up after dinner, the cavalcade started.

We made our way but slowly, heavily laden as our teams were, through the sticky paste of the road, or rather, mud canal—to Dundas, whose smooth liquid surface covered many a dangerous hole; but we began to realize the difficulties of our enterprise when we were ascending the hill above Dundas and had come to the flat about half way up the ascent. Here we were brought to a complete standstill; while on our resuming the steep ascent our two foremost teams stuck fast, and neither "geeing" nor "hawing" nor whipping of which there was too much—nor swearing of which there was much more—could move them. The teamsters, therefore, unhitching the horses from the last two waggons, and putting two teams to each waggon in succession, at length slowly and painfully dragged them to the top of the hill. When we came to the road which branched off to Galt, three of the teamsters announced their determination to take that route, as they were sure, they said, their team could not take them through the "short road". The other three said they would venture it. Our party thus separated, some going with the teams by the long route, the rest, including the women and children, taking the direct road to Guelph. We got on less painfully, though with many a "dird" and shake, till we entered the "long woods" where (as it continued for many years) it was just out of one hole into another.

Loud were the complaints, dismal the groanings, dire the swearings, at the mud holes, the heavy loads—at the unhappy immigrants; while, as if to warn us of our approaching fate, we every now and then met with some shattered wheel, some broken axle, or scattered fragments of some unfortunate waggon. We several times, indeed, narrowly escaped the overthrow of our loads, in which case it would have been impossible for us to have reloaded, on account of the depth of the holes and the unstable footing.

Although the tavern we came to was not very inviting we were glad to get its shelter, and ordered supper for the party. The viands were salt pork, some fry, and bread, black, half baked, the centre tough dough. The landlady made her appearance with the excuse that she was out of tea, and had expected it to-night, bnt it had not come; she, however, had done her best. We had some fragments of bread and meat, the tea was barely tasted and set aside—it was made of some of the Canadian herbs (sassafrass it might be, or hemlock); we asked for water, but alas!—it was a solution of lime nearly as white as milk. We had therefore, no help but go to bed—almost supperless. Fatigue and the jolting made us sleep soundly.

The morning was clear, with a heavy, white frost. We started about six o'clock and reached Black's about ten. Here we had the comfort of tea and excellent well cooked viands. We got to Guelph about one p. m., and proceeded about four miles to a crossway of the direst kind, half broken up, with a mud hole at the end which we tried in vain to avoid, but had no help but to plunge into it, and there the waggons stuck fast. The hole being of unknown depth, it was thought useless and even dangerous for the horses to employ the former expedient of doubling the teams. Happily there were two farm houses near, whither we sent for two ox teams, and by means of doubling them and prying with rails we got the waggons drawn without any serious breakage; the oxen drew on to Blyth's—three young men from the west of Scotland who had recently settled there and built an inn. The house was just roofed, partly chinked, the window frames in, but unglazed, the doorway posted up, but without a door. Though the accommodation thus seemed somewhat unpromising we were glad to embrace it, for it would have been madness to have attempted going further by such a broken and wild track; the teamsters, therefore, in African phrase, untrekked.

We entered under the roof, for it was little more than a roof, only one side of the building being chinked, and the blazing log pile diffusing light and warmth soon melted the ice of ceremony. The young men expressing themselves greatly perplexed as to how they could accommodate us, the lassies volunteered to look after the cooking department, and the married ladies to the beds. They were thus set at their ease, and the joke and the laugh went round.

Our servant Elsy greatly amused them by the fun of her jokes and her smart repartees, and we were soon as merry and comfortable a company as persons who had never seen each other until half an hour before could be. To our supper was added the luxury of venison steaks; and the novelty and strangeness of our circumstances, together with the fatigue and roughness of the day, reconciled us even to the Canada punch. The beds of the principal members of the party were spread along the upper floor, and we slept very comfortably.

We left about ten o'clock next morning to accomplish the last stage of our journey, and reached Elora about three p. m., with less obstruction than we expected, our greatest difficulty being within a quarter of a mile of Elora.

In about two hours we had the satisfaction of seeing the teams arrive that had gone the other way—and with no material damage.

Mr. Watt and his party got immediate possession of the shanty on the north side of the river ; we taking lodgings in the tavern till a house, which had just been raised, should be made ready for us. And here I would gratefully record the courtesy, the kindness and attention shown us by the late David Gilkison, Esq. Warm hearted, intelligent, and having seen a good deal of the world, and with considerable knowledge and experience of Canada, his house and society were an agreeable refuge, and caused many an evening pass pleasantly which otherwise would have dragged heavily ; when any of us needed assistance he was ever as ready to give as we to ask it. His father's purchase here and his own exertion undoubtedly gave the first impulse to the settlement of this flourishing part of Canada West.

As was before mentioned, we took lodgings in the tavern till the house which was preparing for us should be ready for our reception. The landlord, Mr. Martin, and landlady, were exceedingly obliging and attentive, and we were as comfortable as one room, close to the bar-room and serving the manifold purposes of dining-room, bed-room, drawing-room, kitchen and wash house occasionally, and, as it unhappily turned out, hospital also, could allow us to be.

A few days after our arrival Mr. Gilkison had a 'raising,' to which our men were invited. All were willing and even eager to go ; partly to see the (to them) strange sight of putting up a log house. Everything went well till the placing of the uppermost logs, when, by haste or inadvertence, one of them slid and struck down John Robb, one of the handiest of our workmen. When taken up, it was found that his thigh was broken. Mr. Gilkison instantly despatched his man, John Fergusson, on horseback to Guelph, for the Surgeon. Fergusson returned with the Surgeon about eleven o'clock the same night—a wonderfully short space of time, considering the state of the track, for road it could scarcely be called. The fracture was set and bandaged with much difficulty ; and when he returned two or three days afterwards, to dress the wound, he pronounced it to be doing exceedingly well ; and, in the end, his recovery, though somewhat tedious, was effected without much suffering.

The first thing now necessary to be done was to make a practicable road into our new possessions ; it, of course, could only be at first a 'brush' road. The parties who were engaged in making this first road to Bon accord were Messrs. Watt, Mr. John Keith, myself, Mr. William Gibbon, Mr. John Fergusson, and Mr. Sam. Trenholme : the last two were the Engineers and Pioneers. We started from Elora immediately after breakfast, and taking the line between the eleventh and twelfth concessions, by four o'clock in the afternoon completed a very good 'brush' road to the Irvine, making the ford a little above the present bridge The reasons why we took this line rather than the legal one between the twelfth and thirteenth concessions were : first, because it was nearer Elora and would form the front of our farms; but secondly, and chiefly, because this line was much easier and freer from obstructions than the other. We had only one or two short detours to make from the line ; the first to avoid the corner of the swamp on the land first purchased by Mr. Robert Gerrie, and vulgarly called 'Robbie's swoggle'; another short one to the west to avoid the precipitous hill immediately north of Mr. Keith's, and then a slight deflection to the east, into Mr. John Gibbon's lot, to make the most favorable fording place across the Irvine river.

It was now the time to divide our purchase and to apportion the lots to the original Bon accord settlers. These were Messrs. George Elmslie, Peter Brown, Robert Melvin, William Gibbon, Alexander Watt, John Keith and Miss Watt (afterwards Mrs. George Barron).

(Mr. Elmslie adds the names of George Brown, George Cornwall, William Jamieson and W. Carnegie, who, however, did not come to Canada. A list of those who came to Bon accord will be given in another place).

The lands on the whole block being deemed of equal quality, it was my chief desire and care to give to each of the settlers, so far as the position of the lots would permit, a share of the running streams. Messrs. Watt and Keith, and Miss Watt, chose their lots on Concession 11, and I agree to it making the reservation of the Beaver Meadow, Lot 10, which I apportioned to Mr. W. Jamieson, whose father-in-law, Mr. James Moir, senior, with his son and two daughters took possession of it in the ensuing year. To Messrs. Melvin and Brown's I assigned the lots on the 13th concession more particularly giving to Mr. Melvin and P. Brown the four lots through the centre of which the Irvine flows; to George Brown the lot later owned by Mr. Brockie, through which runs a fine streamlet. The lots on the 12th concession were reserved by me more particularly. I appropriated for myself Lots 15, 14, 13 and 12. Lot 15 was afterwards purchased from me by Mr. John A. Davidson, in the name of Dr. Sanger, of London, and Lot 14 by Mr. John Gibbon. One half of Lot 11 was purchased by Mr. J. Wedderburn, and on his leaving was taken up by Mr. William Gibbon; the other half of Lot 11 was bought by Duncan Barber.

We now set about clearing, and raising houses. Mr. Watt let thirty acres to be cleared and fenced, at about sixteen dollars an acre, to Messrs. Nicklin and Elkerton, together with cutting and hauling logs for his house. I let ten acres to be chopped at six dollars an acre; five to be cleared and fenced, and two or three acres, around the house to be cleared, but chopped close to the ground, at twenty dollars an acre. This job was taken by William and Richard Everett, and also the cutting and hauling of logs for the house, forty-two by thirty six feet, for which I gave fifty dollars. The remainder was cleared by Mr. Letson.

Sometime about the beginning of November, Mrs. Elmslie, William Gibbon and I, went to select a site for our house. We were not long in finding one—the top of an eminence sloping up from the Irvine, and at about fifty yards from the stream, and rising gradually from Elmslie Water (as we jokingly called it) on the south and at about seventy yards from its bank.

(This was near what is now the residence of Mr. David Scott, who is the present owner of Mr. Elmslie's farm).

On the twentieth and twenty first of November it was raised. Nearly the whole of the then population of Nichol and Woolwich were there. All the first settlers in Nichol, the English settlers in Woolwich, a great many workmen from Fergus, the first settlers on the Upper Irvine, all our choppers, the carpenters from Elora and its immediate neighborhood, old King Reeves, being our waggoner, carrier, purveyor, &c. The first day the work went rather heavily from the extraordinary size and weight of the logs, so that when night fell, it was little more than half up. Nearly all agreed to see it finished on the morrow. Those who were nearest to the scene of action went home; but the night being mild and dry, a great many remained on the spot and, as there was plenty of viands and punch, they made a large fire, and passed the night very comfortably. Next day all went to it with a hearty good will, and considerably before night, the last log was put up, amid tremendous cheering. As Mr. Watt's raising was to be next day, Messrs. Nicklin and Elkerton invited those who were to stay over the night to the shelter of the shanty. The night being cloudy and dark, a great many stayed, so that the shanty was completely crowded: we had scarcely sitting room: and a scene of mirth and fun, and somewhat boisterous play, without brawling ensued, such as I have rarely seen here, even in those early days. It continued till near morning, for there was no sleeping room. Some, however, took shelter under the thick cedars and hemlocks, which were in abundance on the bank. At daylight it began to rain, which, by the middle of the forenoon, changed into a thick fall of snow, and continued throughout the day, making the work, though far easier than that of the former two days, much more cheerless and uncomfortable. An accident had like to have put an end to my further clearing the forest. The "corner-men" were vieing with each other who should lay his corner most quickly; the falling snow made the axe handles slippery, and the axe of one of them slipped and whizzed past my head with great velocity, almost grazing my cheek. This was one of the providential deliverences I have experienced during my life. The raising was finished early in the afternoon, and we went to our quarters cold and dripping.

About this time we formed a resolution to have Divine Service on Sabbath, at least once in the day. Our first meeting for this purpose, was in the shanty occupied by Mr. Keith, and Mr. Watt, on the north bank of the river, at Elora. Shortly after, Mr. Gilkison invited us to his house, where were assembled the villagers, and a few of the nearest settlers. We had the usual exercises--singing, praying, reading the Scriptures, and a sermon, sometimes of Blair's, sometimes of Newton's, sometimes of others. We continued this as long as we remained in the village.

Towards the end of December we got into our new lodgings—the building provided for us being now roofed and chinked, the doorway hung, and the windows in and glazed—things which did not always happen simultaneously in those days. Our beds were arranged in this wise: at about seven feet from the western gable a strong beam was fastened from side to side; this was divided into three compartments by white cotton screens; then boards were placed across, and on these were laid mattresses and beds. This was our common bedroom, partitioned off by a white sheet extending from side to side. Our cooking stove was placed towards the other end, and in the centre our common table, formed of the large chests; trunks and smaller boxes were our seats. Thus situated we felt comparatively comfortable, only at times the hive was too small for the swarm.

On Christmas morn we were serenaded with Christmas carols, sweetly sung, and accompanied by the flute—a greatly more pleasant arousing than the tumultuous noise in a Scotch town.

The leader of the choir, we found, was Mr. Patmore, carpenter, an excellent singer and a good musician; and certainly our absence from home for six months, and our position—a small spot, a

"Lodge in a vast wilderness,
A boundless continuity of shade,"

still roamed by the untutored Indian—greatly enhanced the delight of the concert.

The winter, as we were informed, was unusually mild, the thermometer not often going below zero, and seldom as low as that; there was no very great depth of snow; there had been, moreover, a singularly long and beautiful Indian snmmer—the former part of it bright, sunny and deliciously warm; toward the close of it, the thick, smoky atmosphere, and the sun rising fiery red and continuing his march until night as if half eclipsed.

Our sojourn was now and then cheered by visits of acquaintances and countrymen from other parts of the province. One of these, a visit from the Davidsons and the late Mr. Geddes from Cox's Creek, together with Mr. Gilkison, was long kept in mind by us as a "Nox Ambrosiana."

Other events came to enliven and amuse us. There was a birth; Mr. Keith's first born, and the first born of the little colony (now Mrs. Connon).

[Jean Keith, who married the late Thomas Connon, was born on the west side of the Grand River, in Elora, on the 19th of March, 1835, and has been a life-long resident].

On one of these occasions we had taken a round by Squire Smith's, Mr. Swan's, Jonathan Swift's and Yankee Miller's; returning by the Elora and Guelph Road, and close on Elora we came upon the mud-hole I have before mentioned. It was full of water and we would gladly have evaded it, but there seemed no possibility of turning it on either side. My companion, therefore, who was driving, shouting loudly to the oxen, and applying the wand pretty sharply, attempted to dash through it, when, with a sudden jerk, the waggon stuck fast. He geed and hawed and hawed and geed, shouting louder and louder still, making therewith divers threatening gesticulations, but in vain—the waggon could not be moved. Aware that my friend liked driving, and, as was natural, thought his own driving better than mine, I stood still without interfering, but looking carefully around and behind to see whether, by going backwards, we might not more easily get forward, and seeing that the driver was nearly exhausted, I said: "Just let me see what I can do." So he handed me the gad, I think not unwillingly. Having noticed, a few yards behind, a part of the wood on our right thinner and not so much encumbered by fallen trees, I jumped into the hole, unloosed the oxen, turned them round, and, attaching the chain to the hind axle drew the waggon back to dry and firm ground. Then, after yoking them in again, I turned into the forest, now and then shaving rather closely the standing trees, and drove them over rotten wood and fallen trees, some of them by no means small, into Elora. I have no doubt that many of the older residents have a very lively remembrance of this same slough at the very entrance to Elora. Our load only consisted of a few bushels of seed wheat and peas.

[The mud-hole described by Mr. Elmslie was about one hundred yards north from the present G. T. R. station.]

In January the snow fell more copiously, but not nearly to the depth of some succeeding years. When the alternations of frost and fresh had hardened and firmed the surface of it, then for the first time we heard the music of the wolves echoing all around every evening and often through the night. One morning, succeeding a night on which their howling had been unusually appaling, and evidently near, a little before sunrise it seemed to come nearer and nearer the shanty; the choppers rushed to the door, and in a minute a pack of between twenty and thirty were seen rushing in full cry after a deer. The deer went direct through the chopping, clearing by great bounds the brush piles and the logs in her way and dashed across the river in the direction of Elora, evidently gaining upon them. The next morning, the ice being bearing, one of our party, wishing to see the banks of the river above, proceeded upwards for about half a mile and came upon a deer run down and slaughtered but recently, for it was not yet cold. It was a good deal torn and mangled especially in the throat and hips but not much devoured. The choppers conjectured that it was the same deer they had seen driven through the chopping, that the wolves had dogged it all the time, giving it no rest, and at length had driven it on the river, the ice was covered with but a light sprinkling of snow, and on this treacherous surface the poor baited deer was soon within the fangs of its merciless pursuers. It had made a desperate struggle, and the surface all round was imprinted by the tracks of many broad paws. Their prey had scarcely fallen when they were frightened from it, for, as has been said, but little of it was devoured; and we supposed that it was either the fall of a large tree, or the sound of the carpenters hammering on the roof of the house, heard in the calm severity of the frosty morning that had scared them from their banquet, hardly won and scarce tasted.

In conjunction with the subject of wolves, I may relate some of the losses we sustained by them. The first was a valuable cow and our first cow; it occurred about fifteen months after this adventure. That winter and spring had in all respects been a complete contrast to our first. On the 16th of November the thermometer stood more than 20 degrees below Zero, and the snow had fallen to the depth of two feet and in the course of the winter covered the stumps. I well remember on that morning the strange stinging feeling on touching anything; another phenomenon was seen—when we raised the cup to our lips the saucer followed, although the apartment was closely chinked and there was a large log fire blazing on the hearth. The feeling reminded me of Milton's description of the cold of the infernal regions—"The parched ground burned froze, and cold performed the effect of fire." The cow had calved a few days before, the morning was bright and warm, the snow was nearly gone, and blades of green herbage were beginning to peep out. Led on by this she strayed into the neighbouring lot, Mr. Fraser's, where she got into a small swamp and stuck, and being weak was unable to extricate herself. The wolves found her out and came upon her in the early part of the night. A settler, lately came up, who was lodging in a small house not far from the spot, described the triumphant yells of the savage brutes combined with the bellowing and wailing of the poor suffering cow, as the most frightful and appaling sounds he had ever heard and he dared not venture out. In the morning our man brought home all that remained of her—the bell and the strap. I have sustained many losses; to some of which this was but a feather in the scale to a ton, but never any by which I was so much moved; it was in vain that we endeavored to restrain our tears. We left the carcase untouched, and a few volunteered to watch for the next two nights. The first night was very dark, and about midnight they came so near that their tread could be heard among the leaves; but either they had scented some thing else besides the carcase, or some incautious sound had given them alarm, so that in a minute they were heard scampering off, not giving the watchers a chance of a shot. The next watchers heard not a sound during the live long night.

About two years after when we had got the small clearance around the house completely fenced and sown in grass, to save the labor and loss of time and vexation—for even after hours' search we not unfrequently came home without them—in hunting up the cattle, we regularly shut them up in this small field. One night about the end of June we were aroused by the noise of the rushing of the cattle, the ringing of their bells, and an occasional bellow. Starting up I hastened to the door. There was just a faint streak of dawn; and I could just see the whole of them, including two yoke of oxen, four cows, calves and sheep, rushing round in the wildest manner. On my appearance they became still; I ran hastily down the park towards the river, and, as I went, heard the plash of many feet rushing through the water. I immediately came upon a ewe stretched out, bleeding much, and evidently dying; a little farther on I came upon another severely wounded, and breathing hard, and then upon a third, not much hurt as it could sit up and soon after rose. By this time the men came to my assistance, and we took the wounded animals to a shanty behind the house. For the first one we could do nothing, it was dead. We dressed as well as we could the wounds of the second, and under the care of our skilful neighbour, Mr. Fraser, it recovered in a few days. The third had escaped with a scratch.

My last loss by the Wolves happened about a year and a half after this. Our saw-mill dam, which was ever breaking out and swallowing up the profits, and something more, in costs of repair--a constant grievance and vexation—so that I was sometimes tempted to join in the joking anathema of a humourous neighbour, (—Mr. Mair—)—"that d——d dam" had burst out in the midst of a press of work, and we had a "bee" of the settlement to repair it—a hard days work which we finished as darkness came on—and as the work was voluntary we had a feast in the evening. Just as the workmen had gone it began to rain heavily, and I asked the men whether the sheep had been shut up. In the hurry and confusion they had been forgotten. I seized the lantern and hurried out, but when I had gone a little way down the slope, I encountered such a storm of wind and rain that my light was extinguished and I had to grope my way back to the house in intense darkness. In the morning we found three sheep killed and nearly devoured.

For several years I observed that whatever intervals might have occurred, if by any chance or inadvertence sheep were left out, they were sure to be taken—plainly showing that the wolves were ever prowling in the very midst of us; though they never, so far as I am aware, took sheep or calves by day. It was strange too, that though most of the settlers were daily in the woods seeking cattle, not one of them, so far as I have ever heard, ever caught a glimpse of a wolf. It was clear that their habitual cowardice was never to be lulled to sleep. Occasionally, but very rarely, a bear might be seen stalking along, as once was by my daughter between my house and her uncle's (a distance of scarce a quarter of a mile) which stopped and gazed on her for about a minute, and then walked slowly away; but a wolf never showed himself. I have heard their yells, coming nearer and nearer, and, in a minute or two afterwards, detected the sound of their tread among the leaves, but none ever came nearer. We have sometimes hunted and killed a racoon, which had committed sad havoc among our crops; and now and then unearthed and killed a groundhog, but these were the greatest of our hunting exploits. In the earlier years of our settlement a very beautiful animal, the flying squirrel, was sometimes brought in by the cat. Its light silvery gray color, and soft velvety fur, with its "wings," a furry membrane extending from the shoulder to the thigh, expanding in its leap or flight, made us think it the prettiest and most wonderful little creature we had ever seen.

Little else occurred during our first winter's abode in Canada, worth chronicling. I went pretty regularly to oversee the carpenters' operations at the house, coming back to Elora in the evening. Having chinked and partitioned off a part of the house, we removed to it, with all our impedimenta, in the beginning of April—that year a most lovely month, mild and warm, with very mild frosts at night, the forest budding and leafing with amazing rapidity, and Mrs. Elmslie and I, and the servant, contrived to make some excellent maple molasses. We were not prepared for making sugar, and all the other hands were fully employed. But the molasses and milk were a delicious addition to our fare.

We now had letters from our intended fellow settlers, telling us that they were to sail in the beginning of April, by New York, and hoping to be with us by the middle of June, mentioning also some additions to our colony I therefore urged on with all my might the small clearings I had engaged to get done for Messrs Melvine and Peter Brown. No additional hands could be got; it was the end of May ere we could put the seed in the small clearances we could make for ourselves; and it will be seen in the sequel that they had better not been sown. This spring I first took a share in logging—as well as I could. It was hard work, and I first feelingly understood the Scriptural allusion to the 'laborer watching for the setting sun.' After four o'clock, the day still hot, and my ankles sore with the unwonted straining, I often looked wisfully to the sun.

I had just got finished the two or three acres for my friends, when we got word that they were on the way up, and would be with us to-morrow. Next afternoon I set out and met them about a mile below Mr. Reynolds'. The meeting was joyful on both sides; though wearied out and travel sore, and sadly bitten, I was glad to see no signs of discouragement—least of all in the ladies.

It may be easily supposed that after so long a separation and so many adventures by sea and land we were at no loss for topics of discourse; an uninterrupted fire of questions was kept up by me for the greater part of the road, which contributed greatly to enliven the jaded travellers. We got tolerably well over the road and even through the Elora slough till we came to "Robbie's swoggle" where one of the waggons stuck fast, and as the sun was set had to be left behind; while one of the ladies who was walking, left a shoe in the mud which could not be recovered. In about half an hour the whole cavalcade reached Irvinebank where the welcomes and congratulations were renewed. The party consisted of Mr. and Mrs. Melvine, their child, and a man and woman servant; Mr. and Mrs. Peter Brown, six children and a maid servant; Mr. Moir, Sr., his son James, and two daughters; Mr. George Davidson, afterwards Sheriff, making with our own family, &c., about thirty individuals. Next day we rested and on the following day I accompanied the gentlemen to show them their several lots.

I ought to have mentioned that old Mr. Moir stayed in Elora the first night being greatly fatigued. Next morning I perceived a stranger coming through the log heaps, and I was told it was Mr. Moir senior. I went across the burn to meet him and got a right Aberdonian salutation: "Hech man, this is a rough countree."

Among those who joined our colony and came out with this party in June, I omitted to mention Mr. John A. Davidson, who became a useful settler, as well as being an intelligent and agreeable companion, and who lodged with us a considerable time—as did also Mr. Moir senior, with his son and daughters, who remained under our roof till their own house was made habitable.

The newly arrived immigrants were immediately engaged in putting in what crops might yet be sown, in choosing sites for houses, building temporary shanties, &c., Mr. Melvine contracted with the late Mr. Charles Allan for putting up a large frame house, the first frame house on the north side of the Grand River and which he just entered to die. Mr. Moir's house was raised about the end of Summer; the supper after raising was spread on the ground; and it was then that for the first time I heard "The Highland Sergeant," sung by Mr James Moir, Jr., and all present were convulsed with laughter. Darkness surprised us ere all the impedimenta were gathered together, and we went home by the light of cedar torches, making the woods ring, and the owl complain of being disturbed, for the first time, in her "ancient and solitary reign." How cheering was the shout and song and laughter of young men and maidens compared with the music we had been serenaded by during the past winter and spring—the yelling of wolves.

There was a good crop of wild grass in the Beaver Meadow; we resolved to cut and house it. There was not a large quantity, but it turned out to be of **great service** during the ensuing severe winter.

In the middle of July we heard of the arrival of Mr. Smith (seedsman) and family, and their settlement at Cox's Creek. Being known to several of our settlers, some of us determined to go and see them as well as other settlers in that neighborhood. Being in want of some necessaries from Shoemaker's mill we drove down in our ox waggon there and visited our friends on our return, getting a good deal of interesting news of our friends in Aberdeenshire. Mr. Smith brought me the happy intelligence that my elder sister, Mrs. John Gibbon with her family, accompanied by my younger, would be with us sometime in September. We had no letter from them lately and letters at that time were from two to three months in reaching us. One I had took five months, having by some mistake gone round by Nova Scotia. That day was the 31st of July bright and warm, but the evening was unusually chilly. Next morning, the 1st of August, was a severe frost—the fields white with hoar frost all over—the ice nearly a quarter of an inch thick on the water-trough—potatoes, melons, tomatoes, everything was cut down; and of course the late sown wheat, as ours was, shared the same fate. Mr. Smith was appalled: like ourselves not anticipating this he had sown some rare vegetables, and all were destroyed by this untimely frost. When we returned home I found that my worst fears regarding the frost were realized. The crops which but a few days before we left looking so rich and luxuriant were stricken down--the potatoes blackened, the wheat a sickly pale yellow, in a word our first crop was destroyed. I had often heard it objected to Nichol and the adjoining townships that they were so liable to frosts that there was no certainty of any crop coming to maturity; and this mischance seemed to confirm the statement. I therefore took pains to ascertain whether the ravages of this frost were confined to the northern part of the "Gore" district. I found that its ravages were universal, extending over Lower as well as Upper Canada, respecting Niagara and Sandwich as little as Nichol and Woolwich; destroying whatever was destructible in the New England States, and felt even to the Northern line of Virginia.

Worthless as our wheat was, we were fain to cut it down for the sake of the straw; and though we were told by the "old" settlers that cattle would thrive on straw and "browst" almost as well as on turnips and hay, our working oxen were reduced to such a state of weakness, notwithstanding the abundance of "browst" that one of them fell down by the way on our return from Fergus with a small load, and we were unable to raise him till we got a warm mash at John Mason's. We got him home with difficulty, and by getting at an enormous price a small additional quantity of hay brought them through the remainder of the winter.

I now got word from my sisters that they had reached Montreal in safety and would proceed to Hamilton without delay. I went down to meet them. It so happened that I timed my journey most exactly. The very next morning after reaching Hamilton I went to the steamer and found them standing on the deck, and if my memory serves me right, Mr. Wm. Tytler along with them. I cannot describe our meeting; it may easily be supposed it was joyful and affectionate. I instantly procured teams and the same afternoon we were on our way to Nichol. The roads were not yet broken up by the "Fall" rains, and were perhaps in their best state, so that our journey was without accident. We had plenty of amusement by the way—the surprise expressed by the boys at the strange and new scenes—Mr. Gibbon's horror of "corduroy," his humorous and graphic descriptions of ship scenes and ship annoyances, in particular his relation of the sufferings of a "Garrioch" man, described in the genuine Garrioch vernacular, rich, racy and eloquent—these, with news of our near relations and friends, Aberdeen gossip, and of the eagerness with which any intelligence from the new "Bon accord" colony, was sought out—made the long rough road seem short, and diverted the minds of the travellers, inexperienced of Canadian roads, from the many jolts and shakes and thumps they had to bear.

When we got to Irvinebank it was quickly arranged by the 'womankind' that my sisters and family should winter under our roof. Our servant Elsie was tired of the backwoods, and of service in our house, for she said it was as bad as any tavern and worse than some at home for we had not the conveniences. We were thus enabled to let her go. Soon after, Mr. Moir and family moved to their house in the meadow—"the back o' the world" as the old man familiarly termed it. Their company had been a great pleasure to us and, in several respects, a help. We had, ever since they came, nightly concerts of sacred and common music, on fine evenings on the log steps of the front door, overlooking the clearance—in unfavorable weather in the kitchen. These were attended by several of the neighbours, especially by Mr. Peter Brown, who greatly delighted in them. Nor have any of us forgotten or can forget those evenings. Mr. Brown spoke of them with rapture when I saw him in Aberdeen seventeen years later.

The Winter was now approaching, and we had to prepare for it by thoroughly chinking the house and plastering a part of it. Lime could not be got ; we had therefore to manufacture it. We dug an excavation in the slope of the bank near the Irvine about twenty two feet by sixteen, and about ten feet deep at the back where it was deepest. There was abundance of logs above and around it : we had thus only to select or cut the logs to the required length. Limestone lay all about on the surface, and we drew it, the smaller pieces in the waggon and the larger (for the chimney of the house) on a rude sleigh or hurdle. When a considerable quantity of the stones had been sufficiently broken we began to lay a tier of logs in the bottom of the excavation, leaving a square opening in the centre. We then placed a layer of limestone upon the first tier of logs, and then another tier of logs until we thought them of a sufficient height. We had not much labor in placing the logs, as they lay above the pile, so that we had only to take care that they did not roll too fast, and to see that the front log was properly secured. We raised the pile to about twelve feet in height When set on fire it made a vast blaze, at night illuminating the forest far and wide and so bright that we could see not only the outlines of the trees but the leaves and branches. We kept rolling in logs as the pile burned away and in four or five days had a large quantity of excellent lime.

The most pressing business now on hand was the building of the chimney, and as we intended having four fireplaces—two above and two below—it required to be a considerable building ; when finished it formed a large gable. The materials were now nearly all on the spot, and I had secured the builders. These were Messrs. Tytler, Lilly, and Kennedy—"Upright Kennedy," the appellation by which he was long known. The weather was favourable for the first few days, but it afterward broke and became excessively rainy, when our situation became very uncomfortable. We could have no fire in the house and our only substitute was a board shanty open in front, in which all our precautions could not prevent the fire from being not seldom dashed out by the excessive rains. If the situation of the inmates was comfortless, that of the builders and hodmen was more so ; but we were obliged to persevere till at the end of nearly three weeks our labours were ended.

It was during this interval that one Sabbath evening, just as we were retiring to bed, Mr. Mair, accompanied by Mr. William Mackie unexpectedly came in upon us. I had heard from Mr. Brown, who had assigned to Mr. Mair one of his lots, of his intended coming ; our meeting therefore, though at the moment unexpected, was most cordial on both sides. They remained with us that night, and next morning I accompanied them to Mr. Brown's. Mr. Mair, with characteristic energy, set about building a shanty, and was able in a few days to bring up his family ; one girl only, not so robust as the rest, was left in Elora. Mr. Brown and I, having occasion to go to Elora on the succeeding Saturday were requested by Mrs. Mair to conduct her home. The forepart of the day was fair, but in the afternoon it rained heavily and the state of the road was—indescribable. We endeavoured at first to pick our footsteps, but it was useless, and we had to flounder on through mud and pool, as best we could, till we came to Irvinebank. But how get over the brook in front of the house ? There was yet no bridge : a large cedar, fallen across the stream was the only pathway for foot passengers ; it was now quite dark, and the brook swollen by the rains. We dared not venture upon the tree in the darkness, so half leading half carrying Miss Mair we got through the stream with no other damage than drenched limbs. But oh ! miserable reception for a young lady just come from Britain—tired out and drenched from head to foot. There was not a fire in the house, and the shanty fire was drowned out by the rains. Fortunately there remained a little warm water, and Mrs. Elmslie, washing and drying her as well as she could, hurried her to bed. Such was Miss Mair's first introduction to Bon-accord.

The winter was now approaching, and the heavy rains and cold nights gave indications of a severe one. With all our means and appliances, and with abundance of warm clothing, we were but indifferently prepared for it. The best that could be said of our houses and shanties was that they would shelter us from the violence of the storms, and that they were uncomfortable ; our crops had perished ; and we had to weather another year on the interest of our little capital. Yet we were not discouraged : we had agreeable and intelligent society ; and our new and isolated situation had increased friendship to attachment, and attachment to love. There were no jealousies, no backbitings, and no quarrels. If unwonted roughness and privations engendered a temporary fretfulness it was speedily soothed down and made a source of amusement. We were, as was afterwards said by several of us—"as one family." But an event was at hand which saddened us all and threw a gloom over the young settlement—the death af Mr. Melvine.

His constitution was feeble, with a hereditary tendency to consumption. From all that was then known of the climate of Canada, his physician judged that emigration there would be favorable to his health. He appeared and felt invigorated by the sea voyage, and during the summer he entered with eager interest into his new plans and labours ; but the unfavorable weather of the Fall seemed to affect his spirits, and he occasionally appeared more irritable than he was formerly wont to do—the effect no doubt of lurking disease within. It was necessary to run our side-lines ; the morning when the surveyor came up was raw and drizzly, and he and I, as had been agreed on, accompanied him. He was very lightly dressed ; I in pilot cloth ; and I urged him to put on at least a great coat, but he declined doing this. It continued wet throughout the day and we finished our survey by five o'clock p. m., drenched and fatigued. A volunteer Rifle Company had been formed at Fergus and he and I joined it. We were called out to drill on a Saturday. The day turned out fine and we walked down together. He seemed in his usual health, appeared in no way fatigued by the walk, but was more silent than was his wont. During the exercises I observed that he once or twice retired ; and at the conclusion I missed him. The unusual exercise and exposure had brought on an affection of the lungs. He said it was nothing—"It came upon him sometimes—but soon went away—he felt quite well, but only a little fatigued with the long walk and the running." He sat a few minutes and we then walked home The shanty being now very damp, by great exertion on the part of the workmen one end of the new house was comfortably fitted up, and he was removed there, only to leave it for the tomb. The very night after his removal the unfavorable symptoms recurred. Dr. Craigie had been sent for, and he soon arrived—only to pronounce the fatal words," No hope." * * * * *

Mr. Webster sent his horses to take the body to Fergus. The day of the funeral was intensely cold, and the snow about sixteen inches deep. It was indeed in every way a very dismal day to all.

Thus passed away, in his 31st year, the friend and companion of my boyhood and youth. * * * * *

I have been more diffuse in my account of the illness and death of Mr. Melvine because I reckon him one of the chief founders of Bon-accord; for without his presence and co-operation I would never have entered on the undertaking.

Shortly after this the Fergus grist mill was burnt to the ground, not long after its completion. This was not only a heavy private loss, but a grievous public calamity. A considerable quantity of wheat and other grain, together with a number of bags, was destroyed in the conflagration. It caused a grievous scarcity, almost a famine. I was a sufferer among many others. I had purchased a quantity of wheat for provisions and seed, and had sent it to the mill, in new bags brought out to me by Mr. Gibbon. All was lost, and I had nothing remaining but a quantity of wheat of a fair quality but damply got in, hutted not housed, for as yet we had no barn. Meantime I was able to purchase some barrels of flour, which I sold out among my necessitous neighbors, so that it did not last long—I could not keep it while my fellow settlers were in distress. There was no grist mill nearer than Shoemaker's, a distance of about twenty miles. Urged by necessity my neighbour Mr. James Moir, jr. and I resolved to go down together. We set off early in the morning with our oxen, (two yokes of oxen hitched to one sleigh,) and by evening reached Cox's Creek, where we staid over night, and reached Shoemaker's by noon of the following day. When we showed our wheat to our utter consternation he refused to grind it. We urged our necessity and the need of our neighbours; but he answered that he dared not put it through the bolt as it would completely unfit the mill for grinding any more. But he offered to chop it, which would give us all the substance of the wheat, though it would not bake well. He advised us however to take it home again and dry it, in which case it would make very fair flour. Thinking that I might in some way or other shift the difficulty I tied up my bags and replaced them in the sleigh, but my neighbour could not wait, and had his grain chopped. We then returned to Cox's Creek, whence we started next morning and got home by ten o'clock in the evening of an intensely frosty night. I returning after three day's travel, just as I went away--he with his wheat not ground but chopped. When, some considerable time after, we were talking over our bootless journey, I asked him how they managed with their "chop." The answer was brief—"Oh man! but it was tough eatin'.

This winter, began in severity, continued severe throughout, with frequent and heavy falls of snow and tremendous frosts. One morning, at sunrise, I found the mercury compressed within the bulb. It was one of Ramage's instruments and marked to thirty degrees below zero; it was on the north side of the house in the open air, unsheltered. The severity continued unmitigated till April, when Spring instantaneously burst in upon us. On Sabbath morning I went into the woods for the cattle—the trees were as bare as in Janurry—you could have seen any distance in the forest. On the succeeding Thursday they were one mass of green foliage, and you could not see beyond the edge of the wood; no snow but in the hollows, and the ground covered with a profusion of leeks and myriads of little flowers.

Not a few fatal accidents occurred in chopping; three of them within two or three miles of us. In one of them the cause was singular. Two young men were chopping a large tree—in order to fell it in the desired direction they cut a sapling, fixed it as a "pry" or lever, and continued chopping. Either from the strokes, or from a wavy motion in the tree, the lever suddenly sprung, struck the young man in the forehead, and he fell as if shot, never uttering a sound.

I have alluded to the toil, loss of time, and vexations and losses caused us by the cattle when they did not return home regularly. I think it was towards the end of the summer of 1837, that the cows and oxen had not come home for three days. I knew pretty nearly the direction in which they had gone during the season—they had a large sonorous bell, the sound of which was familiar to me, and I made no doubt of finding them. I started about six o'clock, and made for the "meadow," as we called Mr. Moir's lot, stopping occasionally, as I went, to listen for the bell. The family were at breakfast, and Mr. Moir pressed me to share with them. I declined, saying I expected to be home to breakfast. "An ye get hame to breakfast it 'ill be a late ane. We heard your bell last afternoon, and it was gae far awa, and we have na heard it the day. Ye'll best take meat whan it's in yer offer." Happily for me, I took the advice. They then directed me to go a good way west, and afterwards, if I did not hear the bell, to keep south. Having gone a long way in the direction pointed out, stopping, however, frequently to listen for the bell, I came upon a stream, which I knew to be the stream that flowed in front of our house. I now made up my mind to go a good way further, in the same direction, and if I heard no sound, to return to the stream and go home by its banks. I went on, as I thought a long way, till I came to a pretty high eminence which must have been west or south-west of what is now Alma, on the summit of which I stood still and listened. No sound of any kind reached my ears—there was not even the whisper of a zephyr, and it was past noon. After some time, I came upon the stream, and I believed our stream, and kept down its banks; now and then fancying I heard a faint tinkle, and stopping. I went on thus for a long time, till I felt sure I must be in the immediate neighbourhood of Mr. Moir's meadow; but there was no sign of any clearance, the forest before me thick and dark. I looked towards the sun, and then to the direction of the stream; it was running south-west instead of north-east. I had taken the wrong stream—that one which, coming at one point within forty or fifty yards of 'our' stream, takes suddenly an opposite course, and falls into the Grand River, about four miles below Elora—in short the stream which misled the hapless Andrew Dalgarno.

(Andrew Dalgarno, was lost on this creek, for three days, in August, 1836.)

I lay down on the bank, and debated with myself whether I should attempt my way direct home through the woods, or follow the stream down to the Grand River. I resolved on the latter course. I felt sure I would reach it before darkness came on, and then the way, though long, would be plain. I kept rigidly to the bank of the stream till I came to a clearance; it was a large beaver meadow; and keeping to the stream, I had to press through a thicket of brambles, gooseberry and raspberry bushes. At length I got through it and travelled through a beautiful conntry, undulating and knolly, with many a little rill running into the stream whose bank I was following. Tired and exhausted, I lay down about mid-afternoon by the side of one of these rills and drank; but I had not patience to rest. I got up, hastened on, and found the ground steadily descending. After a while I felt completely exhausted, and was compelled to lie down. As I lay I heard the faint sound, as I thought, of rushing

ELORA

water; I started to my feet—it was so, I ran forward about fifty or sixty yards. There, a little way below, was the Grand River—and it was time—the sun was setting.

In this abrupt manner Mr. Elmslie closes his narrative. We are left to conjecture, as we may, how he returned to his home. We see him in our imagination carefully fording the Grand River, near what is now the favorite picnic ground of "Whitelaw's Flats." Arriving safely, after much trepidation, on the east bank of the river he would soon reach the river road, and following that to the north, would stumble forward in his final effort to reach that haven for many a tired traveller—Old King Reeve's Place. Here he would be welcomed and, after a rest, and some refreshment, which he sorely needed, Old King Reeves would hitch up his team of horses, which are said to have been the first horses hereabouts, and drive Mr. Elmslie to his home, passing, on their way, through Elora.

As mentioned by Mr. Elmslie, the settlers for the Bon-accord came in parties, relatives and friends following each other at intervals, and all from Aberdeenshire. We now propose to give the names of the first settlers in something like the order in which they came to the settlement. Seventy years have passed since those hardy settlers left home and comfort to face unknown hardships in the bush and as we look over their names to day we find that in the Bon-accord settlement, in Upper Nichol, there are only two farms now owned by sons of the original owners. These are the farms which were taken up by Mr. Watt and Mr. Keith.

* * * *

John Keith was born at the farm of Kinknockie, in the Parish of Old Deer, Aberdeenshire, Scotland, on the 12th. of January, 1809. When a young man he learned the trade of carpenter and cabinet maker at Stuartfield, about four miles from his home, and, in 1832, while assisting at the building of a Manse at Auchreddie, in the adjoining parish of New Deer, he became acquainted with Alexander Watt and his sisters. This led to his marriage on the 23rd. of May, 1834, with Christian Watt, and to their emigration to Canada. They first met with Mr. Elmslie at Grosse Isle, near Quebec, when on their voyage out, and again, at Toronto where they decided to cast in their lot with the Bon-accord colony.

On their arrival in Elora they found that the only available shelter was a log house on the west side of the river; the one which Henry Wilbee had built the year before to be used by him while he was building the first saw-mill at the Elora Falls. The party of four—Mr. and Mrs. Keith, Mr. and Miss Watt—took possession of this; Mr. Keith opened his 'Kist', or Kit of Tools, and soon made the house very comfortable for the approaching winter. Having provided a home, Mr. Keith then did the carpenter work on Mr. Elmslie's house, afterwards on Mr. Watt's and his own. Men were hired to make a clearing on the farm which he chose, which was Lot 15, on the 11th. Concession. By spring time a log house was built; to one end of it was an extension which he used as his workshop; out of the trees growing about him making many necessary articles for himself and his neighbours. As we turn the pages of his old account book we see the record of his work. In many of the accounts the first items mentioned are a window sash, a water-pail, a table, a wash tub or a churn. But there is a great variety, for the list includes spinning-wheels, threshing-mills, lanterns, clock-cases, cradles and coffins.

Mr. Keith assisted at the building of the first Grist Mill in Elora, in 1843, and afterwards built several houses in the village which are in use to day, monuments to his good workmanship.

Ten years had passed after Mr. Keith settled on his farm, when, late one evening in the Fall of the year 1844, a stranger rapped at his door. Enquiring for Mr. Keith, who was not at home at the time, the stranger returned on the following day and explained the object of his visit. This was, to purchase, or exchange other land for half of Mr. Keith's farm, on which was a water-power. This Mr. Keith most willingly agreed to and on the west half of his farm a busy village grew rapidly; such a thriving place was it that for a few years it seemed likely to be larger than Elora. How this came about is another story and will be described when we refer later to the stranger above mentioned—the late Sem Wissler, the Founder of the village of Salem.

For some years after this the 'back line', as the road to the Bon-accord was called, continued to be used for all the travel between Salem and Elora as well as by those settlers from the upper parts of the townships of Nichol, Pilkington, and from Peel. From her house Mrs. Keith could see these neighbours from the north coming down Watt's hill on their way to Elora. Swinging the crane carrying the kettle, over the fire, in the large open fire-place, the water would be boiled and the tea drawn by the time the tired traveller would reach her door. With a cup of strong, black tea, the best of butter, home made cheese from the milk house by the spring and some of those large Scotch biscuits, with carraways in them, such as only Grandma knew how to make, the visitor would continue her journey much refreshed, after promising to call in on her return.

Thus the years went bye; their farm was cleared, their family grown up, their life work done. Then, like so many others since, they retired, about the year 1870, to spend the remainder of their days in Elora.

One son having gone to live in Grand Rapids, Michigan, Mr. Keith went there on a visit. He was shown through the large furniture factories there where he saw the modern methods of making furniture by machinery. While he often spoke of this on his return, and the great pleasure it had been to him, yet there was a note of sadness mingled with it for how easy it was compared with the laborious way in which he had made so much of the furniture for his neighbours.

Not long after this visit the County Volunteers held their camp in Elora. Before returning to their homes they were entertained by the citizens with a strawberry festival. Only those who were assisting at the festival were admitted to the Drill Hall, but one of his young friends, who was a volunteer, saw Mr. Keith near the door and procured admission for him that he might enjoy the unusual sight. One hundred soldiers were seated at each of the four long tables; the Hall was gaily decorated; numerous young ladies hurried about supplying the guests with an abundance of berries and cream; the whole scene was filled with life and pleasure. Only a few steps from the door of the Hall was the site of the bridge over which he had crossed to make his home in a wilderness, and he had lived to see this transformation! There he stood looking at the hundreds of happy young folks; the whole scene reflected on his kindly face. Turning to his young friend a smile and a tear filled his eye, and then, passing among those crowded about the door—he disappeared.

Some two weeks later, on the 11th. of July, 1878, Mr. Keith died suddenly, beloved and respected by all. Mrs. Keith continued to live in their home, overlooking the C. P. R. Station, until March 16th., 1889, when she, too, passed away in her 79th. year. In their family there was—Mrs. Connon, living in Elora; Mrs. James Henderson, in Toronto; John, married Ann Argo, of Eramosa, is living on his father's farm; Alexander, went to Grand Rapids, Michigan. There he married Isabella Melville. He died on August 13th. 1903; Mrs. David Steven, living in Chesley; George, married Mary Loghrin, of Eramosa, is now living in Elora, and Miss Elsie C. Keith in Toronto.

JOHN KEITH

MRS. JOHN KEITH

ELORA

Alexander Watt was born at Auchreddie, in the Parish of New Deer, Aberdeenshire, on the 15th. of March, 1798. Before leaving Scotland he had some experience in business, for which he was peculiarly fitted. As it was, after the difficulties of the early years in Bon accord were overcome, he became a very prosperous farmer and laid the foundation for the notable career which his sons pursued. For more than a quarter of a century his sons, J. & W. Watt, were known to every farmer in Canada to be among the most successful breeders of short-horn cattle. Mr. Watt was associated with others in several business enterprises, such as the store of Ross & Co., and the company which was formed to establish the first newspaper in Elora. But it was perhaps more for the great interest he took in organizing the first Presbyterian Church that he was best known to the community.

Those religious services which were held in the home of Mr. Keith and Mr. Watt during the first winter that they spent in Elora, were the first steps in the formation of the congregation of Knox Church. After they had removed to their farms in Bon accord those meetings were continued; in their houses at first, afterwards in Mr. Watt's barn, and then in "The Old Log Church" which was built in 1838, on a piece of land donated for that purpose by Mr. and Mrs. Barron, from the north corner of their farm Lot 11, Concession 11.

Then a meeting was held to organize a congregation. Having been ordained an Elder in Scotland, Mr. Watt procured a book in which to keep a record of the work of the church, and in his beautiful Scotch copper plate handwriting wrote the following, dated Irvine Settlement, February 8th., 1837— "A few individuals having in the Providence of God left Scotland, their native country, and settled on the eleventh and twelfth concessions of the Township of Nichol, in the Province of Upper Canada, feeling deeply the value of Gospel ordinances from their being deprived of them, and now completely destitute, met and unanimously resolved to use every means that might advance or obtain from time to time a supply of sermon and a dispensation of sealing ordinances as frequently as they could be secured." The first petition for a "supply of Sermon" was sent to "the Missionary Presbytery of the Canadas in connection with and subordinate to the Synod of the United Associate Church of Scotland, meeting at West Flamboro." This was signed by the following individuals: Alexander Watt, Barbara Watt; George Barron, Elspet Barron; John Calder, Christian Calder; John Keith, Christian Keith; and John Alexander Davidson, the last named being appointed "to proceed with the petition to Presbytery." The Presbytery appointed the Rev. Thomas Christie, of West Flamboro, to come to Nichol and organize the congregation. The Rev. gentleman, though getting on in years, being about sixty, walked the whole way, a distance of fifty miles. At this meeting to organize, held in Mr. Watt's barn, on May 18th, 1837, Mr. Watt was elected the first elder. He continued to serve the Church in that capacity until his death on February 26th., 1896, at the age of 97 years, 11 months and 11 days. On the 20th. of May Mr. John A. Davidson was appointed an Elder and along with Mr. Watt constituted the first Session. On the following day the first Sacrament was dispensed. For two years and more the services were conducted by themselves; only occasionally would a minister visit them until a congregation was formed in the Township of Eramosa. After that they agreed with the Eramosa congregation that when a minister came to the one he would also visit the other; the arrangement being that Eramosa would have two services for one in Bon accord. This continued until the church removed to Elora when each engaged a minister of their own, the congregation at that time having a membership of thirty.

For the first six years the congregation had to content themselves with an average of three or four sermons a year. Among those who preached sermons to them at this early period were the Reverends J. Christie, George Lawrence, James Roy, John Morrison, James Skinner and others. These sermons were the special events of the year, and the facts concerning them are carefully engrossed in the Session records.

It was in 1841 that the Rev. Dr. Barrie came to Canada. On the 2nd. of February, 1843, he was ordained as minister of the Eramosa congregation, and on the day following in the Old Log Church, in Bon-accord, and was pastor of both until 1849. He was a man of untiring energy and great force of character.

The first baptism was before the church records were commenced; that of Mr. Keith's first-born (now Mrs. Connon), and the second, although the first on the church records, was Mr. Watt's eldest daughter, Margaret, who was afterwards the late Mrs. John Hunter.

The congregation of Knox Church has had three church homes. The Old Log Church, 1838—1850; the frame rough cast building in Elora, 1850—1873; the present stone structure,—built in 1873, and has been ministered to by the following pastors:

    Rev. Wm. Barrie, 1843—1849.
    Rev. John Duff, 1850—1869.
    Rev. A. D. McDonald, 1869—1879.
    Rev. S. Fisher, 1879—1883.
    Rev. Hugh Rose, 1884—until his death on August 28th. 1887.
    Rev. M. L. Leitch, 1889—1891.
    Rev. John McInnis, 1891—1899 and since 1900 by the present pastor, the Rev. W. R. McIntosh.

After he had taken up a farm and had a house built Mr. Watt returned to Scotland, where, on the 7th. of April, 1836, he married Barbara Argo, a sister of the late Adam L. Argo of Fergus and the late James Argo, of Eramosa. In their family there was:—Margaret (who was the late Mrs. John Hunter); John married Margaret, daughter of the late Hugh Roberts, of Pilkington and widow of the late Geo. Fordyce, and is living on the old homestead; Barbara, living in Elora; James, who died Feb. 18th, 1873; Isabella (Mrs. Wm. Watson) of Peel Township; Elspeth, wife of Rev. John Ross, of Port Dalhousie; William Barrie, married Isabella, daughter of the late Robert Shortreed. He died on July 1st., 1903, at the age of 56 years and 3 months; and Annie, now living in Elora. Mrs. Watt died on August 5th, 1893, at the age of eighty one.

    *   *   *   *

A second party left Aberdeen on the 3rd. of April, 1835, on board the ship "Brilliant," commanded by Capt. Duthie, the voyage lasting two months all but two days. Of the 108 passengers on board, a few came to Elora, among them being James Moir, who was then a young man of about twenty years of age, and he used to laugh as he told of some fun they had while waiting at Quarantine in New York Harbour. Their vessel lay near the island on which the Statue of Liberty now stands, and on a Sunday afternoon a boat load of dandy Americans from the city rowed about the ship, at the same time making some very uncomplimentary remarks about the Scotch. As James Moir said "They were dressed i' their Sunday claithes an' their appearance was better than their lang'age." "Ane o' oor passengers was Peter Reid, an' when he cam' aboard ship at Aberdeen he brocht wi' him, as part o' his providin', a box of eggs. Noo, ye ken, those eggs were auld some weeks afore, and whan thae dandies were tormentin' us Peter slippit awa' doon an' brocht up his box of eggs. Then, says he, tak' a gowpin fu' the piece lads, an' lean o'er the bulwarks. Waiting for a suitable opportunity Peter says to the rest o' us "Noo lads, gin ye be ready, 'odes sakes, fire! Eh, man! but they were nice to thraw. It was fine to hear them crackin'."

Landing at New York they came by the Hudson River and Erie Canal to Oswego, crossed the lake to Toronto and then to Hamilton. From this they came to Preston, then to Winterbourne, where they left some of their fellow travellers, among them being George Loggie and his wife, and Adam L. Argo who there joined his brother James, who had preceded him.

It was the 10th. of June and they felt the heat very much, and were tormented by the mosquitos, as they came through the long woods between Winterbourne and Inverhaugh, but here, at Mrs. Robinson's, they found pans full of milk floating on spring water "and they were loath to leave it."

It was in this party that Mr. and Mrs. Melvine came, and Peter Brown, with his wife and family. It was not long until Mr. Brown went to keep store for Mr. Webster in Fergus. His wife dying shortly after, Mr. Brown, with his family, returned to Aberdeen where he resumed his calling as an auctioneer. Then there was John A. Davidson, a carpenter, who was a leading spirit during his residence in Bon accord. He wrote some articles for the Aberdeen newspapers regarding life in the bush which attracted much attention at the time, and he kept a diary which would make interesting reading to day. Mr. Davidson's house was across the creek from Mr. Keith's. At the time of the McKenzie rebellion there was much excitement in Bon accord, as elsewhere, and, as he was then unmarried, and could readily leave home, Mr. Davidson thought it his duty to take an active part. He didn't do this, but was preparing for it by hunting up his good clothes, and, after looking all forenoon he went over to his neighbour and said Mrs. Keith, "Div ye ken whaur my Sunday waist coat might be, I canna find it?" "Eh be here man!" was the reply, "you have it on you." Mr. Davidson, with his family, removed to Eden Mills, in Eramosa, where he died. His wife was Catharine Middleton and in their family there was : Sarah, Mrs. Mason, living in Garafraxa ; Robert died in Hamilton ; James died in New York ; Catharine is Mrs. Dr. Walmsley, in Detroit ; Christina is Mrs. Peart, living in Burlington ; Annie, William and Hadassah died at Eden Mills.

There was also James Moir, with his sisters Margaret and Annie, and their father, who spent what were, perhaps, the happiest days of his life, fishing in the creek that crossed their farm. Two sisters remained in Aberdeen, one of them being Mrs. Jameson, whose husband, a ship chandler, had instructed Mr. Elmslie to purchase for him a farm in Bon-accord. Ill health prevented him from coming to take possession of it and it was sold, in Aberdeen, to Thomas Gray. After her husband's death Mrs. Jameson and her sister came to Canada. How often the future career of many persons is changed by circumstances, in which, at the time, they are not particularly interested ! When a joint stock company was formed to build the saw mill, mentioned by Mr. Elmslie, they purchased the machinery for it from a young man in Dundas who was then commencing his very successful career as a mechanical engineer. Having come to Bon accord in connection with his work for the saw mill Mr. John Gartshore met his future wife, Margaret Moir. Her sister, Annie, became the wife of George Pirie, of Dundas, and Jacqueline, (Mrs. Jameson) married James Lesslie, who had been postmaster at Dundas and afterwards lived in Toronto, while another sister, Mary, was Mrs. Fleming, of Galt. Nor was this all, for James Moir met his wife, Margaret Pellett, in Dundas and, along with Dr. Middleton, who was his best man, tramped the fifty miles to the wedding, which took place on the 4th. of January, 1842. On the return journey the bridal party were met at Guelph by Mr. Watt who drove down with his wagon, drawn by the first and only horses in Bon-accord at that time, that he might convey the young couple to their home. James Moir was born in the city of Aberdeen on the 28th. of October, 1815. Before coming to Canada Mr. Moir worked for several years at watch making. For the first year after coming to Bon accord he lived at Mr. Elmslie's and had a room in the attic where he repaired watches, in this way earning enough to buy their first yoke of oxen and a cow. Only then could he commence to clear his farm which his father said was "the back of the world."

Mr. Moir was a tall, well built and handsome man, with a great fund of humor, and a born mimic. Although not a trained musician, he was a remarkably good singer, having a strong, sweet baritone voice, a correct ear, and he sang with perfect expression. He was the life of a party, being gifted with a good memory for the words and music, especially of Scotch songs, of which he knew and sang a great number. Mr. Moir lived retired in Elora for about twenty years prior to his death on April 1st, 1906 at the age of over ninety years. Mrs. Moir died some years previously. In their family there is Mrs. Troxel, wife of Capt. Troxel, U. S. Army, Chicago ; William in Winnipeg ; Alexander in Kent, Washington ; Mrs. Mann, wife of Major W. A. Mann, U. S. Army, Washington D. C. ; Mrs. Qua and Miss Jacqueline at home. Those not now living were James ; John ; Lesslie and Mrs. G Tower Fergusson.

It is a most remarkable fact that there are at present two men now living in Elora who went down to the docks in Aberdeen on that April morning seventy two and a half years ago to see this party sail for "America." These are our old friends Mr. Alexander Harris and Mr. William Gibbon. Mr. Harris was a near neighbour, and playmate of James Moir's and Mr. Gibbon's family were intimate friends of Mr. Melvine's.

The third party sailed from Aberdeen aboard the ship "William Wallace," a new vessel on her first trip. Seven weeks from the day they left Aberdeen they landed in Elora, that being the 2nd. of September, 1835. In this party there was Mr. John Gibbon with his wife, Jean Elmslie, and their sons, William Gibbon who is now living in Elora, and John who died in 1849. Another brother, born in Canada, is Mr. George Gibbon now living near Sundridge, in the Parry Sound District.

Mr. John Gibbon was born in 1798 and before coming to Canada was in business as a Dry Goods Merchant in the city of Aberdeen. He died in 1860 and lies buried in the Old Log Churchyard. He was long remembered by his numerous friends for his kind and cheerful disposition.

Another member of this party was Miss Margaret Elmslie, who became the wife of William Gibbon Sr., who came to Bon accord along with Mr. Elmslie the year before. To explain this somewhat complicated relationship we may say that Mrs. Elmslie's two brothers married Mr. Elmslie's two sisters. As all three also lived on adjoining farms Mr. Elmslie was quite right when he said "They were as one family."

In the family of William Gibbon, senior, there is William and Helen, in Hanover ; Jean was the wife of Dr. Groves, of the Royal Alexandra Hospital, Fergus ; Agnes lives in Fergus and Margaret, in Toronto.

Among those who came on the same ship, but did not settle in Bon-accord, there was Mr. and Mrs. George Beattie, who left Scotland on their wedding day. On the voyage a great friendship sprang up between Mrs. Beattie and Mrs William Gibbon, who was not married then, and they decided that if they ever lived within travelling distance they would visit one another, and if that were not possible, they would write. Mr. and Mrs Beattie made their home in Lower Nichol and, strange to say, although not many miles apart, they seldom saw each other. With the bad roads and slow ox teams of seventy years ago there was little visiting ; and in fact there is yet very little communication between Upper and Lower Nichol. The natural thoroughfare was up and down the river road past Winterbourne In the Beattie family were four sons and nine daughters, as follows :—Mrs. Wm. Hastings, in Lower Nichol ;

ELORA 91

Mrs. Robert Pritchard, in Nichol; Mrs. John Simpson, Wimbledon, North Dakota; Mr. James Beattie, living in Elora; Miss Lizzie Beattie, on the homestead; Mrs. Andrew Hudson, in Elora; Georgina died in infancy; Mrs. John Mutrie, now living in Elora; Mrs. Thomas Pritchard, in Nichol; Mr. Wm. T. Beattie, in Theodore, Saskatchewan; Mr. George Beattie, on the homestead; Mrs. W. J. Patterson, London, Ont.; and Rev. John A. Beattie, Miami, Man.

* * * *

The fourth party came a short time later, in 1835. They were Thomas Mair, his wife and family in which there was—James; Thomas; John, who was at one time Warden of the County; Jane, Mrs. Mackie; Isabella, Mrs. George Fraser; Elsie; Margaret; Catharine, Mrs. James Aiken, who is living in Fergus; and Eliza, Mrs. William Dryden, living near Paisley.

Along with them was William Mackie and his sister; Joseph Wedderburn and his wife, and Alex. Webster, a brother of Mrs Wedderburn's, who remained but a few years and returned to Scotland. Another relative in the party was John Calder, with his wife, Christina Webster, and their family. These were Eliza, Mrs. Wm. Keith; Barbara, Mrs. John Dalgarno; Kirstie, Mrs. Andrew Dalgarno; Alexander; John; Mary, Mrs. Turnbull Allan; Margaret, Mrs. John Dobbin; Isabella; William; Jemima, Mrs. Charles Vosper; and Georgina, Mrs. Black, in Hamilton.

Many of the pioneers could tell doleful tales of the hardships they had to endure, and Mr. Calder gave his experience as follows. "They arrived safely at Montreal where they were told that the Rideau canal had broken out. As there were some 125 emigrants altogether they decided to hire a Durham Boat. They started, and were detained for a day at Lachine on account of some damage done to one of the locks. A steamer towed them across the lake, but during the voyage, the sailors, as well as the captain, got drunk, and remained so, while the passengers were obliged to take command of the boat. In coming up one of the rapids the boat was towed by fourteen horses. The rope broke, and away went the boat, which struck a rock and staved a hole in the bottom, but was pulled ashore and saved. A son of the Emerald Isle, being among the passengers, asked for a new rope to prevent a like occurrence, but was refused by the drunken captain. Paddy threatened, if he did not furnish the rope he would pitch him overboard; and sure he did, and the man would have been drowned had it not been that assistance was at hand. But it had the desired effect, for the crew were all sober men until they arrived at Kingston. It took seventeen days to come from Montreal to Hamilton. Mr. Calder was obliged to store his luggage at Hamilton as he had not money enough left to pay the hire of a team from Hamilton to Elora, which was thirty dollars. Accordingly, Mr. Calder, with his wife and young children, walked all the way to Elora, which they reached on a Sabbath evening, the fourth night after leaving Hamilton. He had spent his last York shilling (12 1/2 cents) at Blythe's that day—hard times, indeed, to begin in a new country. Next morning he started for the Bon-accord, where he got the use of a log shanty from Mr. John A. Davidson. He never knew the want of a window in the house until the cold weather came. Mr. Calder was much indebted to Mr. and Mrs. Keith for the use of many things until he was able to get his own luggage from Hamilton. Straw was even scarce in those days, and shavings had to take the place of feathers. The first job was to root out a stump from under the floor of Mr. Elmslie's house. The next was rather a better one. Mr. Gartshore, of Dundas, was building a saw-mill over the creek on Mr. Elmslie's farm, and Mr. Calder was employed to make the mill race. Again, he undertook to build a stone chimney. The tools were a trowel and a hammer, and the stones were carried from the creek in a bag. In the course of time it was finished, and on that night he dreamed that the chimney had fallen down. He started out of bed, half asleep, to see if it really was the case; but it was only a dream, for the chimney survived the house.

Having earned some money, Mr. Calder walked down to Hamilton to secure his luggage. A teamster was hired, and the boxes loaded on to his wagon. When on the road between Guelph and Blythe's an axle of the wagon broke. Mr. Calder and the teamster did the only thing possible; they placed the goods in an unoccupied log shanty which was near and went off to have the wagon repaired. On their return they found that part of the goods had been stolen; all Mrs. Calder's clothing, and the warm clothing that had been provided for the children had been taken. The winter was coming on, and flour was fourteen dollars a barrel! Placing the empty boxes, along with the others, on the wagon the journey was completed to Bon-accord."

* * * *

About this time a young man came on the scene who was to play a conspicuous part in the community. This was Mr. George Barron, whose native place was Savoch i' Deer, in Aberdeenshire. Coming to Canada, several years before this, he had worked in the vicinity of Whitby. There he heard of the Bon accord colony, and came up to investigate. He returned some time later, and, about Christmas, 1835, married Miss Elspet Watt, who had, up to this time, kept house for her brother. This was the first marriage in the settlement. A few days later Mr. Watt set out on a visit to Scotland, leaving the newly-married couple to look after his house until his return. Having married in Scotland, Mr. Watt again sailed from Aberdeen on the 16th of April, on the ship 'Pacific, and arrived at Elora on the 10th of June, 1836. In this, the fifth party, there was, besides Mr. and Mrs. Watt, James Findlay, who was born in the Parish of New Machar, Oct 5th, 1804, and his wife, Margaret Ruxton, from the Parish of Foveran. Their four eldest children were born in Scotland, their family being: Agnes, Mrs. George Smith, living in Brantford; William is the well known auctioneer and resident of Salem; John is in Victoria, B. C.; David, lived for many years in Salem, died in Windsor; James is in Shoal Lake, Manitoba; Alexander died in Toronto; Robert is in Sudbury, and Charles in Shoal Lake, Manitoba.

In this party there was also Alex. Webster, who remained but a few years and returned to Scotland; Charles Michie; Mrs. Brown and her daughter, Mary; George Fraser; James Fraser (not related) who now lives in Milton; Andrew Dalgarno, with his wife and family; and Alexander Rennie.

In Andrew Dalgarno's family there were: Andrew, in Arthur township; John, in the township of Sullivan; Alexander; Margaret, Mrs. Charles Bye; Barbara, Mrs. George Duncan; and Beatrice, Mrs. Joseph Elkerton.

Mr. Alex. Rennie was born in the city of Aberdeen. He learned the trade of shoemaking at Strichen. His first workshop in Bon accord was in a small log shanty on what is now Mr. Fergusson's farm. He had not been long in the country, when, one night while working late, making shoes by the light of a candle, Mr. Rennie heard the howling wolves as they killed and ate Mr. Elmslie's cow, quite near to his cabin. The unusual light of a candle, and the lonely occupant, attracted the attention of the wolves, and some of them looked in at the window—there were no curtains then. After this experience Mr. Rennie used a room in Mr. Barron's house, and, after that, in Mr. Davidson's; finally locating on the southwest corner of Lot 9, Concession 12; at that time the most northerly limit of civilization on the 'back line.' Mr. Rennie's father, mother, three sisters and a brother, settled in Guelph township. The father came up to see how his son Sandy was getting along. Returning to his family,

GEORGE BARRON

THE OLD MILL AT WINTERBOURNE
Photographed in 1892

he was trying to explain the geography of Bon accord, and his description was, that " Ye would easy ken Sandy's place. It's the yontmost hoose in America."

Alexander Rennie married Margaret Webster, and in their family there are Margaret, Mrs. Harry Almas, living in Hamilton ; Mr. John Rennie, a well-known resident of Elora; Christina, deceased; and Jean is Mrs. Charles Webster, living at Lion's Head, in Bruce County.

* * * *

Joseph Tytler was a native of Kincardine O'Neill, which is twenty-six miles up Dee side from the city of Aberdeen. In April, 1836, he sailed from Aberdeen in the ship 'Universe.' Landing at New York he came by the Hudson River and Erie Canal to Oswego, and by schooner to Hamilton, arriving in Elora on June 20th, 1836. Along with him was his brother Alexander Tytler, and his sister, with her husband, Alexander Gall. Joseph Tytler was the only store-keeper, and the postmaster, in Elora, in 1837.

William Tytler was another brother who came to Canada a year before, and, after visiting different parts of the province, settled in Bon-accord, having advised his relatives and others to do the same. Some time later he married Mrs. Melvine, whose maiden name was Jane Inglis Forbes. At their home in Bon accord they were visited for a considerable time by a nephew of Mrs. Tytler's—her brother's son—who was later known to every newspaper reader as the celebrated War Correspondent, Archibald Forbes.

After her husband's death, in May, 1870, Mrs. Tytler, with her two daughters, came to live in Elora, where she died in June, 1885, at the age of seventy eight years and ten months.

Of the family, Agnes is now living in Toronto ; William has for many years been Inspector of City Schools in Guelph ; Alexander is living in Rochester, N. Y. ; and Barbara, Mrs Kirkman, before her removal to Seaforth, and Toronto where she died, was for a number of years a most successful teacher in the Elora Schools.

* * * *

William Gerrie and his wife Clementina Stewart, lived in the Parish of Leslie, in Aberdeenshire. They had a family of eleven, of whom five sons and four daughters were living. The sons were, Alexander, who lived near Ancaster ; William and John near Winterbourne ; Adam in Eramosa, and James. The daughters were, Janet, Mrs. George Brander ; Dorothy, Mrs. John Durrant ; Isabella, Mrs. William Mitchell and Margaret, Mrs. Samuel Burnett. The daughters lived near Winterbourne ; and there the father died on March 4th 1861, at the age of eighty four. But there was one member of this family who was, for more than fifty-eight years, known to every resident in Elora. This was our old friend James Gerrie, who died on the 17th. of December, 1894, at the age of seventy-six.

Having decided to come to Canada, Mr. Gerrie, senior, arranged with a ship captain in Aberdeen for a passage. Upon further enquiry he found that the vessel was not going to sail as soon as he expected, so gave up his place on that ship, and took passage on another, which was to sail a week sooner. He was to learn that the one who starts first does not always make the best speed. Their ship, an old whaler, sailed from Aberdeen on a Saturday about the 11th. of June 1836,and that day ten weeks they saw America. Two weeks later they arrived in Hamilton. The next day, being the Sabbath, they attended Church, and, to their great surprise, the service was conducted by one they had left behind in their native parish, and who had sailed on the ship which Mr. Gerrie had thought too slow,—the Rev. Alexander Gardiner—afterwards pastor of St. Andrew's Church, in Fergus.

Their passage had been an unusually rough one, the old ship rolled badly, the water came in at the open hatchways, and for some days they expected at any time to go to the bottom. Added to this there was much sickness, especially among the children; Mr. and Mrs. Cruikshank and Mr. and Mrs. Young each burying a child at sea.

It took this party three days to come from Hamilton to Elora. After leaving Winterbourne eight waggons stuck on their way through the "long woods" and had to be left until the next day, when, by hitching many teams together, the wagons were pulled out separately. The passengers had to get out and walk, in the dark, to Mrs. Robinson's, which they reached, soaking wet, and some without their boots, which had been pulled off their feet in wading through the swamp mud.

They arrived in Elora, on a Saturday about the 17th of September, 1836. Here more discomfort awaited them, for there was not proper food for such a number, and for days their principal food was potatoes, while they lived within the walls of a frame house that had not, as yet, a roof.

In this party there were thirty six individuals by the name of Gerrie; among them being William Gerrie, from the Parish of Premnay, who bought two hundred acres of land between Bon accord and Elora. His brothers Robert and John came later and each got fifty acres of the land their elder brother had bought.

The wife of this William Gerrie was Isabella Brake and they had a family of eight boys and three girls, six of whom were born in Scotland. They were William, one of the first settlers in the township of Brant who afterwards lived in Fergus; James is living on his father's farm, near Elora; John lives in Fergus; Mary is Mrs. David Keith, near Chesley; Andrew lived in Paisley; Peter lived on a farm between Fergus and Elora; Alexander died in Fergus; Thomas is in Oakland, Cal,; George, lives in Toronto; Isabella was Mrs. James Johnston; and Margaret is married in Chicago.

Of John Gerrie's family the only one now living in Elora is Mrs. John Gibb, and Robert Gerrie had no family.

The farm which the latter was the first to occupy was that to the north of Elora which was, for several years, until his death a few months ago, the home of Mr. Snell. On the "back line," as the road past this farm was called, one may still see the remains of a corduroy road, which, with many cedar trees growing near, show where the swamp was situated that Mr. Elmslie referred to as "Robbie's Swoggle."

On the same ship as the Gerrie family there was Robert Cromar, his sister Anne, and their father Alexander Cromar; James Young and his wife with their children; their family being Jean, Mrs John Mitchell; Ann; Kirstie, and George. Archibald Cummings, with his wife, Ann Brockie, and some of their family, in which the sons were Alexander; George; Archibald; and James and the daughters, Christina, Mrs. William Brander, and Annie, Mrs. James Harrison.

Besides these, who settled in, or near Bon accord, there were others who settled near Elora. Among them being James Cruikshank and his wife; Alexander Leith Moir, and George Leslie with his wife, Ann Mitchell, and six of their family—Margaret, who was Mrs. Thomas Land; John; Nancy; Ann, Mrs. James Davidson; Mary, now living in Elora, and Jean, who was Mrs. Berwick. Other five born in Nichol were James, who is now living in Elora; Beatrice, who was Mrs. Robert Reid; George, living at Stirton; Alexander, pastor of the Presbyterian Church at Elmwood, and Frank, living on a farm, next to the one his father had, in Nichol.

There was also John Mennie and his wife, Elizabeth Sorrie, who were from the Parish of Insch. In their family there was: John Mennie, the well known Hardware Merchant of Fergus; Alexander, who died recently, having

ELORA

been assessor of Fergus and for many years caretaker of Melville Church; and George, of Bessemer, Michigan. Those born in Nichol were; Peter, who died at Hendricks, Minnesota; James, in Macon, Missouri; William, formerly of Aboyne, now in Fergus; Catharine, Mrs. John Ross, in Portage La Prairie; Mary Ann, Mrs. Menzies Young, now in Fergus; and Maria, Mrs. John Davidson in Fergus.

* * * *

These were followed sometime later by John Brockie with his wife and some of their family. Their sons were: John; William; George; James; Alexander; David; Archibald. The daughters were: Margaret, Mrs. McBain late of Garafraxa, and Catharine.

* * * *

Thomas Gray and his wife, Catharine Gray, from the Parish of New Machar, came to Bon-accord along with Mr. Brockie. Mr. Gray bought his farm before leaving Scotland from Mr. Jameson; this being the next farm north of James Moir's. In Thomas Gray's family there was: William, lived in Nichol, near Alma; Jane, Mrs. John Paterson, in Iowa; Christina; David, in Grand Rapids, Mich.; Barbara, Mrs. Thomas Downing, lived in Bon-accord; James living near Rockwood; George died in Iowa; and Catharine, Mrs. Hugh Reid, living near Holstein.

* * * *

Alexander Fraser and his wife, with one son and two daughters came to Bon-accord in 1837. Their son, George, was one of the party that arrived at Elora on June 10th of the previous year. Their sons were George and William. The daughters were: Jane, Mrs. Thomas Frame; and Mary, Mrs. Alexander Lamont

* * * *

The Rev. James Middleton came about 1838 and settled on Lot 16 on the 12th. Concession on which a small clearing had been made by one, Andrew Gardiner, who had, for a short time, carried the mail between Guelph and Elora. In the Middleton family there was—Catharine, Mrs. John A. Davidson; Dr. William Middleton, for many years a practitioner in Elora; Captain Louis Middleton, a lake captain, whose home was in Kingston; Mary Ann was the late Mrs. Wm. Fields of Salem; James, who continued to live on the old homestead, until a few years ago, when he sold it to his neighbour, Mr. John Keith. After this, he lived retired in Salem for a few years prior to his death, about two years ago; John died at an early age; Christina is Mrs. Charles Keeling, in Cargill; Gavin, is in Carnduff, Manitoba and Jane was Mrs. Wm. H. Fraser.

* * * *

George Pirie with his wife and family came to Bon accord with the Middleton's; Mrs. Middleton and Mrs. Pirie being sisters. A few years after their arrival Mrs. Pirie died and, at the funeral, the neighbours took turn about in carrying the coffin to Fergus, as they had no other suitable means of conveyance. The remains were interred in St. Andrew's Churchyard; this being the third burial there from the young colony; Mr. Melvine being the first and Andrew Dalgarno the second   Mr. Pirie turned his attention to the publishing business. He removed to Guelph, and for a number of years was Editor of the Guelph Herald, a paper that has had sixty years of continued prosperity. In the Pirie family there were—George, who lived in Dundas; William, who will be well remembered by all the older residents of Elora; Catharine; Mary; Gavin; John and Thomas.

William, David, and George Keith, with their sisters Catharine, Ann, and Helen, were younger brothers and sisters of John Keith, and it was at his home they stayed for some time after their arrival. William cleared a farm in the upper part of the township and in later years lived retired near Fergus. He died at the home of his daughter, Mrs. John Simpson, of Shoal Lake, Manitoba. David was a blacksmith in Salem for some years and then was one of the first settlers near the town of Chesley, where some of his family are living. George was a manufacturer in Belleville. Ann was the wife of Hugh Fraser, for many years a shoemaker in Salem; while Helen married Alexander Hamilton and lived near Durham. Catharine was for a time housekeeper for the Rev. Alex. Gardiner of Fergus, and then became the wife of James Walker there. No names in Fergus were more closely associated with its early history, or were more highly esteemed for their large hearted kindness and hospitality than those of Baker Walker and his wife. Their history was the history of Fergus. One of their sons, Mr. William Walker, is a well known resident of Preston.

* * * *

Peter Hay, with his wife, Janet Shand, and their family, were from the Parish of Slains, sixteen miles north from the city of Aberdeen. There Mr. Hay, with the assistance of his father, who was a millwright, built an oatmeal mill, and, after running that for some years, Mr. Cromar, Sr., succeeded him as an oatmeal miller, while Mr. Hay rented an adjoining farm. They were thus close neighbours in Scotland, and, after many changes, became near neighbours in Canada. Having decided to leave Scotland, Mr. Hay, with his family, sailed from Aberdeen in the Spring of the year 1835, on a ship called the 'Amity.' They first lived for some months in the township of Seymour, in Northumberland County, but having heard of the Bon accord settlement from an acquaintance who came to visit them, they left their farm in Seymour and came to Bon accord in the early summer of 1836. The friend who had advised them was Mr. William Tytler, who had come to Canada in the same ship as Mr. Hay and had been in the township of Nichol in 1835, but did not decide to settle there until he had seen different parts of the province. It was while on this prospecting tour that Mr. Tytler visited in Seymour. In Bon accord Mr. Hay was among old friends and acquaintances One of these was Mrs. Melvine, at whose home they remained for a few months, the family employed in clearing and logging, until he could select a farm and build a log house. Mr. Hay wished to be near his friends in Nichol, and he also wanted a farm on the banks of a stream. But all the lots bordering on streams in Bon-accord had been taken up; so Mr. Hay crossed the dividing line between the townships of Nichol and Pilkington and squatted on a farm farther up the stream than that on which Mr. Moir lived—the farm that had up to this time been referred to as 'the back of the world." In doing this Mr. Hay became the first settler in Upper Pilkington, which is that part of the township northwest of the Grand River. We say he squatted on this land, because, at this time, it was not on the market, and he was living here for eight years before the land was surveyed, which was in 1844. When this had been done, and a price fixed, Mr. Hay paid for his farm by yearly instalments, carefully keeping the receipts for money paid; and it was well he did so, for the Canadian Agents of the Pilkington Estate pocketed the money, and did not send it to the owners in England. Mr. Hay never saw the deed of his farm; but his son, Mr. Charles Hay, secured the title from the Estate in England, some time after his father's death. Peter Hay died July 16th, 1854, at the age of 65, and Mrs. Hay on the 7th of November, 1856, at the age of sixty six. In their family were seven sons and one daughter:—William, lived in Pilkington. Ann, who was Mrs. Augustus Howes, lived for many years in Pilkington. She died at the home of a son in

ELORA

Luther, on January 20th, 1902, and was buried in the Elora cemetery. James lived in Pilkington. John lived in Garafraxa for a number of years, then removed to Montana, where he died. George was for many years a resident of Elora, his home being on the corner of Princess and Colborne streets ; he died on October 6th, 1900. Alexander died at the age of eighteen. Charles, who is now living retired in Elora ; and Robert, who lived for many years in Pilkington, and later in Alma. Of these, Charles is now the only surviving member of the family. He continued to reside on his father's farm for upwards of sixty-five years and then sold it to the present occupant, Mr. Marshall Miller. Charles Hay married Sarah Calder and they had three daughters, one of whom is Miss Isabella Hay, residing with her father ; Janet Shand died in childhood ; and Jean, who is Mrs. William Robert Knox, living in Upper Pilkington.

* * * *

When Robert Cromar, with his sister and their aged father arrived in Bon-accord in September 17th, 1836, they, too, stopped for some time at the home of Mrs. Melvine, having been related and acquainted in Scotland. Robert Cromar then followed the example of Mr. Hay by taking the next farm farther up the creek and was thus the second settler in Upper Pilkington. In this way Mr. Hay and Mr. Cromar made their homes as near each other in Canada as they were when they lived near the village of Colliston, in the parish of Slains. Robert Cromar married Elizabeth Day and of their family those now living are : Alexander, who has the next farm south-west of the old home. George, who is the Clerk of the Township, is on his father's farm ; and Henry lives at Beaverton. The daughters are : Mrs. Robert Fisher ; Mrs. George Cumming ; Mrs. E. B Armstrong ; and Mrs. George Renton.

* * * *

The winter of 1836 7 passed without any addition to the settlement. As soon as winter had set in, the ground frozen dry and covered with snow, Indians began to make their appearance. During the first part of the winter they came from the north, a few Indian men coming first for the purpose of arranging stopping places and building wigwams. Then came the others, old and young, and although the total number passing Mr. Hays' farm would be some hundreds they did not all come at one time, but in parties, in which there would be several families. By short daily marches they passed from one camping place to another, their object being, it is said, to pay their annual visit and obtain their yearly supplies at the town of Old Niagara.

Towards the end of the winter they returned in the same way, in small parties ; the trail followed being the same as had been used by their forefathers when, in 1651, they fled before the conquering Iroquois to the shores of the Upper Lakes. This trail was from Hamilton, at the head of Lake Ontario, over to the Grand River, and then up its eastern bank to Elora. Here the river was crossed, and the path led up through the bush to Bon accord, where the trail separated One branch led up the Irvine on the way to Georgian Bay, while the other went up the course of the creek past Fraser's, Barron's, Moir's, Hay's and Cromar's, in a northwesterly direction, leading to the headwaters of the Maitland and Saugeen Rivers, entering Lake Huron.

At many places along the banks of these streams there were Indian camping places, at which wigwams were situated near the trail, like roadside hotels, being used by one family after another. The larger wigwams were oblong, built of poles, shaped like a gable roof, and covered with hemlock or cedar brush. A wigwam like this would often hold from twenty to thirty persons, each family having its own fire, these being placed in a row along the centre of the earthen floor, any smoke the wigwam could not hold escaping through the roof. Other wigwams were circular and smaller, but, like all the first white settlers' log houses, the Indian wigwams were always built near a stream or a spring of water.

One of the favorite Indian camping places in Bon-accord was west of the Irvine River, opposite the creek on Mr. Keith's farm. Other two were also west of the river on Mr. Elmslie's farm ; one being near where the creek enters the Irvine, and a larger wigwam was on that part of his farm which is now near the Grand Trunk Railway Bridge. These, with others on either side of the Irvine River, were used by those Indians who came from the shores of the Georgian Bay. Many other wigwams were found along the banks of the stream which flows through the farms owned by Mr. Hay and Mr. Cromar. On the next farm farther up stream from Mr. Cromar's, the farm which is lot six, concession one, in Pilkington, and which is still well known from the name of a recent owner as the 'Richard Hall' farm, there were several camps. (It is on this farm that two creeks come so close together that several of the early settlers were lost in the bush by mistaking the one for the other.)

Had one been living in Bon-accord towards the latter part of February, 1837, they might have seen the Indians on their homeward journey. They had delayed starting until the lengthening days and warmer sunshine reminded them of approaching spring when the wet, melting snow and swollen streams would prevent them from travelling with snow shoes and moccasins. While on the march several Indian men would lead the way, one following the other in single file, in this way packing a firm track in the snow for those who followed, who did not use snowshoes. The Indian men carried nothing but their gun, which was slung across their back, their hunting knife, and a tomahawk or hatchet.

His squaw was among those following behind, trudging along with all she could carry. On her back was her little pappoose, facing backward. It was wrapped up warmly and tied to a piece of birch-bark which was held in place by buck-skin thongs passing over her shoulders and tied about her waist. By means of a broad strap passing across her forehead she pulled a toboggan, heavily loaded with all their earthly possessions.

Coming along in the rear were the boys and girls who were too young to carry their share of the burden and by those who were too old and feeble. The young men acted as scouts, and on them depended the supply of food for the party.

Very often the first intimation that would be received of a passing band of Indians would be while the settler and his family were comfortably seated near the large, open fire-place. The darkening of the room would cause them to turn their heads towards the light where the wrinkled, wizened face of a squaw would be seen peeping in at the window. Perhaps some eatable dainty caught her eye when she did not hesitate to walk in and ask for it. Such a request was always complied with, not through fear, but from a wish to conciliate and befriend them.

The Indians were always anxious to trade venison or other game, and baskets, for flour or pork. If they could get potatoes, or turnips of which they were very fond, they would immediately place them among the coals and hot ashes in the fire-place and then the whole family would come into the settlers' house and squat upon the floor until the meal was cooked and eaten. Should any of the white man's children show signs of fear at their intrusion the Indians would point their finger and laugh at them. None of the white settlers in this locality ever received any harm from the Indians. As the years went by their number rapidly decreased, although many families, while on hunting or fishing expeditions, continued to revisit the old camping places year after year, often remaining for some weeks at a time. Some of these, from being longer in the vicinity, were on friendly terms with the white settlers, and especially would we mention Chief Wabadik, who camped on Mr. Keith's farm.

Strange though it may seem, the road followed by the early settlers who have been mentioned in these pages was the same trail as that used by the Indians. As a vine grows upon a wall we see first the main branches and a few leaves, followed by many smaller branches and more leaves until every spot exposed to air and sunshine has been covered. In precisely the same manner as the vine upon a wall do human beings take possession of an unoccupied bush country, such as Ontario was before the days of railways. Even the two principal gravelled roads leading to the northward followed the direction of the old Indian trails; the one to Southamption, and the other to Owen's Sound.

The first settler referred to in these pages was Captain Thomas Smith, who settled on the east bank of the Grand River, opposite the Conestogo, in 1806; (See page 7, and top of page 17.)

Following the river road, which is nearly the same as the old Indian trail from Captain Smith's home to Elora, and then up through Bon-accord to the farms taken up by Mr. Hay and Mr. Cromar we have a distance of, about, fifteen miles. For the human vine to grow that distance in this part of Ontario or the progress of settlement to advance fifteen miles, it took thirty years—from 1806 to 1836.

When the Indians had gone, and the snow disappeared in the spring of 1837, the third settler to make a home in Upper Pilkington went up the Creek past Mr. Hay and Mr. Cromar and took possession of an Indian Wigwam on the "Richard Hall" farm. This was John Whiteley and he was joined not long afterwards by his cousin Thomas Whiteley.

One of those peculiar accidents which bring heart breaking grief to the parents and cause the sad circumstances to become indelibly fixed in the memory, occurred on this farm. Mr. Thomas Whiteley was engaged in chopping and his wife came out to watch him at his work, carry her baby in her arms. Seeing that she might help her husband by gathering the underbrush into a heap ready for burning, she placed her baby near the stump of a tree. In falling, the tree which the father chopped rebounded in an unexpected direction and one of the smaller branches struck the child. In this way occurred the first death in Upper Pilkington.

It was in 1841, and some four years had elapsed after John Whiteley came before the next settler arrived. This was William Ewing, who came from near Castle Blaney, in County Monaghan, Ireland. With his sister in-law, Nancy Whitcraft, who kept house for him, and his family of three sons and two daughters he settled on a two hundred acre farm to the south, and adjoining Mr. Hay's; the creek running through the northerly corner of it. Of William Ewing's family his daughter Nancy married William Lockhart and lived in Bon-accord. William and Alexander each got one hundred acres of their father's farm, which their families still own. Mary married Samuel Speers and lived in Salem; and Samuel died when young. Another son died while the family were in quarantine at Grosse Isle, near Quebec. William Ewing, jr., died in January, 1873, at the age of forty-eight, and Alexander in May, 1898 at the age of seventy two.

Another year passed before the next settler came. This was Edward Thomas Day, who was born at Walworth, Surrey, England, on September 6th 1792. Mr. Day had seen many years of service in the British army, in different parts of the world. After seven years spent in India, where he was leader of the band, in the 34th regiment, in the service of the East India Company, he brought his wife and family half way 'round the globe to buy a farm in Canada. The voyage from India to London took six months and they were nine weeks in coming to Toronto, where they remained for a month. It was harvest time in 1842 when Mr. Day arrived in Elora where, for a time, he secured lodgings in Gray's tavern. In a short time he bought a two hundred acre farm, being lots two and three on the eleventh concession in Upper Nichol. The northerly half, which is lot two, is now owned by Mr. William Fairweather and lot three by Mr. Levi Trask. It was on the latter that Mr. Day built his house, as it was nearer to his neighbors, and also because it was beside a stream, which is one of the branches of Carroll's Creek, in Pilkington. For several years this remained the most northerly limit of the settlement. Can we imagine any greater contrast in their surroundings than that experienced by Mr. Day and his family? From the stirring life of a Regimental Band Master to a solitary home in the backwoods of Canada, and from the tropical climate of India to the cold of a Canadian winter! For a few years he was kept busy on his farm, until, with the assistance of his sons, they had some comfort in their home. Then he concluded that farming might be all right but he must have some music mixed with it, so he became the bandmaster of the first Elora band, which was organized in the fall of 1848. He also undertook the leadership of the second band in Guelph which was started about the same time, and later was leader of a band in Berlin and another in Owen Sound. Although the distance from his home to Elora and return was ten miles, and to Guelph and back was thirty-six miles, he always walked to these places to attend every band practice; and at another time he tramped to Dundas and back that he might write down the music of a song that he had been told some one there could sing for him correctly. To his enthusiastic love of music Elora was very much indebted The band under his leadership was something to be proud of and when the Elora Cadets were organized early in 1866 Mr. Day was their band leader; for the membership of fifty included a rattling good fife and drum band of twelve players; the organizer and drill instructor being James Christie who was at that time a merchant in Elora. It made things lively in the village when the Elora Cadets turned out with their wooden guns, their red coats trimmed with blue and white cord across the breast, their neat forage caps, their own band playing lively popular airs, and marching along at the head of them, playing his clarionet, proud of his boys and they of him, was old Mr. Day.

Mr. Day died November 5th, 1868 Mrs. Day, whose maiden name was Mary Ross, was born at Craiglockhart, near Edinburgh, in 1795, and died in 1881. In their family were six sons and two daughters and to show the wanderings of a soldier's life we mention the places where the children were born : Elizabeth, who was Mrs. Robert Cromar, was born at Corfu, an island in the Mediterranean; Edward, born in Chatham, England, and died of cholera in India at the age of fourteen; Thomas, born in Edinburgh lived in the Township of Greenock and then removed to the State of Virginia, where he died; Ebenezer, born in Edinburgh, October 1829, died in July 1903, was a wagon maker, and for about fifty years a resident of Elora; James, born in Edinburgh, is now living in Alma; Benjamin, born in London, is living in Alma; Frederick, born in Hyderabad, India, is in the Township of Keppel; and Mary, born in Bangalore, India, is living in Alma with her brother James.

Mr. Day died November 5th, 1868. Mrs. Day, whose maiden name was Mary Ross, was born at Craiglockhart, near Edinburgh, in 1795, and died in 1881. In their family were six sons and two daughters and to show the wanderings of a soldier's life we mention the places where the children were born : Elizabeth, who was Mrs. Robert Cromar, was born at Corfu, an island in the Mediterranean ; Edward was born in Chatham, England, and died of cholera in India at the age of fourteen ; Thomas, born in Edinburgh, lived in the Township of Greenock and then removed to the State of Virginia, where he died ; Ebenezer, born in Edinburgh, October 1829, died in July 1903, was a wagon-maker, and for about fifty years a resident of Elora ; James, born in Edinburgh, is now living in Alma ; Benjamin, born in London, is living in Alma ; Frederick, born in Hyderabad, India, is in the Township of Keppel ; and Mary, born in Bangalore, India, is living in Alma with her brother James.

* * * *

William Gibbon was born in the city of Aberdeen on the 26th of March, 1826. He was a son of Mr. John Gibbon, and with his parents came to Bon-accord on the 2nd of September, 1835, being then between nine and ten years of age. During the intervening seventy two years Mr. Gibbon has had an intimate knowledge of all that has transpired in Upper Nichol. Seeing an opportunity of buying a farm at three dollars an acre, Mr. Gibbon, in 1844, bought lot five on the eleventh concession of Nichol. This is the next farm farther up stream than that on which John Whiteley settled. In the Fall of 1846 Mr. Gibbon, with his yoke of oxen, hauled the logs which were used in building the first two houses in Alma. These were built by Thomas Whiteley and his brother in law, Samuel Wilson. During the following two winters Mr. Gibbon made a clearing on his farm and built a log house, but his plans were changed a year later by the death of his brother, John It then became necessary that he should go back and help his father on the old home farm, which was situated to the east of Watt's bridge, over the Irvine. In the meantime his farm was rented, but after the lapse of ten years, which included two years spent in the Township of Puslinch, he returned to it, and continued to make it his home for over forty years until he and Mrs. Gibbon retired to live in Elora, in 1898. It was on February 8th, 1854, that William Gibbon married Susanna, eldest daughter of William Reynolds, Esquire, who was mentioned among the early residents of Pilkington, and in their family were : Jane Elmslie, who married Joseph Hall and lived in Peel, she died in 1895 and her husband in 1906 ; William Reynolds, died in 1882 at the age of twenty six ; John Brown is living near Lawson, Saskatchewan ; Francis Henry lives in Manitoba ; George died in infancy ; Mary Eliza married Joseph Powell and is living near New Liskeard ; Susanna Margaret, married Alexander Allan and is living at Stratford ; James Alexander died in August, 1887 ; Owen Henry died in April, 1888 ; Agnes Emily resides with her parents ; Arthur Playford is one of the proprietors of the Woodstock Business College ; and Herbert Addison is now living in Seattle.

* * * *

Having traced the course of settlement as it came up the Grand River, through Woolwich and Lower Pilkington to Elora and Upper Nichol, we must shortly leave this part of the history and give something more about the early progress of Elora.

For ten years after Bon-accord was settled few homeseekers came to Upper Pilkington. When they did, they settled in the upper part of it, because, at that time, before the bridge over the Irvine River in Elora was built, the only road leading to this part of the township was that used by the Bon accord settlers. This was up the "back line" to the "Old Log Church" and then over to "Ewing's

Corner's." From this they either went directly through the bush to their farm, or, if that was farther north they followed the line between Nichol and Pilkington which was then partly cleared as far as Mr. Day's farm. This road was used not only by those who first came to live in Upper Pilkington, but by many of the first settlers in Peel and the other townships farther north, which was then called "The Queen's Bush." This government land was offered for sale at different times after 1844 when Andrew Geddes opened the Crown Lands office in Elora. From this time until about 1872, when the Wellington, Grey and Bruce Railway was opened, Elora was the principal market town for all that northern territory. The older residents living in the towns up north still have many stories to tell about the time when they were teaming on the Elora road, which is the name they gave to the Elora and Saugeen road.

To show how the country to the north was settled it may be mentioned again that the two first houses in Alma were built in the fall of 1846 by Thomas Whiteley and Samuel Wilson, being assisted by Mr. William Gibbon, who is now living in Elora. The first house in Paisley was raised on May 9th, 1851, by Mr. S. T. Rowe. Harriston was started in 1855 by three brothers called Archie, Josh and George Harrison. Archie kept a hotel where the Collison House stands now; Josh had a grist mill and George a saw mill. The first house in Clifford was built in February; 1855, by Frank Brown. He was assisted by Mr. Jacob Huck, who was a resident of Salem, and father of Mr. John Huck in Elora.

William Bent was the name of one of the first settlers who went farther back into the wilds of Upper Pilkington. His house was on Lot three, Concession two, which is the farm now owned by Mr. William Wheeler. His brother Amos Bent lived on the same farm. This William Bent was an Englishman, and by trade a bricklayer. He went to the Township of Minto early in the summer of 1857 and there built a house for himself in which he was assisted by Mr. Andrew Catto who had for two years before that been a foreman for Mr. Wissler in Salem, and was recently living retired in Chesley. The house which they built had this peculiarity, that the logs were placed vertically instead of horizontally, which, being interpreted, means that the logs were set on end. This house, which is said to be still in use and now veneered with brick, was the first house on the land where Palmerston stands.

Many sons of the first settlers in the vicinity of Elora became in their turn the pioneers in those townships northward towards Lake Huron. That, without knowing it, they also followed the old trail which was used by the Indians, when they travelled between Bon-accord and Lake Huron, is well illustrated by the following extract from a Paisley newspaper.

In referring to the death of William Brockie, of the Gore of Greenock, it says:—"He was 79 years and 7 months of age, and was born in the Parish of Belhelvie, Aberdeenshire, Scotland. His father immigrated with the family to Canada in the year 1837 and settled in the Township of Nichol, in what is known as the Bon accord settlement. After helping his father to clear his farm, and seeing a comfortable home established, with good buildings and well stocked with fine cattle, he bethought himself of a home of his own. On the 7th of September, 1854, he, along with two brothers, George and John, his cousin, Louis Lamb, James Mair, George Leask, David Black, James Davie and one or two others who wished to see the country, bade good bye to the old folks at home. "We set out," says one of the two survivors of this little party of pioneers, "for the Valley of the Saugeen, at that time the great northwest of Ontario, whence all looking for land were travelling. Some believed it was the last of the land in Canada upon which white men could live. After an eventful journey of about six days and navigating the Saugeen river on a raft, which took all the attention of the man at the helm, we at last arrived safe at Orchardvale, now Paisley. All the company settled in the Gore of Greenock and went to work full of hope on being lairds of the land they had taken possession of."

* * * *

Looking back upon the pioneers of Bon-accord one thing stands out very prominently, and that is, their sterling character. Descended from a race that had become inured to hardship they made a brave and successful struggle against the many difficulties that surrounded them. They were all intelligent, many of them well educated, and none but felt he was quite capable of forming his own opinion. In their opinions they differed, of course. Mr. Elmslie and his party were tories and still adhered to the old established Church of Scotland. They, therefore, joined St. Andrew's Church, in Fergus. The others, including Mr. Watt's party, were, most of them, seceders, and, therefore, reformers. It was they who built the old Log Church.

It is stated as a curious fact that when the first political contest took place in this district, the candidates being Durand and Webster, there were only nine reform voters in the Towhship of Nichol, which then included Fergus and Elora. Seven of these were in Bon accord, one in Fergus, and one in Lower Nichol. In those days a voter had to have the deed of his farm.

At the time of the Mackenzie rebellion in 1837, a meeting of the Bon accord settlers was held to discuss the situation. The supporters of each party had received notice to march to Toronto and join their respective sides; the tories in support of, and the reformers against the government. The result of their meeting was that they decided not to go to Toronto, or anywhere else, as they were so equally divided in their political opinions that they might as well fight it out at home.

The settlement was not without some excellent amusement which was enjoyed by young and old There was a Library, a Temperance Society organized by the Rev. James Middleton, a Singing School, and the Debating Society. A meeting was held in the Bon accord School House on Wednesday, the 2nd, of October, 1839, Mr. William A. Y. Roy being chairman, and among the resolutions proposed and agreed to were the following.

"That the name of this Society be the Bon accord Mutual Instruction and Debating Society."

"That the object of this Society shall be the discussion of Literary, Scientific and Moral subjects, by essay, lecture or otherwise."

"That no subject of a Theological or political nature, shall be introduced at any of the meetings of this Society."

"That any member coming half an hour late will have to chop firewood for the next meeting."

"That no member, on any pretence whatever, shall mention any of the Society's affairs to any other person but a brother member, under pain of being excluded, and particularly if any member shall reveal any of the speeches or affairs of the Society, with a view to ridicule, or laugh at, any of the rest of the members, he shall be forever excommunicated from the Society."

Under these conditions it would be unfair to "ridicule, or laugh at" any of the proceedings as we read the record of their meetings, and yet they had been laughable. Open meetings or Soirees were occasionally held and the proceeds given to the Bon accord Library. At first the meetings were held every Friday evening in the old School House on Mr. Elmslie's farm, but that was found to be too far away for the majority, some of whom were from Pilkington, so that the place of meeting was changed to the Old Log Church, on Mr. Barron's farm. The subjects discussed were not frivolous, but useful and instructive, and a great benefit to the younger members who had to get books from the Library, or borrow from their friends, that they might read up the subject for discussion. As a result, the community had a reputation for intelligence far above most similar settlements. And reading in the evenings then was by the light from the open fire place. The oil lamps used were of the same shape and not in anyway improved upon those used by the Romans two thousand years before. When sheep became more plentiful, a few years later, the settlers were then able to make tallow candles, which were a great luxury, and at the present time, when we have so many different ways of lighting by means of Electric Power, it is worth recording that the first coal-oil lamp offered for sale in Elora was bought by the late Rev. James Middlemiss, D. D., in 1859 ; the coal-oil, as well as the lamp, being sold by the druggist, Mr. R. C. Newman.

Among those who figured in the Debating Society there was one, who, when he was a young man in Scotland, had been a coachman and general assistant to a Doctor. In this way, by reading the labels on the medicine bottles, he gained quite a knowledge of Latin, which was, like all his other information, turned to the best possible use. When he wished to particularly impress upon the younger men the great advantage derived by one, who, like himself, had a classical education, he would solemnly make quotations such as, "Hydrajorum Muriatus"; that's Latin boys; ye winna ken what that means."

* * * *

A man who forced his way to a leading place in the community was George Barron, Esquire. He was so constituted that he had to be in the lead in everything he undertook. With very little schooling, he had, when quite young, to earn his own living; and when he had saved enough from his earnings at farming and other work to pay his passage, with sufficient set aside to take him back again if he did not like the country, he left Scotland. At first he found employment in older settled parts, where he learned something about Canadian farming, which was a great advantage to him in Bon-accord. He was quite proud of his skill in farming, but much of his success was due to the fact that, after his marriage, he was in easy circumstances and was able to hire assistance when needed, which, together with his own undoubted ability and great physical strength enabled him to keep well ahead with his farm work, where his less fortunate neighbours had to struggle on as best they could and take chances on the weather. In all matters connected with the Church he took a great interest. He was a very successful Sabbath School Superintendent, and many of the older men about Elora, who when they were young were members of his Bible Class, will say that they never heard anyone who could explain the Bible Lesson better. At one time he was a candidate for Parliamentary honors, in the interest of the Reform party, and at an early date he was appointed a magistrate, after which he was often called "Cadi," or "Squire" Barron. Although there was no need for such an official in Bon accord, where, true to its name, all lived agreeably and worked together harmoniously, yet was he called upon to settle some serious matters during the early settlement of Peel. In 1862 Mr. and Mrs. Barron left their farm and retired to live in Elora, where, until prevented by advancing years he continued to act as the presiding magistrate, and few localities, at that time, had his equal. No amount of coercion, or intimidation would prevent him from deciding as he thought right. The dignity of the Law was always quite safe in his hands. After having lived in Elora longer than on their farm, George Barron died on April 6th, 1891, at the age of eighty eight and Mrs. Barron on February, 18th, 1894, at the age of ninety years.

During the later years of Mr. Barron's busy and eventful life we knew him intimately. It was always a pleasure to have him relate stories of his early life, of his trip to America, his early experience in Canada, his arrival in Bon-accord and the events that followed. He never tired telling of his trip to the old country in 1862, during which he visited at Marylebone Road, in London, of the wonderful things he saw there ; not forgetting to mention the wax figures at Madame Tussaud's and the way he was deceived by their life-like appearance. Regularly, every day after dinner, he would come around and take a chair beside the large stove at the back of the grocery store ; a place where many old friends were welcome. First, the Toronto Globe would take up his attention. He would carefully read the leading Editorial, now and again adding some pungent and personal remarks about John A., after which he would fill his pipe and soothe his ruffled feelings with smoke. On a stormy winter afternoon other old friends would soon come in and pull up a chair near the fire. Among them there would be Jamie Gerrie, John Edmonston, Peter Simpson, Sandy Spalding and auld John Webster Then, after answering Jamie Gerrie's question, "Weel, what's new the day ?" the stove would be filled with wood and the storm outdoors forgotten. Previous experience had shown how some general remarks, and a few leading questions, would soon be rewarded with a story, so that the following is only one of many that we have heard Mr. Barrnn tell under such circumstances. It gives a good description of Upper Pilkington, in 1836, before any settler lived in that part of the Township. If it were given a name it might be called—

THE LOST ONE FOUND.

A STORY OF MANY YEARS AGO.

In the year 1836 an incident occurred that threw the new settlement into a state of great alarm, and came nearly precipitating a young and helpless family into mourning. One of those who had arrived from Scotland in June of that year was Andrew Dalgarno and he settled on the southwest end of Mr. Barron's lot, in Bon accord, within a couple of miles of Elora. On a Saturday morning, in the month of August, he left his home, carrying on his arm a scythe for the purpose of cutting some Beaver meadow grass, for winter provender for his cow ; large quantities of this grass being found along the banks of the stream which was known as Moir's Creek. He had taken provisions with him for his dinner and consequently his wife and family did not expect him home until night. It was customary in those days to work from sunrise till dark, but with dark no Andrew came. His poor wife spent a sleepless night thinking about her husband being devoured by wolves, which at that time were very numerous. Indeed it was no uncommon thing to be serenaded by a concert of wolves from about dark until midnight, and this as often as two or three nights a week. On the Sunday morning at daybreak Mrs. Dalgarno went to tell Mr. and Mrs. Barron that her husband was lost in the woods, that she would never see him again—that there was no doubt her Andrew was devoured by the wolves. This dreadful intelligence was speedily circulated through the settlement, and brought together a party of eight persons who, with muskets and horns and in short anything that would make a noise immediately formed themselves into a scouring party. This little expedition started and followed the course of the stream, past Mr. Moirs, and upwards to where it first crosses the townline between the Townships of Nichol and Pilkington. On arriving at that point, without discovering any marks of the missing man, it was thought best to hold a consultation as to how the expedition should proceed. It was finally arranged that two of the party should follow the course of the same stream upward ; that two more should follow the blazed line between the townships of Nichol and Pilkington, as far as the south east boundary of Peel, which is now in Alma, and the remainder of the party, four in number, should take a westerly course. But before separating it was agreed that should any of the parties find traces of the lost one, two shots were to be fired in succession from the same gun.

The expedition having divided into three parties, we now turn our attention to the party proceeding in a westerly direction. It so happened that this party had but one gun, but to make up for the deficiency they had a bugle and a pocket compass. They had not proceeded far when one of their number discovered what appeared to be a large clearing on the left, and various were the conjectures as to what it really was, for it looked like a veritable clearance. Could it be possible that we had neighbors so near and know nothing of them? It could not possibly be, seeing that we lived in a place familiarly known and spoken of as the back of the world! After some consultation it was agreed that we should leave our intended course, turn to the left, and ascertain who dwelt in this newly discovered territory. On arriving at the spot, which had the appearance of a large opening in the bush, it turned out to be a long stretch of beaver meadows, with a considerable stream of water winding its way sometimes down one side, sometimes on the other, and oftener in the centre. It was then agreed that instead of pursuing a westerly course we should follow the newly discovered creek, and, if possible, ascertain where it entered the Grand River.

We had not proceeded far along the banks of this stream until we came to a place where a colony of beavers had been at work, and had cut, or rather gnawed down a number of trees, so as to dam back the creek. Some of the trees cut down by these creatures were about a foot in diameter; and it was most interesting to observe the instinct, the almost human ingenuity and sagacity displayed by them in felling trees, as every tree was laid down in the very spot where it was likely to be most serviceable in damming back the creek. Considerable time was taken up in surveying this place, expecting to see some of the ingenious inhabitants, but none of them made their appearance. Thinking that they might be asleep, we threw several pieces of wood upon their lodge, which appeared to be a mound in the middle of the dam, built of large pieces of wood and mud, and raised about three feet above the surface of the water. We crossed and recrossed several times upon the dam dyke, which was built of trees and large pieces of wood, interwoven, and plastered with mud so as to be nearly water tight. We were all so much interested in this marvellous exhibition of animal intelligence that we had taken no heed of the passing time, until, thinking we had played ourselves long enough, some one of the party suggested that it would be well to proceed in search of Andrew.

We had continued on our way but a short distance when, to our great joy, we discovered, not another colony of beavers, but the print of a human foot, and upon that foot had been a shoe whose sole was full of large iron shoe nails! That shoe must have crossed the sea! And we concluded that it was none other than Andrew's foot which caused the impression. The conclusion, was a rational one, for the foot print was discovered beyond what we considered to be the back of the world, consequently, no human being wearing hob nailed shoes, other than the lost one, could, by any possible chance, be found wandering there. It was now agreed that the signal should be given, so that the other two searching parties might return home. As we had only one musket, it was immediately twice loaded and discharged. We had only gone a short distance down stream when we came upon a spot where a small patch of grass had been cut, evidently with a scythe. We were now quite sure that we were upon the right track, and went on farther down the banks of the stream at quite a pace, sounding the bugle at intervals, hoping that the sound might reach Andrew's ears. It soon became evident that the day was drawing to a close, and that we must either retrace our steps homeward, or make up our minds to spend a night in the bush, for which we were very poorly prepared, having no provisions with us. After some consultation it was decided that we should return to our homes and make such preparations as were necessary for a thorough search on the following day. We therefore turned back and proceeded up stream as far as the beaver dam already alluded to. Here it was thought advisable to cross the creek on the dam dyke, as hitherto we had travelled on the right, or western, bank of the stream. Having done this we thought that by taking a north-easterly course through the bush we would most assuredly strike the blazed line between the Townships of Nichol and Pilkington. It so happened that we were right in our conjecture, for we arrived at the south-west corner of Mr. Moir's farm, lot number ten, Nichol, about sundown. We were there met by the two other searching parties who had returned home on hearing the signal we had given, supposing that we had found Andrew. We were soon after met by our friends who had remained at home, who thought that we had got lost and were unable to find our way out of the bush. To Mrs. Dalgarno our tale, that we had seen her husband's footsteps in the mud, was but poor consolation. A general consultation was held to consider what we should do. It was speedily arranged that, as far as practicable before dark, the whole settlement should be warned out to be ready next day at early dawn. Each one was told to bring rations with him for a three or four day's search, should it be necessary.

Shortly after sunrise, on Monday morning, all the men in Bon-accord who were able to undertake such a journey met at Mr. Barron's home, (which is now owned by Mr. George Wilson). There were fourteen persons in the expedition, all hale and hearty, armed with guns, axes, etc.; each man carried a bag of provisions, for we had found it hungry work. In short, we carried everything we thought would be found necessary during a three or four days sojourn in the wilderness. After the experience of the previous day we found no difficulty in retracing our steps up Moir's creek and then over to the other stream which comes near to it, but flows through Upper Pilkington. On arriving at this stream it was thought advisable, so as to thoroughly explore the country, that the expedition should be divided into two parties, one party to take the right, and the other the left bank of the creek. The day was fine, and nothing worth relating occurred during our downward course, except the occasional shooting of a pheasant, seeing frequently the foot prints in the mud or the marks of the scythe among the grass. It sometimes happened that, owing to what they considered almost impenetrable cedar swamps, the two parties were so far separated that the sound of the bugle was but imperfectly heard. Between five and six o'clock in the afternoon we came to a spot where the land was perfectly dry and covered with hardwood, on either bank of the stream. Here the two parties, who had been so long separated by swamps, met and rested for a short time, the moments being occupied in telling what wonderful things each party had seen, and the obstacles surmounted when separated by these swamps. Some thought it would be best to camp here for the night, while others said they thought they heard the sound of running water. It was finally agreed that we should go on a little farther, and, before we could all get ready to start, voices were heard shouting, "More of these confounded beaver meadows," while, in an instant, another voice cried, "here is a large river." The question now to be decided was, where were we?

This must be the Grand River, but the exact whereabouts none of us could divine. It was known to some in the party, who had travelled over it, that there was a road, or rather a wagon track on the east bank of the river; and it was known, also, that this was the road leading from the Townships of Waterloo and Woolwich to Elora. It was agreed, therefore, that we should cross and proceed in a direction at right angles with the river, and by so doing there was a certainty that we should alight on some part of the road. If we could reach it by dark there was a possibility that we might get to Elora that night, as by this time we had given up all hope of seeing the object of our search in life. After crossing the river, and pursuing the course indicated, we arrived at the Woolwich road about sundown, at a point nearly half way between the Sandy Watson and James Ross farms, although they were not living there then, (Inverhaugh post office is now at the place referred to.) On arriving at this point, the first thing done was to blaze a large maple tree on four sides, and inscribe our names upon it, with the date, and the object of our search. It will be remembered that on setting out from home that morning we took with us provisions, sufficient as we supposed to last us three or four days. But as we have said it was hungry work, and before leaving this spot we had a hearty meal at which we consumed nearly all the victuals we had brought with us, knowing that before we needed another we would be among civilized beings.

On reaching Elora, about dark, we were greeted by the welcome intelligence that the lost one was found. On the morning of that day old King Reeves had heard the sound of what he conceived to be a human voice, coming from the west bank of the river. On proceeding in the direction from which the sound came he crossed the river and ascended the bank, (by the steep pathway at the Cascade,) and now, can you judge of the old gentleman's surprise on being confronted by a powerful man, with a scythe on his arm. A brief explanation of his wandering was now given by the stranger, the place of his abode, &c. &c , when Mr. Reeve kindly assisted him down the precipitous descent, across the river, took him to his house, and Andrew, after partaking of breakfast, started for home as fast as his weary limbs would carry him, no doubt anxious that his wife and family should be sharers of that joy of which he was now possessed.

And now I would introduce you to Andrew himself and give you his own account of how he became lost in the bush on the occasion referred to. As already stated, he left his home with the intention of cutting some grass, and in order to ascertain where it was thickest and best he was anxious to survey the meadow from the lower to the upper end, before he began to cut. As the grass was only to be found at particular spots, the intervening parts, which were covered with thickets of cedar, made travelling by the stream very difficult, so that in following up the course of the stream Andrew had frequently to leave the banks of the creek and proceed on the dry ground. Not knowing that there was another stream of water so near, running in another direction, he unconsciously left the one creek, and wandered on to the other, and it was not until he had gone a considerable distance down the wrong stream that he discovered his mistake. He saw clearly now that he was not upon Moir's Creek, and being doubtful of finding his way back, thought it would be better to keep going down the stream he was on as it would eventually lead to some river and possibly a settlement of human beings. On Saturday all day he was a good deal annoyed in forcing his way through the dense thickets of cedar, but hurried on, as fast as he could When overtaken by night he lay down to rest, but could not sleep, all the time keeping the scythe close by him, as the only defensive weapon he had in case he should be attacked by wild beasts. On the Sunday morning at break of day, he started, scythe in hand, with the intention of travelling towards the sunrising ; but owing to his anxiety of mind he forgot that the sun set as well as rose and kept travelling all day pretty much towards the sun, so that Sunday night found him, as he supposed, not far distant from the spot where he spent the Saturday night. He said he felt drowsy, faint, and hungry, on Sunday all day, having had nothing to eat since Saturday morning but a few cakes intended for his dinner on Saturday. And as he laid down that night he felt completely done and slept in spite of his fears. Through the night he woke up with a start to feel if his scythe was beside him. Then he thought again of his anxious wife and their helpless family, of his old home in Scotland, and at a bound his mind would come back to his present unfortunate position, and then, too tired to think, he slept. At break of day, however, on Monday, he heard indistinctly the most welcome sound that had greeted his ear since he left home, and what do you think it was? The sound of a human voice? The roar of wild beasts? No, surely, but the same sound that awakened Peter of old to a sense of his sin! This was a blessed sound to poor Andrew who forthwith proceeded in the direction from whence the sound came. And from what he told me he could not at this time have been near the stream which our expedition followed but had wandered on to a smaller creek that is nearer to Elora, for, I am told, this one falls almost perpendicularly over the rocks by the river's side forming, no doubt, what I have heard you call the 'Cascade,' whereas the stream which we followed was the larger one of those you see at Middlebrook School House. I believe I have heard it called Carroll's Creek, although for a long time we called it Andrew's Creek; and beside where it enters the Grand River there is a Beaver Meadow, while to one side of that, at the foot of a hill, there was a fine, bubbling spring of water. At any rate, Andrew soon found himself standing on top of the high banks of the Grand River beside where the stream fell over the rocks, but he felt powerless to descend the steep bank and cross the river. Looking down upon the river from the height where he stood he could perceive some timbers near the opposite side, but slightly upstream, and they seemed to have been placed there by human hands, and on looking closer he could see what looked like the foundation of a mill. So, at last, thinking if he could hear the voice of a Rooster where he had been a few minutes before possibly some one might hear his voice. He made the attempt, shouted several times as loudly as he could, and as already stated was heard by good old King Reeves, who acted the part of a good Samaritan.

After a little rest and refreshment Mr. Reeve pointed out to him the road to Elora and a little after noon, on that day, the lost one, now found, was restored to his wife and family.

Poor Andrew was cutting a tree shortly after this adventure when a chip struck him in the eye and blinded him. Not long afterwards he was killed while chopping a tree on Mr. Watt's farm. The tree in falling struck the dead stub of a beach tree, which fell upon him; the loss of his sight on one side preventing him from noticing the danger he was in until too late.

ELORA ❦ Its Early History Continued.

It has already been told how, on the first day of December, 1817, Roswell Matthews became the first settler in Elora. That he and his family lived here for nine years or more, that, having been disappointed in not receiving the deed for the land which was promised them by the owner of the Township, they left their home in Elora and removed to the newly founded City of Guelph, where they assisted at the completion of the first houses there. Their house and barn, and the clearing they had made in Elora was left unsold.

It was also shown how Capt. William Gilkison became the purchaser of this part of the Township of Nichol and it will be remembered that we were permitted to publish a number of letters which Capt. Gilkison wrote to his son, Col. Jasper T. Gilkison, who died at his home in Brantford on Friday, November 16th, 1906, at the age of ninety two and a half years.

In one room of his house he had preserved many valuable documents connected with his own and his father's history, and so carefully were these treasured that even the members of his family did not know of their existence. But after her father's death it then became the duty of his daughter, Miss Augusta Isabella Grant Gilkison, of Brantford, who is now the only surviving member of Jasper Gilkison's family, to examine and arrange these documents. In doing so Miss Gilkison has very kindly placed at our disposal all those relating to Elora. Among many interesting mementos of Captain Gilkison is the diary in which he recorded his doings, his thoughts, his plans, and his comments on what transpired during the months preceding his death, which occurred on April 23rd, 1833. The following brief extracts from this Diary are made, not only for their historic value but because they show the estimable character of the man who gave to Elora its good name It will be noticed that where it has been thought necessary to make the meaning plainer we have added, in parenthesis, a few words in explanation, but otherwise the language is that used by Capt. Gilkison.

On March 1st, 1832, Captain Gilkison left Port Glasgow for New York, sailing on the ship Caledonia and accompanied for forty miles out to sea by his son Robert, who returned by steamer. We find that he arrived at New York on April 6th, was at Niagara on June 2nd, and on the 28th, was at Brantford visiting his brother-in law, William Richardson. Here he buys a larger farm for 500 pounds ($2000) and decides to make it his home. On August 31st, as his diary shows, he is again visiting among his old friends at Niagara, where he learns that the south west half of the Township of Nichol can be bought from the Executors of the late Rev. Robert Addison's Estate for 7 shillings and 6 pence an acre, subject to a discount of $5\frac{1}{2}$ per cent. for cash. He thinks he will buy this land. On September 4th, he has bought it. After this his Diary contains many references to his farm at Brantford, his purchase in Nichol, and his plans for the future City of Elora. We now quote from his Diary:—"Brantford, September 20th, 1832—I have been here since the 11th, and am quite engaged in projecting improvements on my farm of Oak Bank. I have men ploughing those excellent lands for wheat, which I intend to sow this month. I have bot seed wheat from Mrs. Crook's up-land, 50 bushels at a dollar the bushel. I have also bought 94,000 brick, from Silverthorn, and paid him 15 shillings the thousand in cash, in full for them. Friend Richardson has bot for me a pair of 4 year silver gray horses for 225 dollars & they are first rate animals for beauty and strength. He has also furnished me with a waggon, harness & plough, all of them of the best manufacture. The farm is a beautiful piece of land & if well worked will be a good farm to me & mine. I have chosen a spot on the height for my own dwelling house & and the farm buildings will be a little lower down. The situation for Oak Bank house is as pretty as one can imagine. It overlooks Fruit-lands, the village of Brantford with its 350 souls, & the Church of the Mohawk Indians &c., &c. I am exceedingly pleased with all this & am again industriously on the qui vive. October 5th.—Still at Brantford. The view from the heights for 3 miles is beautiful. My house is being repaired. I propose to live in it this winter—it will be tolerably snug.

To morrow, having at last got Burwell, the surveyor, to accompany me, I propose to start for Nichol to see my purchase & have the north end of it surveyed & laid out in 100 acre lots—more or less. At the Falls, which is on my half (of the Township), I purpose to survey a place for a town & to sell to all new comers. Brantford, Friday, October 12th.—Yesterday I returned from Nichol—absent 5½ days. Left Burwell at work surveying the northwest part of my purchase & laying out a village plot at the Falls of the Grand River. I prize my late purchase of this land. I left Mr. McKenna in charge of the works—he is instructed to open a mill race at the Falls & build a log house 42x32 feet—to employ Burlingham as plasterer & have the whole in such a state that I may occupy it, or rather my clerk, in January next. I have given a town lot to Mrs. Peck, but she must build there.

Tuesday, October 16th :—Last night I came here, when at Hamilton I ordered a bedstead & matrass. Saw Thos. Gosforth at St. Catharines, a millwright, introduced to him by Mr. Bowery. He has promised to send a bill of scantling for a saw mill at Elora. Saw Jasper at Hamilton—a nice young man. Saw John Gillieland at St. Catharines who told me that he had no claim upon the Falls farm ; he sold to Green & Baker at James Crooks,—but neither he, or any one, has paid one farthing for the property. (This refers to the farm which Roswell Matthews left). I saw Mrs. Matthews with James Crooks & told her I would give her 300 dollars for the clearing on their farm & she agreed to accept my offer for it. On this farm I have laid out a village & will settle it. Alexander Brown, the agent for the Addison family, had taken possession of this farm & had let it to a person as an agent ; he did right—but if he intends to set up a claim to it I never will sanction his claim. The Addison's paid him 50 pounds a year to act for them, not to take advantage of them.

October 17th —Went to Lewiston by Queenston * * * Mr. Creen, one of the executors for Mr. Addison, on the part of the heirs communicated their wishes for a new bargain with respect to Nichol, which I shall not assent to. They sold their interest in it at 7 shillings and 6 pence an acre & that sum I am preparing to pay them—but nothing more. They must give me the Deed for it in 10 or 12 days when I shall be all ready ; or not—then—my correspondence with Mr. Addison's executors is left with Archy, (his son).

October 19th,—I am going to see Mr. Clark at the (Niagara) Falls about the lands in Nichol.

October 21st.—Yesterday I was at Thomas Clark's at the Falls—he makes many objections to give me a deed of the lands in Nichol. I have seen Mr. Butler. I have given him a letter telling him I would be ready to pay for said lands on the 26th, or 27th inst.

October 25th.—Last night I came to York.

October 30th.—I came from York to Niagara. Brot from York an Order on the Branch Bank here for 2817 pounds 13 shillings being the amount in their hands from sale of my Government Debentures. I intend to pay for lands in Nichol with this & other monies to come from New York.

November 1st.—I have received a letter from New York with receipt for proceeds of my Stock sold &c. amounting to 12,592.85$. The Bank has now above 6,000 pounds in cash of mine. Beautiful weather for last six days.

November 5th.—I fear I shall have much trouble to obtain a deed for lands in Nichol. Mr. Clark throws one obstacle in the way after another.

November 16th.—At York—I have been here 8 days without advancing a step in the deed for my purchase in Nichol: the executors of the late Mr. Addison have promised to obtain a deed from Mr. Clark for me but not a step has been taken as yet; they are losing at the rate of $3\frac{1}{2}$ dollars a day of interest on the purchase money which I am to pay—for said money is in the Bank, 5,200 pounds for their use when the deed is delivered to me.

Saturday 17th November—At York—the weather is & has been delightful for a period of many days; it is the Indian summer. I have made no progress in the deed for the Nichol lands Mr. Clark has not come from Niagara. I have dined with the Governor since I came to Town—he knows all about my purchase of Nichol; he asked me if the purchase had been completed. Dined with Samuel Jarvis. I have called on many families here. Time passes away & I am anxious to return to my farm.

30th November, Friday—I came here this day from Niagara at which place I arrived from York on Monday. On Tuesday went to the Falls where Mrs. Clark barred her dower to the lands of Nichol in presence of Thomas Butler, an authorized agent for doing such a duty. At Queenston I visited my friends there. I left forms of transfer, advertizements, deeds &c., with Archy to have printed—these are for Nichol & the village of Elora in which it is situate. Elora is named after a ruined City near to Bombay—See Encyclopedia.

Mr. Clark signed the deed for Nichol with much reluctance; he had offered for the lands, for which I paid 5,346 pounds in cash, but 3,625 pounds; an obvious reason for his fastidiousness. I paid for Nichol by 2 checks on the Bank.

Mr. Fraser, my clerk, will go to Brantford tomorrow & there wait to assist me in forming books &c., prior to his going to Elora. (In another part of the Diary is this memorandum—"Simon Fraser is my agent at Elora—he is to be paid 400$ a year & find his own board.

Sunday, 2nd December—At Dundas waiting a passage to Brantford. My deeds for Nichol are with Durand for Registry & I have paid him for that duty one pound eighteen shillings and nine pence. Visited Mr. and Mrs. Ewart & dine there this day. James Crooks tells me he has ordered sundry lots to be laid out in Woolwich on opposite side of the road—I dont like this plan—nor will I agree to have a bridge anywhere but within the limits of Elora. In fact I will sell no lots to builders but those some distance within the road between Woolwich and Nichol. (This refers to the road on the south side of the Grand River which separates Pilkington and Elora.)

December 18th,—I have received my deeds for Nichol from Durand— they are registered. The weather is mild like May in England. My goods from Hamilton for house use are in my possession except a few articles which are yet at Hamilton. My Glasgow Trunks have arrived from New York. I have been 2 nights in my own bed after an absence from it of five years—Ye Gods! how I felt—how I still feel on returning to it. I have paid Lewis Burwell for surveying Nichol & laying out the Village of Elora 95 pounds 11 shillings and 4 pence—about 22 pounds 10 shillings of which Mr. Clark is to pay me for running the outer lines of his part of Nichol, as he requested me to have done for him. The whole of the land is excellent & there are several Creeks on it, which have mill seats on them. I have read the Field notes of the survey & the book in my possession gives me great satisfaction. My house in Elora is to be one & a half stories high & 42x32 feet. Fraser goes up tomorrow to see it completed. I have named this farm (at Brantford) Oak Bank. I have caused near 80 acres to be ploughed & have sowed 20 of wheat and 15 of rye—hay is 14 dollars a ton without hauling it—dear. The expense is great on this farm but I will make it an example for imitation if I live another year or two.

LT.-COL. JASPER T. GILKISON

Extensive AUCTION.

The following Stock, &c.

Belonging to the Estate of the Late WM. GILKISON, will be exposed to Sale by Public Auction, on Tuesday, the 15th of March, Inst. at 11 o'Clock, forenoon, at the

Falls of Elora, Township of Nichol,—viz.

1 Black Gelding, 1 Brood Mare, 3 Superior Cows, 1 Pair of Oxen, 1 Pair of young Oxen, 1 Calf, 2 Two-Horse Waggons, 1 Double ditto Sleigh, 1 Single ditto, ditto; 1 Ox Sleigh, 1 pair of Wheels of Cart, 1 Plough, 1 Double Horse Harrow, 1 Ox Harrow, 1 Double Sett of Harness, 1 Single ditto, 1 pair Whipple Trees, Ox Yoke and Bows; Spades, Chains, with a variety of other useful articles.

☞ *Terms*—Three Months Credit under £5. Six Months under £15. and Nine Months for all sums over —with approved *Securities*.

Falls of Elora March 1, 1837.

D. *GILKISON*—Ex.

Printed by G. P. Bull. Gazette Office, Hamilton

19th, Dec.—My old house on the farm has cost me 30 pounds in repairs. It is tolerably snug; I have 2 stoves in it & 3 beds for self & visitors; one servant maid is all the domestic attendance I have, as yet.

Wednesday, 26th December, 1832.—Yesterday my sons Archy & Jasper, with Richardson & his wife & Ann Miller came & dined with me on a day I used to be happy when my late & loved wife presided at my board surrounded by a score of our kith & kin in Glasgow; these scenes are past and gone for ever—the recollection of them alone remains to grieve me.

January 2nd, 1833.—The weather continues mild—the ice is all gone from the river, and my horses are ploughing; such things are in the physical world—I have engaged Johnston Richardson, a youth of 17, as an apprentice to my store at Elora for 3 years—at 20—25 & 30 pounds a year.

January 6th.—Fine weather resembling spring; the Grand River has been very high—it has over-run the road to the Bridge & though this day is Sunday people are repairing the injury.

Sunday, 13th January—This day 30 years ago I was married to my late & loved wife Isabell—and now————

Saturday 18th.—I cant get the goods to Elora—the roads are so bad.

January 30th.—It is now mild & thawing—to-morrow I leave for Elora to endeavor to settle my land matters—plan a Saw-mill—arrange goods in the store—make arrangements for improving the road in Nichol—and do all other matters there which shall seem needful.

February 7th.—Since the 31st, I have been to Elora where I met many settlers but could do nothing; I had not the bonds given to Mr. Clark. I staid in the neighborhood several days; passed through Guelph in going & returning—bot 15 barrels of pork from Shade for Elora at 15$ a barrel to be taken from Galt. My house at Elora will be ready & the shop open about the 15th inst. I have resolved to make a saw-mill though the race will be expensive; as also a Bridge over the Grand River. I have sold some land at 20 shillings an acre & one Town lot for 50$, all on credit.

February 13th.—The other day I contracted for a saw-mill to be set in motion & cut 6000 feet in 24 hours—price 700$. Mr. Lennington is the contractor. To-morrow I propose a jaunt to Niagara &c., to look about me—I am lonesome & solitary, too much so.

Thursday, February 14th.—Dined with James Crooks & slept at Dundas. On the 22nd, being Thursday, I returned to Oak Bank after having been at Fort Erie—the Falls—Queenston—Niagara—Hamilton &c. Visited Mrs. Duff —Wintermute—Kirby—the Hamiltons—McCormick and Mrs. Nichol—no snow.

Sunday, 25th February—Yesterday I presented Mrs Matthews with 75 pounds as a compensation for Lot 1 in Broken front of Nichol; she had no claim on me according to law; but I thought it just to pay her that amount, in presence of her daughter, Caroline.

March 1st.—Nothing particular going on.

Saturday, 2nd March—This morning the thermometer stood 12 degrees below Zero—very cold.

15th March—I returned from Elora 3 days ago—absent about 8 days. Met Messrs Clark & Crooks at that place. Resolved to erect a bridge at the Falls & the saw-mill on the south side of the Grand River. The house will be ready to open goods this week—there is $2\frac{1}{2}$ feet of snow there. I staid at Mr. Lepard's house. Slept at W. Dickson's on my return with Mr. Clark. (Mr. Dickson was the founder of the Town of Galt.) Yesterday I entertained a little party at Dinner. I have several letters to answer—not an idle moment. This farm of Oak Bank will doubtless become the shopping part of Brantford some day.

21st March—For the past few days the weather has been warm and the snow has disappeared; I am going on with various improvements on Oak Bank—clearing, fencing &c., &c.

Sunday, 31st March—A most beautiful day. Indeed the last fortnight has been delightful; yet the frost is still in the ground 3 feet deep in fine soils. Yesterday we burnt a deal of brush on the farm; we have been sowing Timothy seed over the clover which was sowed some weeks ago. My establishment increases as the days lengthen out; I have now 4 men—viz.—an overseer & three laborers; we intend to sow oats & pease &c., next week. The rear of the farm has been greatly beautified by last week's work & when our house—barn—garden &c., shall be completed—next year—this farm will be delightful to look on. We shall fence it in next week with cedar pickets well boarded; 4 feet of these posts will be charred & much pains bestowed in planting and finishing the whole—so that it may last for 30 years; it may be in existence when I shall have rested in peace for many a long year :—but, what signifies years & days—or the life time of a frail human being?"

Here Capt Gilkison closes his diary. When the entries in his diary are closely examined it will be found that there is evidence of some confusion between the dates and the days of the week. For example, if Thursday had been the 14th of February, as it probably was, then the following Thursday could not have been the 22nd, nor Sunday the 25th. In another place he writes "I am dull and stupid," which certainly was not his normal condition and from which we see premonitory symptoms of the approaching end, for he had previously suffered from paralysis. For the last three weeks of his life he was so actively employed that he broke down under the strain and died, as before stated, on the 23rd of April.

And now we turn to Simon Fraser, who was employed by Captain Gilkison as his agent and storekeeper at Elora. Leaving Brantford on Tuesday morning, the 18th of December, he arrived at Elora on Thursday afternoon, as he explains in the following letter written to his employer; and this letter is also interesting because it is the first one written by an Elora business man.

Elora, 23rd December, 1832.

Dear Sir :—I have the honour to inform you that I arrived here safely on Thursday afternoon, being the third day from my leaving Brantford. From the state of the roads I advanced very slowly, the mud being very deep, but when within fifteen miles, or thereabout, from Woolwich, the snow lay to the depth of ten inches on the ground & tho cleaner traveling the road being unbroken rendered it nothing in my favour with regard to dispatch. On my arrival I found the raising of the store had commenced on the Monday previous. Under the disadvantage of snow falling & with the hands that came forward that day 4 rounds of the timber were put up. Wednesday was appointed for the next day but the snow still falling prevented its going forward. Accordingly, with the assistance of Mr. Reeve and others all hands were summoned for Saturday, and the day being fine we got forward so far as to have the beams laid for the upper story, and should the snow which falls at present subside I hope we will have all up and ready for the wrights to morrow, to commence work within. These are already engaged and are assisting us of their free will at the raising. On my part not a moment shall be lost. I expect Mr. Sexton here to morrow with two barrels of whisky, by whom I intend to write Mr. Jasper Gilkison at Hamilton respecting what goods I may require.

I am Sir, yours most respectfully,
SIMON C. FRASER.

And so the winter passed away, the time spent in erecting and completing the first store in the village. This was situated on the east corner of lot number 8 on the south side of Carleton Place, which is that lot on the opposite side of the street from the Armory Hall.

In the month of March, when the snow had disappeared, work was commenced on the mill race. According to the plans made by Lewis Burwell, the surveyor, which Mr. Gilkison decided to carry out, the mill was to be placed on the south side of the river, at the top of the ravine called the Cove. It was intended that the huge water wheel should be placed in this ravine where the bearings would be well supported by the walls of solid rock. To lead the water from the river at the head of the Falls it was necessary that a flume, or mill race should be quarried out of the limestone rock for a distance of nine chains, and to a depth in different places of four, ten, thirteen and seventeen feet. As to the width of the mill race Capt. Gilkison wrote "The mill race must be so constructed that it will contain sufficient water to turn a grist, & as many other mills as possible. Do not allow this point to be neglected—understand the mill race man explicitly on this point of abundance of water—& dig accordingly." There was to be no dam across the river. In view of such difficulties it is not surprising then that Simon Fraser should write "Should it be your desire to carry the race into effect I should wish to have 1000 tin tubes for blasting, as we are much troubled with water entering in between the seams of the rock."

Plans were also being prepared for the erection of a bridge across the river. The Islet Rock, in the centre of the Falls was to form the pier of this bridge and in one of his letters, Simon Fraser, according to instructions received, gives a sketch and the dimensions of the proposed bridge. In his reply Capt. Gilkison wrote "I fear for the island if the Bridge shall be over 12 feet in width. Take care that the bridge builders do not, by any means, destroy the effect of the little island ; it is a great beauty in my eye. An artist may come to take a sketch of the Falls of Elora, & the village, and if he does go up, be sure to point out the most interesting spot, or spots, where he can see them to advantage. Mr. McKenna has good taste in matters of this kind—ask his advice. Give the painter a couch &c., with you. Tell the artist to hoist a British flag upon the little island. I am glad to hear things go on as well as you can reasonably expect ; many people will come to the city by & by."

But the sudden death of Captain Gilkison changed all those plans. The saw mill which was to be placed on the south side of the river at the top of the cove was built on the north side of the river at the Falls and the bridge, instead of crossing the river at the Falls was erected at the foot of what is now Metcalfe Street, as already explained on page 59. The store was soon afterwards closed and Simon Fraser went away, but where he came from or where he went to we do not know. It is said that at the time he was in Elora he was an active young man, a widower, with one young daughter, Lily Fraser, who was kindly cared for by friends in Pilkington during her father's residence in Elora. Having no home in which to keep it he left an oil painting of his daughter with Mrs. Swan in Pilkington, because she, like himself, spoke the gaelic ; but he never returned to claim his daughter's portrait. Long afterwards it was reported that Lily Fraser was married and living near Kincardine.

The name of the first store-keeper in Elora recalls that of Simon Fraser who, in 1806 7, explored the Fraser river in British Columbia. Whether, as their names were similar they were in any way related, we have not the means of knowing.

And now it comes that, to better understand much that follows, it is necessary to relate the following circumstances : Shortly after his father's death David Gilkison, the eldest son, who was then about thirty years of age, and who had for some time been employed by James Crooks, of Flamboro, as a storekeeper, came to Elora to look after the business of his father's estate. A year and a half afterwards he decided to build a log house for himself, the raising of which in the fall of 1834 was described by Mr. Elmslie. During his many journeys up and down the river road between Brantford and Elora he soon became acquainted with the Davidson and Geddes families, who made their homes in Winterbourne in 1834. (See pages 10 and 11).

This led to the marriage on June 10th, 1835, of David Gilkison and Margaret Geddes, who then came to live in Elora in the house that had been prepared for them, which stood on the east corner of High and Walnut streets; and it was near that fine brick residence which was built in 1896 by Mr. James Archibald. Here they lived for two years, during which the Bon-accord and other settlers bought land from him and it may be seen by what they have written how much David Gilkison was respected by them.

Elora had received its first set-back. There was nothing doing; there was much that might have been done but there was no money to do it with, for that was invested in land. Therefore, David Gilkison decided to leave the place. The farm stock and implements which had been sent to Elora by his father were sold by auction on the 15th, of March, 1837; that being the first auction sale in Elora. In David Gilkison's family there were a son and two daughters, William, Margaret, and Frances. After their father's death in Toronto, in 1861, these came back to Elora and lived with their grandfather, Andrew Geddes, in the house their father had built. Here Margaret became the wife of the Rev. C. E. Thomson who was pastor of St. John's Church from 1857 to 1877, and Frances first married John J. Marten of Elora and for her second husband A. H. Abbott, principal of the "Little Blue School" for boys at Farmington, Maine.

* * * *

The oldest house now in Elora is that one on the west corner of High and Woolwich Streets, which was long known as the James Chambers' house. The first to use this building as a store was John Craig, who was one of that party which arrived in Elora on Sept. 2nd, 1835. He used it as a house and a store until the summer of 1837, when he sold out the business to Joseph Tytler and went to Ohio. During the time that Craig had it letters were left there for the convenience of his customers but when Joseph Tytler took over the business it became more like a Post Office, for a slot was then cut in the door so that the mail carrier from Guelph, passing through Elora on his way to Fergus could drop in letters without awakening the postmaster. That door with the slot in it was removed from the building some two years ago because the owner thought it was out of date, being now seventy-five years old, but we bought the old door to save it from destruction and some day it may find an honored place in that long promised, Government owned, Post Office.

The first blacksmith came to Elora in 1833, for, in one of Simon Fraser's letters dated March the 18th, he says "I have engaged a blacksmith at 6 York shillings (75 cents) per day and his board; he has commenced this day to chop wood for his coal" The name is not given, but we have been told it was Campbell, and that there was a daughter born here who was named Elora Campbell. However, he did not remain long and the next blacksmith was Michael Cox, who, after a year or two, went to Winterbourne. From his blacksmith shop and residence being there the village, as well as the stream, was long known as Cox's Creek. He afterwards settled in Arthur township. One of his daughters who was well known in Elora was Mrs. Charles Lawrence. Another blacksmith who came to Canada in 1828 was Josiah Johnston and after living in Lower Pilkington for about eight years he left his farm and came into Elora, where he built a blacksmith shop and house on the south corner of

High and Woolwich Streets. Unlike the others who preceded him he and his wife spent their lives in Elora, where many of their descendants are living. James Gerrie built a log house and shoe shop on the east corner of High and Woolwich Streets, shortly after his arrival in September 1836. He, too, spent his life in Elora and died in December, 1894. A teamster employed by David Gilkison, whose name was John Ferguson, put up a house west of Johnston's, and John Gordon, who was one of the party which arrived in Elora in October 1834, built a house east of James Gerrie's, but in a short time he went to Winterbourne. Still farther east on the face of the hill to the north of the residence now owned by Mr. McQueen—where Mr. Andrich used to live—there lived an American by the name of Peck. He had made a clearing on the Guelph and Elora road which he sold to Joseph Carder in December 1833 and then moved into Elora in time to make the second clearing there; Matthews having made the first; and both men were Americans Peck was one of those restless pioneers who could not be content unless beyond all trace of civilization and he left Elora just when it was becoming settled. Before starting off on his journey he told Joseph Tytler, the storekeeper and postmaster, and George Hay who was present at the time, the route he was to travel. He was going around by the great lakes to Chicago, across to the Mississippi, down it to the Missouri, and then so many hundred miles up the Missouri. To attempt such a journey in those days shows the courage and energy of that type of men who in America have led the way into the wilderness; while around the home he left in Elora, Peck's clearing, and the good raspberries that grew upon it were all he was remembered by.

* * * *

Another, who has been mentioned before, was Henry Wilbee, who came into Elora from Pilkington in 1833. After putting up the first temporary log house on the north side of the river he built a good log house on the west corner of Victoria and Woolwich Streets, which was his home during all the years he lived in Elora.

The solitary log house on the north side of the river in Elora, which had been built by Henry Wilbee and used during the winter of 1834 5 by Mr. Keith, was, for the winter of 1836-7, occupied by James Cruikshank and his wife and their child Barbara. It was on an afternoon in the spring of 1837 that Mrs. Cruikshank, with her baby in her arms, crossed the bridge to visit a neighbour who was sick; no other than Mrs. John Mason, long familiarly known as Mammy Mason, who, with her husband was living for the winter in a part of the Gilkison house on top of the hill. Shortly after Mrs. Cruikshank crossed the bridge she was followed by William Martin, one of the first Elora boys, who had been over on the north side of the river looking for their cow; his father Martin Martin then keeping the only tavern in the village. Having climbed the hill and turned to the right to enter his father's house his dog became greatly excited and barked loudly Turning quickly to see what was wrong that the dog should raise such a disturbance he saw the bridge which he had just crossed swept away by the high, spring freshet. He was safe and at home, but what about Mrs. Cruikshank? By the way she had come, from her home the distance night be three hundred yards, but to return to it now that the bridge was gone was to tramp through the bush to Fergus, cross the river there and come back on the north side, a distance of not less than six miles. This she did, and carried her baby all the way, wading through melting snow and mud; and as if to make her misery more complete she worried all the way because she had left a batch of bread baking by the fire place at home.

Shortly after this Mr. and Mrs. Mason removed to the farm they had bought on the Fergus road, north of the river, which was lot 19 on the 13th, concession. Before going on to his farm Mr. Mason had bought a valuable yoke of oxen at the auction sale already referred to, which was held on March 15th, 1837. Evidently the oxen had not liked their new quarters for as soon as they were at liberty they went straight through the bush for more than a mile toward their former home. They commenced to ford the river at what is now the foot of Geddes street, but as the water was much higher than when they crossed before they were swept over the Falls and killed or drowned, perhaps both.

A day was set and all the men for miles around were called to assist at the raising of a new bridge. Captain Forster was there, from Lower Nichol. Being an experienced salt water sailor, and having and knowing how to use block and tackle he bossed the job. This bridge, like the first one, was very much like a corduroy road raised on posts high above the water, for it was covered with logs laid side by side, the drive way being only wide enough for a wagon.

In the year 1841 Adam Gatherer and his wife, with their son in law Joseph Laird, arrived in the village. They came from Scotland with the intention of settling in Elora, to be near friends already here, and they built a house near James Gerrie's. On their arrival in Montreal they met with Thomas Land and his wife, and three sons, Ephraim, Thomas and Henry, who were travelling westward with the intention of living at Brantford; but the friendship then formed with Mr. Laird caused the Land family to come with them to Elora instead. Mr. Land built a house and shop on the north corner of Victoria and Woolwich Streets, where he and his sons worked; the father being a weaver and his three sons shoemakers.

Of this family, Ephraim Land was best known in Elora because he lived here for fifty-nine years. He was born at Columpton, in Devonshire, England, in 1814. In 1831 he emigrated, with his parents, to Prince Edward Island where they remained ten years and then came to Elora. He died August 9th, 1900, and Mrs. Land on March 30th, 1908, she having been a resident of Elora for seventy two years.

It should be mentioned that, in 1837, George Gray took the place of Martin Martin, who, heartily sick of the hotel business went on to a farm in lower Pilkington. And then, one other should be added to the list of those who lived in Elora before 1842, and that was John Hainan, who, because he did his own thinking and could calculate eclipses was said to be eccentric.

For the nine years, from 1833 to 1842, Elora was at a stand-still. According to the assessment roll for 1842 the property owners in Elora were George Gray, Adam Gatherer, Thomas Land, Henry Wilbee, Josiah Johnston and James Gerrie. Besides these, who were residents, there were the heirs of the Gilkison estate who were assessed for 33 acres of cultivated land; and Alexander Watt and James Ross, who, under the name of Ross & Co., were assessed for 15 acres, besides the saw-mill. The assessable property in the village amounted to 226 pounds, or 904 dollars; the items being:

```
3 horses, assessed at......   £8— £24
4 oxen         "         ......   4—  16
6 cows         "         ......   3—  18
1 saw-mill     "         ......      —100
1 hewn log house ........            — 20
48 acres of cultivated land..   1—  48
                                    ————
                                    £226
```

The owner of the house "built of squared or hewed logs" was Thomas Land. All the other house-holders got off free because their houses, although fully as large and as comfortable as his, were built of logs in the rough. We may laugh at such methods of assessment, but what improvement can we show to day after the lapse of two thirds of a century? For now, as then, those who try to improve and beautify their property are fined by the community that is benefitted thereby, while others, who apparently care nothing about the appearance of their home, but enjoy the same privileges from the corporation, escape with lower taxes.

It will be noticed that in Elora at this time even the assessor could not find a store. The saw-mill was so conspicuous that the assessor was in duty bound to mark that down, although it was not then in working order. The only bright prospect was the interest taken in the village by Alexander Watt and James Ross, or Ross & Co., as the firm was called. Early in the year 1842 they purchased from the Gilkison estate the water-power at the Falls and the land on the north side of the river up as far as the present Town Hall. Then, having done this, they found a man to join with them who made the village grow. This was Charles Allan.

* * * *

Charles Allan was born in the parish of Lethendy, Perthshire, Scotland, in February 1801. After having learned the trade of carpenter at Lethendy from David Steven, father of the late George Steven of Guelph, Mr. Allan carried on the business of a builder in the village of Coupar-Grange, in the adjoining parish of Bendochy.

It was on the 6th of August 1833 that he left his native land to make his home in Canada. On his arrival in Toronto he met with William Lyon Mackenzie, who came from the same part of Scotland. Mr. Mackenzie had also been acquainted with the family of Andrew Burns who was employed by Mr. Allan in Scotland and emigrated with him to this country. Mr. Mackenzie found shelter for both their families in a house of his own, and got them to fit up a hall for his political meetings. (A Mr. McLagan who afterwards befriended William Lyon Mackenzie also learned to be a carpenter with Mr. Steven in Lethendy, but he did not live in Elora).

It had been Mr. Allan's intention to settle on the Canada Company's lands, and he had all his luggage addressed to Goderich, before he left Scotland; but soon after arriving in Toronto he went to Niagara to call on one for whom he had built a house in Scotland, the Hon. Adam Fergusson, who was then staying there. The result of this visit was that he contracted with Mr. Fergusson to erect a dwelling house and stabling on the farm of Woodhill, in the vicinity of Waterdown, which Mr. Fergusson had recently purchased. Mr. Allan spent the summer and fall of 1833 at Woodhill, carrying out his contract there, and was led by Mr. Fergusson to change his intention of proceeding to the Huron Territory and to make choice of the Township of Nichol as his final destination. He purchased from Fergusson and Webster a lot in their then recently laid out Village of Fergus, and two hundred acres of farming land in the vicinity. Having built a log house in the village of Fergus he moved up his family in the spring of 1834.

On settling down Mr. Allan engaged in his former business as a builder and many of the first buildings in Fergus were erected under his superintendence. One of his first contracts was building the first St. Andrew's Church in Fergus, a rough cast frame building which was opened on August 23rd, 1835. When the Owen Sound Road was opened to the northward he, in company with Messrs. Perry and Garvin, entered into a contract with the Government to build a dam and saw mill in the village of Arthur.

It was early in the year 1842 that the first contested election in the township of Nichol was held. The object was to elect a representative to the District Council, and the competing candidates were James Webster and Charles Allan. Politically Mr. Webster was the conservative and Mr. Allan the reform candidate; but although we could give a list of the voters and the side on which the votes were cast that would be no indication, in this case, of the political leaning of the voters; and for this reason. Mr. Webster, as the merchant and miller in Fergus, had been a very good friend to the first settlers and to those in Bon accord especially. When, in January 1836, the Fergus mill was burned with wheat belonging to the settlers the efforts which Mr. Webster made at that time to help them tide over their loss gave him a prior claim on their votes. The result was that Mr. Webster was elected by a majority of three; he having received eighty two votes and Mr. Allan seventy-nine. This election was held in St. Andrew's Church in Fergus, but it was never used as a polling booth again. Each of the candidates ascended the stairs to the pulpit and thanked the electors for the very liberal support given them.

Immediately after this election Mr. Allan entered into partnership with Alex. Watt and James Ross and came to live in Elora. Some changes in the firm took place later when Arthur Ross, David Henderson and others became interested.

Under Mr. Allan's management a new dam was built in the summer of 1842 and the greater part of it is still there to show that the work was well done. A bridge was built for the first time on the site of the present Victoria Bridge. The object was, not only "to bring grist to their own mill," but customers to their store. They had opened a store, temporarily, in the David Gilkison house until they could build a new store at the north west end of the bridge. This was a story and a half building on the same corner as the later one for so many years occupied by Mrs. Sinclair.

In April 1843 work was commenced on a large frame flour mill and a new saw-mill; the machinery being supplied by Gartshore, of Dundas. Among the carpenters who worked at it were William Reid, David Henderson, David Foote, Andrew Burns and John Keith. On the south side of the river a carding mill was built. This first woollen mill was a frame building and the business was carried on by Peter Paterson.

The log house which Mr. Allan built for himself is still standing on the face of the hill north from the bridge. It has, ever since it was built in 1843, been the home of the Allan family, and it is now the oldest house on the north side of the river in Elora; although the "James Chambers' house," on the south side of the river, is ten years older.

The company had much to discourage them at the commencement of their business in Elora, for the country was in a very depressed state and produce was almost unsaleable; oats, for instance, only bringing ten cents a bushel, and that not in cash. As soon as the flour and woollen mills were in operation Elora began to be one of the most go-ahead backwoods villages. Under Mr. Allan's liberal management business was attracted to Elora from a large district of the surrounding country.

About 1850 the company's store business was sold to Messrs. James and Robert Philip, and two or three years later the mills were sold to Mr. McNaughton, of Galt. Mr. Allan then engaged in land speculations along with Mr. Mathieson of Hamilton and afterwards with Mr. James Geddes, son of Andrew Geddes, of Elora.

Although unsuccessful in his first election contest Mr. Allan afterwards defeated his opponent, Mr. Webster of Fergus, and was elected a member of the District Council. On the organization of the Township of Pilkington Mr.

ANDREW GEDDES
Crown Lands Agent

CHARLES ALLAN

Allan become its first Reeve and was for two years Warden of the County. In December 1857 he was elected a member of the Provincial Parliament—again defeating Mr. Webster. He was unseated on very trivial grounds, but had on difficulty in securing his return a second time; the way in which he had been treated by the Election Committee putting more energy into the efforts of his friends and gaining for him the sympathy of some of his opponents.

But he was not long spared to enjoy his parliamentary honors, for he died suddenly at Hamilton on Thursday, January 13th, 1859. He had left Elora a few days before, in apparently good health and spirits, to proceed to Hamilton to close some business connected with a piece of property which he owned on top of the "mountain." After completing this business satisfactorily he left, apparently quite well, to take the afternoon train for Toronto, intending to return home from there. When at Hamilton station he felt a pain in the region of his heart, and called a cab that he might return to his hotel. But on the way he felt so uncomfortable that he asked the cab-driver to let him out at the home of his friend Mr. Mathieson, which he did, and a quarter of an hour after entering the house he breathed his last.

Great was the consternation in Elora when Geordie Forbes, the first telegraph operator in the village told every one he met that he had received a telegram for the Rev. James Middlemiss, pastor of Chalmers Church, of which Mr. Allan was a member, announcing Mr. Allan's death. But a short time before, farmers for miles around had formed a procession which went from Elora to celebrate at The Old Log School House, in Fergus, his election to parliament; and now, on Tuesday the 18th of January, a still greater number met in Elora to follow his remains to their last resting place, only a few yards from the scene of his late victory, for he lies buried near St. Andrew's Church, in Fergus. Mrs. Allan died October 13th, 1880, in her eighty second year.

Three brothers and a sister of Charles Allan came to reside in, or near Elora. These were James, George, David and Henrietta.

In the family of Charles Allan, senior, there were Charles, who was born in Scotland December 1st, 1828 and died in Elora on May 30th, 1905; Adam Fergusson who was the first child born in Fergus and named after its founder; Henrietta, Mrs. (Doctor) Middleton; James; Jemima; Grace, Mrs. (Doctor) Walmsley, of Elmira; and David, who died young.

Those of the second generation now living are Charles, a well known resident of Elora; David, who is Lieut Colonel of the 30th. Regiment; Miss Jemima, who resides with her mother in the old family home in Elora, and Martin, a druggist, of Salt Lake City.

* * * *

With regard to the commencement of the Methodist Church in Elora Mr. Joseph Carder wrote "From 1836 to 1843 we were nearly as badly off for religious meetings as we were for schools. In the winter of 1835, a Wesleyan minister, Mr. Poole, preached in the evening, once a fortnight, at Mr. Peck's. The Colonial Missionary Society sent out the Rev. Mr. Wastell, a Congregationalist, to Guelph, who, once a fortnight, preached at James Gerrie's in the afternoon and at Mr. Middleton's, in Bon accord, in the evening. So soon as the Rev. gentleman left Guelph these meetings were discontinued. On Messrs. Ross, Allan & Co., purchasing the Falls the Rev. Ezra Adams, who was stationed on the Guelph Mission, took up an appointment in Elora, at Rowley Wood's, in a log house opposite where the school was afterwards built. He was succeeded by the Rev. Stephen Brownall. As Ross, Allan & Co., had the use of the David Gilkison house they gave Mr Brownall the use of the large room, which used to be crowded with hearers. Some time after this the Company opened a store and the large room was occupied for that purpose.

This compelled the Wesleyans to look out for new quarters. Our village blacksmith, Josiah Johnston, immediately fitted up his log stable tor preaching in, and it answered very well, as it was summer time. I think the Rev. Mr. Barrie preached several times in this place. Before the winter commenced our noble old log school house was ready for occupation, which afforded us comfortable quarters." "As the congregation in the school house became crowded, a subscription was started for the purpose of collecting funds wherewith to erect a new Wesleyan Church. The members were few in number and not being able to put up a frame building they concluded to put up a log one, 30x36. The logs were cut and hauled by a "bee," to which 34 ox-teams turned out the first day, and 14 the second. The Rev. Stephen Brownall made us a present of the lot, and when the church was finished it was very comfortable."

This first Methodist Church was built on the east corner of Victoria and Woolwich streets. It is still standing, in good repair, and it makes a very comfortable dwelling.

The corner stone of the present brick church on the north side of the river, was laid on July 10th, 1862 and the church was opened on March 1st, 1863.

* * * *

The old log school house was built during the summer of 1842 on lot 6 on the south side of Woolwich street. It was used as a school and general meeting house for many years, but now, like the old Methodist Church, it is used as a dwelling house.

* * * *

Andrew Geddes was born in Banffshire, Scotland, on June 2nd, 1782. When he was a young man he was sent to Denmark as a clerk employed by an Aberdeen shipping firm. He was in Copenhagen when, on April 2nd, 1801, Lord Nelson, with the British Fleet forced his way into the harbour and destroyed 28 Danish ships, and he used to tell of hearing the cannon balls crashing through the buildings 'round him. The office he was employed in was destroyed and he returned to Aberdeen aboard a British war ship ; the "Pompey," one of Nelson's fleet. After this Mr. Geddes was employed by the large mercantile house of Farquharson & Co., in Aberdeen. In 1812 he was appointed Manager of the Aberdeen Lime Company and held that position for twenty-one years. He then, with his family, came to Canada, reached Quebec in September 1834, and, along with Mr. James Davidson and his family, with whom he was acquainted in Aberdeen, he settled in Winterbourne. (See pages 10 & 11). It was while his home was in Winterbourne that David Gilkison became his son in law, which afterwards caused Mr. Geddes to take an interest in Elora. For a short time in 1839 Mr. Geddes was in Elora but there was nothing that he could do. He then removed to Hamilton and lived there until 1844 when, through the influence of Sir Allan MacNab and Lord Metcalfe, Mr. Geddes was appointed Crown Land Agent for the United Counties of Waterloo, Wellington and Grey. On the separation of the counties Mr. Geddes retained the agency for the County of Wellington. But the reason why Mr. Geddes made his home in Elora and established the agency for Crown Lands here was that he was also the agent for the Gilkison estate. In the twenty-one years that he was a resident of Elora he was well known and respected by all. In him every new settler found a ready and reliable adviser. No one could be more punctual or methodical in attending to business. His early training had given him such exact business habits that they had become like second nature to him. While he was living in Elora in 1839 Mr. Geddes joined very heartily with David Gilkison and Squire Reynolds in organizing the congregation of St. John's Church and through their efforts the first church building was opened for public worship in August, 1842. (See page 30)

Of the Gilkison and Geddes families a friend who knew them well writes "They had much to do with the early times in Elora. They brought from Scotland not only means, but education and talents of a very high order ; and although they have now passed into oblivion they have left a mark of refinement in every place they lived in. Churches and church music would have been poorer without them ; Hamilton, Brantford, Elora, Mount Forest and Meaford have benefitted by them, and many of the early clergy of the English Church have accepted their hospitality."

Andrew Geddes died on March 7th, 1865, at the age of eighty two years and nine months and Mrs. Geddes died November 12th, 1850, at the age of sixty-eight. Their remains were recently transferred from the burying ground of St. John's Church to the Elora Cemetery.

The two principal streets in Elora to-day are named "Geddes" and "Metcalfe" streets ; the first one after Andrew Geddes and the other in honor of Lord Metcalfe to whom Mr. Geddes was indebted for his appointment as Crown Land Agent.

The welfare of Elora was always with Mr. Geddes an object of intense interest. Every proposal calculated to secure the prosperity of the village had, in him, a warm and earnest advocate. But his experience was like that of many others since and is best described in the following extract from a letter which he wrote to Jasper T. Gilkison in November, 1855. "Since I came to Elora I did not think that I could do enough for it. My constant and untiring study has been to lay out and improve every spot and part in and about the village and connected therewith—far beyond my slender means—until I rendered myself a poor man."

In Andrew Geddes' family there were—James. who was a lawyer in Elora. About 1860 he removed to Mt. Forest, and later to Meaford where he died in 1883 at the age of 74 ; John was a sea captain ; Andrew died in Hamilton ; Margaret was first Mrs. David Gilkison, and after his death, by a second marriage, was Mrs. Derry. Another sister, May, was Mrs. Staunton, who died at Simcoe in 1883 ; and Miss Anne Geddes, who, after her father's death lived at Meaford, and Toronto, where she died at the home of her nephew, the Rev. C. E. Thomson, in 1891.

* * * *

In the year 1845 there were twenty five dwelling houses on the south side of the river in Elora. Among the names of residents not mentioned before were those of—Thomas Chambers ; George Blaney,—Maston ; Morris Jones, a waggon-maker ;—Jardine, a storekeeper ; John Black ; Thomas Craig ; Francis Headley ; Rowley Wood ; Joseph Kerr ; James Ritchie ; David Henderson and Ned Hatcher. On the north side of the river there were five householders—Charles Allan ; his brother James Allan, who was a blacksmith and farrier ; William Reid, a carpenter ; Alexander Jack, a miller ; and James Skinner.

* * * *

In the three years, from the spring of 1842 to 1845, the enterprise of Charles Allan and his partners had given Elora a good start, but no sooner was their business established than a formidable rival appeared in Sem Wissler, the founder of Salem, a village not more than a mile distant from Elora.

Sem Wissler was born in Clay Township, Lancaster County, Pennsylvania on the 21st of March, 1819. He was the youngest in the family of Jacob Wissler and his wife Anna Eby ; and a descendant of a Jacob Wissler and his wife who emigrated from Switzerland and settled in Pennsylvania in the year 1720. Sem Wissler's father, Jacob Wissler, was one of the many Germans from Pennsylvania, who, during the first few years of the 19th Century bought land in Waterloo County, Ontario. Between 1802 and 1805 Jacob Wissler bought over 7000 acres in the Township of Waterloo, but although many years later he sent several of his family to Canada, he remained in Pennsylvania, where he lived all his life on the same farm. With the exception of two farms, he gradually sold all the land he had bought in Canada at a handsome profit. In 1834 the father gave the two farms, which he had reserved, to his son John who had learned the business of a tanner. John Wissler came to Waterloo township in 1834 and on the west bank of the Grand River, about two miles north from the village of Bridgeport he built a tannery long known as Eagle Tannery, and subsequently built a large brick dwelling for himself and a number of homes for his workmen. Here he carried on a large and profitable business, having, besides Eagle Tannery, a store, saddler shops, shoe shop, and farm. In 1837 his brother Levi came from Pennyslvania and entered into partnership with him, remaining four years. On the 24th of August 1839 Sem Wissler came to Eagle Tannery and worked for his brothers until 1841. His father was anxious that he should return home and take the homestead but he preferred to remain in Canada. On the 4th of May, 1841, he received $2,650 from his father and bought the interest of his brother Levi in the business at Eagle Tannery. Levi then returned to Pennsylvania and received the old homestead from his father. In 1845 a sister, Mary, and her husband Levi Erb, came to Canada and Mr. Erb, being a currier by trade, was at once taken into the firm.

In 1841, Jane Robertson, a Scotch lassie of fourteen years of age, came to Eagle Tannery to nurse John Wissler's children, and being clever and pretty, with fair hair and rosy cheeks she at once became a great favorite with John Wissler and his wife. Jane Robertson was a daughter of John Robertson and his wife Janet Harvey and was born on October 15th, 1826, at Largie, in the parish of Insch, Aberdeenshire, Scotland. About 1830 her father died, leaving her mother and three children. In the spring of 1837 her mother married James Sims and they all sailed for Canada. The following winter was spent at the home of her aunt, Mrs. Arthur Walker, on their farm, lot 12, on the 16th concession of Upper Nichol, which is on the Owen Sound Road, north of Fergus. In the spring of 1838 they moved to Galt and in the fall of that year Mr. Sims took up a farm near Hawkesville. After this Jane Robertson lived partly at home, sometimes with Mrs. Arthur Walker and sometimes with the Rev. Alex. Gardiner, minister of St. Andrew's Church in Fergus, who had been appointed her guardian by the Court, in Scotland. But in 1841 the Rev. Alex. Gardiner died and Jane Robertson went to Eagle Tannery to nurse John Wissler's children.

The reader may ask, what has all this to do with Salem? And yet it will be seen that had there been no Jane Robertson, if she had not had her aunt to visit, and if her aunt, Mrs. Arthur Walker, had not lived north of Fergus, the chances are that there would have been no Salem.

Sem Wissler and Jane Robertson were married on the 6th of August, 1843 and after that when Mrs. Wissler visited her aunt, Mrs. Arthur Walker, she was accompanied by her husband. On his different trips through Bon accord Sem Wissler saw several opportunities for developing the water power on the Irvine River and with that keen eye for business which always distinguished him he saw that in the south west end of Mr. Keith's farm with its water power and timber, money could be made. For in the neighborhood of Eagle tannery tan bark was becoming scarce and the firm was beginning to look for a suitable place in which to start a new tannery.

On the 28th of October 1844 Sem Wissler brought his brother John to look over the situation. Evidently John Wissler was favorably impressed with

SEM WISSLER

SALEM IN NOVEMBER, 1856
From an Oil Painting by Thomas Connon

RESIDENCE OF SEM WISSLER

SALEM IN 1870

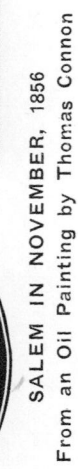

WISSLER'S MILL AT SALEM

what he saw for that same day he wrote offering to buy lot number 16 and the west half of lot 17, on the 11th concession of Upper Nichol for $700.

In his reply Jasper T. Gilkison wrote on the 31st of October: "I am not very anxious to dispose of these lots of land, but as I understand it is your intention to improve them and erect a tannery, and as I am desirous of promoting the prosperity of the township I will therefore sell you 100 acres in lot 16, and 58 acres in lot 17, for 25 shillings ($5.00) per acre; 100 pounds to be paid down and the remainder, 97 pounds 10 shillings, in two equal payments at 12 and 18 months,"—which offer was accepted.

Sem Wissler then completed an arrangement he had made with Mr. Keith (see page 86) and exchanged on terms that were mutually advantageous, the north east half of lot 16 for the south west half of lot 15, and on this the principal part of Salem now stands. He then hired Robert Barkwell and James Longman to clear part of the land, which was then a dense and unbroken forest, and to erect a log shanty with a hemlock bark roof for himself and family.

On a bright summer morning, the 9th of June, 1845, Sem Wissler with his wife and child, now Mr. J. R. Wissler, who was then nine months old, moved to the Township of Nichol and took up their residence in the log shanty prepared for them, and Mr. Wissler called his place Salem. For sixteen months they lived in this log house which was situated on the same site as he afterwards built his stone residence, and which is now owned by his son, Henry Wissler. For a cellar Mrs. Wissler used that small cave in the limestone rock which is a little east of the smaller bridge now crossing the Irvine.

During the first season he built the dam, the flume, the saw-mill, and part of the tannery. In 1846 the tannery, which was a building 40 feet by 120 feet with basement of stone and upper storey and attic of frame, was completed, part of this large building was fitted up for a dwelling, part was used as a store another part for a shoe shop, and the rest for a tannery; and in the mechanical construction of his buildings, water-wheels and other machinery, his principal adviser and assistant was John Keith, from whom he had purchased the land and waterpower.

From the very commencement there was a great trade done in Salem. The tannery and saw mill were worked to their utmost capacity, the general store did a large business, and in the shoe shop from fifteen to twenty shoemakers were constantly employed.

Mr. Wissler had great business ability; he successfully managed his large business with little apparent effort, and as is the case with all strong characters he made no fuss about it, but did it quietly.

Such was the beginning of Salem.

The first blacksmith shop was built by David Robinson. It was on Lot 8, on the east side of James St., near the upper dam on the Irvine river, where, at that time, before a bridge had been built, the road crossed the river. Near the blacksmith's shop, on lot 6, on the east side of James St., John Pearson erected a tavern which was the stopping place for many a tired traveller as he journeyed northward to make his home in the woods. Among other early residents were James Mutch, Gottlieb Brindley, Hugh Fraser, Charles Keeling, Christian Goldner, Florence Smith, Michael Murray, and William Tamlin. It was Mr. Tamlin who built the first brewery, which was situated on lot 5, on the west side of Union St., a position selected owing to the abundance of spring water. This first brewery was burned in August, 1865 and rebuilt by Conrad Dorbecker, who afterwards sold it and built the present one which is west of the river.

In 1848 Mr. Wissler, although a non-resident, was elected by the residents of the Township of Peel as their representative in the District Council, or County Council as it is now called, and on October 8th, 1849, he secured the passage of a By Law for the purpose of opening the present road between Elora and Salem. Early settlers spoke of that, and the opening of a roadway northward from McCrea's Corners, or Alma as it has been called since November 1855, as the two greatest improvements in those early days. By this means all the traffic caused by the rapid settlement of Peel and the other townships northward was diverted from the older Bon-accord road and brought through Salem, making it a very busy place and attracting many workmen to the village. In 1853 Levi Erb, who was Mr. Wissler's brother in law, and a business partner in the firm of Wissler & Erb, came to Salem and built the stone flour mill which is now owned by Messrs. Copeland & Ziegler. This was a great benefit to the village and gave it a fresh start.

When John Wissler, Sem Wissler and Levi Erb had finished their annual stock-taking at Eagle Tannery in 1855 and found they had done so well, John Wissler told the others to go home and build a comfortable residence for each of them, which they did.

It was in 1856 that Mr. Wissler built the large stone flour, oatmeal and pot barley mill farther down the Irvine river from Erb's mill.

In 1857 the period mentioned in their partnership having expired, each member of the firm then pursued his own course. John Wissler sold Eagle Tannery and went to Columbia Furnace, Virginia ; Levi Erb retained his mill and residence in Salem until 1866 when he sold them and with his family also removed to Virginia, and Sem Wissler retained the saw-mill, tannery, shoe shop, store, farm and other property in Salem.

After the dissolution of partnership Sem Wissler continued to prosper greatly and money seemed to roll in. As his business increased Salem grew to be a thriving village, with a large number of happy and industrious citizens. Every year saw great progress made. Roads were improved, bridges built and not a stone was left unturned by Mr. Wissler to provide for the continued prosperity of Salem. It was carefully and thoroughly founded. The one object of his life was to build up a lasting village—not one of mushroom growth ; and all who look to day upon the substantial character of the buildings must agree in awarding to his memory the praise he so honestly and perseveringly endeavored to deserve.

But man is the sport of destiny. Twenty years had almost passed after Mr. Wissler's arrival in Salem when, at about five o'clock on the morning of the 18th of May, 1865 he was just rising from his bed when he fell back and died immediately. Prior to this there had been no apparent symptoms of any organic weakness. He was buried in a vault erected in the Elora Cemetery, the land for which had been sold by him to the corporation of the village of Elora the year before.

Mr. Wissler's death was a great calamity to Salem from which it has never recovered. He died intestate, leaving all his children minors, so that his estate could not be wound up or sold, except at great expense, until the youngest child should attain his majority. In Canada at that time all legal matters were costly and cumbersome and there was no legal provision for dealing simply and economically with such a case. It was found, for example, that to convey to the purchaser a village lot which Mr. Wissler had sold shortly before his death for $25.00, the legal expenses would amount to $400.00. Under these conditions the property of the estate could be used, but not sold, even although it was quite evident that conditions affecting the different industries were changing rapidly. As the surrounding country became cleared, tanbark could not be obtained for the tannery and without the tannery no leather was available for the shoemakers. As the land was cleared saw-logs could not be had in sufficient quantities to make the saw mill pay. With their farms cleared farmers found it to their advantage to go into the feeding of live stock which gradually cut off the supply of grain for the mill ; while the changes which at that period occurred in the milling business itself made it necessary to refit the mill with new and expensive machinery. This included a powerful steam boiler and engine, for, owing to the deforestation of the land and the drainage necessary for cultivation the rainfall was reduced, and the water in the Irvine river, which before that had continued throughout the year in a fairly steady stream then came in periodic floods And as if these uncontrollable difficulties were not sufficient in themselves, the Wellington, Grey & Bruce Railway was built northward from Guelph to Elora and instead of continuing in the same direction in the shortest and most natural way through Salem to Alma, the bonus hunting promoters carried it around by Fergus fully five miles out of its way. The expense of teaming grain and flour to and from the Elora station was too great a handicap and the milling business ceased to pay.

After Mr. Wissler's death the business was carried on by his eldest son, John R., for a few years until his second son, Ezra, became of age, after which it was conducted by the two brothers under the name of J. & E. Wissler until the first day of January, 1887, when the estate was wound up and divided among the different members of the family. These were—John R. Wissler, who is Clerk of the Township of Nichol, has been closely associated with Municipal affairs in that Township since 1867 and was one time Warden of the County. He is also a director of the Nichol Mutual Fire Insurance Company and several other companies and is now living retired. Ezra, at the time of his father's death was attending a Business College in Poughkeepsie, New York, and after graduating there he returned to assist in managing his father's estate and always kept the books and the store and post-office. Mrs. C. H. Biggar, who is living in Toronto ; Mrs. G. W. Field, in Salem ; Levi Erb Wissler, who owns his father's farm in Salem ; Henry Wissler, a Barrister, practising law in Elora, who resides in the old family home in Salem ; and Sem Wissler, who is a Fire and Life Insurance Agent in Elora and lives in Salem in the house built by Levi Erb. Mrs. Wissler Sr. continued to live in her home in Salem where she had seen so many and great changes until her death on June 3rd, 1907 in her eighty-first year.

* * * *

By this time there was much need of a bridge over the deep Irvine river ravine at Elora. For several years after the upper part of the township of Pilkington was surveyed, in 1844, the only means of access to this part of the township for any sort of a conveyance was by fording the Grand river several miles down stream from Elora, by fording the Irvine at Salem, or by crossing at Watt's bridge and following the old Bon-accord road to Ewing's corners. After Mr. Wissler had been conducting his business in Salem for two years a bridge over the Irvine at Elora became a necessity. Such being the case two young carpenters were found who undertook to put a substantial bridge over the Irvine for four hundred dollars. These were David Foote and John Cattanach.

* * * *

David Foote was born at Millhaugh farm, in the parish of Kettins, Forfarshire, Scotland, on the 27th, of June, 1823. He was educated in the parish school of Kettins, and having a retentive memory and good natural ability became a scholar of more than ordinary attainments. His teacher was James Gibb, who was one of that type of parish schoolmasters who did so much to make Scotchmen famous in all parts of the world. James Gibb was teacher in Kettins for a period of forty-eight years, from 1825 to 1873, and his whole effort was to teach his pupils anything and everything that might be useful to them in later years. One of his former pupils, on returning to visit Scotland after many years residence in Canada, told how he found that, on the whitened walls of the old school room this grand old teacher had neatly painted the names of all who had attended his school. No wonder, then, that a teacher who thought so much of his scholars should have been so kindly remembered by them.

Leaving school at the age of twelve or thirteen years David Foote engaged as Clerk to his uncle, John Foote, who was then factor on the estate of Neil Malcolm, of Poltalloch, in Argyleshire, and he often referred to this as one of the brightest spots in his early life. He retained a vivid recollection of the grand scenery of the locality, and a keen remembrance of the warm hearted Highlanders, whose kindness he then experienced and never forgot. On leaving his uncle's employment he was placed in a lawyer's office in Coupar Angus, a village about three miles from his home, but he did not care for the intricacies of law and always looked back upon this two years of his life as misspent. Returning to his home he again attended school for a short time, and after that commenced a three years apprenticeship with David Steele, a millwright, at Fowlis, near Dundee. But after having served two years at this trade his father unfortunately lost a large part of his estate by going security for another. He learned by bitter experience, as countless others have done, that "He that is surety for a stranger shall smart for it." Having decided that in their reduced circumstances they would have a better chance in Canada. David gave up his position at Fowlis and along with his uncle John, the Factor, came to Canada; his father, step mother and the rest of the family coming out in the following year. Arriving in this country in 1842 David Foote speedily found employment upon the Rideau Canal, where Alexander Mackenzie, afterwards Premier of the Dominion, was then engaged as a stonemason. In the spring of 1843 his uncle rented a farm on the Owen Sound road near Fergus and his nephew then joined him. Shortly after he arrived at his uncle's David Foote learned that a mill was being built at Elora, so he at once found employment at the building of it and afterwards assisted Mr. Gartshore to instal the machinery. After this was completed he helped Andrew Burns to do the carpenter work of the first Melville Church in Fergus.

It was in the fall of 1847 that David Foote and John Cattanach took the contract of building the first Irvine bridge at Elora. One, and perhaps the best mechanic in the settlement, wrote out an estimate, intending to tender for the job of building the bridge, but took a little time to think it over before committing himself. During the night he could not sleep for thinking of it. He had carefully figured on the work of preparing the material for the bridge, but how would he put it to its place after the material was all ready? In the morning he burned his estimate, and because he had a large family of young children and could not afford to run such risks of losing, decided to have nothing to do with it. But that was not the way with the contractors. During the winter of 1847—8 they commenced operations by searching for a number of tall rock elm trees. These were felled, hewn square and drawn to the bank of the river ready to be put in place. Then they had to face the problem which had been foreseen by the other, and older mechanic. How could the first heavy timbers be put across the ravine which is here about 105 feet in width, or 120 feet between supports of bridge, and 70 feet in depth? For a time the contractors were at a loss to know how they should proceed, but a sailor helped them out of their difficulty. Jamie Gairns was at that time working as a baker in the village. He had been a sailor, and at his suggestion the contractors found several others who had some experience as sailors who could assist him. Jamie Gairns was let over the steep bank with a rope and in the face of the rock he cut notches. Into these the ends of long timbers were placed which were to form braces for the support of the main timbers, the outer ends being temporarily held in position by guy ropes. Pulleys, with ropes,

DAVID FOOTE

ALEXANDER SPALDING
Wonderful Violin Player of Scottish Dance Music

Born at Kettine, Forfarshire, Scotland, September 13th, 1820; came to Canada in 1854; to Elora in 1855; died October 5th, 1889.

were attached to the tops of high trees growing close to the ravine, one of the long timbers was moved forward endwise over the chasm as far as possible without overbalancing, and the back end was weighted down to keep it from upsetting. These operations were repeated at each of the four corners of the bridge, there then being the ends of four long timbers projecting over the river, but not meeting in the centre. Having succeeded so far, another heavy timber was slid lengthways along the top of those already in place on either side of the bridge, in this way bridging over the space between the projecting ends. When these were bolted to their places the main portion of the first cantilever bridge in America was completed ; and a good bridge it was, for it lasted fifteen years without any expense for repairs and was only replaced when the timbers were considered unsafe.

When they had paid those who worked for them and had settled their board bill at William Smith's tavern, which before him had been kept by George Gray and Martin Martin, the two partners found that out of their four hundred dollars they only had twenty dollars between them in return for all their difficult and dangerous work. In those days an event of such public importance as the opening of Irvine bridge could not be allowed to pass without some fitting celebration to commemorate it, so they negotiated with their landlord, Mr. Smith, who for and in consideration of the twenty dollars by him received did that night provide for all their friends a ball and dinner that was long remembered in Elora.

After the ball, the day after, and that was in October 1848, David Foote did some serious thinking. He had succeeded in completing a very difficult engineering feat, had done a lot of hard work but had nothing for it, and he was no nearer having a home of his own. Perhaps there was also another reason why such thoughts should have suggested themselves at that time, for, on the previous day two young ladies had arrived in Elora from Martintown, Glengarry, to join their brothers Roderick and Alexander Smart who were already here. As it turned out David Foote married one of these, Barbara Smart, in April 1849 ; her sister married John Cattanach, and still another sister, who came to Elora a couple of years later, became the wife of James Allan jr. But the result of David Foote's meditation on the day after the ball was that he at once went to Fergus to take counsel with his uncle, who advised him to purchase the farm on the Fergus road adjoining Elora, which was afterwards his home, and is now occupied by his son. This he did, but he did not move on to it until 1852 ; having by that time built a log house and made extensive clearings on it. In connection with his farming operations it may be said that he was one of the pioneers of turnip culture in this locality and did much to demonstrate the productive qualities of that main stay of the Wellingstock raiser.

In 1848 Mr. Foote assisted in the erection of the old Elora Hotel at the south east end of Victoria bridge, which was put up by his landlord William Smith, father of the late T. P. Smith and his sister Mrs. Charlie Allan sr., who is now living in Elora. In 1849 Mr. Foote put up the frame work of the first Knox Church building, to which the congregation removed from Bon-accord, and in 1852 he built the old Gilkison bridge which crossed the Grand river near Mr. Bissell's foundry. Besides other minor contracts he built, in 1855, the frame work of the first Chalmers Church, and strange to say, after both Knox and Chalmers Church buildings had served their purpose for 24 and 21 years respectively, Mr. Foote bought the old buildings and turned the material to other uses. In 1858 he went into a losing venture when he developed the water power and built an oatmeal mill at Aboyne, between Elora and Fergus. Mr. Foote was elected as a councillor in the township of Pilkington, when Elora formed part of it, and upon the incorporation of Elora in 1858, was made one of its first councillors and selected by the Council as its first reeve. In the following year he was appointed Assessor, and acted in that capacity until he was again elected reeve of Elora, which position he filled from 1881 to 1888 inclusive. In 1869 he was appointed one of the County High School trustees in Elora, and continued in office until the time of his death.

For forty-eight years, David Foote was closely identified with Elora, and in whatever capacity he acted he invariably attempted to do his duty, and convinced, even those opposed to him from time to time, that he was honest in intent. It could not be said that he was proficient in the refinements of, so called, aristocratic society; he called a spade a spade, and, if necessary, with suitable emphasis. He was well read, abounded in folk lore, and knew the inner history of every Scottish regiment; and if anything pleased him more than to talk with his old schoolmate, John Small, the Crimean Veteran, about his life as a British soldier; it was to listen to another schoolmate, Alexander Spalding, playing on his violin, as only he could play, the old Scotch songs, strathspeys and reels. David Foote died on the 10th of October, 1891, and Mrs. Foote in July 1880. Of their family of two sons and six daughters all are living excepting James, who was drowned in the Columbia river in 1885. In the family are Mrs. Sharpe, Elora; Miss Annie Foote, teacher, Calgary; Mrs. Henry Wissler, Salem; Mrs. J. D. Maitland, Nichol; Miss Bella Foote, in Elora; Miss Mary Foote, teacher, Toronto; and David, living on the old home farm adjoining Elora.

* * * *

While the Irvine Bridge was being built, Mr. Allan and his partners purchased about forty acres of land, west of Geddes St., and between Colborne St., and the Grand river. This plot of ground was surveyed into village lots, and these were sold by auction in the Fall of 1848. Besides the liquid refreshments which were usually provided on such occasions, a brass band, from the village of Bridgeport, was engaged to furnish music. It was owing to this visit that, as soon as the Auction Sale was over, a Brass Band was organized in Elora, under the leadership of Edward Thomas Day, a retired Military Bandmaster, who had settled in Upper Nichol. Among the members of this first Elora Band were :—Edward Thomas Day; Charles Lawrence; Thomas Vickers; David Foote; John Cattanach; Robert Wallace; John MacDonald; Alexander Smart; George Hamilton; Thomas Day, jr.; Alexander Laird; James Mutch; George Forbes; John Dillon; Allan MacDonald; and also Caesar Coxhead and two brothers named Mitchell from the Township of Pilkington.

These were neatly dressed in bright uniforms, having red jackets with brass buttons, black pants and black peak caps.

In a year or two this musical association was so popular and proficient that they went on an extended tour and gave very successful band concerts at Guelph, Galt, Hamilton and Bridgeport; the vocalists on these occasions being James Moir, from Bon-accord; Henry Wilbee, of Elora, and Thomas Fisher, from Peel.

* * * *

On the village lots which were sold at the Auction Sale in 1848, houses were soon erected. One of the first of these, on lot 2, on the east side of Princess St., was built for Miss Grant, who taught a private school in it for several years, so that it was called the Academy. Miss Grant became the wife of the late Hugh Roberts, who came to Elora in 1842, and a few years later, as soon as the land was surveyed, settled on a farm west of the river in the Township of Pilkington.

ELORA

This academy was not the first one in Elora, however. Two brothers and two sisters by the name of North occupied a frame building on lot 6, on the south side of Woolwich Street. The brothers kept a store, and the sisters a private school that was spoken of as Quaker North's Academy. This school was patronised by young ladies and gentlemen from all over the province, one of Toronto's merchant princes, Mr. W. R. Brock, having attended that school when a boy.

From another source we learn that in the North family there were three brothers, one of whom was married, but that there were no sisters. They came from, and returned to, Rockwood, Ontario, where it is quite possible that they were associated in some way with the founding of the, long noted, Rockwood Academy.

* * * *

So many came to live in Elora during the few years following 1848 that it would be impossible to give an account of each family ; and it would be needless, too, for of the many who for a few years made Elora their home, no descendants are now living here. We will, therefore, briefly mention a few of those who played a more or less prominent part in the community.

One of these, who came in 1848, was Dr. John Finlayson ; a gruff, but kind hearted old doctor from Glengarry County, Ontario. It was he who employed Mr. Keith in that year, to build the residence in which he lived for about thirty years, and which is now owned and occupied by Mr. William Snyder. His only daughter married W. H. L. de Lapenotiere, a public land surveyor, who some years after the doctor's appointment as postmaster, became his assistant and successor.

* * * *

Andrew Gordon was born at Elgin, in Morayshire, Scotland, on the 10th of October, 1821. After learning the trade of harness making he bought out a business in the town of Ballater, in Aberdeenshire. There he married Mary Skieff, who was born in Ballater on May 24th, 1820. In the spring of 1848 Mr. and Mrs Gordon, with their eldest son sailed for Canada in the ship Berbice ; and on the same ship were Peter Laing and his wife—old Mrs. Laing, who was caretaker of the Elora Public School for so many years. Another vessel, the Lord Metcalfe, arrived at Quebec at the same time and on board of it were the Forbes family, who preceded them to Elora and were life-long neighbours of the Gordons. For some months Mr. and Mrs. Gordon remained with relatives who came out with them and bought a farm near Ancaster. They then moved into Dundas, where Mr. Gordon found employment ; and there he met Mr. Mathieson, a wholesale merchant in Hamilton, who was interested with Charles Allan in his land speculations. Through the influence of Mr. Mathieson, who pictured the future of Elora in growing terms, Mr. Gordon decided to come here. It was in the spring of 1849 that Mr. Gordon loaded his household goods, which were not very numerous, on to a wagon owned by Mr. George Bye. Perched up on top of the load, Mr. Gordon held the little boy, John, while Mrs. Gordon took great care of her baby girl, Maggie, and in this way, although often Mrs. Gordon felt it was safer, and walked, they completed their journey, over very rough roads, to Elora. They found shelter for some months in part of a house owned by the Forbes family, on the village lot adjoining their own. The rain often streamed through the roof, but they were young and hopeful then and made light of their difficulties. As Mrs. Gordon would say "The happiest time that ever I had was when all my bairns were young."

When Mr. Gordon looked about him he found, that so far as his trade of harness making was concerned, very few farmers, as yet, owned any horses ;

and many of those who did were not going to buy any harness as long as they could make shift to do without by using pieces of rope, or old chains, with sometimes horse collars made of wood.

On the corner of Geddes and Colborne Streets, which is now known as "The Business Corner," and occupied by Carswell Bros., Departmental Store, a Mr. Sutherland had opened a small grocery shop. Mr. Gordon purchased his stock of goods and on the next lot north east of this on Colborne Street he got David Foote to put up a small building, part of which was used as a store and part for their house, to which he added more as it was needed. This small business was the first in the upper, or northern part of the village and was carried on for several years until the growing demand for harness was sufficiently remunerative. By the year 1865 his business had so increased that he built the "peak" portion of that brick "flat-iron" building on the corner of Geddes and Metcalfe streets. The larger part of this brick block was built by Mr. Robert Dalby, for an hotel, and was long known as "The Dalby House" but is now called "The Iroquois." For thirty years before Mr. Gordon built on this corner, all the land between him and Irvine Bridge, and eastward past Connon's corner had remained a common. This part of the village had been chopped clear of trees in the year 1835, by John Marriot and Sam Darby, and it was logged and burnt over in the following year. It was, therefore, a most suitable place on which to hold a cattle market, when, in April 1852 Lord Elgin, who was then Governor of Canada, saw fit to graciously permit a fair or market to be held in Elora on the first Thursday of April and September in each year. This continued until 1859 when it was decided by the village Council to hold a fair on the first Tuesday of every month, on this common, around and about the site of the present Town Hall. This monthly fair had grown to be an important event in the business of the village, for it was patronized by all the farmers to the northward. Slowly, but surely, the business of the village was growing towards this fair ground At first all the business places in the village were on top of the hill on the south side of the river; later on the business was principally along Mill street, where it was supposed to be established. But there is nothing constant but change. Great efforts were made by property owners interested, to keep the business of the village on the south side of the river, and along Mill street. The Village Council for the year 1865 not only built the Armory Hall on the south side of the river against the expressed wish of the large majority of the ratepayers, and caused a stone with the image of a bantam rooster to be placed over the door way as an emblem of defiance. Clothed in a brief authority, which was taken from them a few week's later, they in November 1865, passed a celebrated By-Law (number 63), by which they tried to compel farmers and others not to offer any live stock for sale in any part of the village except on the ground adjoining the Armory Hall, or the Drill Shed as it was then called; and three hundred copies of this by-law were printed and distributed among the farmers.

On the morning of the following Fair Day, which was Tuesday, Dec. 5th, 1865, a fine, clear cold day, with no snow on the ground, Andrew Gordon was up bright and early as usual and was out taking his morning constitutional around the northern part of the village. He, evidently, had a presentiment that something was going to happen. The first farmer to come in with a cow for sale that morning was Mr. Nesbit, from Bon-accord. He asked Mr. Gordon where the fair was going to be held. The reply was "Right here; here is the first beast right here." "Well, Mr. Gordon, would you mind watching her until I go and get some breakfast?" "Why no, certainly not," (he was always willing to oblige a friend.) But Mr. Gordon soon found that the cow was hungry too, and was also inclined to wander away in search of its breakfast, so he then had a happy inspiration. He remembered that over at his home, which was not a

ANDREW GORDON

Yours truly
Charles Clarke

hundred yards away, he had a barrell of salt and he was not long in procuring a handful, which he sprinkled on the grass. This had the desired effect and the cow was quite content to stay where the salt was. But by this time more cattle had come upon the ground and, having once tasted the salt, did not want to leave it. Then, seeing that a handfull of salt would keep so many cattle where he wanted them, Mr. Gordon procured more and spread it around liberally.

With regard to this celebrated Fair Day, the "Elora Observer" said, "From an early hour crowds began to roll in from the surrounding country, and cattle dropped in at first by ones and twos, and by droves as the day advanced. A few of the first comers were in a state of glorious uncertainty as to the whereabouts of the Fair Ground, and as some of them were from the extreme back country they were not well posted in our local doings. They were met at the entrance to the village Fair Ground by sundry officials, big with the importance of their position, who ordered them, in stentorian tones, to go to "the other side of Jordan." They found it "a hard road to travel," but not knowing any better, some of the more timid ones submitted to the powers that be, and went. But it was amusing to notice how naturally the old sellers, who have made our fairs what they are, turned upon the old sod, and with what an air of determination they sold, openly and undisguisedly, regardless of the constable and his oft repeated threats. One lady, who deserves special notice for her pluck, gallantly led her cow by a rope upon the forbidden ground with an air of triumph, and loudly expressed her wish that she had a vote at the next municipal election in Elora, saying, "If I had, wouldn't I send these Councillors to the "right about?" The sales were numerous, the prices good and large droves left the village. We haven't made our usual note of them, for obvious reasons, although we have a long list which sundry dignitaries would probably like to read."

It may be seen from the foregoing, how the arbitrary action of the reeve and his Council, in 1865, aroused a spirit of opposition between the two sections of the village, which, before that, had not existed, and the effects of their misguided action are quite evident to-day. The business portion of the village has been completely changed; the Town Hall now stands on the ground where the grass was salted, and no business stand in Elora to day is more central than Andrew Gordon's old harness shop, which is at present occupied by Mr. W. Arthur, the barber. Perhaps these changes would have come about anyway, but one of those seemingly trifling incidents, which sometimes produce great results, was the sprinkling of Andrew Gordon's handful of salt.

Mr. Gordon was a tall, strong, well built man, full of restless energy, fearless and impulsive. As an example of these latter qualities, the following incident may be related.

The first bridge over the Irvine river ravine was so constructed that the ends of square timbers, which were laid crossways to support the joists and planking, projected for several feet beyond the railing of the bridge. These timbers were about four feet apart, or so far that a jump was required to step from one to the other. On a Sunday afternoon, while out for a walk with two companions, the question arose as to whether the ravine could be crossed by stepping on the projecting timbers. No sooner was it spoken of than Mr. Gordon commenced at one end of the bridge, and, by long, running strides crossed the river. A mis step, a defective timber, or any hesitation would have cost him his life, for he would have fallen seventy feet to the rocks below. While he crossed it safely, his companions stood horrified, helpless witnesses of what they expected might, at any moment, be a tragedy.

Mr. Gordon was an ardent reformer, and his shop was a place where many congenial spirits met to discuss the political and other questions of the day, on which he was well informed. He was a great admirer of the Toronto Globe, and read it regularly, at a time when few daily papers came to the village. One day, during the very exciting general election of 1878, the Globe failed to arrive at noon, as it should have done. His son, George, who worked with him, procured a copy of the Toronto Mail, which was the leading conservative paper. Neatly pasting the head lines of an old Globe on to the Mail, he folded it and laid it carelessly in the customary place, and went on with his work. A few friends arrived, to hear the latest news, which Mr. Gordon would give them as he read the newspaper. Mr. Gordon came in from his dinner, picked up the paper, turned to the leading editorial and commenced to read. He took off his glasses, wiped them and tried again. He looked as if the earth was falling away from under him. Of all things, the Globe had gone back on its party in the midst of an election! The eruption that followed was described as simply volcanic.

Generous, obliging, and always loyal to the interests of Elora, Mr. Gordon was one of the principal movers in the efforts made, in 1879, to build, by subscription and voluntary work, the stairs and pathways down the "Rocks," which had, up to this time, remained an unknown wilderness to all but the more venturesome. There was in Elora at that time a group of public spirited men, who, without seeking to benefit themselves, worked together for the good of the community, and it is to them that we are indebted for Irvine Park. Andrew Gordon died April 10th, 1883, at the age of sixty one. Mrs. Gordon, who is now in her eighty ninth year, has continued to live on the same lot for over fifty-nine years. Bright, cheerful, hopeful and happy in the face of many trials, Mrs. Gordon has been a good friend and kind neighbour to many during her long residence in Elora. Of the family, the eldest, John Gordon, has lived for nearly twenty years in Brooklyn, N. Y.; Mrs. Robert Tribe lives at Emo, Ontario; Isabella, who is living at home with her mother; George and William are deceased and Joseph Gibson Gordon lives in Preston.

A sister of Mr. Gordon's, Eliza Gordon, spent her early days at his home in Elora. She went to New York, where she married Joseph Gibson, who died a few years later. Mrs. Gibson is yet living at 140 Maple Street in Jersey City, which has been her home for forty years.

* * *

Walter Perkins Newman was born at Cheltenham, England, April 19th, 1819. When little more than a boy he had such a desire to see the world that he was sent to a relative in Australia. He returned to England some years later and then came to Canada. For a short time he ran a country store business in West Flamboro' and about 1847 came to Elora. For a year or two Mr. Newman was employed in Ross & Co's store and post office, but gave that up to engage in a conveyancing and real estate business. After the arrival of his elder brother, Edward, in Elora, this developed into Newman Brothers private Banking business, which was afterwards formed into a company under the name of the Farmer's Bank. For nine years after the incorporation of Elora, W. P. Newman was the Clerk of the Municipality. He was very methodical in business and for a long time had an intimate knowledge of everything pertaining to all local financial matters. He was mechanical too, and as early as 1849 invented a form of turbine water-wheel, and a method of using it, which was some years ahead of its time. Fond of flowers, of order and neatness in everything, Mr Newman was one of those who sought to improve the pathways about the "Rocks" and scattered seeds of many garden flowers among the crevices. W. P. Newman died May 7th, 1881 and his wife, Caroline Farrow, January 18th, 1888.

Edward H. Newman, brother of the former died in Elora, February 11th, 1881, in his sixty-ninth year, and another brother, Richard Newman, who was a druggist in Elora, died in Toronto. Of their different families which at one time were well known here, none are now living in Eiora.

* * *

James Philip was the elder son of James Philip of Kingindee, and was born in Old Meldrum, Aberdeenshire, Scotland in 1812. He was educated in Inverurie and came to Canada in 1839, merely on a tour, intending to return to Scotland after a year or two. In course of his travels he arrived at Niagara Falls, where he made his headquarters at the old Clifton House. At this time the Welland Canal was being built and, becoming acquainted with the contractor, Mr. Philip was offered, and accepted the position of book keeper and paymaster. On the completion of this work Mr. Philip proceeded to Hamilton, where, by this time, his younger brother, Robert, was employed in Mr. Mathieson's wholesale grocery establishment. This was the same Mr. Mathieson who had urged Mr Gordon to come to Elora. Through him Mr. Philip was also induced to visit Elora, when he was so attracted by the opportunities then existing that he purchased from Charles Allan and his partners the store business that had been carried on by them. Having done this, Mr. Philip's younger brother, Robert, came to clerk for him. The business was increased by adding a distillery, which was built early in 1853, on the site of what is now that part of the T. E. Bissell Mfg. Co's property which is used as their office and moulding shop Alongside of this, and now forming part of the main building at the T. E. Bissell Co's Works, Mr. Philip built, in 1856, the first steam flour mill in this part of the country. It was some years later, when the property was owned by Ross & Bonallie, that a dam was built and the mill run by water power. On top of the hill, overlooking the mill and distillery, Mr. Philip built his large stone residence, which is now the home of Mr. John Mills.

In 1853, Robert Philip left his brother's employ and in company with his father-in-law, Mr. George Elmslie, built and commenced business in that large three story stone building which is now Mr. Fischer's furniture store.

James Philip married Mary Brown from Aberdeen, Scotland, who was mentioned among those who arrived in Bon-accord in June 1836. Mr. Philip died in Fergus on August 23rd, 1889, leaving a widow and six of a family.

* * *

Charles Clarke was born in the city of Lincoln, England. on the 28th of November, 1826. After receiving a good education he was apprenticed, when about the age of fourteen, to a linen draper, a premium being paid for his instruction ; but before the three years of his apprenticeship was completed his widowed mother married Mr. John L. Kirk and, with him, sailed for Canada in 1843. Much against his will Mr. Clarke remained with his employers for a few months longer until, on the last Sunday in April 1844 he left his native place and was driven by a friend to Nottingham, where he took the train for Liverpool. There he took passage on an old ship, the "Superb," which went to the bottom some months later. After a six weeks voyage he landed at New York, came by the Hudson River and Erie Canal to Buffalo, and on the 23rd of June 1844, reached Port Robinson, on the Welland Canal. His mother and step-father had preceded him and about seven miles from Dunnville, Ontario, had purchased a poor, played out farm. There Mr. Clarke spent the next four years, and there he might have remained had not severe attacks of fever and ague rendered a removal necessary.

From a commercial traveller in Hamilton, who had become well acquainted with the settled parts of Upper Canada, Mr. Clarke heard of a place called Elora where fever and ague and all such troubles were unknown. After consulting Mr. Kirk it was arranged that they should accompany the commercial traveller, who was about to visit Elora. Stopping at a roadside tavern on the way, within twenty miles of their destination, the proprietor asked where they were going; when they replied Elora, he said "I never heard of no such place hereabouts," but when, after further questioning, he found out where the place was he remarked "Oh, that's the Falls on the Grand River; I know where that is."

Arriving at Elora late one evening in the spring of 1848, Mr. Clarke and his friend, with Mr. Kirk, put up at the village tavern. Although it was late in the evening and would soon be dark they could not rest until they had seen something of the place about which they had heard so much. Crossing over the bridge to the north side of the river, passing Ross & Co.'s store and the mill, Mr. Clarke, for the first time, saw "The Falls." Overlooking the river, in a recess on top of the river bank, about where the mill stabling is, there was at that time a lime kiln owned by Geo. Watson, father of Senator Robert Watson. The bright light from the lime kiln fire illuminating the river and surrounding trees, the dark smoke streaking across the evening sky, and the roar of the dashing water produced a scene of such weird and fascinating grandeur that Mr. Clarke has not forgotten it. When viewed by daylight the beauty of the situation lost nothing of its charm and they decided to make Elora their home. They left their farm in the Township of Canboro', which they afterward sold, and drove to Hamilton. There they met with James Ritchie, a teamster for Ross & Co.'s mill, whom they engaged to drive their household goods to Elora. The building first occupied by Mr. and Mrs. Kirk was that which was built for Captain Gilkison, nearly opposite the present Armory Hall. Here, in that part of the building which had been used as a store, Mr. Kirk resumed work at his trade of shoemaking. Subsequently, when the newly surveyed lots on the north side of the river were offered for sale, Mr. Kirk bought Lot number 6, on the east corner of Church and Princess Streets, where he had his house and store. Later he built a brick residence and store on the south east corner of Church and Geddes streets, which has been the family home ever since. In February, 1861, the firm of Kirk & Clarke moved their large and varied stock of merchandise into the three-story brick building which they built on the south-east corner of William and Metcalfe streets. At that time this was considered to be one of the best business blocks and most complete stocks of goods in the county.

Shortly after their arrival in the village, after Mr. and Mrs. Kirk were comfortably settled, it was found that there was no suitable employment for Mr. Clarke in Elora, and as they felt that he should have some more experience before engaging in business he therefore set out and walked the forty miles to Hamilton, where he secured a situation in a drug store. To occupy spare moments Mr. Clarke contributed articles for publication in the Hamilton "Journal and Express," of which, the Editor, Solomon Brega, thought so much that Mr. Clarke was employed for a time as assistant Editor, which gave him experience that proved very useful to him when at the end of three years he returned to Elora.

On February 10th, 1852, a company was organized for the purpose of publishing a Reform newspaper in Elora. The capital stock was two hundred and fifty pounds, or one thousand dollars, consisting of one hundred shares of ten dollars each. Among those who bought stock in this company were: Charles Allan, James Philip, Charles Clarke, James Stocks, Walter P. Newman David Foote, William Smith, John Smith, John Copp, James Ross, Alexander Watt and Peter Paterson. There was no delay in commencing work: a building was leased, being that which still stands on lot number 8 on the east side of Geddes street, a supply of second-hand type was purchased which had formerly been used in printing the Hamilton "Spectator," and the first copy of "The Elora Backwoodsman" was printed on April 3rd, 1852. On this eventful occasion Mr. Malcolm C. Cameron removed the first paper from the press and handed it to Mr. Clarke, who has carefully preserved it.

The practical printer on this paper was Francis Frank and the first Editor, William Mowat, who was followed by Burton Campbell. Although these were nominally the Editors it was well understood that the one who did most of the Editorial work was Charles Clarke. While the population was yet too small to make this first newspaper a financial success, the publication of "The Elora Backwoodsman" was a great benefit to the village and it was published with varying success for six years or more.

Another publication which appeared at irregular intervals during the years 1857, 58 and 59, was "The Elora Satirist," a small, four page paper, which, as its name would indicate, ridiculed all local celebrities. The name of the Editor was not given, nor was there any clue to the publishers of it so that those who felt they had been libeled (and they were many) were at a loss to know who was responsible. All they knew was that Andrew Spalding, who was then the printer's devil in the Backwoodsman office, found a ready sale for the papers at five cents each. As he has long been beyond the reach of the law it will do him no harm now to say that the Editor of this cleverly written paper was Charlie McLusky, a bright young man, at that time a resident of Elora, who died near Buffalo in 1863.

On May 24th, 1859, a smart, active young man arrived in Elora, from Guelph, and made his presence known by beating all local runners in the foot races being held to celebrate the Queen's Birthday. He did not come to Elora for that purpose, but to purchase the Backwoodsman newspaper company's printing outfit, which for a year or two previously had been situated in a frame building near the mill gate, on the plastered walls of which may still be seen some old advertisements of that period. Two weeks later, on June 8th, 1859, the first copy of "The Elora Observer" appeared and with it the young Editor, Mr J. M. Shaw, commenced his career as a printer in Elora and the old files of the "Observer" show with what energy and enterprise it was conducted ; but the Editorials and many other communications appearing in this, as in the Backwoodsman, were penned by Mr. Clarke. Ten years later Mr. Shaw sold the "Observer" to John Smith, who had the distinction of having been the first Mayor of Guelph. After an absence of about three years Mr. Shaw returned to Elora and commenced publishing an opposition paper called "The Elora Lightning Express." Owing, perhaps, to a short circuit, or to defective insulation, or to many changes in ownership since that date this paper has lost its lightning, but still continues as the Elora Express, owned and edited by Mr. R. E. Mills.

When we look through the old copies of the Elora Observer what a history we find of the stirring events occurring at that time! How these caused a Volunteer Rifle Company to be formed in Elora may be seen from the following succession of events :—

In November, 1860—Abraham Lincoln was elected President of the United States.

January 1861—An unsuccessful attempt was made to take back to the United States a runaway negro slave, named Anderson, who had found refuge in Canada.

March 4th, 1861—Lincoln was inaugurated President.

April 4th, 1861--A report that civil war was expected in the United States.

April 12th, 1861—The bombardment of Fort Sumter.

April 19th, 1861—Several regiments of American soldiers from Northern States marched through the city of Baltimore, the streets lined with an excited crowd. " A blacksmith in a red shirt and leather apron, his arms bared to the elbows, sprang from the sidewalk into the open space between the troops and the gutter, lifted a paving stone high above his head and hurled it with all his might straight against the soldier nearest him. The soldier reeled, clutched at the comrade next him, and sank to the ground. Then, quick as an echo, a puff of white smoke burst out down the line of troops and a sharp, ringing report split the air. The first shot of the American civil war had been fired."

June 15th, 1861—It is proposed that a Rifle Company be formed in Elora.

July 21st, 1861—The Battle of Bull's Run.

July 30th, 1861—A public meeting was held in the Temperance Hall, at which Charles Clarke was chairman and W. P. Newman secretary, when the following resolution was carried unanimously : "That in the opinion of this meeting, considering the unsettled state of affairs in the neighboring Republic, it is highly desirable that a Volunteer Rifle Company be organized in Elora, and this meeting recommends that steps be immediately taken for that purpose." The membership roll having been placed on the table 31 persons agreed to join the Company by writing their names thereon. At this meeting, Captain Donaldson, an old army officer, offered his services as drill-instructor free of charge.

One week later, on August 6th, the Company, then numbering about fifty, assembled, without uniforms or rifles, in the newly built stone woollen mill, and were drilled for the first time, after which they were drilled regularly all winter. In October there was great excitement in Canada over the Trent affair, and war with the United States was expected daily. The membership of the Volunteer Company was at once increased, but the winter passed without being called to arms ; the principal event of the season being a grand Rifleman's Ball, which was held on February 14th, 1862. Towards the end of April rifles and overcoats arrived for the Volunteers ; the rest of their uniform, costing about twenty dollars, had been made by local tailors and paid for by the men themselves. To decide on the most suitable color for the uniform, experiments were made on what was then a common, in the northern part of the village, where men were placed at different distances and covered with various samples of cloth, when it was found that a cloth of a dark fawn color, which was then manufactured in a woollen mill at Galt, was the least conspicuous and the most economical. The orders of the military service specified green as the rifleman's color, but this was a case where "The man that pays the piper calls the tune." The officers and men who were paying for their uniforms insisted on choosing the color, and that is why the Elora Company was the first one in Canada to wear the color that has been found to be the most serviceable, and anticipated by many years the use of what is now called the khaki uniform.

The Volunteer Company paraded outdoors for the first time on May 24th, 1862. After a march to Salem and back (along with the Fire Company, Hook and Ladder Company, and the Elora Brass Band) the Volunteer Rifle Company was drawn up facing the building to the south, at the foot of Metcalfe street, while with a camera placed at an upstairs window they were photographed by the writer's mother, his father being one of the Company. This photograph, like so many others relating to the history of Elora, has been preserved.

The members of the first Volunteer Rifle Company of Elora were :—

   Thomas Donaldson, Captain. Charles Clarke, Lieutenant.
   Walter P. Newman, Ensign.   Andrew Spalding, Bugler.

William Leech	John MacDonald	George Sinclair
Thomas Connon	David Foote	Edward H. Newman
Richard Ferguson	James K. Crossman	William J. Davidson
Ben. Taylor	William Allan	James Davidson
David S. Ritchie	Thomas Strachan	Francis Dalby
John M. Shaw	John Godfrey	Peter Simpson

Alexander Smart	Alexander Shields	Alexander Johnston
Robert Milne	Thomas Farrow	Alexander Laird
William M. Kerr	James Gerrie	Arthur Farrow
Thomas Lawrence	Thomas Biggar	James Fraser
Arthur H. Paget, M. D.	Wm. James Duncan	Henry Scott
Fred Farrow	Edward Coates	George McKenzie
William Gibbon, jr.	James Gairns	Robert Hughes
George Sheppard, jr.	John H. Lawrence	Charles Rollitt
John Wilkinson	John Bain, jr.	Robert Shields
John Simpson	Francis Shields	Turnbull Allan
John Crawford	Robert Simpson	John Watt
John W. Hele	John Jacob	David Findlay
John Potter	Malcolm O. Macgregor	Thomas Land
John Stevenson	William Thomson	William McKenzie

(List of Names dated September 12th, 1861.)

On the 15th of August 1862 a grand military picnic was held on the Tribe farm, near the Cascade. On this occasion a Bugle was presented to the volunteer company, by the ladies of Elora.

When the excitement over the Trent affair abated, interest in the volunteer company was not allowed to fall off, for so long as the American war continued it was believed that at any time Canadians might be called upon to fight. Officers from British regiments sent to Canada at that time were distributed among the different volunteer companies and drilled them thoroughly. One of these, Sergeant Ward of the Coldstream Guards, was a great favorite with the Elora company during 1862 and 63. He was, in later years, a well known officer on the Toronto police force.

It was in February 1864 that Captain Donaldson resigned and Lieutenant Clarke succeeded to the command of the Elora Volunteer Company. That the officers and men were very much in earnest may be shown by the fact that they met for company drill seventy four times during the next twelve months. By this time Lieutenant Clarke had his company in a high state of efficiency; but it was none too soon, for there were many rumors of a Fenian invasion, and these threats increased as the American war was drawing to a close.

There was a song often heard at this period which was very popular, because it so truly expressed the heart felt wish of all the people in the United States; and Canada, too, for there were many Canadians engaged in that war, of which Elora furnished its share. Some of the words of that song were :—

"We're tired of war, on the old camp ground.
   Many are dead and gone
Of the brave and true who've left their homes,
   Others been wounded long.

Many are the hearts that are weary to-night,
   Wishing for the war to cease.
Many are the hearts looking for the right,
   To see the dawn of peace."

It so happened, that, early in April 1865 Mr. Clarke was in New York for the purpose of purchasing goods for his store in Elora. It was past midnight, and he was sound asleep at his hotel, when he was awakened by the shrill, piercing cries of the newsboys on the street as they sold an extra edition of the New York papers announcing the fall of the city of Richmond, which was immediately followed by the surrender of Gen. Lee, and the close of the war.

A year passed by, during which there were so many rumors of a Fenian invasion that Canadians were tired hearing of them, when on Saturday the 31st. of March 1866 Lieutenant Clarke received orders to hold the Elora company in readiness for active service. The company assembled in the Armory Hall that evening and so great was the enthusiasm that many more than the required number of men offered to go, and the most difficult task that Lieut. Clarke had was to strike off the names of those who had to be left at home. While waiting for orders on Monday and Tuesday the time was spent in drilling. Then at five o'clock on the morning of Wednesday the 4th of April, hundreds of their friends found their way to the Armory Hall to see them off. They drove to Guelph in wagons where they arrived at 8.40 and had breakfast. They were in London for dinner and reached Chatham at 10 p. m.

The following is a list of those who went to Chatham:—

Lieutenant—Charles Clarke.

Sergeants—William Leech; Robert Simpson; David S. Ritchie; Malcom O. Macgregor.

Corporals—Frank McFarlane; Alexander Johnston; Robert Tribe; Thos. Farrow.

Bugler—Andrew Spalding.

Privates—Frank Mutch; John R. Wood; George McKenzie; George Lillies; Benjamin Farrow; William Forbes; George Mutch; James Ritchie; William Gerrie; Thomas Gerrie; Samuel Hill; Richard Harper; George Leslie; George Mathieson; Edwin Crossman; William Reynolds; George Blinco; William Gibson; William Whiteley; John Young; Everett Everett; William Ritchie; James Land; John C. McLean; George Gerrie; Albert Land; George Wallace; Thomas Godfrey; John Potts; James Skinner; James Gallagher; Henry Roberts; John McGregor; James Algie; Charles Findlay; James Moir; Thomas Carlton; James Findlay; James Gairns; William Mutch; John Brady; John Keyworth; Joseph Whiteley; James Clarke; William Davidson; Angus McPherson.

What most astonished the men on their arrival in Chatham was the sudden and unexpected change of climate. At Elora, on Monday April 2nd, they stood upon the ice on the river to have the Company photographed, and wore their overcoats. On their way to Guelph they passed through deep drifts of snow, while on their arrival in Chatham they found fine summer weather, with dust blowing on the streets.

The Elora Company drilled six hours daily while at Chatham, and was fortunate in having, in addition to those of its own officers, the services of Sergt. Major O'Reilley and Capt. Boyd of the Royal Canadian Rifles, under whose instructions they quickly acquired the confidence and bearing of "regulars." While waiting six weeks for the threatened invasion to take place, there were several promotions in the Company. Lieutenant Clarke became Captain; Sergeant M. O. MacGregor, Lieutenant; Sergeant Leech, Ensign, and Corporal Alexander Johnston, of Salem, Sergeant.

They left Chatham for home on the 17th of May, receiving a great ovation from the Mayor and Citizens. At the old Great Western Station in Guelph they were met that evening by friends from Elora, and then, with the Salem Brass Band leading the way and playing lively popular airs they marched down to the town, where wagons were waiting to convey them to Elora. "The Elora Observer" of that date said. "The boys struck up "Tramp, Tramp" and sung it with a will. Arrived at Ellis' Hotel, a short halt was made and the men were then marched into the large dining room, where Mr. Ellis, at his own expense, and without suggestion from any other source than his own liberal heart, furnished a repast for the boys, which they disposed of in true soldier like fashion. After the eating was pretty well disposed of the teams were ordered out, the boys piled into the wagons and stages provided for them, the signal was given, and the Company was again en route for home. At Hirsts' another halt was made, and he, with the whole souled liberality which ever distinguishes him, was on hand with refreshments, which he gave out with no stinted hand. The procession was soon under way again, and shortly after midnight reached our village. No sooner was the roll of the wheels heard, than a huge bonfire was lit, near the (old) English Church, the village Band struck up, the old cannon boomed forth in its loudest tones, cheer after cheer rent the air, and the boys, one and all, felt that they were home again. The Company speedily formed fours and marched through the village to their Drill Shed, which was brilliantly lit up for their reception. Here they found a still greater crowd of citizens, and citoyennes, awaiting them, and after a hearty hand shaking, AND SO ON, the order was again given to march, and the Company proceeded to Biggar's Hotel, where an ample supper was spread, to which due justice was done. About two o'clock the Company was dismissed, with orders to "fall in" upon Friday afternoon. On Friday it was resolved that a still better reception should be given to the boys, in which the girls could take their part, and no better plan for this purpose could be thought of than a Ball, to which all in Volunteer uniform, with their partners, should be invited. In the afternoon the Company marched through the village, presenting a very fine appearance and showing the good effects of their sojourn in Chatham, and after going through various evolutions upon the green near the English Church with a precision which took all by surprise, proceeded to the Drill Shed and were then dismissed from active service by Captain Clarke, who said that he was proud of the conduct of his men while in Chatham and felt sure that if ever called upon again, the same men would turn out as promptly as before, behave themselves as well, and return home with as good a character as that which they had earned upon this occasion."

One week later, the Volunteer Company took part in the Queen's Birthday celebration, after which they settled down to the work in which they had formerly engaged. But they were only becoming accustomed to their several occupations when they had to hurriedly leave their work and go to the "Front" once more.

On the morning of Saturday the 2nd of June, at a few minutes past eight, Capt. Clarke received a telegram with orders to report, with his Company, in Guelph at once. The Bugle sounded the call to arms, the different members of the Volunteer Company quickly dropped the work they were at and in less than an hour were assembled at the Armory Hall. Several teams of horses, with wagons, including the large Salem Band wagon, had been hurried to the spot, the men bade their friends good bye, quietly took their places and without wasting time on formal ceremony they went up over the hill "to drive the Finnegans back." Before noon they arrived at Guelph and there received orders to proceed to Point Edward, near Sarnia.

While in Guelph they learned that the Orders which Capt. Clarke received on the morning of Saturday the 2nd of June, should have been delivered to him more than twelve hours before. The delay in transmitting this important telegram was never satisfactorily explained, and the men, who had drilled so diligently to prepare for such an emergency, ever afterwards regretted that through this delay they had been prevented from taking part in the Battle of Ridgway, which was fought that day. While the conclusion generally arrived at was that some one through whose hands it had to pass had intentionally delayed the message, there was one thing quite certain, it was not caused through any neglect in the Elora office. During this exciting time, John Hele was in constant attendance at the telegraph office, where news from the front was eagerly sought for. Such a crowd gathered around the office on Sunday the 3rd of June that the telegraphic reports received were given to the Editor of the Observer, Mr. J. M. Shaw, who printed and distributed a supplement giving the latest news of the Fenian invasion, and reports of the Battle of Ridgway.

Owing, perhaps, to the fact that it was nipped in the bud, there is a feeling among the present generation that this intense interest in the Fenian invasion was all foolishness, but when the volunteers left the village on that June morning, mothers, wives and sweethearts bade their dear ones farewell and felt that they might never see them again. A wave of patriotic enthusiasm spread throughout Canada at this time and in every village in the land men were eager to join in the defence of their country. In Salem, for instance, a Company was unofficially formed and drilled by Sergt. Robert Simpson, the wagon maker. This Company was drilled in the oatmeal grainery at Wissler's mill. In a pasture field at Ewing's Corners on the Alma road some thirty or forty young men on horseback were drilled by a retired cavalry officer. Every young farmer had a gun and knew how to use it, so that when drilled as mounted Infantry, as these were, they would have been quite effective in repelling invaders. This outburst of patriotism found expression in the words of a song which was often sung by the volunteers when on the march, although it was a parody on one used by the Americans during the civil war. The Canadian version was:—

> In a cottage by my side
> Sits the darling of my pride,
> While our happy children 'round us are at play;
> But the news spreads through the land
> That the Fenians are at hand,
> And our country's call we cheerfully obey.
>
> CHORUS—
>
> Tramp, tramp, tramp
> The boys a marching;
> Cheer up, let the rabble come—let them come;
> For beneath the Union Jack
> We will drive the Fenians back,
> And we'll fight for our beloved Canadian home.

The words of another, and it may be a more popular version, ran something like this:—

> Old Maloney, wanting cash,
> Says he contemplates a dash
> With his troops upon our shores to make a raid;
> But he'll find to his dismay
> That the thing will never pay,
> Then perhaps off British soil he'll wish they'd stayed.

Upon the next morning after the arrival of the Elora Volunteer Rifle Company at Point Edward they attended service at church, it being a Sunday, and as it was expected that at any hour the invaders might attempt to land, each man carried sixty rounds of ammunition. In the afternoon Sergeant Alexander Johnston, of Salem, was sent out in command of a party of men to patrol the Grand Trunk Railway line, which for some miles west of Point Edward runs near the south shore of Lake Huron. Returning late in the afternoon he reported all well, and in the evening, when it was near dark, he was sent out again, with the same men. Standing on the rear platform of the special train on which they rode, and when near Camlachie, Sergt. Johnston saw two vessels near the land, and he could also see that men on board were signalling to some one on shore by means of lighted lanterns. He called the attention of the train conductor to this and together they watched the signalling, the conductor remarking that although he knew that locality well he had never seen vessels come in there before. The conductor then pulled the bell rope as a warning to the engineer to stop the train, the engineer whistled for brakes, and immediately afterwards the signalling ceased—like Tam O'Shanter's experience at Alloway Kirkyard, when, "In an instant, all was dark." Whatever may have been the object of those on board the vessels in attempting to land in this unfrequented spot, their project did not succeed.

The only other event worth mentioning occurred a few weeks later, when some of the volunteers who were fishing saw a vessel pass down the river, on which the green flag of the Fenian Brotherhood was conspicuously displayed; the result, it was said, of a wager made by the ship captain to carry the flag on his vessel from Chicago to Cleveland. About this time the men who were fishing heartily wished they had their rifles instead of their fishing rods, for the river is narrow here and the men on the vessel were within easy range. But then, what fine shots we see when we haven't got a gun! As it was, this incident came near causing trouble between the United States and Canada.

The raid was over, having lasted three days, and as all was quiet again on the frontier the Elora Volunteer Company returned home on Thursday the 5th of July, 1866. They were enthusiastically welcomed and the celebration included a monster village picnic which was held on Friday, the 20th of July. As announced in the "Observer," it was "A day set apart by the inhabitants of Elora and surrounding country, as a public holiday, for the purpose of giving a great welcome home picnic to our gallant volunteers As there is no desire to make money out of the affair it has been resolved to conduct it upon the voluntary principle and no charge will be made to cover incidental expenses, those have been provided for by the municipality. This will be the greatest popular demonstration which Elora has ever seen."

Besides the Elora Rifle Company, and their guests the Fergus Rifle Company, there were at this picnic the Elora and Salem Brass Bands; the Elora Cadets, drilled by Mr. James Christie, with their own fife and drum band under the leadership of that old veteran bandmaster, Mr. E. T. Day; and a number of the children of the village sang choruses in which they had been trained "under that prince of juvenile musical instructors, Prof. J. W. Youmans." Speeches and presentations were the order of the day, among which the "Elora Observer" mentioned that "Captain Clarke then stepped to the front of the platform, and, after a few appropriate introductory remarks, presented Bugler Andrew Spalding with a handsome six shooter revolver, something near the same style and finish as that which but a few moments previously was presented to himself."

Shortly after this the 30th Wellington Battalion was formed, and as part of it the Elora company went to camp at Thorold in the following September with Captain Clarke promoted to be Major of the Battalion. During this camp there was a continuation of wet, disagreeable weather, which was the cause of the first death in the company, that of Sylvester Dalby, a young man in his 24th year, who died on the fourth of November.

In June 1871, when the 30th Wellington Battalion went to camp at Goderich, the regiment was under the command of Lieutenant-Colonel Clarke. So successfully did 'Colonel' Clarke fill this position, and so popular was he with the rank and file that he was persuaded to retain command of the regiment for upwards of twenty-two years, finally retiring from military service in 1893. During the years in which he was in command of the 30th Battalion, the regimental Band was established in Elora, which, for the greater part of the time was under the leadership of a popular and efficient bandmaster who was familiarly and commonly called "Billy." Gay, his proper name being William Gay.

Colonel Clarke commenced his political career, when, on the 22nd of January, 1858, he took his place at the Council Board of the then newly incorporated village of Elora. The members of this first village Council were David Foote, (who was elected Chairman, and was, therefore, Reeve,) Charles Clarke, John Potter, John Godfrey and John Mundell. In the years 1859—'60—'61—'62—'63—'64—'67 and '68 Charles Clarke was elected Reeve of Elora and a member of the County Council. He had acquired these eight years of preparatory experience in the transaction of public business, when in

1871 he was offered the Liberal Nomination to represent the Centre Riding of the County of Wellington in the Provincial Legislature. At this time the Centre Riding, as it was called, included the Townships of Erin, Eramosa, Garafraxa, Nichol and Pilkington, the town of Orangeville and the villages of Fergus and Elora. In the election which followed Col. Clarke defeated his opponent by a majority of 600, and this figure was about maintained in each succeeding election until his retirement in 1892 to accept the clerkship of the House of Assembly.

So flagrant were the abuses in those days of open voting that Col. Clarke had for some time, on the platform and through the press, been advocating the adoption of a system of voting by ballot. Immediately after his election, therefore, he procured information from the various countries where this system of voting was in use and introduced a bill before the Legislature to have the vote by ballot adopted in all Ontario elections At first an attempt was made to turn down this great reform, but Col. Clarke urged its adoption, when, by a vote of the Legislature on February 6th, 1873, the members, not voting on party lines, showed by a vote of 50 to 14 that, individually, they were in favor of it, and in the following year it was introduced as a government measure and became law. In the Ballot Forms at the end of the Act some of the names used for the purpose of illustration are the same as those used by Colonel Clarke in his original bill; some showing him to be an ardent admirer of Dickens, in the names of Chuzzlewitt, Copperfield, Bardell and Snodgrass; others show loyalty to his old friends and supporters, such as Charles Allan, James Argo, John Brown and other names slightly changed, besides those which indicated his nationality in John Bull. To his industry in gathering information and his energy in pushing the matter to a successful conclusion Col. Clarke is fairly entitled to the honor and credit of causing the ballot to be used at both municipal and parliamentary elections in Ontario.

Among other important bills which he introduced in the Ontario Legislature he was the first to introduce a measure to make the covering of the tumbling rods and other exposed parts of the machinery of threshing machines compulsory. Before this bill became law many accidents were constantly occurring, owing to the clothing of farmers being caught in the rapidly moving machinery.

Being a lover of nature, especially of flowers, and knowing how valuable birds were as insect destroyers he had an Act passed making it unlawful to destroy any insectivorous bird; and had his parliamentary usefulness been limited to the introduction of this one Act, Colonel Clarke would have earned the everlasting thanks of present and future generations.

To him also much credit is due for the introduction of a system of County Poor Houses throughout the Province.

As chairman of the public accounts committee, and of the House when in committee he showed ability which was recognized in 1880 when he was elected Speaker and continued in that position under two parliaments, for seven consecutive sessions. In 1892 Col. Clarke accepted the position of Clerk of the Assembly which he occupied until January 1907, during this period holding commissions which, in case of need, authorized him to act as Lieutenant Governor. At the request of the Premier, Sir Oliver Mowat, he compiled "The Member's Manual," a book of rules governing parliamentary procedure, which has become the standard guide to successive legislators.

Upon retirement in 1907 from his many years of activity in political life, Col. Clarke at once engaged in writing and publishing a book in which he relates many interesting recollections of his "Sixty years in Upper Canada," to which the reader is referred.

The story of John Smithurst was written for the first time in September, 1921. It was better known in Elora two-thirds of a century ago than it is today.

It is more than twenty years now since the following letter was sent to a young lady friend, who proposed to enter a course of training as a professional nurse.

"My Dear Jean:—

"Did I ever tell you the story about another girl who wanted to be a trained nurse? This young lady was born at Florence, in Italy, but her father owned estates at Embley Park, in Hampshire, and at Lea Hurst in Derbyshire, England.

"Her cousin, a young man employed by a merchant in London, fell in love with her. To break off this attachment, her parents took her from her home and for several years travelled on the Continent. The young lady wanted to be a nurse and at all the cities which they visited, she learned what she could of nursing as it was then, and of hospital organization.

"But what did her lover do? Come to the cemetery at Elora, Ontario, and on that free-stone cross you may read the inscription:

" 'John Smithurst, Clerk in Holy Orders, died September 2nd, 1867, aged 59 years, 11 months and 23 days. A native of Lea Hurst, Derbyshire, England; 12 years missionary to the Red River Settlement; nearly six years Incumbent of Elora; afterward resident at Lea Hurst in the Township of Minto and missionary to that township.'

"Now you will want to know who she was. When the very urgent need came for nurses during the Crimean War, the only one in England at the time, who had studied hospital work and knew how it should be organized, was this young lady, who became the heroine of the British Army—Florence Nightingale."

This letter was an attempt to tell the story as it was generally known in Elora while Mr. Smithurst was living. But gradually, like falling leaves in autumn, those who knew him intimately have passed away, until now it is merely a tradition.

Experience in collecting local history shows that very often the most important information is found where one would least expect to find it.

During the few years following the potato famine in Ireland, in 1846, many Irish immigrants took up farms in "The Queen's Bush," as it was called. The Township of Peel was the first to be settled because it was, at its nearest part, only six miles from Elora, where the land was sold by Andrew Geddes, the Crown Lands Agent. One of the first settlers in this township was Bill McConnell, who, two or three years later, sent for his father, mother, three brothers and a sister, Mary. It was to Mary McConnell that we were partly indebted for Mr. Smithurst's story.

The McConnell family, although Irish, did not come from Ireland, but from Ashton-under-line, near Manchester, England. While living there, Mary, being the youngest, had acquired the habit of using such expressions as "I says" and "Says I," which, with her native Irish, made her talk interesting.

The father, mother and Mary remained at the British Hotel in Guelph while her brothers went up into the bush to prepare a house for the family in Peel, or "Pale beyant" as it was commonly called. As she said, "Mr. Thorpe, who owned the British Hotel in Guelph, was something akin to my mother; aye, he was her cousin." "When my brother Hugh came back to Guelph from Peel, I says to him says I what do you think of that new country, says I." "Well, Moll, says he to me (for that was what my brothers called me) says he, if it was not for you and mother being here, I'd go back to England tomorrow." "Well" says I, "that's bad, very bad, but now that we are here, we will just make the best of it. And for all my brother Hugh lived in Peel and died in it, and acquired a lot of property, he never liked Canada."

The Reverend John Smithurst came to St. John's Church, Elora, about the last day in the year 1852 and commenced his duties on New Year's Day of 1853.

His second marriage ceremony was that of James McCague and Mary McConnell of the Township of Peel, on February 1st, 1853. What a fine couple they were! What a happy home they had! Then a woman from Hamilton visiting in the neighborhood brought the infection of scarlet fever and their family of three daughters died within two days.

Some years later the old couple retired to live in Elora. In the course of years—it was in 1894—Mr. McCague died. All the friends and neighbors attended the funeral from the house. After the service was over, without leaving her simple invitation to the friends to be given by the undertaker, the old lady came to the door, which was many steps up from the ground. Calmly looking over the friends gathered there, she said: "Now thin, if any of yez would like to see the last of Jamie McCague, just come this way." She faced all her misfortunes with the same quiet courage as when she said, "But seeing we are here, we will just make the best of it."

Having been a resident of Elora for nearly six years, Mr. Smithurst bought a farm of four hundred acres or more in the Township of Minto, which was then just open for settlement. His home in the bush, which he called "Lea Hurst," was two and a half miles east of the village of Clifford and about thirty-five miles north-west of Elora. When making his frequent trips to and from Elora, during his residence in Minto, Mr. Smithurst always found a kindly welcome at the home of Mr. and Mrs. McCague, and to them he told his story.

John Smithurst was born at Lea Hurst, Derbyshire, England, on September 9th, 1807. In early manhood his attention was given to mercantile pursuits and for a time he was employed with the then well-known firm founded by Sir Richard Arkwright, one of the inventors of machinery for spinning yarn. But a change came in his career, for, according to Mrs. McCague, he and a cousin fell in love with the same girl, who was also their cousin, Florence Nightingale. John Smithurst told Mrs. McCague, as he had told others, that he and Florence Nightingale had been engaged, but that she decided not to marry.

As Mrs. McCague told it: "Then, says John to Florence, says he, what would you have me to do? says he." "Well, then, says she to John, says she, I would like you to be a missionary to the Indians in North America, says

REV. JOHN SMITHURST

REV. JOHN SMITHURST'S GRAVE
IN ELORA CEMETERY

she." Then John Smithurst gave up his position in the business he was engaged in and went to the Mission at Islington to prepare himself for the work of the Church Missionary Society.

Shortly after his ordination, he was sent out by this Society as a missionary to the Red River Settlement, in the Hudson's Bay Territory. He arrived at his destination on the 20th of September, 1839. For twelve years he was Superintendent of the Mission and Chaplain to Fort Garry, which is now Winnipeg. For particulars of his work there the reader is referred to a small book printed long ago, called "The Rainbow in the North," by Miss Tucker.

In 1851, after this lonely life for twelve years, Mr. Smithurst returned from the Red River Settlement to England. He remained about twelve months. Why he did not remain longer in England we do not know. It was said that the climate did not agree with him; but would it not be more than likely that he went home to see the girl he loved and ask her if she had changed her mind?

However that may be, he returned to Canada, but this time to Ontario. For a short time he was stationed in the Township of Grantham, which is near St. Catharines, but about the last day of the year 1852, he came to Elora and commenced his duties in charge of St. John's Church on New Year's Day, 1853. He brought with him to Elora a set of Communion Silver, three pieces of which are still used in St. John's Church, but one other piece is missing. On the under side of one of them, that which is called a Platen, is engraved the following inscription in Latin:—

> Dono Dedit
> hoc munusculum
> Rev. Ioanni Smithurst
> amico dilectissimo
> alumnus ejus
> Ebenezer Hall
> officiorum in se grate
> memor
> A. D. MDCCCLII

A translation is said to be about as follows:—

"Acting as agent, or factor, for someone, Ebenezer Hall gives as a gift this set of communion silver to Rev. John Smithurst, a very dear friend, in grateful recognition of his many kindnesses, A. D. 1852."—the someone in this case being Florence Nightingale.

Of her history we know nothing but what we have noticed in the daily papers and magazines. We have read that her parents thought it beneath the dignity of a lady to be a nurse. However, what we wish to point out is that about the time John Smithurst returned to Canada, Florence Nightingale at last received her parents' permission, very much against their will, and from that time devoted her life to the study of nursing. From a newspaper we read, "From this time, after her declaration of independence and the beginning of her serious training for the work of her life, there is never a syllable in diary or letters which denotes anything but happiness and satisfaction. A New Year's letter of 1854 says, "I have never repented or looked back, not for a moment. And I begin the New Year with more true feeling of a Happy New Year than ever I had in my life."

After leaving home, she immediately began training as a nurse; first at Kaiserwerth, on the Rhine, under Pastor Fliedner and his wife, and afterwards at the Maison de la Providence in Paris; then, returning to London, she undertook the post of Superintendent of the Harley Street Hospital for Sick Gentlewomen. It was at Harley street, in October, 1854, that her call to the Crimea came. The story has often been told how a friend who knew her, Mr. Sydney Herbert, then Secretary of War, wrote to Miss Nightingale asking her to undertake the work of evolving order out of chaos in the Military Hospital at Scutari, and how his letter crossed one from her to him offering her services. This was on the 15th of October, 1854. On October 21st, she started for the Crimea, accompanied by a band of forty-two trained nurses.

During the Crimean War, Mr. Smithurst was in Elora. Think of what it meant to him when the name of the girl he loved was on the lips of everyone. And was he not proud of her? To the writer's father and to other intimate friends he told of his former engagement at that time.

Of his later years spent on his bush farm, the workmen from Elora who were employed by him to put up buildings long remembered the winter evenings when, seated around the large, open fire-place with its blazing logs, Mr. Smithurst read novels to them in his deep, rich voice, or related even more interesting tales of that far-off and little known region, the Canadian North West, or of his early life in England.

When failing health made it necessary that he should have medical attention, Mr. Smithurst returned to his former home at St. John's Parsonage in Elora, where he received every care from his successor, the Rev. C. E. Thomson. He was attended during his last illness by Dr. Paget, who came to Elora in May, 1858. The old doctor, after practising his profession in Elora for about sixty years, is now living retired in Toronto. When Florence Nightingale died, in August, 1910, Dr. Paget happened to be in Toronto for a short time. We wrote to him with reference to the romance associated with her name and received the following reply:—

Jarvis street, Toronto, August 17th, 1910.

Dear John:—

I had the pleasure of knowing the late Rev. John Smithurst, of Lea Hurst, Minto, a fine, well educated gentleman.

He was engaged to the late Florence Nightingale.

I attended him, with Dr. Clarke, of Guelph, during his last illness.

Yours sincerely,

A. H. Paget.

We have a good photograph of Mr. Smithurst and also his large, well-kept garden at his home in Minto, and of a beautiful beaver meadow near by. These were made by the writer's father, for, as has been stated, he was one of his intimate friends while Mr. Smithurst lived in Elora and visited him at hs bush home near Clifford which was then called Minto Village.

After Mr. Smithurst's death, his farm was sold to a Mr. Taylor, whose son and daughter, Mr. John Taylor and Miss Hannah Taylor, are living retired in Clifford. Miss Taylor gave the writer Mr. Smithurst's old, well worn Bible, which they found in the house when they took possession. It was printed at Edinburgh in 1795 and had belonged to a sister or other near relative, for, on a fly leaf is written:

> Elizabeth Smithurst
> her Book.
> Departed this life
> the 4th day of January,
> aged 15   1806

In another place it has his earliest attempts at writing his own name and the date, February 19th, 1811.

If that old Bible could tell its story, what a story it could tell!

*   *   *

With coal at three-quarters of a cent a pound, the present day residents of Guelph build large houses in the most exposed situations, where they receive the full force of every wind that blows. For some years after that City was founded in April, 1827, they were free to locate where they pleased, for it was all new, and they built small, but comfortable homes down in the sheltered spots by the river side. The business portion was then in the southern part, where it was protected from the cold north-west winds by the bush growing on the high hill, where the Church of Our Lady now stands. Here, on the sloping ground where the snow melts first in Springtime, they built their homes and their shops; while right at their door, fire-wood could be had for the cutting!

Down on Nottingham street you will find the first school house still standing at numbers thirty-two and thirty-four. It has long been the home of Mr. Lambert. Across the street from it you will be shown the house where "Old Doctor Clarke" lived, he whose son was, not long ago, the Lieutenant-Governor of Ontario. The neighbors will also say: "And there is where Dr. Orton lived; and in that two-storied square house, built of cut stone, at number twenty-one where Mrs. Monkhouse lives, the Bank of Montreal did business; while a large space around here was a common on which the monthly fairs were held."

It is with this old house at number twenty-one that we are particularly interested just now; for in the years between 1847 and 1857, there lived in that home a man whose name should be remembered with gratitude by every Canadian—the man who saved that priceless heritage we call the Canadian North-west, for Canada. His name was John McLean.

He has never received credit for what he did. The Canadian public did not know what part he played when, in 1869, at the time of the Alabama Award, politicians in London and Ottawa were going to give away all west of Lake Superior to the United States. The politicians, and public generally, were deceived by the stories circulated by the Hudson's Bay Company that the North-West Territory, which they had occupied and wanted to keep, was a cold, Arctic region unfit for the homes of white men.

John McLean was born in the Isle of Mull in the year 1800. At Montreal in the month of January, 1821, he entered the service of the Hudson's Bay Company. He was first sent for some months to the Parish of Petit le Mask, where, in the home of Father Gibert, who had been born and educated in France,, he became proficient in writing and speaking French. After that, he was stationed at different Hudson's Bay Posts in the district of the Ottawa River. In April, 1833, he wrote, "I had now served the Hudson's Bay Company faithfully and zealously for a period of twelve years, leading a life of hardship and toil, of which no idea can be formed except by those whose hard lot it may be to know it by experience. And what was my reward? No sooner had I succeeded in freeing my district from opposition than I was ordered to resign my position to another, who would enjoy the fruits of my labour. When I arrived at the Company's Headquarters at Lachine, to take my departure for a remote district, I was ordered to provide for myself until I embarked. And, when enjoying myself in the bosom of my family, to suit the convenience of one of their correspondents, I was torn away from them prematurely and without warning; treatment which caused one of them so severe a shock as nearly to prove fatal."

For a few months he was at Norway House, on Lake Winnipeg. Of the Indians there he wrote: "Of Christianity, they have learned just as much as enables them to swear; in other respects they are still Pagans."

From there, in August 1833, he was sent by way of Athabasca and the Peace River to Fort St. James in British Columbia. Here he arrived at the end of October, 1833. After about three years and a half he was again removed; this time from the one extreme to the other; from British Columbia to Fort Chimo in northern Ungava.

He commenced this trip on February 22nd, 1837. His route was past Kamloops to the Okanagan and Kootenay Valleys; over the Rocky Mountains, with their deep snow, and across the great prairies on which the wheat grown each year is now measured by the hundreds of millions of bushels. John McLean saw all this country, and remembered it.

He left York Factory on Hudson's Bay, on August 22nd, and arrived at Ungava on September 11th, 1837. As even at that early date it might be frozen in, the vessel left on its return trip two days later.

Fort Chimo, which was to be John McLean's headquarters during his (almost) four years in Labrador was established in 1831. He wrote: "Whatever may have been the Company's real motives in forming a settlement in this quarter, the profits derived from it added but little to the dividends." "I was directed to push outposts into the interior, to support my people on the resources of the country, and at the same time open a communication with Esquimaux Bay, with the view of obtaining in future my supplies from there by inland route—there being no question of the practicability of the rivers— So said he who had not seen those rivers."

He lost no time in carrying out his instructions. On January 2nd, 1838, he left Fort Chimo on a trip that lasted until the 26th of April. He had four companions. No party of Arctic explorers ever endured greater hardship and came through alive. Each summer after this, he continued his efforts to find a possible route of communication across the country from north to south.

All these trips furnished useful information but the journey of 1839 was the most eventful.

After a most difficult trail of about four hundred miles from Fort Chimo, their canoe was launched on the Hamilton River. The date was about August 9th, 1839. This is how he described it: "One evening, the roar of a mighty cataract burst upon our ears, warning us that danger was at hand. We soon reached the spot, which presented to us one of the grandest spectacles in the World, but put an end to all hopes of success in our enterprise." "About six miles about the fall the river suddenly contracts from a width of six hundred to four hundred yards, then, rushing along in a continuous, foaming rapid, it finally contracts to a breadth of about fifty yards ere it precipitates itself over the rock which forms the fall; when, still roaring and foaming, it continues its maddened course for about a distance of thirty miles, pent up between walls of rock that rise sometimes to the height of three hundred feet on either side." "This stupendous fall exceeds in height the Falls of Niagara, but bears no comparison to that sublime object in any other respect, being nearly hidden from the view by the abrupt angle which the rocks form immediately beneath it. If not seen, however, it is felt; such is the extraordinary force with which it tumbles into the abyss underneath that we felt the rock shake underneath our feet as we stood two hundred feet above the gulf. A dense cloud of vapor, which can be seen at a great distance in clear weather, hangs over the spot. From the fall to the foot of the rapid—a distance of thirty miles—the zig-zag course of the river presents such sharp angles that you see nothing of it until within a few yards of its banks. Might not this circumstance lead the geologist to the conclusion that the fall had receded this distance? The mind shrinks from the contemplation of a subject that carries it back to a time so very remote; for if the rock, syenite, always possessed its present solidity and hardness, the action of the water alone might require millions of years to produce such a result."

"After carrying our canoe and baggage for a whole day through bogs and swamps and windfalls, in the hope of finding the river accessible, we at length gave up the attempt and with heavy hearts and weary limbs retraced our steps."

Some fifty-two years later, on September 2nd, 1891, this immense waterfall was again visited, this time by Mr. Henry G. Bryant and Professor C. A. Kenaston, of Washington. Their experience was given in the Century Magazine for September, 1892. In this Mr. Bryant said: "Unquestionably the first white man to gaze upon this remote cataract was John M'Lean, which he discovered in 1839." "Twenty years after M'Lean's visit, Joseph MacPherson was guided to the spot by an Indian. It does not appear that the latter ever gave an account of his visit to this region." "These are the only white men, who, previous to September, 1891, are known to have seen the Grand Falls."

Two or three years later a Canadian Government explorer was there and gave the height of the Fall as 302 feet. Mr. Bryant and Prof. Kenaston measured it by means of a strong cord, with a block of wood attached to it. They found that the river dropped 32 feet in the steep incline or chute, immediately above the brink of the Fall and 316 feet in the Fall itself, making 348 feet of drop at that place. Including the rapid below, the total fall in twelve miles was 760 feet! Such a fall is not unusual in a mountain cascade but with a large river whose flow is compared with that of the Ottawa River at Ottawa, the amount of water power is extraordinary. If the hopes of Nikola Tesla are ever fulfilled, and it becomes possible to successfully transmit electric power to any distance without the use of wires, this great power will be better known.

For those who wish to know something more about that desolate country, we would say, let them read "The Lure of the Labrador Wild," which tells of the tragic death from starvation of Dr. Leonidas Hubbard, Jr., on October 18th, 1903. Mrs. Hubbard afterwards succeeded in crossing Labrador, from Hamilton Inlet to Ungava, but she did not visit McLean Falls. This adventurous journey she was enabled to make only by having three of the most skillful Indian voyageurs who came from the James Bay district to assist her. One of these was George Elson, who had accompanied Dr. Hubbard so loyally on his disastrous expedition. In 1908, Mrs. Hubbard wrote "A Woman's Way through Unknown Labrador." Be sure to read it.

It is most remarkable that three of those who have taken part in the exploration of Labrador should have been in Elora. As will be seen, John McLean lived in Elora for twenty-five years. Mr. Hubbard came to Elora to see his future wife, Miss Mina Benson, of Peterborough, who was then on a visit to her sister, the wife of Mr. Underhill, principal of the Elora Public School in 1900, 1901 and 1902.

Having completed his last trip across Labrador from Fort Chimo to North-West River, John McLean found letters from the head office in London giving him permission to visit his old home. On August 18th, 1812, he embarked for England on board a small schooner of sixty tons, deeply laden with fish and oil. He landed at Plymouth on the 3rd of September and on the 20th, arrived at the spot from which he started twenty-three years before.

This was a small hamlet called Dervaig, about twenty miles from Tobermory, the principal town in the Isle of Mull. Quite near to Dervaig is Calgary Castle, where John McLean's mother was born. Both his parents were McLean's of the same Clan but not closely related. They traced their descent in an unbroken line back to the first McLean, of the Island of Coll, in the year 1100. Like so many other Highland families, they lost all for Prince Charlie. As he wrote, "The meeting of a mother with an only son, after so long an absence, need not be described."

He sailed from Liverpool on December 15th, and arrived in New York on January 17th; started up the Hudson River on the 5th of February; spending the remainder of the winter in Montreal. On May 2nd, 1843, he was again sent on a long journey which took him as far as Fort Good Hope on the Mackenzie River. He spent the winters of 1843-44 and 1844-45 at Great Slave Lake.

What John McLean thought of Sir George Simpson, Governor of the Hudson's Bay Company may be learned from a few brief extracts from a letter which he wrote to Governor Simpson in July, 1844. He said: "I cannot avoid remarking that the treatment I have on this and so many other occasions experienced from you is unworthy of yourself, and as unworthy of the high station you fill, as I am undeserving of it. You are pleased to jest about the hardships I experienced while battling with opposition during a period of

JOHN McLEAN

REV. JAMES MIDDLEMISS, D.D.

twelve years in the Montreal Department and the privations I afterwards endured in New Caledonia (now called northern British Columbia). From there you sent me to Ungava, where you say you are not aware I experienced any particular hardships and privations. You are aware of the circumstances in which I found myself when I arrived there.... This consideration, however, did not interfere between me and my duty and I accordingly traversed my desolate country in the dead of winter, a journey which nearly cost myself and my companions our lives. I then continued to explore the country during the entire period of my command and finally succeeded in discovering a practicable communication with Esquimaux Bay and determining the question so long involved in uncertainty as to the 'Riches' the interior possessed. By so doing I saved an enormous expense to the Company. The Honorable Committee are aware of my exertions in that quarter, as I had the honour of being in direct communication with them while there."

Then, in 1846, after serving a soulless corporation, with a heartless Governor, for twenty-five years, he resigned.

One of the schemes used by the Hudson's Bay Company to hoodwink the public in England was to employ a few missionaries to look after the spiritual welfare of the Indians. Those missionaries were in greatest favour with the Company who confined their efforts to baptising, marrying and burying. One of another sort, who was not employed by them, found his way into the North-West Territory. This was the Rev. James Evans. He was born at Kingston-on-Hull, England, in 1801; came to Canada when a young man and taught school. In 1833, he was ordained into the Methodist ministry, his second appointment being to the congregation at Sarnia, Ontario.

When he commenced work in the North-West, he converted some of the Indians, who, therefore, were taught that it was sinful to work on the Sabbath Day. Was the Hudson's Bay Company going to have their work interfered with; have their voyageurs delayed on long trips because a few of them had been converted? Any one who was in their employ had to work Sunday and every other day and the missionary who taught anything else had to suffer. Of course, the Company dared not oppose Mr. Evan's missionary work openly for the dear public in England would hear of it. All the same, the work of James Evans was carried on under great discouragement.

As the Cree Indians among whom he was living had no written language, Mr. Evans sent to London for a printing press and type, that he might translate the Bible into the Cree language, using ordinary letters. But the Company prevented the press from being shipped to him. This caused Mr. Evans to invent an alphabet to suit their needs. With an ordinary pocket knife he cut type from leaden bullets, and, with a rude, home-made printing press he, assisted by his good wife, printed hymns and prayers for the Indians. It is with these Cree syllabic characters, invented by the Rev. James Evans, that the British and Foreign Bible Society print the Bible for all the Indians of our Canadian North-West today. Lord Dufferin said: "Many a man who did nothing comparable with this has been honoured with a burial in Westminster Abbey."

Mr. Evans went on a visit to his old home in England. He still hoped to continue his work and it is said that among the many who were interested, they provided him with a printing press. Almost on the eve of his return to Canada, on the evening of November 23rd, 1846, after speaking on missions to a large audience at Keilby, in Lincolnshire, he retired to the home of a friend and suddenly passed away. He was laid to rest in the Waltham Street Chapel, Hull, after seventeen years in the ministry.

The reader may ask: "What has all this to do with John McLean? Simply this: that John McLean had married a daughter of Mr. Evans and it was with the intention of having a home in a civilized country that they came to live in Guelph. He was Agent of the Bank of Montreal at No. 21, Nottingham street. The office was in a room on the north-east side of the house. While living in this house in 1849, John McLean wrote "Notes of a Twenty-Five Years Service in the Hudson's Bay Territory." These books are now very rare—and valuable.

Among his assistants was one who had also been a former employee of the Hudson's Bay Company. This man received nothing but kindness from Mr. McLean and repaid it by stealing a large sum of money belonging to the bank. This was in November, 1855. Honest, honorable and upright himself, John McLean did not suspect his assistant, although Mrs. McLean, with a woman's instinct, distrusted him.

The loss of this money was, for about twenty years, a complete mystery and put an end to Mr. McLean's banking career. It meant financial ruin to him, for he gave up all the savings of his strenuous lifetime trying to make restitution for the loss the bank sustained. Owing to this, all his later life was a continual struggle. Years went by, but Mr. McLean lived to see the truth revealed. The man who stole the money died, leaving a large sum to a hospital in an Ontario town. He received credit for being a philanthropist from those who did not know the facts. And, Oh, the irony of Fate!. In a geological map of Canada, issued in 1913, a lake in Labrador is given the name of the man who stole the money, while John McLean, who explored the country, is not mentioned.

It was a token of respect from those who knew him best, and a compliment to Mrs. McLean and her mother, when Mr. McLean was requested to lay the corner stone of Norfolk Street Methodist Church in Guelph, in April 1855. And then, toward the end of 1857, the family came to Elora. Not long after that, Mrs. McLean having died, her mother, Mrs. Evans came to live with the family and took charge of them.

John McLean was an only son, but had three sisters. One of these married a Mr. McDonald, who lived at St. Laurent, near Montreal. Mr. McLean also had some cousins living in Canada, one of these, is was said, being Chief Justice McLean. Another, we have been led to believe, was Mrs. Catharine Fraser, mother-in-law of Dr. Finlayson, for many years a doctor, and later postmaster in Elora, at whose home Mrs. Fraser died at a very old age. Still another relative was John McLean Bell, the first Grammar School teacher in Elora. A sister of the latter was the wife of Mr. E. H. Kertland, a Public Land Surveyor whose name appears on many early maps of town sites in this part of Ontario. While in Elora he did this work, but, later, was for a long time a Doctor of Medicine in Toronto.

In John McLean's family, two of the older ones, a boy and a girl, died in the same week, of cholera. Clara married Capt. Charles McMillan; Margaret married a brother of the former, Lt.-Col. A. G. McMillan, a barrister who practised in Elora and later in Whitby; Archie was for many years a resident of Buffalo, where he was editor of a newspaper. He died suddenly, sitting in his office chair, June 8th, 1925. The youngest was Eugenia, named after her mother. She married Dr. O'Brian.

For twenty-five years and more Mr. McLean lived in Elora, where he was Clerk of the Division Court. He often wrote to the Toronto Globe, the Montreal Witness and other papers telling of the value of the North-West for settlement; and especially did he write, and quite forcibly, during the first weeks of 1869, urging the Dominion Government to secure this land, which they did about the month of April, 1869. Only recently, early in 1925, were some of the matters in dispute finally settled.

As a sample of what he wrote at that time, we give the closing paragraph which is as follows: "Ere I conclude, I would submit that the foregoing remarks are founded on personal observation. I have visited every part of the Territory which I have attempted to describe, and therefore know whereof I speak. I began to write on this subject about nineteen years ago, when the people of Canada knew little of the North-West Territory and cared less. The value of the Territory is now perfectly understood, and it affords me no small satisfaction to find that all who have visited the country since—Noblemen, clergymen, men of science, officers of the Army and Navy, have confirmed my report in every particular.

"In my former correspondence with the Press I generally wrote over the signature of 'Viator', but I see no reason why I should retain my incognito any longer and therefore subscribe myself,

Yours truly,
JOHN M'LEAN.
"Elora, April 27th, 1889."

Mr. McLean was very much respected by many friends who admired him. Tall, erect and active up to the age of eighty three, when he left Elora; even in the coldest, stormy weather he did not miss his morning walk.

He was quiet, reserved, and, in later years lonely, for his family had grown up and were away. His thoughts ran back to the years spent in the silent places; in the great lone land where, for months at a time, he had faced death by famine, frost and flood. He did not boast of what he had done, but to his friends, of whom my father was proud to count himself one, he told of the great falls in Labrador and I heard of those falls from my father long before I read of them. Comparing the different parts of Canada, he said: "And the Peace River is the pick of it all."

The photograph which accompanies this was made over sixty years ago by my father, the late Thomas Connon. Through their friendship, I was led to what he had done, as well as knowing Mr. McLean personally, I was led to preserve much of his history. I have the only copies of the Elora papers containing the letters which he published and hope that when loyal Canadians come to realize what John McLean did for them, some means may be found to reprint all he wrote about this, then, unknown part of Canada.

Leaving Elora early in June, 1883, accompanied by his daughter, Mrs. O'Brian and her two children, they went by way of Buffalo to San Francisco, up the coast to Nanaimo, B.C., and later to Victoria, where, at the home of his daughter, Mrs. O'Brian, he died on March 11th, 1890, at the age of ninety years. He was buried in Aisle 25, lot 72, in the Presbyterian Plot in Ross Bay Cemetery, Victoria, B.C.

Is it too much to hope that a monument to which Canadians may point with pride, should take the place of the modest marble cube which at present marks the spot?

*   *   *

Rev. John G. MacGregor was born at Alva, Stirlingshire, Scotland, in 1799 He received his preliminary education at the local schools and then took his Arts course at Glasgow University. After passing this he went to Edinburgh Divinity College where he took his Divinity course and was licensed to preach For some time he devoted his energies to private tuition in Edinburgh but in 1836 he came to St. Johns, New Brunswick. He remained in St. Johns until 1847. Having received a call from the congregation of Knox Church, Guelph, he was inducted there on June 23rd, 1847.

In 1852 he accepted the headmastership of the Elora Grammar School, which he held until his retirement about 1874. He was said to have been a thorough classical scholar and turned out a number of pupils who made their mark in the world.

Mr. MacGregor died in Elora on December 22nd, 1881. His wife, whose maiden name was Jane Stirling, survived him and died in Elora in April 1891 at the age of 89.

Of their family: Helen married the Rev. Mr. Stewart and lived at Kincardine; Jane, after the death of her mother, lived in Kincardine; Malcolm O. MacGregor, was a Barrister and Police Magistrate in Mount Forest; Alexander lived in Galt; Charles at Stratford; John and Robert at Minneapolis, Minnesota.

*   *   *

Rev. James Middlemiss, D.D., was born in the town of Dunse, Berwickshire, Scotland, on February 23rd, 1823. His father dying when he was only three months old, he became the care of his mother's father and brother until he entered the Edinburgh University at the age of fifteen. After his first session at the University he maintained himself, and paid all the expenses of his education, by money received from scholarships and private teaching.

At the time when Dr. Middlemiss was receiving his education in Edinburgh, two sisters in that city were conducting a boarding school for young ladies. These were Miss Elizabeth Menzies and her younger sister, Miss Mary Menzies, daughters of Captain Duncan Menzies, for forty years in the Royal Navy, who retired in 1815 to spend his later years at Dura Den, near Cupar-Fife, Scotland, and died in 1846 at the age of 86.

On August 23rd, 1855, after a long acquaintance, the Rev. James Middlemiss married Miss Mary Menzies, in view of his settling in Canada, and on the 11th of October, 1855, they arrived in Hamilton. On the evening of Saturday the 3rd of November, Dr. Middlemiss arrived in Elora, making his home with the kind family of Mr. James M. Adie, and preaching on the following day. The friendship with Mr. Adie's family, thus commenced, continued to the last, although, latterly, his family lived in Clifford. We shall leave Dr. Middlemiss to tell the history of Chalmers Church, just as he wrote it.

But, outside of all his Church work, he deserves credit for something which he did while he was working his way through college. On the recommendation of one of the teachers in Edinburgh, Dr. Middlemiss was, for two years, the private tutor to a young lad who afterwards became the greatest mathematician of the nineteenth century. The tutor was at that time from sixteen to eighteen and his pupil was from eight to ten years of age. To mention what his pupil, Professor James Clerk Maxwell did, would take too much space. You will find that given in the Encyclopedia Britannica. In Astronomy, in Electro-magnetism, and in Optics the results of his mathematical ability are accepted without question to-day. But there is one of his many useful inventions, which, even the doctors who make daily use of it, do not know where the idea came from; and Maxwell was the originator of it. We refer to the Opthalmoscope, an instrument used for examining the interior of the living eye. Light from a candle, as it was in his day, is placed at the side of the patient's head and is reflected into the eye by means of a small concave mirror. The interior of the patient's eye, or throat, is thus illuminated, and can be viewed through a small hole in the centre of the mirror, and may be magnified by means of lenses, if necessary.

On Whitsun Eve., 1854, Maxwell wrote to a relative— "I have made an instrument for seeing into the eye through the pupil. The difficulty is to throw the light in at that small hole and look in at the same time; but that difficulty is overcome, and I can see a large part of the back of the eye quite distinctly, with the image of the candle on it. People find no inconvenience in being examined, and I have got dogs to sit quite still and keep their eyes steady. Dogs eyes are very beautiful behind, a copper coloured ground, with glorious bright patches and networks of blue, yellow and green, with blood vessels great and small."

Again he wrote, on May 15th, 1855: "I have been perfecting my instrument for looking into the eye. I have found a dog which sits quite steady and seems to like being looked at; and I have found several men who have large pupils and do not wish to let me look in. I have seen the image of the candle distinctly in all the eyes I have tried, and veins of the retina were visible in some; but the dog's eyes showed all the ramifications of veins, with blue and green network, so that you might copy down everything. I have shown lots of men the image in my own eyes by shutting off the light till the pupil dilated and then letting it on."

Why is it that so many are deprived of the honour due to them? Prof. James Clerk Maxwell had a short life, but a busy one. He was born in July 1831 and died in November 1879. His biography was written by Prof. Lewis Campbell of St. Andrew's University, in Scotland. In doing this, Prof. Campbell was dependent for the information concerning Maxwell's younger days upon an aunt of Clerk Maxwell's. She seems to have had a grudge against the young divinity student, who was the tutor in the same house, for a short time. She, apparently, had an ambition to be a minister's wife. Because James Middlemiss did not help her to fulfil that ambition, she, forty years later, gave an unfair report of his work as tutor.

Whenever Maxwell published a book, his old tutor, out of his limited means, bought a copy; and, owing to the cost of publishing and the limited sale such books have, they were expensive. Because the writer was one of the few whom he had met, who knew what Clerk Maxwell had done, Dr. Middlemiss gave him those books which he could so ill afford to buy.

Carefully pasted in this biography, we find the following:

"Card from Professor Campbell to Professor Clerk Maxwell's tutor." "Professor Campbell has received Mr. Middlemiss' interesting letter, and hastens to assure him that he will do what he can to remove from the record some details which he now perceives to be calculated to give an unfair and exaggerated impression. He knew nothing of the relative ages of the parties, and was unaware of much which through Mr. Middlemiss' communication he now understands. He can only now express his regret, but when the opportunity arrives, which may be within a few months, he will do his best to retrieve the mistake. St. Andrews, December 4th, 1883."

This unfair reference to his work as tutor hurt Dr. Middlemiss very much. It was so undeserving. Clerk Maxwell's life-work showed the influence of h's tutor in his thorough knowledge of the Bible and his early mastery of geometry and algebra; in all of which Dr. Middlemiss was, himself, not surpassed by many.

It was on the first of November, 1860, that Dr. Middlemiss commenced to keep an accurate record of the weather and temperature, at his home in Elora. Twice a day, week after week and year after year, he carefully rcorded the thermometer readings, stating whether clear or cloudy, with incidental remarks as to the arrival and departure of the migratory birds, and the first appearance of garden flowers. With very few gaps, this evidence of his exact care and perseverance was continued until the end of August 1899—within two months of thirty-nine years. And this, not for any government salary or hope of reward, but all due to his mental make-up which insisted that what he knew should be exact, not a guess.

The Manse of Chalmers Church was that stone, two-storied cottage near the junction of the Irvine with the Grand River, which is now the home of Mr. W. D. Samson, editor of "The Elora Express". This, with the trees growing about it was a sanctuary for the birds that came up the rocky gorge of the Grand River. The ancestors of those birds had followed the same course, generation after generation, ever since there was a river; and their descendants would continue to do so to-day, in even greater numbers if there were a few more homes where they would be fed, welcomed and protected as they were during all those years at the home of Doctor and Mrs. Middlemiss.

It was in the summer of 1873 that Miss Menzies came from Edinburgh to make her home with them. The two sisters, refined, educated ladies, were the embodiment of self-forgetfulness and generosity, continually helping those who were sick or in need. One treasure from her father's home, Miss Menzies brought to Canada: a wonderful chair which is said to date from the time of the Italian Renaissance, about the year fifteen-hundred.

Miss Menzies died April 19th, 1892, at the age of 84; Mrs. Middlemiss on June 29th, 1892 at the age of 79, and Dr. Middlemiss, after a lonely life of fourteen years, on March 11th, 1907, at the age of 84.

Dr. Middlemiss was possessed of an acute sense of humour, which had been continually suppressed, to be in keeping with the dignity of his profession. However, the writer was one of those who knew him more intimately and enjoyed that humour which others never guessed at. And we can say this, that some of his best sermons were comprised within one sentence. We shall give two, in illustration.

On a summer's afternoon, we were standing on the platform of the C. N. R. station at Elora. A locomotive, attached to a freight train, was waiting for orders to pull out. We had been talking over a variety of subjects, when we spoke of the working of the engine in front of us. It was then our old friend said, "Is it not most remarkable that the greatest powers are those we cannot see?" "In the boiler of that locomotive there is steam. When admitted into the cylinder of the engine, its expansive force moves the train. But, not until after the steam has done its work and has come in contact with the cooler air does it become visible in the form of minute drops of water. Even although the engine were made of glass, the steam is invisible. And then we have Electricity and Magnetism and Gravitation and even Life itself. Yes, all the greatest powers are those we cannot see."

During the earlier years of his ministry, there was a man who had lived in Elora for a short time. He had tried to succeed and failed, for the same reason that so many failed then, as they do now. He, therefore, decided to go to some other town and make a fresh start. But, before leaving, he called to have a talk with the pastor of Chalmers Church, where he had attended. To him he told his difficulties, and how he thought by going to another community he would be away from the companions and the temptation he had found in E'ora. Carefully bringing the tips of his thumbs and fingers together, as was his habit, Dr. Middlemiss said, "Yes, yes, but one must go a long way before he gets away from himself."

* * *

HISTORY OF CHALMERS CHURCH, ELORA
Written About 1906 by Rev. James Middlemiss, D.D.

In the early fifties of last century, when Elora, which for a number of years had been only a hamlet, was rapidly becoming a village of growing importance, the minister of Melville Church, Fergus, the Rev. George Smellie, felt it due to the increasing number of his people in the rising village to give them a fortnightly service. About the middle of the decade, early in 1855, a growing desire to enjoy regular Sabbath services manifested itself in the erection in summer of a frame church building of moderate dimensions; and later in the year, application was made to the Presbytery of Hamilton for stated supply of service by appointment of the Presbytery's Home Mission Committee. It so happened that, having been commissioned by the Colonial Committee of the Free Church of Scotland, to the Presbytery of Hamilton, the Rev. James Middlemiss reached Hamilton on the 11th of October, two days after the Presbytery had consented to the application. He was almost immediately directed to proceed to Elora to labour there as a Home Missionary until he should receive further instructions. Beginning his work on Sabbath, the 4th of November, he preached morning and afternoon in the

Temperance Hall, with occasional exceptions, during the winter; and the congregation having been duly formed on the 21st of February, the usual steps were taken with a view to his settlement as pastor, which took place on the 3rd of June, 1856. In the course of the winter, the Church had been seated and opened for worship. The membership numbered sixty-six, separated by certificate from Melville Church, Fergus. But thirty-eight names were added to the Communion Roll on the occasion of the first Communion, which was observed in July, the late Dr. Reid, according to the old practice, assisting the minister. In the course of the summer and fall, elders and deacons were appointed, the full organization of the congregation being completed on the 31st of October, when the Deacons were ordained.

(Mr. Middlemiss had been settled only a few weeks, when it became a matter of common report that he was unorthodox in his publc teaching; and the Kirk Session, on his request, petitioned the Presbytery to make a thorough investigation. Fortunately, with one exception, the sermons alleged to be unsound were written in full; and on investigation it was found that the charges were groundless; and the author of them, who, being a minister, it was thought, had been disappointed in his hope of having the care of the new congregation in addition to his mastership of the Grammar School, was suspended from his functions and privileges on the charges of slander and falsehood. The suspension was removed some months after, on due apology made, and at the same time, Mr. Middlemiss was, on recommendation of the aged Clerk of the Presbytery, appointed his successor in office—a position he occupied a number of years, resigning it eventually in favour of Dr. Torrance.)

In the summer of 1861, the manse of Chalmers Church was built; and now with improvements from time to time on the house and on the adjacent grounds, but little is needed to make it one of the finest, if not the finest, of the manses in the province. In 1868, the congregation had so increased in number,—the membership being over two hundred—that is was thought necessary to make an addition to the building to the extent of one hundred and twenty sittings, the former capacity having been three hundred.

In 1874, the old building of 1855 showing signs of decay, the congregation resolved to erect a new building of stone, capable of accommodating five hundred and seventy. It was begun in the fall of 1876, and was opened for public worship on the 11th of November, 1877, Principal Caven preaching morning and evening, and Mr. Middlemiss in the afternoon. At the inception of the undertaking. it was calculated that the cost would be twelve thousand dollars; but with unforeseen requiremen's and the interest of borrowed money during nine years, it cost the congregation fifteen thousand dolars before the debt was entirely removed in 1886. It may be mentioned here to the credit of the congregation, that, though its membership has never been large—never exceeding two hundred and sixty—i thas the campartive'y rare distinction of having carried to a finish the burden incurred in the erection of its new church, without asking the Presbytery for leave to mortgage it.

In 1886, the Senate of Knox College conferred on Mr. Middlemiss the honorary degree of Doctor of Divinity; and in 1893, he was, after a ministry in Elora of thirty- years, released on the seventieth anniversary of his birth. from the active duties of his pastorate. A few months after—in August of the same year—his successor, the Rev. H. R. Horne, LL.B., an alumnus of the University of Toronto, and a graduate of Knox College, was ordained to the Christian ministry and inducted as pastor of Chalmers Church. After a ministry of twelve years, he accepted last year the position of Secretary and Agent of the Religious Tract and Book Society. unanimously offered him by the Directors.

This reminds me of what, perhaps, I should have mentioned earlier in relation to my income as pastor of Chalmers Church. When I was settled as its pastor, it was on the promise of an annual stipend of one hundred and five pounds, Halifax currency, or four hundred and twenty dollars, the Halifax pound being four dollars. Without having promised it however, the congregation from the first paid my house rent of eighty dollars during the five years of my occupancy of the house now belonging to Mr. Alex. Davidson. In 1861, my stipend, including house rent was raised from $500 to $600. When the manse was built that year, I received $600 and rent free, equal to $100— in all, $700. Then in 1869 the stipend was increased to $800; and, the membership still continuing to increase, another hundred was added about the time of the opening of the new church; so that, including the manse, my income from that time was $1000.

*   *   *

David Boyle was born at Greenock, Scotland, on May 1st, 1842. With his parents he came to Canada in 1856. For a short time his father carried on a blacksmithing business near the Wissler Mill in Salem, which had just been completed. For the two years previous, the Crimean War had caused such a demand for Canadian wheat and flour that the milling and every other business in Canada was prosperous; to be followed some months after the sudden termination of that war by the greatest financial crash this country has ever seen. Commencing about 1852, when the Grand Trunk and other smaller railways were being projected through Ontario, a real estate boom flourished. Villages were surveyed in the most absurd places and town lots were sold and resold at high prices—until the boom burst. Such were the conditions when Mr. Boyle and his parents came to Canada.

Mr. Boyle, Sr., being a superior workman and having had considerable experience on engine work at his former home at Greenock on the Clyde, the birthplace of James Watt, the greatest improver of the steam engine, and at Birkenhead, near Liverpool, he found more suitable employment with the Great Western Railway Company at London, Ontario. Of Mr. Boyle, Sr., it was said that he forged and set the tires for the first locomotive built in Canada for that company.

When the family removed from Salem, David Boyle was apprenticed to his uncle, Andrew, a blacksmith at the small village of Eden Mills, at the south end of the Township of Eramosa. The good folks of that quiet village were never at a loss to know upon whom the blame should be placed for the many practical jokes played upon them during his sojourn there. His resourcefulness in contriving ridiculous situations seemed to be without limit and continued until late in life.

It was while David Boyle was at Eden Mills, in the year 1857, that the reaction following the close of the Russian War became serious. There was a sudden fall in the price of wheat. The real estate boom collapsed. Merchants who had given credit found that they could not collect their accounts. The whole country was bankrupt. But a strange thing happened. When all material prosperity was at a standstill, and every one was just as poor as his neighbour, people turned to intellectual matters. Each locality had its singing school. Libraries were formed, lectures were well attended; the subjects being mesmerism, phrenology, physiognomy, and occasionally astronomy. Before the close of that year Guelph was visited by Elihu Burritt, the learned blacksmith, who, by his own efforts had secured an education that gave him international fame. David Boyle walked to Guelph and back, which would be about ten miles. to hear that lecture, after a hard day's work at his trade. That was the turning point in his career, for what he heard that night aroused his ambition and he forthwith determined to acquire an education. For days after hearing that lecture he talked of Elihu Burritt and the way in which he had educated himself. To one of his companions he said, "If he could do it, I can."

After being about three years in Eden Mills, Mr. Boyle returned to Elora, where he secured employment at his trade with the late Hugh Hamilton. Later on he attended the old Grammar School when the Rev. J. G. MacGregor was the teacher and here he was grounded in all the doctrines which were then considered necessary to procure a teacher's certificate. While attending the grammar school,in June 1864, Mr. Boyle was given a prize for English composition, a subject of which he made good use in later years. Toward the end of the year, as a newspaper report of the time says, "After the requisition of the law had been complied with, in respect of evidence by some responsible party, of the good moral character of the applicants, the examination was proceeded with." Up to this date the examinations were oral. Random questions were asked by members of the examining board, who were usually ministers; for, until the invention of the coal-oil lamp and a method of refining petroleum, about 1858, few working men got a chance to read. At work all day, they could not read long by candle light and it is a peculiar fact that until coal-oil lamps came into general use there were no daily newspapers.

At the suggestion of the Rev. James Middlemiss an important change was brought about, which came into use at the mid-summer examinations, in 1865. We find in the "Elora Observer" of that date, "The examination was conducted by means of printed questions to which written answers were required, a mode of examination which necessarily occupies more time, and may thus appear more of a hardship to those from a distance from the place of meeting but one whose superiority in the majority of cases, in the results elicited, must counter-balance minor considerations."

In January 1865, Mr. Boyle commenced teaching in what is best known as Middlebrook School. The school was thus appropriately named by Mr. Boyle because it is situated between two beautiful trout streams locally known as Carroll's Creek and Bosomworth's Creek. This school is about three and a half miles from Elora, in Upper Pilkington. It was first opened in 1852, the teacher being Miss Farrell; the second was Robert Godfrey; the third, Thomas Frankland; the fourth, John McCatty, and the fifth, David Boyle.

There was a rough element in that school section when Mr. Boyle commenced to teach. Former teachers had much trouble with some full grown men who would attend school just when it pleased them. Their only object seemed to be to show the other pupils what wonderful men they were, at the expense of the teacher. Fights between pupil and teacher had been a common occurrence; but Mr. Boyle took a different plan. On the day school opened, he talked to the scholars for more than an hour explaining to them the value of a good education, and how those who neglected their opportunities in procuring that education were at a disadvantage all through life. Then he referred to the young men and to what he had heard of their former conduct. He told them he had prepared a document which he would ask them to sign before going on with the school work. This was a pledge stating that while in the school or on the school property they, on their honour as gentlemen, would behave themselves. There was some hesitation at first; but each one who signed shamed the others until he had thirty names on that pledge. After that he had little trouble. If those young men were to be considered gentlemen, they could not break their word of honour.

It may be interesting to record that the salary was $340.00 a year.

Mr. Boyle continued to teach in Middlebrook until the summer of 1871, when he became principal of the Elora Public School, his predecessor being John Tait and his successor Alexander Petrie.

When Mr. Boyle came to the Elora school he found a few hundred books piled in a ha'lway which joined the two buildings. Those old books were all that remained of a library which had been organized many years before. At his suggestion, and with the assistance of others the Elora Library was re-organized a few months later. He took a lively interest in the library, both in getting up the entertainments necessary for its support and in the selection of books. This gave him the opportunity he had long wished for, to read the latest scientific books. From this reading, he became much interested in the study of biology and geology. With the oldest forms of life which have left their imprint in the rocks lying exposed to view on the magnesian-limestone banks of the Grand and Irvine Rivers at Elora, Mr. Boyle entered into the study of geology with an enthustiastic interest, and his discovery of several hitherto unknown fossils brought him before those interested in that science.

As a teacher, Mr. Boyle was very successful. Having had to follow original methods in procuring his own education, he did not follow hard and fast rules in teaching others. Interesting items in the daily papers, or any natural object would form the subject of a lesson and in this way his method of teaching by object lessons led to the valuable collection of Canadian birds and animals, historical and Indian relics, together with a collection of geological and mineral specimens which, in his day, was referred to with pride as "The Elora Museum".

For ten years Mr. Boyle taught in E'ora and, on leaving, took with him an extensive and valuable collection of Indian relics and many curiosities which he had procured in exchange for local geological specimens. These he presented to the Canadian Institute in Toronto, and this formed the nucleus of the Provincial Archaeological Museum in the Normal School, which mainly through his efforts, ranks among the finest on the American Continent.

Mr. Boyle had charge of the Ontario Mineral Exhibit at the Cincinnati Exhibition in 1888, of the collection of minerals for the Imperial Institute, London, at which was shown a colossal map of Ontario planned by himself. He prepared the collection of Ontario Minerals exhibited at the World's Fair at Chicago, in 1893. There, the amazing mineral wealth of Northern Ontario was first shown to the World. Occupying a prominent place in this exhibit were two 16" x 20", direct print, photographs of the Elora Rocks, made by the writer.

Mr. Boyle was a humorous writer in the Scottish dilaect; his first efforts in that line appearing in the Elora Express under the name of Sandy McTocher.

Not long before leaving Elora, Mr. Boyle wrote "The Adventures of, or the Ups and Downs of Number 7", being a full, true and correct account of what happened in the said School Section during a period of twelve months, more or less, and some things that were enacted beyond its limits."

This paper covered book of a hundred pages, was supposed to relate some of his own experiences as a teacher. It caused much amusement while the parties described were living, and gave a good description of the trials and difficulties teachers had to contend with at that time, with practical suggestions for improvement.

The closing years of Mr. Boyle's life, a period shadowed for him by constant ill-health, was brightened by one of the greatest honours that came to him during a career that brought him honours at every turn. In recognition of his eminent services in the field of science he, on June 12th, 1909, received the degree of Doctor of Laws from the University of Toronto. The conferring of the degree took place in the bedroom of Mr. Boyle's home, his illness preventing him from attending the regular convocation of the University.

The Editor of the Scottish American wrote— "It is with great sorrow that we announce the death on February 14th, 1911, of our friend and contributor for nearly thirty years, Mr. David Boyle, L.L.D., who was the first provincial archaeologist in Ontario, the first superintendent of the Provincial Museum, and the first secretary of the Ontario Historical Society. About two years ago he was laid aside by paralysis, and during his long illness the frequent demands upon us for letters from "Andra McSpurtle, formerly of Auld Kiltulliegorach," showed how greatly Mr. Boyle's contributions under that pseudonym were appreciated by our readers. His English contributions were faultless in style, displaying great ability and erudition on whatever he dealt with, while the doric and humour of "Andra McSpurtle's" letters were alike unique and peculiarly his own, and always showed that in thought and feeling he was a Scotsman to the backbone." In 1895, he published "Notes on Primitive Man in Ontario"; in 1896 "The History of Scarboro; while between 1886 and 1909 appeared his annual "Archaeological Reports", which are known throughout the world by students of folklore; besides editing the annual reports etc., of the Ontario Historical Society. At its meeting of February 18th, 1908, The Cayuga County Historical Society, of New York State, awarded the Cornplanter Medal for Iroquois Research, to Mr. Boyle, he being the first one outside of the United States to receive this medal.

DAVID BOYLE, LL.D.

ICICLES ON THE BANKS OF THE GRAND RIVER
AT ELORA
Photographed February 1885

Mr. Boyle's humorous letters were not all sent to the Scottish American. Here is one, of the many sent to the writer's father.

Toronto, November 2nd, 1894.

Weel My Auld Cronie:—

Hoo are you? I was much pleased to hear from you to-day and I can assure you that nothing would give me more pleasure than to accept your kind invitation, and spend a short time in Elora both under your own hospitable roof, and the ditto ditto of others. Do you know that as I read your note, I said to myself, 'Connon is feeling blue—he has been engaged in reminiscences—Hallowe'en has set him athinking of all his old friends and foes who have joined the great majority as well as a few who are yet 'In the land of the living and the place of hope'. He has been causing to pass in review the 'old corps' —Robert Chinneck, Hugh Hamilton, Dawvit Foote, Sandy Spalding, Andrew Gordon, J. M. Fraser, Richard and Walter P. Newman, Henry Kirkland, John Hele, Rowley Wood, John Bain, Geordie Thomson, Billy McDowell, Sem Wissler, Jimmy Allan (the auld farrier), the Raiverin' Duff, Dr. Finlayson, Dr. Middleton and so on, just as they came into his noodle. He has also taken into account that he is himself older than he once was and that he made a narrow escape frae the deil no' lang syne. Thus he longs for a blink of a weel-kent face, and the soun' o' an auld clapper, and he said to himself, 'Well it'll relieve me a wee if I write to Boyle—who knows but he may take a run up, and then couldn't we have a canty time rehearsing old stories, and fighting old fights over again'. Now, was it not something of this sort that was in your head? Well, if it wasn't, I can tell you that such thoughts often take full possession of my own pow, and I would like real well to see Connon, or some other old friend to talk with.

But why should I suggest such sad and such serious thoughts? Let us think of something else. At any rate, I have no doubt that if we were together for a little while we could make the rafters dirl with laughter, notwithstanding our united hundred years, and our corresponding frozen pows.

I was greatly pleased to see John and have such a long talk with him during Fair time—he gave me all the news.

Do you know Connon, it often occurs to me that we had in Elora a lot of very odd old customers, and some equally young ones, too—of course you and I would not be included in either category! What a lot of funny sketches might be written about them!

Yes, thank you, we are all quite well, especially every one of us. Sus is lecturing at the College, and physicking generally—Jim is in his third Medical year. Annie runs the house and all the family, and Willie is at the technical school.

Now, how is Mrs. Connon? I would like to see her and to have a talk with her too. When you write to Tom, remember me to him, as also, in your correspondence with Mrs. Grant.

Now, I am sure you are sorry you wrote to me, but it serves you right.

Say, give my respects to my old boss, Sandy Cuthbert.

Yours truly,

David Boyle.

(Note: Sandy Cuthbert was a blacksmith in Elora. J.R.C.)

Toronto, November 6th, 1903.

John Connon.

My Dear Old Boy,—

I have been wondering for some time not only how your general health is, but how your throat is? I shall be glad to know also that your prospects are good for the issue of your local history. This reminds me that I am in doubt as to whether I ever thanked you for the photographs of local characters you sent me some time ago. What a charming book of illustration you can have for the History of Elora. I am sure no other place in the province has been so well pictured. Yours will be an "embarrassment of riches". There will be no money in it. You must never be original in this country unless you want to remain poor.

       Your old teacher,

          David Boyle.

I fain would hope that Death does not end all,
....
But if I'm wrong and worst should come to worst!
Shall I be blamed for what I could not see?
Shall I be asked why I did not from the first
Believe with others what seemed wrong to me?

    David Boyle.

On May 24th, 1867, David Boyle married Martha S. Frankland, who, at this date, April 1926, is living at Richmond Hill, Ont.

In their family—

Dr. Susannah Peel, (Trinity) married Dr. A. S. Hamilton, in 1902, a noted neurologist of Minneapolis, Minnesota.

John B. married Ella Manning, and has lived in Detroit, Vancouver and Los Angeles.

Dr. James Frankland, Toronto, married Millicent Flett. He lived and died in Edmonton in 1917.

Anne Anderson, married William Cowan Perry, 1900. Lived in Winnipeg and Toronto, widowed in 1906. A journalist since 1912.

William Robert married Eva Wilson. He has been employed by the Robert Simpson and Hudson Bay Companies in the principal cities from Vancouver to Montreal.

      *   *   *

In the month of October, 1834, the first of a number of settlers from Aberdeenshire, in Scotland, made their homes in that part of the Township of Nichol, on the banks of the Irvine river, about two miles north of Elora.

They called their settlement Bon-accord; that being the motto on the coat-of-arms of Aberdeen City.

Five years later, on October 2nd, 1839, a meeting was held to organize a Debating Society and a Library. The object of the Society was "to discuss Literary, Scientific and Moral subjects, by essay, lecture or otherwise." "No subject of a theological or political nature shall be introduced at any of the meetings of this Society."

Books were contributed by those who had them and in this way they formed a library. Open meetings, or soirees were occasionally held and the proceeds given to the Bon-accord Library. At first, the meetings were held in the old school house, which was on the back of Mr. Elmslie's farm (near the railway bridge over the Irvine), but this was found to be too far away for the majority, so that the place of meeting was changed to the Old Log Church, on Mr. Barron's farm. Here the meetings continued until the Congregation moved to their Church in Elora, which was built in 1850, and called Knox Church. Among those who should be given credit for the formation of this Library, three should be mentioned. They were the Rev. James Middleton, who had been a Presbyterian minister in Scotland. His brother-in-law, Mr. George Pirie, who, a few years later founded the Guelph Herald newspaper, and Mr. George Elmslie, who, not adapted to farming spent the remaining thirty-five years of his life as a teacher in Ancaster. Hamilton, Guelph, Elora and Alma.

In Elora Village, a similar library, supplied with books from those interested, was kept, voluntarily, by Mr. William Reid, a carpenter, in 1843 and for some years later.

A Public Meeting, to organize The Elora Mechanics' Institute was held in the Commercial Hotel on Thursday evening, November 26th, 1857. At this meeting the following officers were elected:—

President, E. H. Kertland (Then a surveyor; afterward for many years a doctor in Toronto). Vice-presidents, John W. Burke and William Morrison. (Mr. Burke was also a surveyor, and, later an Anglican clergyman in Belleville.) Treasurer, Robert Haig. Secretary, John S. Crossman. Committee, Charles Clarke (afterward Lieut. Colonel and Clerk of the Legislative Assembly); William H. Frazer; John Duncan; John Wilkinson; John Bain; John Henderson; Andrew Gordon; Ephraim Land and Conrad Eisenhut.

Among the names of 76 members who were enrolled, should be mentioned that of John McLean, who, during his 25 years exploring for the Hudson's Bay Company discovered one of the wonders of the World, the Grand Falls in Labrador, and in 1869, by his knowledge of that country saved the Canadian North-West, for Canada, when politicians were going to give it away to the United States.

At a meeting held on April 2nd, 1869, the following resolution was passed, "That in consequence of the small support which the public has given to the Institute, it has become advisable to dissolve it, and it is hereby resolved that it be discontinued, and that Mr. E. H. Newman he requested to realize as much as possible out of the assets and report to a final meeting to be held in the Council Room, on the 16th of April at 7½ o'clock". "Memo. April 16th, 1869. Attended at Council Room in accordance with above resolution; two members only attended."

After the mid-summer holidays in 1871, a teacher commenced his duties as Principal of the Elora Public School. This was Mr. David Boyle, who, ten years later went to Toronto where he became the leading Canadian Archaeologist. Mr. Boyle found, stored in a hallway in the school, the books of the library which had dissolved two and a half years before, and was the means of re-organizing the Elora Mechanics' Institute in October 1871. In doing this he had the assistance of Charles Clarke, Fred Cornwall, William Crackle, Thomas Connon, D. M. Potter, William Snyder and Robert Mitchell, who was for many years the Librarian; and he was succeeded by his daughter, Miss Agnes Mitchell; while she in turn was followed by Miss Land, who died on August 25th, 1928.

This organization has continued since October, 1871, and is now known as the Elora Public Library.

*   *   *

Away back, about the close of the 18th Century, some surveyor ran a line upon which the geography of this part of Western Ontario is built. Just what date it was, we could not learn when enquiry was made at the Survey Office at Parliament Buildings, in Toronto.

At that time, the home of Chief Joseph Brant was at Burlington, on Lake Ontario, near Hamilton.

Starting from Joseph Brant's House there, the Surveyor ran a line in a north-westerly direction, or, as they say it, North, 45 degrees West. This line he continued about fifty miles, until he came to a stream which he thought was the head waters of the Thames, or some other river running into Lake Huron. When he arrived at this stream and that conclusion (which was wrong) he stopped.

The stream, it was learned later, was the Conestogo, which runs into the Grand River near a village of the same name. Look it up in a good map of Ontario. The point at which the line came to this stream is now the Village of Arthur.

The Six Nation Indians, who remained loyal to Britain during the American Revolutionary War, were promised a tract of land if they would come to Canada. Their descendants live near Brantford to-day. The tract of land which they were promised was to be six miles on either side of the Grand River, from its source to Lake Erie. (As you will see, they never received any above Fergus; and the river has come more than thirty miles before it reaches Fergus.)

This strip of land which had been given to the Indians, was very soon sold to private individuals, or sold back to the Government, which, in turn again gave it to private parties for their military or political services.

When other surveyors came later to set apart this strip of land, six miles each way from the river, they commenced from this base line which crosses the Grand River a little above Fergus. Measuring from this point to a distance of half the width of the proposed township, they found a spot at the east corner of the County Poor House Property and about four hundred yards up stream from the railway bridge which crosses the river half way between Elora and Fergus. From this point as a centre, they measured six miles to either side of the river and in this way formed the Township of Nichol. While the upper side of this township is the north-eastern boundary of Fergus, the lower side is at the junction of the Irvine with the Grand River in Elora. The other townships farther down the river were formed in a similar manner. They curve to suit the general course of the river like the steps of a winding stair.

If we place a ruler on the map; one end of it at Hamilton and the other at Southampton it will be found that the line passes this spot, at the junction of the rivers. Elora is, therefore, "In the Centre of the Map". So much for the geography of Elora.

ELORA

One of the first owners of the Township of Nichol was Colonel Thomas Clark, of Niagara Falls. His remains are buried in the graveyard of Trinity Church, Chippawa, near the Inlet of the great Hydro Power Canal. When Col. Clark was the owner of the township, it was so inaccessible that he could not get anyone to settle in it until a mill was built. He, therefore, persuaded Roswell Matthews to go to the Falls on the Grand River, as it was then called, and build a mill. He promised Matthews one-hundred acres for each of his family. This they never received, for, no sooner had they arrived at the Falls on the Grand River than Col. Clark heard that Major-Gen. Pilkington, the owner of the adjoining township, was going to build a mill. Col. Clark abandoned his project and Matthews undertook to build the mill about 1½ miles farther down. This mill was built, and, by being constantly repaired, it was used by for three years; but Matthews could not succeed in making the dam strong enough to withstand the current, because the bed of the river was full of pot-holes. The mill was moved to a smaller stream and supplied the wants of the few settlers until one was built at the Falls on the Grand River in 1843. But it was not built by Matthews. In great poverty and hardship Matthews and his wife, with a family of nine children struggled on for nine years, until in 1827, they heard that work might be had in Guelph, which was just starting. With what they thought was a better prospect, they left their home and clearing behind them. Shortly after going to Guelph, Roswell Matthews met with an accident and, through unskilful treatment, died. His was the first grave in the City of Guelph.

The family scattered. John Matthews, the first Elora boy who was in Elora from his ninth to his eighteenth year, died at Santa Catalina Island, off the coast of California at the age of 97. Hardship and plain living in his childhood did not shorten his days, but, on the other hand it was only because he was very strong that he lived through it.

The next to take an interest in the place was Captain William Gilkison. In October, 1832, he bought half the Township of Nichol; being a strip twelve miles long and about one and seven-eighths miles broad. He at once had the village surveyed; and that was on the clearing made by Roswell Matthews, on the south side of the river overlooking the falls. The date on this original map of Elora is November 10th, 1832, and on it, for the first time was the name Elora. It was so named as a compliment to his youngest brother, Capt. John Gilkison, who on the building of a new ship for himself, had called it the 'Elora'. In this vessel he made regular trips from Port Glasgow to Bombay, in India. Capt. John Gilkison had named his ship after the wonderful Cave Temples of Elora, in India, which were hewn out of the granite face of a mountain—by hand; Temples side by side for a mile and a quarter! The caves in our Elora were not made by hand.

At the time he bought this land, Capt. Gilkison lived in Brantford, but had been there but a short time. He sent a Clerk to Elora to have a store built while he was busy gathering and forwarding supplies for the new Settlement. This included the machinery for a saw-mill; for the water-power at the Falls on the Grand River was the object in view; with Matthews and with Gilkison and those who came later.

Six months later; on April 23rd, 1833, Capt. Gilkison died from a stroke of paralysis; brought on by the driving energy with which he was working. He was 56 years old.

For ten years, from 1833 to 1843 Elora lay dormant. The capital that Capt. Gilkison would have used to develop the water-power and the village was divided among his seven surviving sons, the eldest of whom was thirty years of age.

Charles Allan was a carpenter. He had helped to build the first houses in Fergus, only three miles away. He formed a small company which included besides himself, James Ross, father of the prosperous lawyer, James L. Ross of 20 King St. East, Toronto, and Arthur Ross, father of the Rev. Dr. John Ross of Brussels, Thorold, Toronto and sometimes California.

In April 1843 this Company commenced to build a grist-mill, a store and a bridge. For fifteen years Elora went ahead fast. It was the market for all the country toward Lake Huron. The building of the Grand Trunk Railway main line from 1852 to 1854, and other smaller railroads brought on a mania in Canada for buying town lots. The Crimean War followed when prices for all farm produce went high. Everybody felt they were becoming rich. Mr. Allan and some others had town plots surveyed in different places. The little village of Alma, sold by auction in January 1856, for $18,500. That was when it was all bush. Now, with the buildings in it, no one would want it at that price. These sales were generally held at an hotel. Champagne and bogus bidding made the bidding brisk. The Crimean War ended suddenly. At once, wheat, which had sold for more than two dollars a bushel became unsaleable. The whole country became bankrupt.

But Mr. Allan had made money and while he lived, Elora prospered. As the result of winning a law suit, a dispute over some real estate deal, Charles Allan died suddenly at Hamilton on January 13th, 1859.

In 1845, Sem Wissler founded the Village of Salem which is part of Elora in one way. He did so because there was good water power on the Irvine River there. For twenty years it grew. They had two flour mills, a saw-mill, a tannery, two breweries and six hotels—then called taverns. They manufactured shoes, shoe-losts and shoe pegs.

On the morning of the 18th of May, 1865, Mr. Wissler was rising from his bed when he fell back and died immediately, at the age of forty-six.

He left no will. At that time there was no way to administer an Estate in such a case. It had to wait until the youngest son was of age, which was in 1887. By that time there was not much left.

On the first of July, 1870, a railway was opened from Guelph to Elora and Fergus.

In 1873 the railway was continued north-west to Southampton and at once every small place to the north became as good a market for farm produce as Elora had been.

The industries in Elora long ago were, first, the saw-mill; then a grist or flour mill, a woollen mill, a foundry where they made agricultural implements a planing mill and all these were run from 'The Falls on the Grand River. Up stream, there was a smaller water-power. It ran the first Ingrain Carpet Factory in Canada. It was a good industry. Had it not been, it would have been allowed to remain in Elora; but it was wrecked by Toronto Directors and a factory built in Toronto that should have been in Elora. That was from 1873 to 1875. So, you see, it is a sad story of hardship, death and disappointment.

There were other industries, if they can be so-called. We had in Elora two distilleries. After the Crimean War when wheat was unsaleable; and before that when much of it was frozen every year, whisky was sold for eighty cents a pail, for cash, or one dollar if it was booked! We can remember when there were eight taverns in Elora. At that time there would be a population of 1500 or perhaps 1600. Now, it is sad to relate, there are about 1200. That is, in Elora proper. Outside the corporation, in Lot 18, as it is called, being the number of the farm on the map; and in Salem, there are, it may be, 400 more But it is safe to say that Elora has less of a population than it formerly had. It is not safe to rely on old statements of population, for the more it could be made out to be the more liquor licenses could be issued by the village council; and as the village received the money from the issue of licenses (before the Crooks Act of 1876), they rather encouraged the assessor to make the population as high as he could. It was surprising how quickly boarders changed the hotel at which they were stopping about that time.

So, the reason for Elora's existence was the Falls on the Grand River. There was no other reason.

The cause of its decline is that the land about the sources of the river has been completely denuded of the trees that grew there. Nature's way is best. The land where the Grand and Irvine Rivers take their rise is a large plateau. It was one large swamp which acted as if it were a huge sponge. When rain came, or snow melted, the sponge absorbed it all and gradually all the year 'round the water escaped from thousands of springs. I have photographs which my father made of the Elora Falls in 1860. Saw logs are shown on the face of the dam. There was not sufficient water—no flood to wash them over; and there they stuck. Now, in Spring time a large part of the water which should and did come down in a regular flow, comes down in a few days. The water-powers are of little use now. They can not be depended upon for power.

As to the future, Elora has many good buildings which would cost little to buy or rent. They should be useful for small industries that could use Hydro Power.

We have, in 1926, two furniture factories, a planing mill and a disc harrow and steel land roller industry. One of the best industries in the country is the White Lime Company, which will continue to be a money-maker.

Owing to the railway cutting off trade from the north, south and east, Elora has a very limited store trade.

The manufacturing possibilities are great. Summer tourists come in ever-increasing numbers to see the rocky gorge on the Grand and Irvine Rivers.

We look forward to the time, and that in the near future, when Fergus, Elora and Salem will form one large manufacturing centre.

*   *   *

We propose to trace the relationship of several family groups, or those from the same localities, who were more or less associated with the History of Ontario, and, in some cases, of Elora and Fergus. This may be uninteresting to the general reader, who merely reads from curiosity, or to be entertained, but we believe that long years after this it will prove useful to those who really wish to know the history of our country.

It was on the 13th of September, 1759, that the British force of a few thousand men captured Quebec. General Wolfe found, as he had shortly before read, that "The path of glory leads but to the grave". General Montcalm the brave commander of the French, also sacrificed his life for a France which, at that time, did not deserve it.

While General Wolfe was taking Quebec, another army of fourteen-thousand men was coming to his assistance by way of Lake Champlain, while a third expedition captured the French fort at Niagara and then went down by way of Lake Ontario and the St. Lawrence to Montreal, where, about the 6th of September 1760 all three armies met within a few hours of each other.

Commodore, The Honorable Alexander Grant was born on May 20th, 1734, being a son of Patrick Grant, the 8th Laird of Glenmorriston, Invernesshire, Scotland.

At an early age he was a midshipman in the British Navy and left it in 1757 to join the Montgomery Highlanders, and with them came to Canada. On Lake Champlain it was found necessary to build and use sailing vessels. Therefore, the General, Lord Amherst, called for volunteers who had experience as sailors. One of these was Lieutenant Alexander Grant, who, on October 11th, 1759, was put in command of a sloop of sixteen guns. So much were his services appreciated that, in 1763, he was placed in charge of all vessels between Niagara and Mackinaw. Some fourteen years later, when half the width of these lakes passed under the United States Flag, he was re-appointed to suit the new conditions, as follows. May 25th, 1778. Sir: His Excellency, the Commander in Chief in his letter to me of the 23rd October 1777, informed me that he has appointed Capt. Alex. Grant to be commanding officer of the Naval Department upon the Lakes Ontario, Erie, Huron & Michigan. Signed Mason Bolton, Lieut. Col. To Capt. James Andrews. Commandant of Niagara.

This fleet also had to be built. In 1780 it was said that the captains and crews of nine sailing vessels were under pay at Detroit, and nearly all those were built there. They ranged in size from the largest of about 200 tons down and carried from one to fourteen guns.

On July 8th, 1792, Alexander Grant was one of those appointed by Lieut. Governor Simcoe to form the first Executive Council of Upper Canada, now Ontario, and in 1805 was acting as Lieutenant Governor.

During the first session of this Executive Council, in 1792, their time was taken up in organizing the Province. But at the second session, on July 9th, 1793, they passed a law of which all Canadians may be proud. In brief, it said: there shall be no slavery in Canada.

His residence, called Castle Grant, together with about two-hundred and fifty acres of land was at Grosse Point, about ten miles up from Detroit and is now said to be the summer home of Mrs. T. Parsons Hall. But he had another home at Fort Malden, of which he no doubt changed the name to Amherstburg in honour of Lord Amherst, who gave him his first promotion.

The Commodore was of a commanding appearance, a good officer and a general favorite. This is well shown by a document signed by James Madison, President of the United States, dated June 17th, 1812, in which he confirms to Alexander Grant the title to his home at Grosse Point, which was in the United States. This was just at the commencement of the war of 1812-14 and was an unusual mark of respect to one who had served on the border for so many years. His Highland hospitality was shown to Tecumseh, Joseph

Brant and their warriors who were often his guests. For 57 years he was in His Majesty's Service.

Commodore Grant died May 11th, 1813 at the age of 79, and his wife on November 11th, 1810, at the age of 53. They are buried in St. John's Anglican Churchyard at Sandwich.

All this leads up to the fact that there was a family living at Detroit by the name of Barthe. Even then they were old settlers in Detroit.

Theophile Barthe, Armurier du Roy, married in 1718 Charlotte Alavoine, daughter of a Montreal merchant. Their two sons, Charles and Pierre settled in Detroit. Charles married, in 1747, Therese, daughter of Louis and Marie Louise Compeau, of Mackinaw. In their family were Marie Archange, Jean Baptiste, Bonaventure, Charles Andre, Louis Theophile, and Therese.

Of these, Marie Archange married Col. John Askin, the founder of the numerous families of that name. Their home still stands on the bank of the river between Windsor and Walkerville.

Bonaventure married Major Mercer, of the Royal Artillery, who died in England.

Therese, born 1756, married Commodore Grant in September 1774.

The children of Commodore Grant and his wife, Therese Barthe, were:

Therese, born 1776, married Dr. Wright. Both died on board ship, of fever, while returning from Jamaica. They had a daughter, Maria Julian Wright. She married Colonel Robert Nichol, after whom the Township of Nichol received its name. Their home was at Lundy's Lane, near Niagara Falls. One evening he dined at the home of Thomas McCormick, at Old Niagara town. On his way home in the night, on horse-back, he lost his way in the dark and fell over the high bank of the Niagara river between Queenston and the whirlpool, May 6th, 1824. His body was found next morning near the water's edge and was buried in Stamford cemetery. Some years later, Mrs. Nichol married Captain Boyd. They have descendants living in Toronto.

It was this Mr. McCormick mentioned above who, on August 28th, 1832, suggested to Capt. Wm. Gilkison that he should buy half of the Township of Nichol from the heirs of the Rev. Robert Addison. On August 31st Capt. Gilkison made an offer for it. On September 4th he bought the south-west half of the Township of Nichol, being about 13,816 acres at 7/6 an acre, payable when the deed was delivered to him. And, at the same time, he bought from Mr. Woods a farm which is now called West Brantford, for £500.

Isabel'a, died young;

Nellie, died young;

Maria Julia married William Robison. They lived, latterly in Scotland.

Archange married Thomas Dickson, a brother of William Dickson, the founder of Galt, and of Walter Dickson of Niagara-on-the-Lake. Mrs. Dickson died in Glasgow.

Isabella, born December 26th, 1783, married \Capt. William Gilkison, founder of Prescott in 1811, and of Elora in 1832. She died in Glasgow February 10th, 1828.

Phillis, married Alexander Duff. They lived at Chippawa. She died at the home of her daughter, Mrs. G. McMicking at Niagara Falls, Dec. 3rd, 1858.

Nancy, married Alexander Miller. They lived in Chatham.

Elizabeth, born February 1787, married James Woods. They lived at Sandwich and then at Chatham. She died at the home of her son, Judge R. Woods, of Chatham.

Nellie, married George Jacobs and lived at Windsor. She died at Chatham January 30th, 1861.

Alexander, born March 17th, 1791, was not married. He lived and died at Brockville where he was known as Major Grant, or 'Big' Grant.

Jane Cameron married William Richardson, went to Brantford as a bride in 1824; died in Ottawa April 1875. She was buried from the home of her nephew, Lieut. Col. Jasper T. Gilkison, in Brantford.

This William Richardson was a son of Dr. Robert Richardson, an officer of Simcoe's Rangers, and a brother of Major John Richardson, the author of "Wacousta".

William Richardson was one of the very first residents of Brantford. It was because he lived there that his brother-in-law, Capt. Gilkison, bought land in Brantford and made it his home during the winter of 1832 and 1833. The house he lived in is still at number 71 Gilkison street. He called this farm "Oak Bank" after the home he had in Glasgow. While Capt. Gilkison was living in this house he was planning to build a much larger one on the high ground farther from the river, where the Sanitarium is now. That it was to be large enough to entertain his many friends, may be judged from the fact that 92,000 bricks had been ordered for the building of it. The house in which Capt. Gilkison lived was at that time perhaps the nearest house to Brant's Ford, which was between the railway bridges now used by the T. H. & B. and the Electric Road to Port Dover.

But, very much in the way he expected, as recorded in his diary, Capt. Gilkison died suddenly, on April 23rd, 1833. His grave is on the north side of the old Mohawk Church. There is no monument to mark the grave. We asked his grand-daughter, Miss Augusta Isabella Grant Gilkison, of Brantford, the only one living who knew to point out to us the exact spot. It is from six to eight feet out from the wall, opposite to the third window, counting from the front. The next grave farther from the wall is that marked by a marble slab to the memory of "Harriot Lugger, wife of the Rev. R. Lugger, missionary to the Indians, who departed this life Jan. 12th, 1829, aged 38 years."

The Mohawk Church at Brantford is said to be the oldest in Ontario. With its grand old trees, its well kept grounds and its many historical associations it is well worth visiting; and while you are there take a look at that lonely spot where lies Capt. William Gilkison.

There were three men who, in their different ways, did much for Canada. In the order in which they were known to the public they were Sir John A. MacDonald, John Galt and, quite unknown until we commenced to publish this history in 1906, the third was Capt. William Gilkison. To place them in the order in which they were in Canada they should read Capt. Gilkison, John Galt and Sir John A. MacDonald, for the first commenced sailing on Lake Erie in 1797, when the great city of Buffalo had only five inhabitants. He made regular trips between Buffalo and Detroit, taking up supplies for the North West Fur Company and bringing down furs.. In those days sailing vessels did not have steam tugs to assist them but had to wait for a favorable wind to carry them up against the current of the river to Detroit. It was in this way that

Capt. Gilkison met and married the daughter of Commodore Grant, whose home was at the mouth of the river at Amherstburg. When the Commodore was getting old it was Capt. Gilkison who managed his large estate, comprising land both in the United States and Canada. Going home to educate his sons, in June 1815, Capt. Gilkison made his home in Glasgow. There he renewed his friendship with John Galt, who was his cousin, and both were born at the town of Irvine, in Ayrshire. From him John Galt heard of this great country called Ontario. Then, long years after, John A. MacDonald came to Canada, and he was, as the Highland Scot counts it, related to Capt. Gilkison. From the record Miss Gilkison, of Brantford, has, John A. MacDonald's grandmother and Commodore's Grant's father, Patrick Grant, the 8th Laird of Glenmorriston, were brother and sister. We leave that to be traced by those who draw a Government salary for doing such work.

In "Picturesque Canada," on page 482, it is stated that "On Galt's advice Capt. Gilkison purchased at the Grand River falls a tract of fourteen thousand acres". The writer of the letter press in that publication was a good one but he did not get that information from a reliable source. Capt. Gilkison did not have to learn anything about Ontario from John Galt, but John Galt learned from Gilkison who was here about thirty years before him.

* * *

For the purpose of educating their seven surviving sons, Capt. Gilkison and his wife went to Scotland in the summer of 1815, hearing from a passing vessel in mid-ocean of the Battle of Waterloo. Mrs. Gilkison died in Glasgow, February, 1828, and three years later Capt. Gilkison gave up his home there and decided to return to Canada.

On Friday, May 13th, 1831, he records in his diary: "The Ellora—a barque my brother John commands—was this day launched at Dunbarton and towed by a steamer to Port Glasgow. I was one of a large party to behold this nautical scene; a scene always pleasant to an old sailor; and particularly so to me, since all my brothers are interested in this fine ship of 334 tons; which is built for £ 10/ a ton—& when she sails will cost her owners £16 a ton. She is intended for the Bombay trade.

Among the collection of old and rare books which the writer has is one printed in 1825 entitled "The Wonders of Elora, or the Narrative of a Journey to the Temples extending upwards of a Mile and a Quarter, at Elora in the East Indies," by John B. Seely. This book was written by a soldier who had spent years in India. He visited the Temples of Elora in October, 1810. He said: "It is my humble opinion that no monuments of antiquity in the known world are comparable to the Caves of Elora, whether we consider their unknown origin, their stupendous size, the beauty of their architectural ornaments or the vast number of statues and emblems, all hewn and fashioned out of the solid rock!"

Capt. William Gilkison and all his brothers were sailors. The youngest one, Capt. John Gilkison, sailed regularly between Port Glasgow and Bombay. He may have heard the name Elora while in Bombay, from which it is distant about forty miles in a direct line, as by an aeroplane, or about 200 miles by the road usually travelled; or, it is quite possible, and, who knows, but he may have first read of the Elora in India in this identical old book, which was printed six years before he launched his new ship Ellora, which is recorded in this old diary, May 13th, 1831.

Capt. William Gilkison travelled about in Scotland and England visiting his many friends before leaving his native land. On August 1st, 1831, he is in London. On the 2nd he says: "Went by water to London Bridge & saw the splendid tents erected on it, where the King & Queen & 1600 other guzzlers were keeping up a farce yesterday for the New London Bridge was opened that day."

Friday, 5th: "Went to the Opera with Mary Dickson to hear Paganini—a surprising player on the violin—tickets 10/6 each." (Mary Dickson was his niece and he was one of her guardians, her mother having died. J.C.)

August 16th: "I am sick tired again. I must off to America at an early day to solace my mind, if that be possible, in the vast grandeur of that great continent."

London, Sept. 3rd: "John Galt, James Crooks & I dined together."

Thursday, Sept. 8th: "The King & Queen were crowned: I saw the procession & I heard the multitudes cheering. The people of Europe must have some demigod to worship or to condemn. The Reform Bill passed the Committee last night. This is of more importance than fifty Coronations, if it will lead to fair play; time will show."

Sept. 10th: "John Galt, James Crooks & I dined together. This morning, while walking with Mr. Galt, he complained of giddiness & unpleasant feelings. I told him I had similar feelings & asked his opinion why we should both be so effected & he replied laughingly: 'These are warnings for us both that we shall be called away at no distant day.' And I am of the same opinion with my sagacious & most talented friend. We must go—God knows when, nor does it matter much as to me."

Sept. 11th: "Dined with Mr. Galt & James Crooks. We had a pleasant day"

Monday, 12th: "Left London."

March 1st, 1832: "This morning at ten I left Liverpool for New York in the 'Caledonia.' "

Thursday, 9th March is entered in this memorandum book "because it is the birthday of the scribbler, who was ushered into this planet (where he had been before) on the 9th March, 1777, at Irvine in Ayrshire, Scotland, & that is enough for any man to say of himself."

He arrived in New York on April 7th, 1832, and he adds: "Am living at Mrs. Laidlaw's boarding house—54 Broadway—at 7 dollars a week." He at once met many old friends in New York, where he was well acquainted.

Monday, May 14th: "The weather is delightfully pleasant & I feel better these few days past. Paid boarding bill; they have charged me one dollar a day, which is 28/ sterling a week. In London I used to live in a similar house at the rate of 45/ a week.

Wednesday, May 16th: "Left New York and came to Albany in 11 hours, by steamer, the distance was 144 miles."

Thursday, 17th: "I came from Albany to Schenectady by the rail road—a miserable production when compared with the one between Liverpool and Manchester. There seems to be a total disregard of good management in this establishment. It has cost in its half finished state 800,000 dollars— 100,000 more may finish it." (This "Mohawk & Hudson" was the first seventeen mile section, from Albany to Schenectady, of what is now the great New York Central Railway. This combination of horse railway, inclined planes, and steam railroad was chartered April 17th, 1826; commenced building about August 1830; was officially opened on September 24th, 1831. Over the road of which this now forms a very small part, trains now run from New York to Chicago in twenty hours.—J.C.)

Wednesday, 23rd May: "At Utica. Visited the 'Oneida Institute.' It is 3 miles from the village; the object of the Institution is to bring up young men for the Church; they work 3 hours at gardening and farm work and the rest ?"

Monday, 28th May: "I arrived at Queenston after having passed through Syracuse, Geneva, Canadaigue, Rochester, Lockport & Lewiston. The towns through which I passed have become extensive compared with what they were a score of years ago." "The evening of the 28th: I went to Niagara & met my two sons, Archy & Jasper. They are very well & I was delighted to re-unite with them; they are promising lads."

The 29th and 30th: "I went to Queenston, the Falls and Chippawa & saw Clark, Duff, Street, my old friends of other and bygone years, who live in these places."

June 1st. Friday: "I returned to Niagara where I stay in a Tavern."

June 4th: "At Niagara. I dined with Charles Richardson & have visited William Dickson, an old friend, & to-morrow am to dine with him. He has invited me to spend some days at Galt & I propose to accept, when my son Daniel shall arrive from Brockville."

"This is Wednesday, 13th June, 1832, & I am at Niagara but on Saturday last I went to Chippawa & saw the 'Adelaide' steamer launched. Visited my friends in that quarter & returned on Sunday, which day as well as the succeeding ones have been exceedingly warm & close. I am tired and uneasy though I sleep and eat well—on fish and vegetables—yet am not as I used to be. Yesterday I paid my respects to Mr. and Mrs. Attorney General Bolton, of York, who were here and they kindly asked me to visit them."

Tuesday, June 19th: "Yesterday we have learnt the Colera is at Quebec & Montreal & everyone is fearful of the disease coming to this quarter."

20th June at Niagara. Yesterday a man died in a vessel at the wharf and the usual contradictory medical opinion is given of the case having been Colera. At any rate, the man died in the course of a few hours. I think of leaving this place when Daniel arrives but I do not know where to steer to avoid the coming pestilence. The minds of people are wonderfully agitated by it. We have reports of all sorts. One story is that 100 people died at Montreal on Thursday last, June 25th. At Niagara. Weather very warm. Daniel came on Friday & to-morrow I propose to go with him & Jasper to the head of the lake. Jasper goes into the service of Colin Ferrie & Co. at Hamilton. His wages are to be £30 for the first year; £40 for the second and 50 for the third. (That was, in Canadian currency, $120—$160—$200 a year. This was the start of Lieut. Col. Jasper T. Gilkison, who was the principal promoter of the Great Western Railway Co., and its first secretary. He was the projector of the first telegraph line into Canada via Queenston etc. and of the first railway Suspension Bridge at Niagara.—J.C.) June 26th. Left Niagara for the head of Lake Ontario with Jasper & Daniel & slept at Hamilton—Inn detestable. June 27th.—Passed the day at this village and visited my old acquaintances.

June 28th. Came to Brantford, found Richardson. His wife, my dear sister-in-law is absent. I have taken up my quarters here for a few days, with my friends, but the heat & solitude of the place will drive me away again. What a restless creature I have become.

Saturday 7th July. At Brantford. The weather has been exceedingly warm for eight days, the thermometer ranging from 88 to 93 degrees. We hear of Colera in Lower Canada where its effects have been dreadful. In one 24 hours there were 149 deaths. I shall buy the Woods farm on the other side of the Grand River. It has 180 acres by Burwell's survey.

Friday 13th July. We have heard of 2 cases of Colera in London, and both fatal. Slept at Ancaster.

Saturday 14th. Arrived at the hospitable mansion of my kind friend Crooks & am received, as always have been by Mrs. Crooks, with that urbanity which so characterizes this good lady. Mrs. Ewart, Mrs. Arnold & Miss Crooks are here and the family well. This is a very pretty part of the District of Gore and the lands are good. It is on the mountain top, 600 feet above the level of Lake Ontario.

Saturday 21st. Yesterday I was at Dundas & we had a delightful ride round part of Burlington Bay. There is a canal from the bay to Dundas & when it shall be finished there will be water for steamers and sailing vessels to come to the village. It will render Dundas the port for much of the connection with the western country.

I cannot account for my feelings—but I am sure they are happier—have been more calm ever since I came to America than they were when I was in Europe last year. I begin to think I may yet find a few years of happiness in Canada—but this idea, like many others I have formed, may pass away like a vision—a dream of summer night: in the meantime I may enjoy as much happiness of mind as most men of my age & my health is better than it was.

My friend Crooks has 1st, a cloth manufactory; 2nd, a grist mill; 3rd, a saw mill; 4th, a blacksmith factory; 5th, a distillery; 6th, a paper mill; 7th, lime-kilns; 8th, cooperage; 9th, potashery; 10th ? ?; 11th, a merchant shop; 12th, a beautiful farm with 200 acres cleared & many conveniences; 13th, a tavern very well let for $200 a year; and last—though not least—an excellent & hospitable wife, with a fine large family of 10 sons and daughters to do him and her credit in the decline of life. (Note—The home of The Hon. James Crooks was at what was then called "Crooks's Hollow", in West Flamboro'. One of the sons in this family was the one-time well known Hon. Adam Crooks Minister of Education for the Province of Ontario. He was the man who introduced the Crooks' Temperance Act about 1876.)

To-morrow, Mr. Crooks proposes to convey me to Guelph that I may see where my dear son, David, toiled for many a day. Sunday 29th July. At West Flamborough, where I had the pleasure of receiving a letter from Mary Dickson.

Last Wednesday I went to Guelph, distant 30 miles & slept there. Looked at the saw mill which had been built by my son David. It has made no profit since he left it 3 years ago, but it is valuable in its way—perhaps worth

£500 though no one could be found to offer more than £320 for it. It has 10 acres of land in the Town & on the river bank. The situation of Guelph is good & it may continue to be a town for ages to come. I know nothing of futurity, & somehow or other, I care little about it; so let Guelph and its future consequences pass.

On Thursday I went to visit Mr. Dickson at Galt, in Dumfries, the situation is good & the manor house comfortable. I slept 2 nights there. 400 acres immediately above Mr. Dickson are for sale for £400. There are mill seats on the lots. There are 80 acres for sale below Mr. Dickson for 12 dollars an acre; it is partly cleared and has a small house. If these lots are not sold to 2 persons whom I met at Mr. Dickson's, I shall buy them on speculation. My friend, James Crooks, came to Mr. Dickson's on Saturday and we left the hospitable mansion of our obliging friend in the forenoon of that day for West Flamboro'. On the road we measured an oak of 60 feet to its lower limb, the bottom of which measured 25 feet. I never before saw the monarch of the forest. It is a beautiful tree & may be 500 or 600 years old. The heart of this magnificent tree is in rapid decay. The land on which it grows is of beautiful rich mould. I passed through Waterloo in my rambles. This is a rich & well cultivated township. The Upper Canada Gazette contains 25 notices of applications to Parliament for leave to make railroads and Lord knows what. People are mad.

Wednesday 1st August 1832. I left Hamilton for Niagara in a steamer. We were 4 hours from the Beach to the wharf. On Monday I visited the premises of old Lyons, one of the first settlers at the head of the Lake, & he has made a large & valuable property by sheer industry & farming talent—perhaps eight or ten thousand pounds in the course of 40 years of undeviating attention. His barn, outhouses & sheds form a wooden square of 250 feet. It is there his numerous cattle are sheltered from the winter storms. His horses have excellent stables; his pigs their apartments & all are distinct. He has a granary too & everything under lock & key. This is the best establishment I have met with in Canada.

There were several deaths from Colera at Hamilton while I was there. Indeed, this disease is now universal over Upper and Lower Canada as well as the State of New York.

Monday 6th August. Left Niagara & came to Niagara Falls to idle away time—indeed I do little else. My life ebbs on & it will soon be at an end. The rumbling noise of the Falls & its most singularly beautiful appearance have never changed since I knew them 34 years ago. I am at a window which overlooks the scene—a scene that will soon be lost to me—for time—to a man—is but a dot in existence. I am well.

Saturday 11th August. For the last 5 or 6 days I have been living at the Inn close to Niagara Falls. Here I met, accidentally, two sons of James Lumsden of Glasgow & was delighted for one is always charmed to meet with those one has known—perhaps in happier times. I have visited my sister-in-law, Mrs. Duff, & her family at Chippawa—the Clarks & the Streets. Several cases of Colera have been in the neighborhood—generally fatal. Few people come to gaze on the stupendous falls—Colera is the terror of the spot.

Thursday 16th. August 1832. At Buffalo in the United States. On Monday last I was at Forsyth's & on Tuesday came here to take the warm Bath, being afflicted with rheumatic pains. This is a place, a city, of 10,250 by the population returns of last year. I was first here in 1797. Then the total of its inhabitants were five. In fact, there were not 50 settlers at that time between Batavia & this place. More than 100 sailing vessels & 10 steamers come to this port & trade to the westward. Weather exceedingly warm. Colera is in this town; so am I in it. The dinner bell rings & I am hungry—no bad sign in these times of ill health.

Friday, August 17th. I have looked at Buffalo once more. Its advance since I first saw it in 1797, with a total population of five, is remarkable. I called on Mrs. Towbridge. This lady has now a large family, though my sons, David & Alexander, wer her playfellows in 1813. The inn is good but I shall return to Canada to-morrow.

Saturday, August 18th. I returned to Canada this morning and spent the day among my old friends—Kirby, Warren & Douglas. I must again remark on the disease which so alarms all classes of the people of North America, for Colera is everywhere destroying mankind.

Monday 2th August.—Yesterday dined with my old friends & re'atives, the Duffs, at Chippawa, & in the evening came to the Inn which is on the bank of Niagara river and overlooks the stupendous falls.

Tuesday 28th.—I have written Wm. Richardson (his brother-in-law) to accept Woods' offer of £500 for his farm at Brantford. John Brant died of Colera 27th inst. This disease continues its tremendous conflict with frail humanity. It has carried off about one in forty in this town (Old Niagara) & is equally severe everywhere around. Mr. McCormick suggests that I should purchase land in Nichol. I have made an offer to the heirs of the Rev. Mr. Addison for their half of the Township of Nichol. I am advised by Wm. Richardson that my offer for the Woods farm at Brantford has been accepted.

September 4th—I have this day bought the Addison half of the Township of Nichol, payable when the deed is delivered to me. Last week I passed four days with my friends, Hamilton and R. Grant, of Queenston. It is to be remarked here—I feel much obliged to T. McCormick who has been persuaded by me to manage the affairs of Mrs. Nichol & he is to make a regular charge for his time and labor. (Mrs. Nichol was the widow of Robert Nichol, after whom the township was named. J.C.) The Court is sitting here & I drank tea last night with the Chief Justice.

Friday, 7th Sept. 1832.—I propose to start to-morrow for Brantford, taking Sandy Brown on my way to obtain from him, at the suggestion of Mr. Clark, a report on the Township of Nichol. Have asked Mr. McCormick to advertise my lands in Cramachie, Sidney, Murray, Aldborough & Delaware for sale.

"Thursday 11th.—Yesterday came to Brantford, having seen James Crooks on the route. Went over my purchase of the Woods farm; it is in such complete disorder that 200 pounds must be spent on it immediately. Mr. Burwell, the surveyor, will meet me at Guelph after the 20th inst., to survey the N. W. part of Nichol.

"I have an answer from The Bank at York. It has refused to lend on security of my debentures but it offers to buy them. This is the way Canada Banks act. They will discount a man's bill of whom they know little, while they refuse to lend another man who has thousands of Government securities in their possession. Such is my own case. I consider this a most unjust proceeding. Recently, £75,000 was subscribed for bank stock of the York Bank & one-tenth of that amount will be taken by the bank. Persons who do not think of the monetary system of the Province viz: a paper system—imagine this to be a proof of Provincial wealth; but I differ from such an opinion in toto. My paper is as good as bank paper but if I were to issue more of it in bills than I am worth in money, sooner or later I would fail in my engagements I would be bankrupt. Why shall the York Bank, which issues treble its capital, be exempt from such a fate? I do not believe that all those who subscribed not long ago for £75,000 of bank shares could, among them, muster one quarter of that amount if called upon."

"October 30th.—Brought over from York an order on the Branch bank here (Niagara) for £2817, being the amount in their hands from the sale of some of my debentures. I intend to pay for lands in Nichol with this and other monies to come from New York."

"November 1st, 1832.—I have received a letter from Gillespie & McLeod of N. Y. who have sent me Prince Ward & Co.'s receipt for proceeds of my Stock sold. amounting to $12,593 paid them for the Bank of Upper Canada in my name, said bank to give me the money here at one per cent. as exchange. Showed the receipt to Mr. McCormick."

* * *

How sound, and almost prophetic Capt. Gilkison's ideas on finance were is shown by the following. This Mr. Thomas McCormick was the first and only local manager of the Bank of Upper Canada at Old Niagara. He held that position from 1821 to 1864, when the bank failed and he lost all his money when he was eighty years of age. He died the following year, in 1865, at the home of Mrs. Wm. Griffin, his youngest daughter, who lived in Hamilton. His remains were taken by boat to Niagara, accompanied by Mrs. Griffin and Lieut Col. Jasper T. Gilkison, and buried in the family plot in St. Mark's Church grounds.

Thomas McCormick was married in 1810, at Queenston, to Augusta Jarvis, second daughter of Capt. William Jarvis, first Provincial Secretary to Governor Simcoe. Among those in their family were Marie, who married George Hamilton, the founder of the City of Hamilton; Hannah married Alexander Hamilton and lived in Queenston; Elizabeth married William B. Robinson, brother of Sir John Beverly Robinson; Mary Elizabeth married Lieut.-Col. Jasper T. Gilkison, of Hamilton and Brantford; and, as mentioned above, the youngest daughter was Mrs. Wm. Griffin, of Hamilton. From 1810 to 1821, Mr. McCormick lived in Queenston but when appointed manager of the Bank of Upper Canada he removed to Old Niagara, where the old home still stands at the corner of Front & King streets. It is still in good condition, and occupied. The last family gathering in that house was in 1854, when 13 grandchildren were present. The only survivor, this May 1926, Miss Augusta Isabella Grant Gilkison, of Brantford, in writing of this says "We drove from Hamilton; got stuck in a snowdrift at Grimsby, but arrived all right".

"When reminded of such family gatherings—and who has not had experience of similar ones—we recall the words of the song "Far Away," which so fittingly describes them.

"Where is now the merry party I remember long ago?
Laughing 'round the Christmas fires, brighten'd by the ruddy glow,
Or in summer's balmy evenings, in the field, upon the hay?
They have all dispersed and wandered far away, far away.

Some have gone to lands far distant, and with strangers made their home;
Some upon the world of waters all their lives are forced to roam;
Some are gone from us forever, longer here they might not stay;
They have reached a fairer region, far away, far away.

There are still some few remaining who remind us of the past,
But they change as all things change here, nothing in this world can last;
Years roll on and pass forever, what is coming, who can say?
Ere this closes, many may be far away, far away.

* * *

As fully explained in a former part of this history, Capt. Gilkison completed the purchase of the south-west half of the Township of Nichol and had Lewis Burwell survey a village at the Falls on the Grand river, which Capt. Gilkison called Elora after his brother Johnnie's ship, which before that had been named after the Cave Temples of Elora in India.

He then employed Simon C. Fraser to be his agent and storekeeper at Elora. On Dec. 18th, 1832, Capt. Gilkison wrote: "My house in Elora is to be one and a half stories and 42 x 32 feet. Frazer goes up to-morrow to see it completed."

Writing from Elora to his employer, on Dec. 23rd, Simon Fraser said, "I have the honor to inform you that I arrived here safely on Thursday afternoon, being the third day from leaving Brantford. From the state of the roads I advanced very slowly, the mud being very deep, but when within fifteen miles or thereabouts, from Woolwich, the snow lay to the depth of ten inches on the ground and tho' cleaner travelling, the road being unbroken rendered it nothing in my favour with regard to dispatch. O my arrival I found the raising of the store had commenced on the Monday previous. Under the disadvantage of snow falling and with the hands that came forward that day four rounds of the timber were put up. Wednesday was appointed for the next day but the snow still falling prevented its going forward. Accordingly with the assistance of Mr. Reeve and others all hands were summoned for Saturday, and the day being fine we got forward so far as to have the beams laid for the upper story, and should the snow which falls at present subside I hope we will have all up and ready for the wrights to-morrow, to commence work within."

And then we added, on page 115, "But the sudden death of Capt. Gilkison changed all those plans. The store was soon afterward closed and Simon Fraser went away, but where he came from or where he went to we do not know. It is said that at the time he was in Elora he was an active young man, a widower, with one young daughter, Lily Fraser, who was kindly cared for by friends in Pilkington during her father's residence in Elora."

Many years have passed since that was written. When, from January 1906 to February 1909, the first 144 pages of this book were being printed through the generosity of Mr. Richard E. Mills in his paper, The Elora Express, the writer's mother, his only companion, was in poor health and, owing to her death on May 22nd, 1909, any further work on this local history had to be laid aside. Early in this year of 1926, through the kindness of Mr. J. C. Templin and his son, Mr. Hugh C. Templin, the Editors of The Fergus News-Record, a second effort is being made to complete what was commenced twenty years before. In some ways this has not been a loss, so far as the history is concerned, for each year has brought additional information, which has caused some repetition, but if some one in the future re-writes the material given, this may easily be remedied. One good illustration of the advantage gained by the delay is the following, to explain which we must digress a little.

In Goderich, as also in Guelph, some effort is being made preparatory to celebrating the centenary of their foundation next year—in 1927—for both were started by John Galt and his Canada Company about one hundred years ago. With this in view, a belated effort has been made to organize an Historical Society in Goderich and the writer's brother, Mr. Thomas G. Connon, the C. P. R. Agent there has been appointed secretary of that society.

A picture of some old men living in Goderich, and some reading matter about them appeared in a Detroit paper a few months ago. This paper fell into the hands of a lady living at Mt. Clemens, Michigan. The name of Goderich and the pictures of those old residents at once recalled what she had heard of the childhood of her husband's mother. Very little could this old lady tell of her childhood, or of her family history. She knew that she had lived in the home of Capt. Dunlop in Goderich, and that she had attended a private school kept by two maiden ladies there, and that was about all. On the slight chance that it might be possible to learn more, the lady who read the paper, who is the wife of Dr. E. G. Folsom, Mt. Clemens, Michigan, wrote the following letter:

155 North Avenue,
Mt. Clemens, Mich.,
March 4th, 1926.

To Mr. McEwen,
The Hon. Mayor,
Goderich, Ontario.

Dear Sir:—I was greatly interested in the picture of the Octogenarians in your town, and article, as printed in one of the Detroit papers recently; and I am writing to enquire if, thru some of those elderly men I might be able to obtain a little information regarding some of the early settlers. My husband's mother, relict of the late Rev. George P. Folsom, D.D., lived in Goderich as a little girl, and in Capt. Dunlop's family, he being, or his wife, a relative. Mother Folsom's name was Lillias Graham Fraser and she attended a school kept by two maiden ladies. Her parents came with her from Scotland when she was very young and both died within a few years.

If you can ascertain something of the teachers and of the Dunlop family, if any descendants, without inconveniencing yourself too much, I shall be very grateful.

Respectfully yours,
Harriet M. Folsom.

The Mayor of Goderich handed this letter over to my brother and he replied to it, giving what information he thought might be useful to the enquirer. In a second letter which he received from Mrs. Folsom she said—"Mother Folsom was born in the Isle of Islay in 1827. Her mother was a Graham and her father's name was Simon C. Fraser."

For some years my brother, Thomas G. Connon lived in New Westminster, near the mouth of the Fraser river in British Columbia. On his return, I asked him if he knew whether the Simon Fraser who explored the Fraser river had a second name, and showed him several letters which I have that were written by Capt. Gilkison's agent in Elora. For this reason, as soon as my brother saw that name—Simon C. Fraser—he recalled the fact that I had shown him those letters and he at once sent Mrs. Folsom's letter to me. Of all the miraculous things that happen, how did that letter fall into the hands of the only one between Elora and the North Pole who knew that I was seeking information about a man of that name? Verily, this is the strangest World I was ever in!!!

Before concludng her letter, Mrs. Folsom wrote—"I realise that it is difficult now to secure any data concerning her early life but thank you for your letter and am glad to know the name of the school ma'am who taught her. Thanking you for your kindness and also for the interest shown by Mayor McEwan in giving my letter of inquiry to you.

Respectfully yours,
(Mrs. E. G.) H. M. Folsom.

Adding the information which Mrs. Folsom has now supplied to that which we printed years ago the story is something like this.

The Bonnie Isle of Islay lies off the coast of Scotland, about eighty miles in a direct line west from Glasgow, although by water the sailing distance is twice that. On the margin of an old gravestone in the cemetery at Kilarow in Islay there is the following inscription.

"HEER LYES THE CHILDREN OF DAVID FRASER VIZ
JAMES DANIEL CHARLES MARY SIMON
AND JEAN DUFF HIS WIFE

One thing we know; there were a great many by the name of Simon Fraser in different parts of Scotland. In the above inscription we find two names—that of Simon Fraser and Jean Duff, his mother. When Capt. Gilkison was at Niagara he visited with his relatives, the Duffs, who lived at Chippawa.

Almost without exception we find that those coming to make their home in Canada settled near relatives who had preceded them.

Simon C. Fraser and his wife, Lillias Graham, were from the Isle of Islay. Their daughter Lillias Graham Fraser was born in Islay about 1827. Somewhere about 1831 or 1832 they came to Canada and lived at Niagara, where Simon Fraser had a brother, James Fraser. During his visits up and down the river between Chippawa and Old Niagara Capt. Gilkison must have heard of the sad death of Simon Fraser's wife, who was probably related to his friends the Duffs, at Chippawa, and also to the Dunlop family who were so intimately associated with his cousin and friend John Galt, in the operations of the Canada Company and the founding of Guelph and Goderich. And were they not all interested in, or from that, then, rapidly growing City of Glasgow?

Lily Fraser was about five years old when she came with her father to Elora and found a temporary home with the Nicklin and Swan families in Pilkington. There was not a suitable home for her in Elora at that time

When the Hon. Adam Fergusson arrived on the evening of October 6th, 1833 he wrote, "Mr. Frazer, who has acted as agent for the Gilkison family, insisted upon our taking quarters in the "manor house", as the tavern was in a rather rough state. There had been a "Bee" held for two days and the jollification. had yet scarcely subsided. We got a most comfortable supper, however, and kind reception for which we were sincerely thankful. Some respectable settlers from the adjoining township of Woolwich (now Pilkington) spent the evening with us and communicated much useful information. On the following morning, our host, Mr. Frazer, volunteered to ride with us after breakfast up the banks of the river to view the object of our visit. The only trace of a road consisted in blazes or chips taken from the bark of the trees."

The result of this visit was that Mr. Fergusson purchased from the Hon. Thomas Clark the north-easterly quarter of the Township of Nichol, containing about 7,367 acres. Associated with him in the enterprise was Mr. James Webster, who had accompanied Mr. Fergusson from Scotland. From the foregoing it will be seen that Simon C. Fraser piloted the Hon. Adam Fergusson on his first trip to the town which is now named after him—Fergus—and that date—Otcober 7th, 1833—should be ever memorable in the annals of that place.

This is the last record we have of Simon C. Fraser at Elora. Shortly after this date of October 1833, he had gone away, taking his daughter, Lily, with him. Apparently they had gone back to Niagara. From there he went to London, Ontario, where misfortune still followed him. In February, 1835, he is ready to leave London and not long after that he had gone still farther away and this explains why it was so difficult to learn what had become of him He had gone down the Mississippi river to the City of Vicksburg! The following letter was written by him, addressed to his daughter——

Miss Lillias Graham Fraser,
Care of
James Fraser, Esq.,
Niagara, U.C.

This was written June 21st, 1838, but posted a month later, on July 21st. The postage on it was 25 cents.

Vicksburg, Mississippi,
Dated 21st day of June, 1838.

My Dear Lilly:—

I have no doubt but you think strange at my not writing you before this time but when I inform you the cause of my delay you will be no doubt satisfied.

In this part of the world we have nothing but shin-plasters for our currency, and such money would not answer my purpose travelling to Canada Therefore I have not come to see you this summer.

I wish your uncle and aunt to send you to Buffalo, to learn dressmaking and other branches of education you may require, and your uncle can draw on me for the amount quarterly; otherwise he can write me what they charge a quarter and I will send it forthwith before you enter.

Life in this warm climate is so uncertain that I deemed it necessary to make a Will in your favour of one-thousand dollars, being the proceeds of my Estate at this time.

In the event of death, I have by my last will appointed Mr. John M. Henderson and Mr. Peter Scrimshaw my lawful executors who will pay you the aforesaid amount, if anything should happen me this Summer or Fall.

The reason of my writing after this manner is that I have taken the command of the Steam Boat Signal and will leave this place for Texas about the 15th September; sooner if I can settle my other business. As you can see from the paper I sent you of date 20th July, I am agent for Mr. Scrimshaw, and have the settlement of his business, and any letters coming from you to me in my absence, I have authorized him to answer as if I were present, therefore you can address as usual.

The Gulph between Galveston Bay and Houston is very rough, as well as all along the coast, which is very alarming in stormy weather. It is the principal cause of my addressing you in the manner that I have done, though at the moment I apprehend no danger. Henceforward I will write you every month, until I can get some hard Mexican dollars to answer my purpose, then I will come after you and take you to the City of Houston, Texas, one of the finest climates in the world, at least I think so.

In hopes that your uncle and aunt Fraser (at Niagara. J.C.) will attend to my request I will conclude by saying that I will some day, if I live, reward them for trouble, or expenses, they may be put to on your account. Please write me on receipt and if I should leave before your letter arrives I can receive it in Texas in ten days from this City. Let me know when uncle heard from home and if any of uncle John's sons came to Canada. I wish I had one of them here now.

Dear Lilly—Write me what your expense at a boarding school in Buffalo may come at per quarter, and to whom your aunt may have a notion of sending you. With love to you all I remain

Your affectionate Father,

S. C. FRASER.

21st July, 1838.

N.B. When a person takes a fever in this city he don't live more than three or four days, and at present we have a great many cases tho' nothing to what it likely will be in a month from this time, the only objection I have to the south. S. C. Fraser.

This was her father's last letter. What an agony of suspense for the eleven year old daughter, hoping against hope for some word from her father in Vicksburg. But nothing more was ever heard from him, nor from his executors. Perhaps they, as well as Simon Fraser, had been swept away by the scourge of yellow fever.

As to Lily Fraser, we can only surmise that she continued to live in the home of Capt. Dunlop, at Goderich, at least until his death on February 28th, 1841.

After that she seems to have gone to Monroe, Michigan. There she met and married the Rev. George P. Folsom, D.D. He was born at Buffalo, N.Y., and after attending Williams College, graduated from Auburn Theological

Seminary. Mrs. Folsom, Sr., (Lily Fraser) outlived her husband by five years and passed away at Mt. Clemens, Mich., in November 1909, at the age of 82.

The mind of a child under five years of age retains but a few distinct impressions on into later years. Stored away in her brain, Lily Fraser remembered one young woman who had loved her dearly, just after Lily lost her mother, and twenty six years afterwards found where this woman was then living and wrote to her. Here is the reply.

Lockport, N. Y., August 21st, 1858.

My Dear Long Lost Lillie:—

Am I dreaming? Or do I really hold in my hand a letter from one, who in her childhood days, by her affectionate disposition, gentle manners and guileless, innocent ways, entwined herself into the innermost recesses of my heart, and for the past twenty-six years has remained sacredly enshrined therein. How I loved you then, and what it cost me to part with you, God and my own heart alone know. And may His holy name be praised for hearkening to my prayer and permitting me once more to hear from her whom I had so long mourned as dead. May my future life attest my gratitude.

Dear Lillie, do not think me wild or visionary. Had a voice from the tomb called unto me, it could not have awakened greater surprise, or deeper emotion than the receipt of your welcome letter. For one moment, every faculty was hushed—My very heart stood still! Then came the reaction—my pulse beat wildly, almost to bursting—and an intense desire to see you took possession of me. Could I have annihilated space, you would have had me that night for a guest, instead of my tossing upon a sleepless pillow.

You ask if I have forgotten you. I answer, when the Sun forgets to yield us light or the Heavens gentle dew, or my heart is cold in death, then, and not till then will I forget how very dear you once were to me. And how I long to know if my affection for you, or any part of it, is, or ever was returned. You were so very young, scarce five years old, that I hardly dare hope it. Yet it would break a charm of my life to know it was not so, and some few sentences of your letter bids me hope you have cherished my memory, at least tenderly. Will you enlighten me on this matter? For I shall hope to have you hereafter a constant correspondent. Write to me, dear Lillie, in future freely and confidentially as you would to your own Sainted Mother, were she now living. And if your feeling toward me corresponds at all with mine for you, you could not confer a greater blessing than to permit me, as far as our circumstances will allow, to fill to you, in a measure, that dear Mother's place, unless it has already been better filled. In that case I will be satisfied to remain your friend.

I do so long to know your history since last we parted. Every detail, however trivial, will be interesting to me. Write me also of your father, of his whereabouts, and how the world fares with him, and if he is near you, or in your correspondence. Please convey to him my kindest regards. It is possible he may recollect me.

The foregoing letter, which was from Mrs. Elvira A. Ransom, of Lockport was the commencement of a correspondence which continued at intervals for twenty-nine years, for we find the following letter was written from 95 Transit Street, Lockport, N. Y. ,September 29th, 1887.

My Dear Mrs. Folsom:—

How swiftly your letter carried me back over a space of fifty-five years to a little village on the shore of Lake Ontario, where, one bright sunny morning a little girl clad in deep mourning was placed in my charge to keep for a time in safety from the contagion of "scarlet fever". She was an affectionate, winsome little thing and soon won her way to my very heart of hearts and it was very hard for me to part with her. But fate was stronger than love, and I gave you up to your natural guardian and my Lillie passed from my sight, but not from my memory. After an interval of many years, she bloomed in my pathway again for a very brief time, and then the silence of the tomb seemed to come between us. And now again in my "old age" that same Lillie that I loved so well in my youth suddenly springs up again to brighten my lonely hours, with words of love and kind remembrances.

With every prospect that in coming to Elora he would have a home for many years to come, Simon Fraser brought with him an oil painting of his wife. When father and daughter left Elora, they could not take that painting with them. It was large, about 20 x 24 inches; roads were merely bush trails and their future plans very uncertain. So, the painting was left in a home in Pilkington, until called for.

A boy in that home had watched where his mother kept her supply of cut-loaf sugar, a form of white sugar cubes that were quite common then, but are seldom seen to-day. This sugar was kept in a bureau drawer in the room where the painting hung. When the boy went in to that room to steal the sugar, those eyes of hers in the painting seemed to follow him and watch every move he made. One day, in a rage, he took his bow and arrow and shot holes through the canvas where the eyes were. The painting was completely destroyed.

The painting was there while Lily was, but it did not love her as her good, kind girl friend in Niagara did and the painting left no lasting impression on her mind. She did not remember it at all, and yet it was the portrait of her Mother!

*   *   *

Thomas Connon was born on the farm of Tillyeve, in the Parish of Udny, Aberdeenshire, Scotland on September 14th. 1832. When about eight years old the family removed to the farm of Elfhill, near Stonehaven. He received a good education at the school there and then served an apprenticeship in a wholesale grocery in the City of Aberdeen.

But that love of adventure which has peopled the earth with Scotsmen was part of his inheritance and he came to Canada in August 1852. Perhaps if there was one thing more than another that he wished to see it was Niagara Falls; and yet, although he spent the first winter within a few miles of it, at Beamsville, nine years passed before he saw Niagara. Early in March, 1853 he came to Elora.

As a young boy, the greatest treat his sisters could fetch home for him from the nearest town was a lead pencil and some drawing paper. He was always fond of drawing and this led to oil painting.

Shortly after coming to Elora he experimented in photography, being led to do this through reading the 'Art Journal', which was published to describe the exhibits shown at the Great London Exhibition of 1851; and through which were articles showing the, then, latest improvements in photography.

THOMAS CONNON

MRS. THOMAS CONNON

It was in 1859 that he commenced to make photographs for money. In August 1867 he sold his general store business; visited Scotland, where he photographed his father, brothers and sisters and his old home; saw the Paris Exhibition and returned to Elora, to carry on the photographing business in a building erected for the purpose at the corner of Geddes and Moir streets.

In the Fall of 1881 he designed what was afterward called a roll-holder, in which the gelatine emulsion upon which the photograph was made was to be placed upon something like a roll of ribbon, instead of, as fomerly, on glass plates. No doubt such an idea had occurred to others but the strange part of it was this. He wrote to a firm of photo supply dealers with whom he had long been acquainted in Toronto, asking them if they could suggest some way of making use of that idea. At the bottom of the letter was a neat drawing of the roll-holder. The reply was that it was too expensive for the Canadian market.

Four years later this roll-holder, without any essential improvement, was described in the Scientific American of October 17th, 1885, as an American invention. On being asked to return the letter he had sent, the firm in Toronto wrote that they had carefully searched their files but could not find it. Before leaving this we would like to say that neither my father nor myself ever supposed that the firm to whom it was written had anything to do with its disappearance. There are many ways in which a letter may be taken from a file while the heads of the firm would know nothing of it. The fact is, they received the letter; they carefully looked for it expecting to find it where they put it and it was not there. Their letter of October 28th, 1885, says so.

It was in August 1887 that the writer received his American Patent No. 369,165 for the first camera ever made which would photograph the entire circle at one exposure. Such cameras, built upon the same principle, are in common use to-day. When designing this panoramic camera the rolls were placed in the front corners of the camera. When consulted about this in July 1890, a reputable firm of patent lawyers in New York said "The idea of placing the rolls of film in spaces not heretofore utilised is covered in the Panoramic Camera Patent No. 369,165. It was the placing of the rolls of film in the front corners of the camera which made the small size film camera possible. This whole circle panoramic camera was patented in Britain the United States and Canada.

Of the different efforts to make use of this invention after it was completed, it would take too long to tell. It was invented too soon; for the camera was made three years before there was transparent film to use in it. Sample pictures were made by using negative paper and these were shown in New York in August 1887. Later, pictures were made by the writer in New York in February and March 1890, using the very first transparent film that was sold in New York.

Looking back over this record of forty years there is a certain satisfaction in knowing that the first whole circle panoramic camera was made in Elora. We not only have the patents, but all the cameras and experimental pictures; all the letters and other evidence. When we think of the way in which a corporation became rich by using what was not their own our sympathy goes out to the original inventor of the transparent celluloid film now universally used. This was the Rev. Hannibal Goodwin, a Clergyman living in Newark, New Jersey. One of his hobbies was chemistry. He realized the need of a transparent, flexible support on which to make photographs. His application for a patent for transparent film was dated May 2nd, 1887. There can be no other conclusion than that the granting of a patent to him by the American Patent Office was delayed until a huge monopoly could get time to make similar experiments. You will find the miserable story on page 249 of the Scientific American for March 21st. 1914.

After years of litigation, carried on at great expense, the Supreme Court of the United States decided that the Rev. Hannibal Goodwin, of Newark, New Jersey was undoubtedly the original inventor.

But what about him? After struggling on in poverty and suspense for more than thirteen years, he died on the last day of the Nineteenth Century, December 31st, 1900.

On November 4th, 1854, Thomas Connon married Jean, eldest daughter of John Keith, one of the first Bon-Accord settlers in Upper Nichol.

Commencing in May 1885, failing health gradually necessitated a discontinuance from all work and Mr. Connon passed away on January 10th. 1899. Mrs. Connon survived him ten years and died May 22nd, 1909.

Of the family, Elizabeth married James Grant. They lived for many years in Chesley, Ontario. Mr. Grant died July 12th, 1911. From injuries received falling down a stair in the University at Saskatoon, Mrs. Grant died on Christmas morning, 1925.

Next in the family is the writer of this, John R. Connon.

The third is Thomas G. Connon, who married Matilda Carswell. They live in Goderich, where he is an Agent of the C.P.R. and Secretary of the Goderich Historical Society.

When referring to the death of Mr. Connon in the Elora Express, the Editor, Mr. J. M. Shaw, wrote——

"The writer first made the acquaintance of Mr. Connon in 1859. soon after becoming a resident of Elora himself. He was then one of the foremost men of the rising village, and took an active part in everything pertaining to the welfare of its inhabitants. He served on the school board for many years acceptably and filled the responsible position of village auditor so carefully and trustworthily that it was a pleasure to look upon his work. His artistic eye saw so many new and ever recurring beauties about the Elora rocks that he was intimately acquainted with every nook and corner of both the Irvine and the Grand Rivers for miles up and down stream, and many are the gems photographed by him from time to time. The old Indian bridge was a hallowed spot in his memory, and ere it was destroyed by an over loving mother for her son's safety he secured photos of it at various seasons of the year. The people of old Elora are passing away rapidly and ere long the village will be peopled by an entirely new generation."

ELORA

LIST OF VOTERS WHO WERE PRESENT AND VOTED AT THE FIRST CONTESTED ELECTION IN THE TOWNSHIP OF NICHOL IN 1842

The contestants were James Webster, of Fergus, associated with the Hon. Adam Fergusson in the founding of Fergus and Charles Allan, also of Fergus, but who, as a result of this election moved to Elora. Webster was a Conservative and Allan a Reformer but, in this election politics were very much forgotten. Owing to the burning of the first mill in Fergus, in January 1836, many of the first settlers were almost starving, for their grain was at the mill and burnt. Mr. Webster, having the second store in Fergus, helped the settlers through this period of hard times, and they did not forget him when they voted in this election.

The result of the voting, Webster 82; Allan 79. The voting took place in St. Andrew's Church, Fergus.

VOTED FOR WEBSTER

Robert Mitchell
William Gerrie
Robert Gerrie
John Gibbon
Wm. Tytler
Wm. Gibbon
George Pirie
Alex. Tytler
John Brockie
David Morris
George Elmslie
Joseph Wedderburn
John McCrodden
George Leslie
George Fraser
Arthur Walker
John A. Davidson
Peter McLaren
Alex. Walker
Leonard Dobbin
James Bergen
Alexander Gaul
James Young
Alex. Patterson
Michael Cox
James Middleton
Morris Cushing
Patrick Daly

James Robertson
Batt. O'Connor
Patrick Clifford
Hugh McAnnany
Arch. Cummings
Denis Clifford
Barney McCarrol
John Bryden
George Barron
W. Carter
Charles Michie
Edward Noble
Wm. Mackie
David Giliss
Wm. Gunn
Wm. Kilpatrick
Arch. Nichol
Thomas W. Valentine
John Valentine
James Mutch
James Gordon
Thos. Ogsden
John Mennie
Thomas Webster
George Dickinson
Geo. Hamilton
Richard Alexander
John Merrit

Alex. Watt
Alex. Leith Moir
Joseph Carder
Alex. Burr
Wm. Moorhead
Robert Henderson
Thomas Mair
Geo. Gray
Wm. Buist
D. Mikisock
James Foster
Geo. Robertson
Henry Hudson
James Moir
A. D. Fordyce
John Keith
Thos. Gray
John Garry
John Stevens
John McCluskie
James Morrison
James Findlay
John Mason
Bernard Kelley
James Gaul
A. D. Fordyce, Jun.

VOTED FOR ALLAN

Alex. Masson
William Beattie
James Davidson
Robert Pourie
John Sweeney

James Cattanach
Wm. Black
Timothy Clifford
Nicholas Morphy
Peter Stuart

John Gunn
Alexander McGladdery
Thomas Boys
Edward Robinson
Eugine Scanlin

ELORA

George Beattie
David Allan
James Ross
Andrew Burns
George Wilson
John Cunningham
James Miller
Oliver Lasby
David Henderson
Alex. Harvey
John McPhail
Samuel Cunningham
David Munroe
George Royal
Robert Dryden
John Cormie
Robert Garvin
Archibald Sheritt
Alexander McDonald
Daniel O'Connor
Wm. Reid
Edward Ford

Thomas Lochrin
James Davidson
John Orr
John Elmslie
Peter Butchart
Wm. Reid
James Perry
John Watt
James Dow
Daniel Cummings
Wm. Gibbon
Peter Grassock
James Reid
Wm. Crisstisson
James Flewwelling
Patrick Scanling
George Elgie
John Cooke
Thomas Monroe
Wm. Flewwelling
Robert Scott
John Monroe

Samuel Broadfoot
James Jackson
Hugh Black. Jun.
Thomas Dow
H. Metcalf
Charles Milne
Robert Cooke
Wm. Stewart
Fairly Milne
A. B. Flewwelling
Francis Anderson
John Gerrie
James Duguid
Francis Anderson, Jun.
James Gill
James Robertson
Samuel Trenholme
David Smith
T. C. Allardice
Gregor McGregor

* * *

NAMES FROM ASSESSMENT ROLL OF NICHOL FOR 1850

County of Waterloo

To Wit——I, James Davidson, collector of the Township of Nichol, in the said County of Waterloo, do hereby solemnly swear that the annexed is a true copy of the Collector's roll of said township and that it contains the names of all the freeholders and householders in the said township.

JAMES DAVIDSON, Collector.

Sworn before me at Fergus, this sixth day of January A.D. 1851.

JOHN WATT, J. P.

Anderson, David
Archibald, Robert
Allan, James
Archibald, John
Allardyce, William
Anderson, James
Anderson, Francis sr.
Allardyce. Thomas C.
Allan, David
Anderson. Francis jr.
Allan, Charles
Black, Hugh sr.
Broadfoot, John H.
Butchart, James
Butchart, Edward
Butchart, William
Broadfoot, William

Butchart, Peter
Buick, James
Birt, Charles (Burt?)
Beattie. William jr.
Beattie, John
Beattie, George
Beattie, William sr.
Beattie, James
Broadfoot, Samuel
Boyce, Thomas
Barron, George
Brindley, Gottlieb
Barnhart, George
Brander, William
Bates, Thomas
Brown, John
Brockie. John

Burns, Andrew
Burr, James
B'ack, William
Black Hugh
Brown, Peter
Carder, Joseph
Carter, William
Cowie, Alexander
Cormie, John
Cowie, James jr.
Clark, Alexander
Cunningham, Samuel
Connor. Daniel A.
Cushing, Morice
Cox, Michael
Cull, Harvey
Clifford, Dennis

ELORA

Cook, Robert
Cook, John
Cunningham, John
Cummings, Daniel W.
Cummings, John
Cunningham, William
Cattanach, James sr.
Clifford, Timothy
Connor, Daniel A.
Craig, John
Craig, Robert
Cooper, John
Campbell, Samuel
Coady, Michael
Calder, John
Cummings, Archibald
Cummings, George
Clark, William
Campbell, John
Cadenhead, John
Cadenhead, Brebner
Cadenhead, Alexander
Cattanach, James jr.
Cattanach, John
Chambers, Thomas
Campbell, William M.
Cattanach, Archibald
Dickinson, George
Dow, Thomas
Dow, Peter
Daley, Peter
Davidson, James
Dow, James
Driscoll, Florence
Donachy, James
Donachy, James
Duggan, Timothy
Dow, Thomas sr.
Day, E. T.
Downey, Thomas
Duguid, James
Davidson, James
Davidson, James
Depew, James
Davidson, James
Dolman, George
Ewing, John
Elmslie, James
Elmslie, James jr
Elgie, George
Emslie, John
Emond, Robert
Edwards, James
Eby, Jonas
Fasken, John
Flewwelling, James
Finnegan, Thomas
Flewwelling, Abram J.
Flewwelling, William
Findlay, James
Fraser, Alexander
Fraser, George
Faulkner, William
Foote, David
Farrell, Trevor
Fordyce, A. D. sr.
Foote, James
Ford, Edward sr.
Ford, Edward jr.
Fergusson, David B.
Forrester, Andrew
Finlayson, John
Field, William
Forbes, George
Gordon, James
Gillies, Donald
Gibbon, William
Grenside, Edward C.
Grassick, Peter
Gray, Thomas
Grant, Peter
Geddes, Joseph
Gibbon, William
Gibbon, William jr.
Gibbon, John
Gerrie, Robert
Gall, James
Gall, Alexander
Gibson, William
Gerrie, John
Gerrie, William
Gill, James
Garvin, Robert
Grant, Andrew
Glover, Adam
Galbraith, John
Galbraith, William
Garrow, John
Geddes, Andrew
Gray, George
Gerrie, James
Geddes, James
Gairns, James
Gordon, Andrew
Hastings, David
Heffernan, John
Hudson, Henry
Heffernan, John
Hawkins, John
Howse, Augustus
Heffernan, Thomas
Heffernan, Morice
Heffernan, Patrick
Henderson, David
Hatcher, Henry
Hatcher, Edward
Hamilton, George
Hay, William
Hatcher, James
Holman, John
Harvey, Alexander
Irwin, James
Jameson, Samuel
Jackson, Joseph
Joice, John
Jardine, George
Johnston, Robert
Jones, Morris
Johnston, Josiah
Jack, Alexander
Kilpatrick, Hugh
Kesson, Edward
Kennedy, Patrick
Keith, William
Keith, John
Knox, Robert
Kerr, Robert
Kilpatrick, William
Keys, James
Kelleher, William
Keys, Cowan
Kirk, John L.
Leslie, George
Laird, Joseph
Larter, James
Loghrin, Thomas
Lamont, Alexander
Lilly, Alexander
Low, Charles
Logan, William
Land, Thomas sr.
Land, Thomas jr.
Land, Henry

ELORA

Land, Ephraim
Milne, John
Milne, Fairley
Moore, John
Morrice, James
Moir, Alexander L.
McQueen, James
McArale, Barnard
McGregor, Gregor
McIssac, James
McDonald, Alexander
McSweeny, John
McMillan, Archibald
Maitland, Francis
Michie, William
Murphy, Nicholas
Munroe, John
Masson, Alexander
Milligan, Robert
Felix McGinn
Moultrie, John
Metcalf, John
McNee, Alexander
McLeister, Michael
Millar, James
Millar, John
Moir, James
Mutch, James
Mackie, William
Michie, Charles
Mulligan, John
Middleton, James
Mair, Thomas
Mason, John
Mair, James
McHardy, George
McGillivray, Robert
Muir, George
Muirhead, William
Moore, William
Mockler, William
Mennie, John
Macaulay, Michael
McDonald, John
Morrison, James
McRory, William
MacNamara, John
McRory, John
McKee, John
Mutch, William
Martin, James

McLaren, Peter
Martin, John
McFarland, Charles
Milne, William
Middleton, W. G.
Nesbit, Joseph
North, William
Orr, John
Owens, Samuel
Ogston, Thomas
Pritchard, Richard
Peter, Robert
Paterson, Archibald
Pearson, John
Prendergast, Patrick
Powrie, Robert
Perry, James
Preston, Henry
Piper, William
Peterson, Peter
Philip, Robert
Philip, James
Robb, Charles
Rennie, Alexander
Robb, Joseph
Robertson, George
Robertson, David
Reid, William
Ritchie, James
Reid, James
Royal, George
Roy, Alexander
Ross, James
Ross, Arthur
Ross, David
Robertson, Thomas
Shortreed, Robert
Shea, Patrick
Smith, Henry
Scanlan, Eugene
Sherratt, Archibald F.
Scott, James
Scott, Thomas
Scott, Robert jr.
Stockford, William
Scott, William
Smith, Florence
Smart, Charles
Shields, David
Stephen, John
Skinner, James

Smith, David
Skein, George
Skeoch, John
Storey, Thomas
Shannon, John
Smith, James L.
Stewart, George
Small, Samuel
Small, Joseph B.
Stocks, James
Smith, William
Smith & McDougal
Taylor, Robert
Tytler, William
Trenholm, Samuel
Todd, Gilbert H.
Thomson, Andrew
Vickers, John
Valentine, John
Valentine, Thomas
Wilson, William
Wilkie, David
Wyllie, William
Wilson, Robert
Wells, Charles
Watt, Alexander
Wissler, Sem
Wilson, Samuel
Whitely, Thomas
Wilson, Hugh
Wedderburn, Joseph
Whitelaw, George
Walker, Alexander
Walker, Arthur
Watt, John
Webster, James
Waters, Robert
Wilson, John
Watson, L. W.
Walker, James
Warmington, Richard
Webster, Henry
Wilkie, Alexander
Williams, John
Wallace, James
Watson, George
Wilson, Thomas
Wood, Rowley
Williams, Thomas
Young, James
Young, James

ELORA 195

NAMES FROM ASSESSMENT ROLL OF PILKINGTON FOR 1851

Woolwich, December 30th, 1851.
I, William Reynolds, do hereby solemnly swear that the within list is a true and correct list of the inhabitants of the Pilkington Tract, extracted out of the assessment roll of the Township of Woolwich, to the best of my knowledge and belief. So help me God.

WILLIAM REYNOLDS,
Collector of the Township of Woolwich.
Sworn to before me this first day of January, 1852.

ALEX'R WATT, J. P.

List of the inhabitants of the Pilkington Tract, extracted from the assessment roll of the Township of Woolwich.

Ayars, Robert
Astell, John
Allan, John
Ariss, Mrs.
Allardyce, William
Anderson, William
Anderson, William jr.
Auger, Samuel
Arthur, Humphrey
Astell, William
Amy, Cotton
Ariss, John
Bauer, Andrew
Berberick, John
Berberick, Adam
Bye, John
Bye, George
Bye, William
Blythe, John
Blinco, George
Boys, Thomas
Burnett, Alexander
Bent, William
Bain, George
Barrett, Patrick
Barrett, James jr.
Boulding, Charles
Bettchen, Gilgian
Borton, Edmund
B'ack, David
Badley, Edward
Blinco, William
Beal, William
Beal, Thomas
Burns, Denis
Barrett, James
Bergin, Rhodolphus
Bonallie, John

Bosomworth, Christopher
Bosomworth, Thomas
Birney, George
Birney, James
Batters, Thomas sr.
Batters, Richard
Bosomworth, John
Boyd, Robert
Boyd, George
Blinco, John
Barrett, Joseph
Brown, George
Carrol, Peter
Carrol, James
Campbell, William
Cromar, Robert
Coxhead, Caesar
Coxhead, Thomas
Currie, John
Clarke, William
Coffee, John
Coffee, Patrick
Caldwell, Gavin
Caldwell, David
Caldwell, William
Cummins, Thomas
Cummins, William
Cruikshanks, James
Coxhead, William
Cameron, Donald
Duggan, Cornelius
Dunbar, Joseph
Dumphy, Patrick
Donaldson, George
Day, Joseph
Elkerton, David
Elkerton, Benjamin
Elkerton, William

Elkerton, John
Everett, William
Ewing, William sr.
Ewing, William jr.
Edwards D. C. George
Fergusson, William
Fletcher, Adam
Fasken, George
Fasken, Robert
Fry, John
Franck, Martin
Fahrer, Anthony
Francis, Thomas
Grey, George
Grain, Thomas
Glover, Michael
Gillis, Donald
Garland, Matthew
Green, John
Gordon, Alexander
Gale, John
Gordon, James
Goodwin, Eli
Gray, George
Hill, John
Holloway, William
Hughes, Richard
Hess, Ignatz
Holm, John P.
Harvey, Francis
Harper, Richard
Howard, Charles
Hay, Peter
Halls, William
Howse, Augustus
Hay, William
Howard, William
Harrison, William

Hurst, George
Hughes, Griffith
Howse, James
Hall, Henry
Howse, Thomas
Howse, George
Howse, Benjamin
Howse, William
Hall, Thomas
Hall, Joseph
Hall, Edmund
Holman, Henry
Hauser, Ignatz
Hall, James
Hanna, J. Richard
Hunter, Alexander
Haig, Robert
Jones, Robert
Jones, Richard
Jones, Morrice
Jones, David
Johnston, Robert
Jack, Alexander
Irvine, Robert
Kelly, John
Kingshott, George
Kayworth, John
Keating, Thomas
Kirby, Michael
Kirby, Thomas
Kelleher, Timothy
Kremer, John
Kurtz, Gottlieb
Knepfler, John
Kellier, George
Kelly, Michael
Kelly, Thomas
Kaum, Patrick
Kilpatrick, Thomas
Knox, William
Lasby, Joseph
Larter, Henry
Lilly, George
Lisco, Thomas
Lines, Zechariah
Lilwall, William
Lennox, Thomas
Luckitt, George
Larter, William
Linseman, Joseph
Lambrick, Andrew

McGovern, James
McGovern, Barney
Mepner, Anthony
McKenzie, George
McPhee, Alexander
McEwen, Lawrence
Mason, Alexander
MacDonald, Allan
Marshall, Edmund
Morrison, James
McGarry, Barney
Mitchell, Alexander
McNeil, Edward
Meer, Ustus John
Martin, Martin
McQueen, Richard
McDonell, Allan
Marriott, John
Milne, David
Murray, Michael
More, George
Mutrie, James
McClarting, Michael
Moran, Patrick
Murphy, Arthur
McKay, John
McKay, Archibald
McTaggart, Donald
Mitchell, Benjamin
Mitchell, John
McQueen, James
McQueen, Thomas
McQueen, Alexander
McQueen, Malcolm
McFarlin, Malcolm
McRea, Robert
McRea, Alexander
Neagle, Thomas
Nickison, George
Newman, John N.
Nicklin, George
Neagle, James
Neagle, Richard
O'Connor, Bartholomew
O'Connor, Daniel
O'Brian, Thomas
Ormandy, William
O'Neil, Hector
Philip, James
Pasmore, Edward
Pollard, William

Preston, William
Patmore, Edward
Patmore, Samuel
Pritchard, Hugh
Peacock, Thomas
Pulkinghorn, John
Peckover, Daniel
Pollard, Edward
Rowden, John
Robins, Daniel
Rumby, David
Reeve, George
Reynolds, William
Robinson, Samuel
Ryan, Jeremiah
Roberts, Owen
Ross, James
Roberts, Hugh
Robb, Samuel
Roth, Lorenz
Reinhart, Francis J.
Reinhart, Francis Weaver
Reinhart, Martin
Reinhart, John
Schroeder, Andrew
Shifter, Leander
Shone, Joseph
Strangways, Charles
Simpson, John
Snider, Henry
Stewart, John
Scott, Robert
Sheppard, Alexander
Short, Thomas
Short, Thomas jr
Short, Leonard
Short, William
Short, George
Stickney, John sr.
Stickney, John jr
Stickney, William
Snider, Henry
Swan, John
Tribe, Mrs.
Taby, Henry
Tuckey, William
Thomas, Peter
Thomas, John
Toner, John
Toner, Neil
Thring, William

ELORA

Tilly, Frederick
Tilly, Henry
Thomson, Joseph
Weiler, Anthony
Weiler, Valentine
Wissler, Sem
Winfield, John
Wilson, Thomas
Whitelaw, George
Williams, Richard
Wallace, Donald
Wallace, Hugh
Wright, James
Wright, Nicholas
Ward, James
Weadick, William
Watson, Alexander
Weiler, Dumas
Zinger, Joseph
Zimmerman, Joseph

* * *

A list of the leading men and heads of families living in Elora in 1853, when Thomas Connon came. Written as he gave them from memory.

Adie, James M.—merchant.
Allan, Charles—carpenter
Allan, Charles jr.—clerk in store.
Buckley, John—weaver
Brydon, John—cooper
Campbell, W. M.—tinsmith
Cattanach, John—carpenter
Clarke, Charles—merchant
Cope, or Copp, John—foundryman
Chambers, Thomas.
Dolmage, George—hotel keeper.
Duff, Rev. John—pastor of Knox Church.
Davidson, James—miller
Dixon, or Dickson, John—miller
Eby, Jonas—cabinet maker
Foote, David—carpenter
Forbes, George sr.—tailor
Forbes, George jr.—tailor
Field, William—distiller.
Farrow, Thomas Algar—retired
Farrow, Edward—pump-maker.
Finlayson, Dr. John
Gordon, Andrew—harness maker
Gatherer, Adam—retired
Gerrie, James—shoe maker
Geddes, Andrew—Crown Land Agent
Geddes, James—lawyer
Gray, George—hotel keeper
Gairns, James—sailor and baker.
Haig, Robert—postmaster
Hill, Samuel—framer
Jack, Alexander—miller
Johnson, Josiah—Blacksmith
Jones, Morris—waggon maker
Kertland, Edwin H.—surveyor
Kirk, John L.—merchant
Land, Henry—shoe maker
Land, Ephraim—shoe maker
Land, Thomas—shoe maker

Laird, Joseph—mason
Lawrence, Charles—brick layer
Mundell, John—cabinet maker
Mowat, (?) —Editor of 'The Backwoodsman')
Middleton, Dr. W. G.
Morrison, William—surveyor
Moore, Thomas—carpenter
Murdoch, Hugh—baker
McIntyre, John—tailor
MacDonald, John—carpenter
Normandy, William—employed in woollen mill
North, William, and Brother—conducted "Quaker North's Academy", which was in some way connected with the Rockwood Academy of a later date.
Newman, Walter P.—accountant
Pepler, Philip—hotel keeper
Philip, James—merchant
Philip, Robert—merchant
Paterson, Peter—woolen manufacturer
Ritchie, James—employed at Allan's mill.
Stocks, James—merchant
Smith, John—hotel keeper
Smith, Thomas—bailiff
Smart, Alexander—cooper
Skinner, James— (?)
Small, Dr. Joseph B.
Smith & MacDougal—merchants
Simpson, Peter—carpenter
Vickers, Thomas—carpenter
Webster, Samuel—tinsmith
Williams, Thomas—blacksmith
Wood, Rowley—
Watson, George—farmer (Father of Senator Robert Watson).
Wilbee, Henry—carpenter

ELORA

Some of the boys in Elora, in 1853——

Thomas Johnson	John Ritchie	James Land
Oliver Johnson	Thomas Wilbee	Peter David Land
James Chambers	John Wilbee	Thomas Land
David S. Ritchie	Edwin Wilbee	John Gordon
William Ritchie	William Land	Joseph Laird
James Ritchie	Albert Land	James Skinner

*   *   *

LIST OF NAMES FROM THE ASSESSMENT ROLL OF ELORA, FOR 1855

Allan, Charles sr.
Allan. Charles jr.
Allan, James jr.
Armstrong, Rev. R.
Alexander, John
Bain, Alexander
Beck, Thomas P.
Black, John
Boyd, Daniel
Brand, Thomas
Bunton, John
Chambers, Thomas
Campbell, William M.
Connon, Thomas
Cattanach. John
Clarke, Charles
Davidson, James
Dalby, Francis
Dillon, John
Dolman, George
Dorwood,   (?)
Duncan, John
Duncan, James
Duncan, George
Dunbar, Joseph
Duff, Rev. John
Elliott, Elihu A.
Farrow. Thomas Algar
Finlayson, Doctor John
Fields, James
Foote, David
Forbes, George sr.
Forbes, George jr.
Frank, Francis
Fries, Peter
Gaul, James
Gatherer, Adam
Geddes, Andrew
Geddes, James
Gerrie, James

Gerrie. John
Godfrey, John
Godfrey, Alexander
Gordon, Andrew
Gordon, James
Gray, George
Haig, Robert
Hamilton, Hugh
Hamilton, James
Hay, George
Henderson, David
Hes'em, Charles
Halley, Maurice
Inglis. John
Johnson, Josiah
Johnson, Thomas
Kertland, Edwin H.
Kievell, William
Kilpatrick, John
Kilpatrick, William
Knowles, William
Kirk, John L.
Kirkendall, Mrs. E.
Kirkendall, George
Kirkendall & Ormandy
Kribs, Daniel
Land, Henry
Land. Thomas
Land, Ephraim
Laird, Joseph
Lawrence, Charles
Leech, William
Lowthian, George
Mathieson, James
MacGregor, Rev. John G.
McNaughton, Duncan
McNaughton, John
McBain, Duncan
McIntyre, John
McGuire, Hugh

Middleton. Dr. William G
Mundell, John
Moore, Thomas
Newman Brothers
Newman, Walter P.
O'Lone, Bernard
Preston, Henry
Philip, James
Philip, Robert
Pepler, Philip
Potter. John
Rattray, Alexander
Reid, William
Reeve, George
Ritchie, James
Robinson. Thomas G.
Rose, James
Sauvey, John
Schroeder, Henry
Simpson, Peter
Skinner, James
Smith, Robert
Smith, David
Smith, John
Smith, Mrs. E.
Smart, Alexander
Somers, J. G.
Spence, John
Stork. William
Spalding, Alexander
Tamlyn, William
Topping, John
Taylor, Benjamin
Tribe, Jonathan
Webster, Samuel
Wilkinson, John
Williams, Thomas
Winfield, James
Wood, Rowley

MEMBERS OF THE ELORA MECHANIC'S INSTITUTE, ORGANIZED THURSDAY EVENING, 26th NOVEMBER, 1857

Adie, James M.
Allan, James
Allan, William
Allan, Charles
Bain, John
Biggar, John
Blake, George
Bradley, J.
Brown, John
Burke, John W.
Clarke, Charles
Campbell, W. M.
Chinneck, Robert
Crewson, W. M.
Crossman, J. S.
Duncan, John
Duncan, J. George
Douglas, Moses
Elmslie, George Sr.
Eisenhut, Conrad
Eby, John
Forbes, George jr.
Farrow, Thomas
Frazer, W. H.
Fraser, James
Frank, Francis
Foote, David
Gordon, Andrew
Garrard, Seaman H.
Gray, William
Greathead, Thomas
Gibbon, William
Geddes, James
Gibbon, John
Haig, Robert
Henderson, James
Henderson, John
Henderson, David
Jennings, Arthur
Jackson, Hugh
Johnston, Alex.
Johnston, James
Kertland, Edwin H.
Kirkendall, Geo. W.
Land, Ephraim
Laird, Alexander
Morrison, William
Maw, Robert
Moore, Rev.
Mundell, John
McDonald, Peter
McLean, John
McKenzie, Valentine
McCluskey, Charles
McDonald, Donald
Newman, Ed. H.
Newman, Richard C.
Newman, Walter P.
Newman, Robert M.
Noble, Robert
Owens, T. J.
Philip, James
Potter, John
Rollett, Charles
Ross, James
Reid, William
Shaw, Charles
Smith, Alexander
Sheppard, Jacob
Sheppard, William
Scott, Charles
Stafford, William
Smart, Alexander
Scott, Archibald
Simpson, Peter
Spalding, Alexander
Simpson, John
Simpson, Robert
Taylor, Benjamin
Wilkinson, John
Wilson, James
Total 81.

ELORA

(By Alexander McLachlin)

O lovely Elora! Thy valley and stream
Still dwell in my heart like a beautiful dream,
And everything peaceful and gentle I see
Brings back to my memory some image of thee.
I've roamed this Dominion, allured by the gleam
Of the wild woodland beauty by mountain and stream,
From lone Manitoulin all down to the sea,
But found ne'er a spot, Sweet Elora, like thee.

There's lone rocky grandeur away at the Sound,
And down the St. Lawrence wild beauties abound;
Quebec, towering proudly, looks down on the sea,
And lone Gananoque there's beauty in thee;
And Barrie! The lady that sits by the lake,
O, that I could sing a sweet song for her sake,
But here in thy beauty a-list'ning the Fall,
O, lovely Elora! Thou'rt Queen of them all.

If friends should forsake me or fortune depart,
Or love fly and leave a great void in my heart;
O, then in my sorrow, away I would flee
And hide my misfortune, Elora, in thee;
Away from the world, with its falsehood and pride,
In yon lonely cot where the smooth waters glide,
I'd commune with nature till death set me free,
And rest then, forever, Elora, in thee.

Index

ACADEMY, "Quaker North's" ... 130 131
ADAMS, Rev. Ezra 121
ADDISON, Rev. Robert 50 52 110 111 173 180
ADELAIDE, Launching of Steamer 177
ADIE, James M. 157 197
ADSETT, Thomas 15 16
AIKEN, Mrs. James 91
AITCHISON, Andrew and Family .. 42 43
ALABAMA AWARD 149
ALBANY 176
ALGIE, James .. 140
ALLAN, Adam Ferguson, (First born in Fergus) 121
ALLAN, Charles, of Fergus and Elora 43 79 119 120 121 123 129 131 135 136 170 191 197.
ALLAN, Alexander, and Family, of Winterbourne 11
ALLAN, Absalom Shade (Sheriff and M.P.P.) 11
ALLEN FAMILY, (of Lower Pilkington) 36
ALMA ... 126 142 167
AMHERST, General Lord 172
AMHERSTBURG . 175
ANCASTER. 7 131 167
ANDREW'S CREEK 109
ARCHEOLOGICAL MUSEUM .. 163 164
ARCHIBALD, James 116
ARGO, Adam L. and James 88 89
ARISS, Benjamin and Family (of Lower Pilkington 34
ARMOURY HALL 59 132 136 140
ARTHUR VILLAGE 168
ASIA (Vessel) 7
ASKIN, Col. John 173
ASTELL, Joseph .. 35

ASSESSMENT ROLL OF NICHOL ... 192
ASSESSMENT ROLL OF PILKINGTON 195
ATKINSON, William 42
AYNHO 33
BADLEY, Edward 32 39
BAIN, John Jr 139; John Sr. .. 165 167
BAND, ELORA 100 130 141
BANKS, Upper Canada 180 181
BARBER, Duncan . 74
BARRIE, Rev. Dr. 88 122
BARRON, George 87 92 104 105 107 167.
BARRON, Mrs. George 73 87
BARKWELL, Robert 125
BARTHE FAMILY, of Detroit 173 51
BATTERS, Thomas 15
BEALE FAMILY, of Lower Pilkington 37
BEATTIE, George and Family of Lower Nichol 90 91
BEAVER MEADOW 70 109
BECK, Mrs. Fred . 32
BELL, John McLean (First Grammar School Teacher) 33 154
BEMIS, Benjamin Bowman and Family, of Winterbourne ... 10
BENNER, Jacob .. 14
BENNER, Joseph .. 9
BENNER'S BRIDGE 14
BENSON, Miss Mina 152
BENT, William and Amos 102
BERBICE (Ship) . 131
BERWICK, Mrs. .. 94
BETCHEN, William & Family 36
BEVERLY TOWNSHIP 6 7 14

BIBLE 149 153
BIBLE SOCIETY . 153
BIG BEND 46
BIG RIDGE 14
BIGGAR, Thomas . 139
BIGGAR'S HOTEL 141
BLACK, David ... 43
BLACK, John 123
BLACK ROCK 8
BLANEY, George . 123
BLATCHER, Elizabeth 50
BLINCO FAMILY, of Lower Pilkington 37 140
BLOOMINGDALE . 8
BLYTH, Annie ... 41
BLYTH'S 72
BOLTON, Lieut. Col. Mason 172 177
BON ACCORD SETTLEMENT .. 64 103 132 135 166 167
BONALLIE, Mr. and Annie 19 40
BORTON, Elizabeth 36 38
BOSOMWORTH'S Creek 162
BOOMER, Dean .. 11
BOULDING, Henry, Lottie, Mary Ann 36
BOYD, Capt. .. 140 173
BOYLE, Dr. David and Family 45 161 to 167
BRADY, John 140
BRANDER .. 12 93 94
BRANT, Capt. Joseph 19 168 173
BRANT, John ... 180
BRANTFORD 169 174 178 180.
BROADFOOT, Elizabeth, James, Allison 38 42 42
BROCK, W. R. .. 131
BROCKIE FAMILY 95 102
BROCKVILLE 174 177
BROLEY FAMILY 28 50
BROWN, Mrs. Andrew (Winterbourne) . 11
BROWN, Mrs. and daughter Mary 92 135

INDEX

BROWN, Capt. (of S. S. Polynesian) .. 58
BROWN, Frank (of Clifford 102
BROWN, Peter (of Bon Accord) .. 73 74 78 79 81 89
BROWNALL, Rev. Stephen 121 122
BRYDON .. 39 60 197
BUCHAN, James . 41
BUCKLEY, John . 197
BUFFALO . 10 135 155 156 179 180.
BURNS, Andrew 120 128
BURLINGTON 168 178
BURKE, John W. .167
BURWELL, Lewis ..54 115 178 180 182
BYE FAMILY 36 42 43 92 131
CADETS, Elora 100 143
CALDER FAMILY 87 91 92 97
CALLAWAY, Joshua and Ellen 25 28 49 (Also in page of corrections).
CAMPBELL, W. M. 197
CAMERON, Malcolm Crooks 137
CARPET FACTORY 170
CARSWELL BROS. STORE 132
CARD, Samuel 42
CARDER FAMILY .. 41 42 61 62 63 117
CARLTON, Thomas 140
CASCADE 27 40 45 139
CATTANACH, John 127 128 130 197
CATTLE MARKET 132
CATTO, Andrew .. 102
CHAMBERS, James 59 116 120 198
CHAMBERS, Thomas 123 197
CHATHAM ... 140 172
CHIMO FORT 150 151 152
CHINNECK, Robert 165
CHIPPEWA 169 173 177 180 184
CHOLERA, ...177 178 179 180
CHRISTIE, James 100 143
CHRISTIE, Rev. Thomas 87

CHURCH, The Old Log 87
CHURCH, Chalmers 157 161
CHURCH, St. John's Anglican 140 146 147
CHURCH, Knox .. 167
CHURCH, Methodist 121
CHURCH, St. Andrew's (Fergus) 115
CLARKE, Lt. Col. Charles.. 135 144 167 197
CLARKE, "Old Doctor" of Guelph 149
CLARK, Colonel Thomas, of Chippewa 47 49 52 54 60 169 177 185
CLEMONS, Elvira .. 9
CLIFFORD, Village of 146 149
COATES, Edward. 139
COLBORNE, Lieut. Gov. Sir John .. 65
COMPEAU, Louis and Marie, of Mackinaw 173
CONESTOGO, ... 7 8 12 169
CONNON, Thomas 76 138 155 165 167 188 190.
CONNON, Mrs. Thomas 75 86 88 190
CONNON, Elizabeth 190
CONNON, John R. 190
CONNON, Thomas G. 190
CONNON'S CORNER 132
CORNELL, Martha 14 15
COPE, John 197
COPELAND AND ZEIGLER 126
COX, Michael and Mary 11 37 116
COXHEAD, Caesar 130
CRAIG, John, Thomas 116 123
CRAMER, Adam .. 49
CRAWFORD, John 139
CRESS HOUSE (Preston) 14
CRESS FAMILY 42 94 97 100
CROOKS, The Hon. James 8 24 27 29 47 176 178 179 180
CROOKS, Thomas 12 13

CROSSMAN, James K., Edwin, John S. 138 140 167
CROWN LANDS AGENT 11 145
CRUIKSHANKS FAMILY.. 39 40 94 117
CUMMINGS FAMILY (of Bon Accord) . 94
CUTHBERT, "Sandy" 165
DALBY FAMILY 39 132 138 143
DALGARNO FAMILY 35 36 43 84 91 92 95 105 108 109
DOLMAGE, George 197
DARBY, Janet 15
DARBY, Sam .. 38 132
DAVIDSON FAMILY, (of Winterbourne) 10 11 122
DAVIDSON FAMILY, (of Bon Accord) 74 79 87 89 138
DAVIE, James 102
DAY FAMILY .. 100 30 97 130 143
DERRY, Mrs. 123
DICKSON FAMILY (of Niagara and Galt) .. 11 113 173 177 179
DICKSON, John .. 197
DOWNING, Mrs. Thomas 95
DUFF, Alexander (of Chippewa) .. 173 177 179 180 184
DUFF, Rev. John 88, 165, 197
DUNCAN, John .. 167
DUNCAN, William James 139
DUNDAS 12 71 131 178
DUNLOP, Capt. William ... 183 184 186
DUNWOODIE, Mr. .. 60
EAGLE TANNERY 124
EBY, Sarah, Anna, Jonas 43, 123, 197
ELKERTON FAMILY 35 36 74 92
ELMSLIE, George and Family ...... 64 to ..74 90 103 135 167
ELORA, Assessment Roll for 1855 .. 198
ELORA, Backwoodsman Newspaper 41 136 137
ELORA Satirist Newspaper 137

INDEX

ELORA, Observer Newspaper 133 137 162
ELORA Express Newspaper .. 137 158 183
ELORA BAND 100
ELORA, Business Directory for 1853 . 197
ELORA, Mechanics Institute .. 163 167 199
ELORA, Museum.. 163
ELORA, Public School 163 167
ELORA, Grammar School.. 154 156 160 162
ERB, Levi 124 126
EVANS, Rev. James 153 154
EVERETT, William, Richard, Everett 39 74 140
EWING FAMILY .. 99
FALLS, ELORA 26 44 56 67 69
FALLS ON GRAND RIVER .. 136 170 171
FARRELL, Miss (Teacher) 162
FASKIN FAMILY 42 43
FARROW FAMILY 134 139 140 197
FENIAN INVASION .... 139 to 143
FERGUS .. 60 69 144 168 170
FERGUS, Rifle Company 143
FERGUS News-Record 183
FERGUSON, Richard 138
FERGUSSON, Hon. Adam 60 64 119 185 191
FERRIER, Alexander D. 21
FINDLAY FAMILY 92 139 140
FOLSOM, Dr. E. G. 183
FOLSOM, Rev. Geo. P. 183 186
FOLSOM, Harriet M. 183 184
FOOTE, David and Family 120 127 128 130 132 136 138 143 165 197
FORBES, Archibald (The Noted War Correspondent) 93
FORD FAMILY 36 38
FORSTER, Capt. 38 118
FRANK, Francis 41 137

FRANKLAND, Martha S., Thomas, Mary 166 162 39
FRANCIS, Francis and Family 36 39
FRASER, Simon C. (The first storekeeper in Elora) 38 55 114 115 182 184 186 188
FRASER, Lillias Graham, his daughter ...... 115 182 to 188
FRASER, Alexander & Family (of Bon Accord) 91 92 95
FRASER, Rev. Donald 31
FRASER, Mrs. Catharine 154
FRASER, Hugh 96 125
FRASER, J. M. .. 165
FRASER, William H 95 167
GAIRNS, James 128 139 140 197
GALL, Alexander . 93
GALT, John .. 51 174 176 183 184
GALLAGHER, James 140
GARDINER, Rev. Alexander 93 124
GARTSHORE, John 89 91
GATHERER, Adam 118 197
GAUKEL, Emanuel & Family 8 14
GEDDES, Andrew and Family 11 30 75 102 120 122 123 145 197
GERRIE FAMILY 73 93 100 105 117 139 197
GERRIE William Thomas 93 94 140
GIBBON, Agnes 64 90 101
GIBBON, William Sr. 65 67 73 74
GIBBON, William Jr., son of William . 139
GIBBON, John. 90 101
GIBBON, William, son of John Gibbon 101 102
GIBSON, William . 140
GILKISON, Capt. William 38 47 50 to 58 64 110 to 114 136 169 170 173 to 176 181 182 184
GILKISON, Lt. Col. Jasper T. ... 52 58 59 110, 174 177 178 181
GILKISON, Augusta Isabella Grant ..52 110 174 175 181
GLENNIE, William Jessie 16 14
GOLDNER, Christian 125
GODERICH .. 143 183
GODFREY, John 138 143
GODFREY, Robert 162
GODFREY, Thomas 28 140
GOODWIN, Rev. Hannibal (Inventor of transparent Photographic Film) .189 190
GOODWIN, William 16
GORDON, John (came to Elora, Oct. 1834) 13
GORDON, Andrew and Family .... 131 132 ..133 134 165 167 197
GORDON, John, son of Andrew 131 198
GRAIN FAMILY .. 38
GRANT, Commodore, The Hon. Alexander .. 51 172 173 174 175
GRANT, Miss 130
HAIG FAMILY ... 39
HAIG, Robert 167 197
HAMILTON, Alexander Banker at Queenston 181
HAMILTON, George, Founder of Hamilton City 181
HAMILTON, Hugh, Blacksmith in Elora, ... 162 165
HAMILTON, James, Miller at Winterbourne 9 11
HAMILTON, Rev. A. M. Minister at Winterbourne 10
HARRIS, Alexander 90
HARPER, Richard 140
HARRISTON 102
HARRISON, Archie. George, Josh ... 102
HASTINGS, Mrs. William 90
HATCHER, Ned. . 123
HAY, Peter and Family 96 97
HEADLEY, Francis 123
HELE, John W. 139 141 165

INDEX

HENDERSON, David 43 120 123
HILL, Samuel 140 197
HEWITT, Elisha and Family 9 12 15
HOLMAN, Alexander 19 43
HOLMWOOD, John & Family .. 8 12 13 14
HORNE, Rev. H. R. 161
HOWSE, Thomas and Family 33 34 35 36
HOWSE, Mrs. Augustus 96 97
HUBBARD, Dr. Leonidas 152
HUDSON'S BAY Co. 147 149 150 153 154 166
HUCK, Jacob 102
HUGHES, Hugh and Family ...31½ 32 63
HUGHES, Robert . 139
IMLAY, Sandy 10
INDIANS, Six Nation 19 97 98 99
INDIAN BRIDGE . 45
INVERHAUGH 15
IRVINE, Thomas 14 30
IRVINE BRIDGE, building of 128
Pier of 37
JACK, Alexander 123 197
JACOB, John 139
JARDINE, Mr. ... 123
JOHNSTON, Josiah & Family 24 29 116 122 197 198
JOHNSTON, Alexander 139 140 142
JONES, Edward and Family 32
JONES, David and family 33
JONES, Morris 33 123 197
JONES, Hugh (Ned Jones' Father) .. 32
KEELING, Charles 95 125
KEITH, John and Family 71 73 74 75 85 86 91 96 99 125 190
KEITH, Jean, Mrs. Connon 76 190
KEPKE, Isaac 15
KERR, Alexander . 41
KERR, Joseph .. 123
KERR, William M. 139
KERTLAND, E. H. 154 167 197

KEYWORTH, John 140
KENNEDY, Catharine 8
KENNEDY, "Upright" 81
KILPATRICK FAMILY 41 42
KIRK, John L. 135 197
KIRKLAND, Henry 42 165
KNOWLES, Mr. .. 63
KNOX, Mrs. William Robert 97
LAING, Peter 131
LAIRD, Alexander 130 139
LAIRD, Joseph 118 197 198
LAMB, Louis 102
LAND, Thomas and Famliy 118 119 139 140 167 197 198
LAND, Ida 169
LANPHIER, Thomas H 11 12
LANPHIER, Capt. Henry 12 63
LANPHIER, Eliza 11 12 63
LANPHIER, Lucia 11
LAPENOTIERE, W. H. L. de 131
LARTER, Eliza, William, Nancy 35 38 43
LASBY, Charles and Family 13 16 28 29
LAWRENCE, Charles .. 16 37 116 130 197
LAWRENCE, George 15 16 37 38
LAWRENCE, Henry 37
LAWRENCE, Fanny & Thirza 37
LEASK, George .. 102
LEECH, William 138 140
LEITCH, Rev. M. L. 88
LEPARD, Squire 21 22
LEPARD, Mary Ann 14 21
LESLIE, George and Family 94 140
LETSON FAMILY, ... 13 22 62 74
LILLIES, George .. 140
LINES FAMILY .. 35
LOCKHART, William 99
LOGGIE, George . 89
LONGMAN, James 125
LONDON BRIDGE, Opening of 176

LUCKITT, George and Thomas 34 36
MACDONALD, Allan 130
MACDONALD, John ... .130 138 197
MAC EWAN, H. J. A. (of Goderich) .. 183
MAC GREGOR, Rev. John G. and Family ... 139 140 156 162
MACKIE, Jane 16
MACKIE, William, ... 81 91
McCATTY, John .. 162
McCONNELL FAMILY 145 146
McCORMICK, Thomas and Family (Banker at Old Niagara) 51 54 58 173 180 181
McCREA'S CORNERS 126
McDONALD, Hugh and Family of Inverhaugh 40
McDONALD, Rev. A. 88
McFARLANE, Frank 140
McGREGOR, John. 140
McINNES, Rev. John 88
McINTOSH, Rev. W. R. 88
McINTYRE, John 197
McKAY, Hiram 14
McKAY, Ann 14 41 60
McKAY, Redrick 41 60
McKENZIE, George & Family 11 41 60 128 139 140
McLEAN, John (Explorer for the Hudson's Bay Co.) 149 150 151 154 155 167
McLEAN, John C. (Eldest son of the former) 140
McLEAN, Alexander 59
McNAUGHTON, Mr. 120
McPHERSON, Angus 140
MAIR FAMILY 78 82 91
MAITLAND, John .34
MARRIOTT, John. 24, 38, 132
MARTEN, John J. 116
MARTIN, Martin and Family 34 38 43 59 69 73 117

INDEX

MASON, Mrs. Robert 36
MASON, Mrs. 89
MASON, John 62 80 117 118
MASTON, Mr. .. 123
MATHIESON, Mr. 131 135
MATHIESON, George 140
MATTHEWS, Roswell and Family (The first family in Elora) 7 27 45 to 50 55 59 110 169
MECHANIC'S INSTITUTE 167
MELVINE, Robert 73 74 78 79 82 83 89 95
MELVILLE CHURCH (Fergus) 128 159 160
MENNIE, John and family 94 95
MERCER, Major . 173
MICHIE, Charles 70 92
MIDDLEBROOK School 162 163
MIDDLETON, Rev. James and Family 64 89 95 103 121 165 167 197
MIDDLEMISS, Rev. James, D.D. .. 104 121 156 to 162
MILLARD FAMILY 13 14
MILLER, Alexander, of Chatham, ... 173
MILLER, "Yankee" 39
MILLS, R. E. 137 183
MILNE, David and Family 42 43
MILNE, Robert .. 139
MITCHELL, Robert & Agnes 167 168
MITCHELL, ... 15 41 42 93 94
MOCKRIDGE, Rev. James 31
MOIR, James and Family .. 74 79 80 83 88 89 90 130 140
MOORE, Thomas 197
MOREILL, Richard and Family 16
MORRISON, Rev. John 88
MORRISON, William 167 197
MOWAT, William 137 197
MURRAY, Michael 125
MURDOCH, Hugh .197

MUTCH, James and Family (of Salem) 125 130 140
NESBITT, Mr. .. 132
NEVITT, Katie . 21 22
NEWMAN FAMILY, ... 104, 134, 135 136 138 165 167 197
NICHOL, Col. Robert 51 173 180
NICHOL TOWNSHIP 11 17 50 51 144 166 168 169 173 180 182
NICHOL Voters at first Election (1842) 191
NICKLIN FAMILY 29 38 50 74 185
NIGHTINGALE, Florence 145 146
NORMANDY, William 197
NORTH, William 197
ORMANDY, William 39
O'REILLY, Sergt. Major 140
OPTHALMOSCOPE, Inventor of 157
PAGANINI, Violinist 176
PAGET, Dr. Arthur H. 139 143
PAISLEY, Ontario 102 103
PALMER, Rev. Arthur 30
PANORAMIC CAMERA, Inventor of 189
PARSONS, James .37
PATERSON, Peter 120 136 197
PATMORE FAMILY 35 36 38 40 75
PEACE RIVER DISTRICT 150 155
PEARSON, John . 125
PEART, Mrs. 89
PECK, Mr. 62 117
PECKOVER, Donald 36 38
PEPLER, Philip .. 197
PENFOLD FAMILY 14 15
PHILIP, James ... 120 135 136 197
PHILIP, Robert 64 120 135 197
PHOTOGRAPHY 188 189
PIRIE, George and Family .. 89 95 167
PILKINGTON Estate 7 13 20 21 33

PILKINGTON TOWNSHIP 7 8 13 17 18 19 33 44 96 144
PILKINGTON, General 20 31 32 34 169
POTTER, John 139 143
POTTER, D. M. .. 167
POTTS, John 140
PRESCOTT, (First house in).... 52 173
PRESTON, Charles 40
PRITCHARD FAMILY 33 91
QUEEN'S BUSH 102 145
RAILWAYS, W. G. & B. 14 17 102 127
RAILWAYS, Grand Trunk .. 142 161 170
RAILWAYS, Great Western 140 161 177
RAILWAYS, Guelph & Goderich 15
RANKIN, Mr. Surveyor 65 66
REEVE, George ("Old King Reeves") 16 23 26 28 31½ 74 85 108 182
RED, William 120 123 167
RENNIE, Alexander and Family .. 92 93
REYNOLDS, Squire, and Relatives 20 21 24 29 30 31 32 33 38 101 140 195
REYNOLDS, Susannah (Mrs. William Gibbon, Jr.) 24 101
RICHFIELD, Mr. . 62
RICHARDSON, Charles (of Niagara) ... 177
RICHARDSON, Major John 174
RICHARDSON, Dr. Robert 174
RICHARDSON, William (Earliest resident of Brantford) 110 174 177 180
RITCHIE, James and Family 123 136 138 140 197 198
ROBB, John 73
ROBERTS, Hugh and Family 20 33 88 130
ROBERTS, Mrs. Owen and Family 15 33 45
ROBERTS, Henry 140
ROBINSON, Thomas .. 22 23 37 38 40 62

INDEX

ROBINSON, David 125
ROLL HOLDER, Photographic, Inventor of 189
ROLLITT, Charles 139
ROSS, Arthur and Family 43 120 170
ROSS, James (Of Ross & Co) .. 43 136 170
ROSS, James (of Inverhaugh) .. 23 40
ROSS, Rev. John, D.D. 88 170
ROSS and Co. .. 43 87 119 134 136
ROSS & BONALLIE 135
ROSE, Rev. Hugh . 88
ROWE, S. T. (Built first house in Paisley 102
ROY Rev. James . 83
ROY William A. Y. 103
RUXTON, Margaret 92
RYAN FAMILY (of Inverhaugh 40
SALEM 11 125 133 142 161 170 171
SALEM BRASS BAND 140 143
SAMSON, W. D. . 158
SANDILAND, Mr. (of Guelph) 63
SCOTT, David 74
SCOTT, Henry .. 139
SEACH, Thomas ... 62
SEXTON FAMILY 8 9
SHADE, Absalom 11 46 49
SHAW, J. M. 46 137 138 141 190
SHEPPARD, George 139
SHIELDS, Alexander 139
SHIELDS, Francis 139
SHIELDS, Robert . 139
SHORTREED, Robert 88
SIMS, James 124
SIMPSON, Peter 105 138 197
SIMPSON, Robert 139 140 142
SIMPSON, John 96 139
SINCLAIR, George 120 138
SKINNER, Rev. James 88
SKINNER, James 123 140 197
SMALL, John 130

SMALL, Samuel .. 32
SMALL, Joseph .. 32
SMALL, Dr. Joseph B. 197
SMART, Alexander 120 130 139 197
SMELLIE, Rev. George of Fergus) 159
SMITH, Captain .. 7 ..8 12 13 14 17 49 99
SMITH, Cushman 8 17
SMITH, Alpheus 8 12 17
SMITH, Thomas (The old Squire) 24
SMITH, Theophilus 24 40
SMITH, John (Editor of Observer) .. 137
SMITH, William 129 136
SMITH, T. P. 129
SMITH, Thomas .. 197
SMITHURST, Rev. John ... 145 146 147
SNYDER, William 131 167
SPALDING, Alexander 105 130 165
SPALDING, Andrew 137 140 143
SPEERS, Samuel.. 99
SPENCER, Anna (wife of John Matthews) 48 50
SPENCER, Hon. Benjamin 48
SPENCER, Rev. James 48
SPIEZ, Michael .. 15
STEVEN, Mrs. David (of Chesley) 86
STEVENSON, John 139
STOCKFORD, Elizabeth, Charles and Richard .. 16 37 38
STOCKS, James 136 197
STORK, Mrs. George 9
STRACHAN, Archdeacon 65
STRACHAN, Thomas 138
STROH, George. 7 13
SUGG, Annias, William Samuel 15 16
SULLIVAN, Benjamin 50
SUSPENSION BRIDGE (At Niagara) .. 177
SUTHERLAND, Mr. 132

SWAN FAMILY 38 39 185
SWIFT, Jonathan . 39
TABLE ROCK 67
TAMLIN, William .125
TASSIE, Dr. 11
TAYLOR, Benjamin 138
TAYLOR, James (of Galt) 21
TAYLOR, Miss Hannah and John, of Clifford 148 149
TEACHERS' EXAMINATIONS 162
TEBBY, Miss Annie & Henry 35
TECUMSEH 172
TEE-A-HO-GA 49
TEMPLIN, Hugh .. 183
TEMPLIN, J. C. 183
TESLA, Nicola .. 152
THOMAS, Miss Elizabeth, Peter and John 32 34 35 39 46
THOMSON, Joseph 19
THOMSON, Rev. C. E. 116 148
THOMSON, George 165
THOMSON, William 139
THRING, Mr. 19
TOVEL, Mark 35
TOWNSEND, Thomas 49 50
TRENHOLME, Samuel 62 73
TRIBE FAMILY 14 15 134 140
TUCKEY Family .. 38
TYLEE, Edward, George and Robert 20 21 24
TYTLER FAMILY 80 93 96 116
UNDERHILL, Mr. 152
UNGAVA. 150 152 153
VAN NORMAN, Mr. 61
VEITCH FAMILY, Annie, Mary, William 40 43 41
VICKERS, Thomas 130 197
VOLUNTEER RIFLE Company 137 to 143
VOSPER, Charles . 91
WABADIK, Chief . 99
WALKER, Arthur (Owen Sound Road) .124
WALKER, James (The old Baker, of Fergus) 96

INDEX

WALKER, Mary (Mother of Capt. Gilkinson) 51
WALLACE, William 20
WALLACE, Robert 130
WALLACE, George 140
WARD, Sergeant. 139
WASTELL, Rev. Mr. 121
WATT, Alexander .. 65 67 71 73 74 75 85 87 88 136 195
WATSON, Alexander .. 40 41 63 136 197
WATSON, Senator Robert 136
WEADICK, Ann .. 41
WEAVER, Mary and Ann 7 8
WEBSTER, James (of Fergus) 60 69 89 103 120 185 191
WEBSTER, Stephen, (of Winterbourne) 16
WEBSTER, Samuel (Tinsmith of Elora) 197
WEBSTER, John . 105
WEEDON-BECK .. 20
WEICHEL, Mrs. Adam 32
WEST MONTROSE 8 13 14 15

WHITCRAFT, Nancy 99
WHITELAW'S FLATS 85
WHITELY, John, Thomas, Joseph 99 101 102 140
WIDDERBURN, J. 74 91
WIGGINS, Sarah .. 36
WILBEE FAMILY 7 8 17 24 25 30 39 60 117 130 197 198
WILSON, Mr. 69
WILSON, James and Family 24
WILSON, James (Of Monkland Mills, Fergus) 59
WILSON, Samuel 101 102
WILLIAMS FAMILY 32 33 38 42 197
WILTON, Elizabeth 14
WILKINSON, John 139 167
WINFIELD FAMILY 39 42 15 32
WINTERBOURNE 8 9 10 11 12 13 62
WISSLER, Sem and Family 39 86 123 to

127 130 142 161 165 170
WOOLCOT, William 19
WOLLIS, Edmund and Family 16
WOOD, Christopher & Family 25 40 62
WOOD, Rowley 24 26 39 121 123 197
WOOD, John R. .. 140
WOODS, James and Judge R. (Of Sandwich and Chatham) 174
WOOLNER, James . 9
WOOLWICH .. 7 8 9 10 13 15 17 18
WORSLEY, Mrs. (Had a store in Guelph) 63
WRIGHT, Dr. 173
WRIGHT, Maria Julian 173
WRIGHT, Mr. (Had a Bakery in Guelph 63
YOUMANS, Prof. J. W 143
YOUNG, James and Family 94
YOUNG, Mrs. Menzies 95
YOUNG, John 140
ZUBER, Jacob 14
ZUBER'S CORNERS 14

CORRECTIONS

Page 22—The name of Joshua Callaway was omitted by the printer. He was one of the twelve first settlers in Pilkington, and was a brother of Mrs. Lepard. Joshua Callaway later moved to Bayfield on Lake Huron. A son of the same name was well known in Winnipeg at the time of the boom, 1880-1881.

Page 45, Line 35—For 150 feet read 135.
Page 45, Line 20—For 1880 read Sept. 1878.
Page 52, Line 19—Mrs. Gilkison died 1828, not 1826.
Page 147—"Platen," in the 22nd line, should be "Paten."
Page 155—The date of the letter beginning on this page should be "April 27th, 1869," not "1889."

ELORA 31½

The first of these Welsh families was that of Griffith Hughes, with his wife and three children, Helen, Hugh and Mary, who sailed from Liverpool on the 3rd of April, 1831, on the ship 'Milton' bound for New York. From there they came by the Hudson river and Erie Canal to Buffalo; crossed the Niagara river to Fort Erie, and got a conveyance to take them to old Niagara. An employee in the tavern at which they stopped overheard Mr. and Mrs. Hughes talking to each other in Welsh and spoke to them. They had been discussing how they could get to Little York, now Toronto, intending to go to Hamilton from there, but their friend told them that was out of their way and directed them to a brother of his—an Ebenezer Evans—living in Hamilton. From Hamilton the father walked (about fifty miles) to King Reeve's place, when Mr. Reynolds soon found means to fetch the mother and her family to their new home. Two yoke of oxen brought the wagon from Sexton's to Tom Robinson's, and he came to meet them, bringing a pail of water, with bread and cheese. The Hughes family moved into a house near King Reeve's place, on the Lepard farm, and lived there until 1838, when they all returned to Wales. In 1841, the son, Hugh Hughes, came back again, followed in 1842 by his parents and sisters.

The following correction, for the second printing of the WLU reissue, November, 1974, was reported by Mrs. Margaret Kilpatrick Gordon, R.R. 5, Rockwood, Ontario:

> Page 42, line 16 — James Kilpatrick married Helen Broadfoot, not Alison. Alison Broadfoot married John Maitland.

Also, Edna Staebler (nee Cress) of R.R. 3, Waterloo, reports that the "CRESS FAMILY" listing in the Index, page 202, is wrong. The Cress name occurs on Pages 9 and 12. The page numbers listed originally (43, 94, 97, 100) probably were meant for the CROMAR family, a name inadvertently dropped from the index. The name CROMAR is cited on those pages, and, following alphabetical order, would appear next in the Index.